THE HEROIC LEGEND OF
ARSLAN

STORY BY
YOSHIKI TANAKA

MANGA BY
HIROMU ARAKAWA

1

THE HEROIC LEGEND OF
ARSLAN

TABLE OF CONTENTS

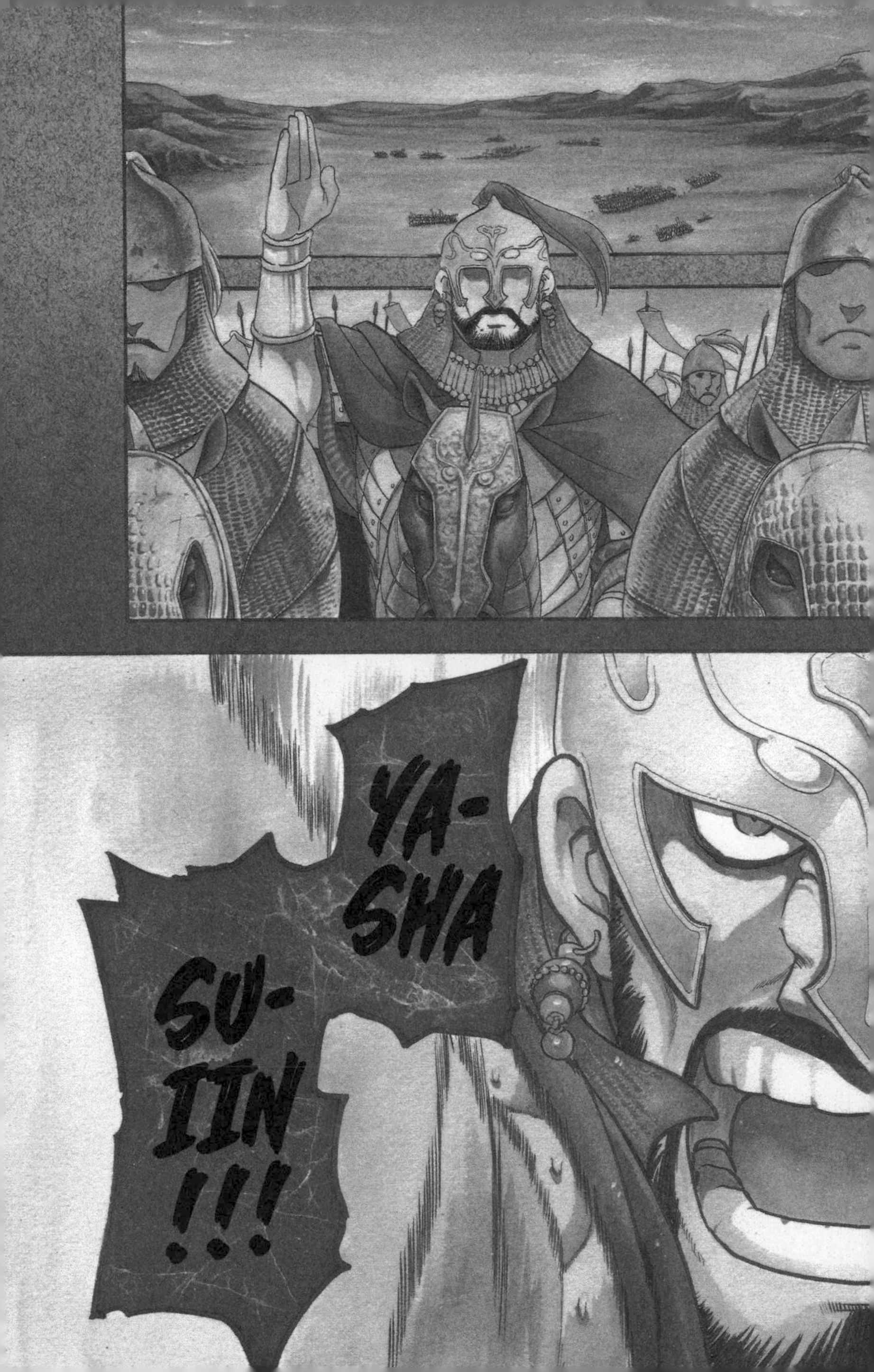
YA-SHA
SU-IIN!!!

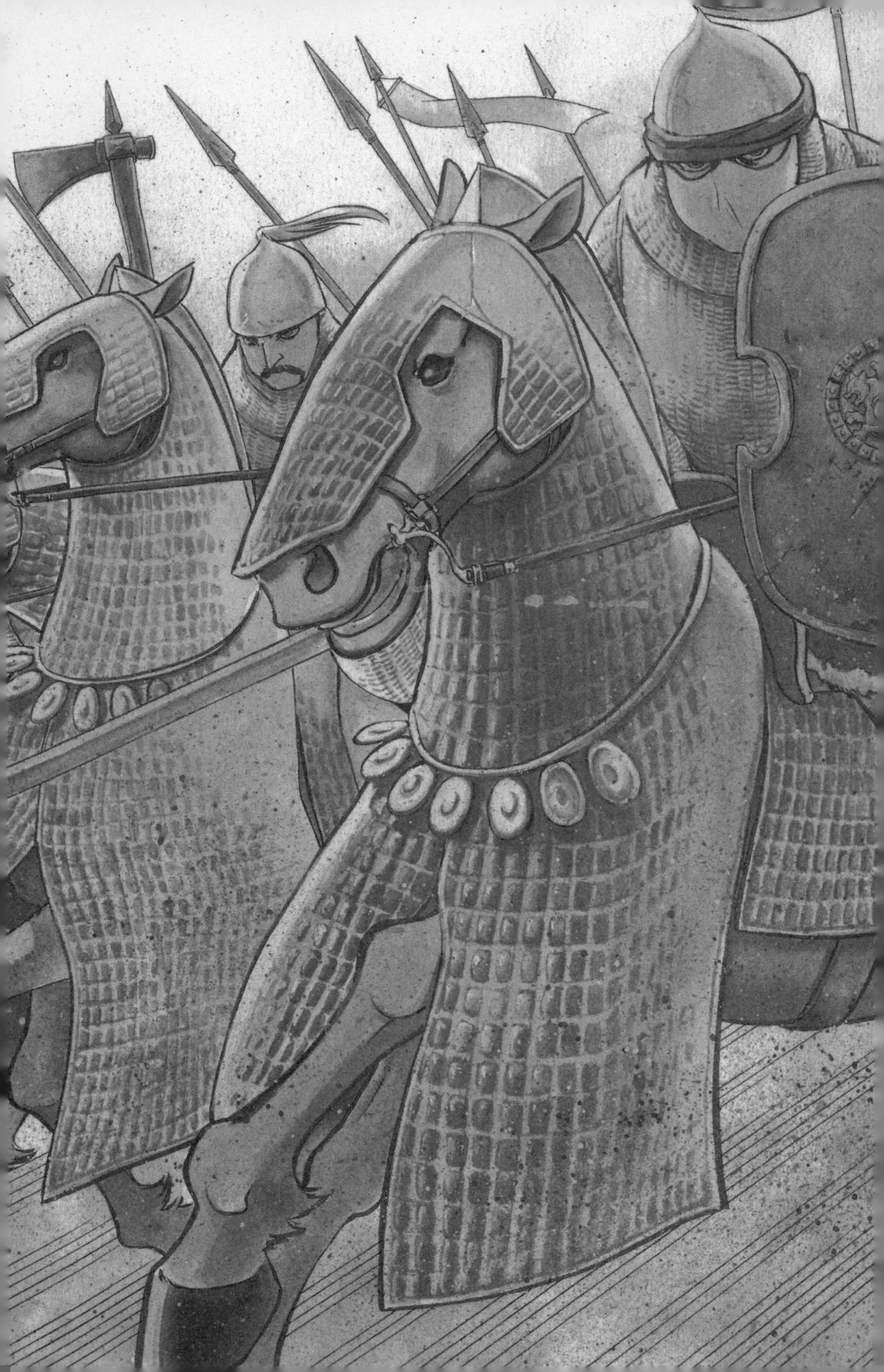

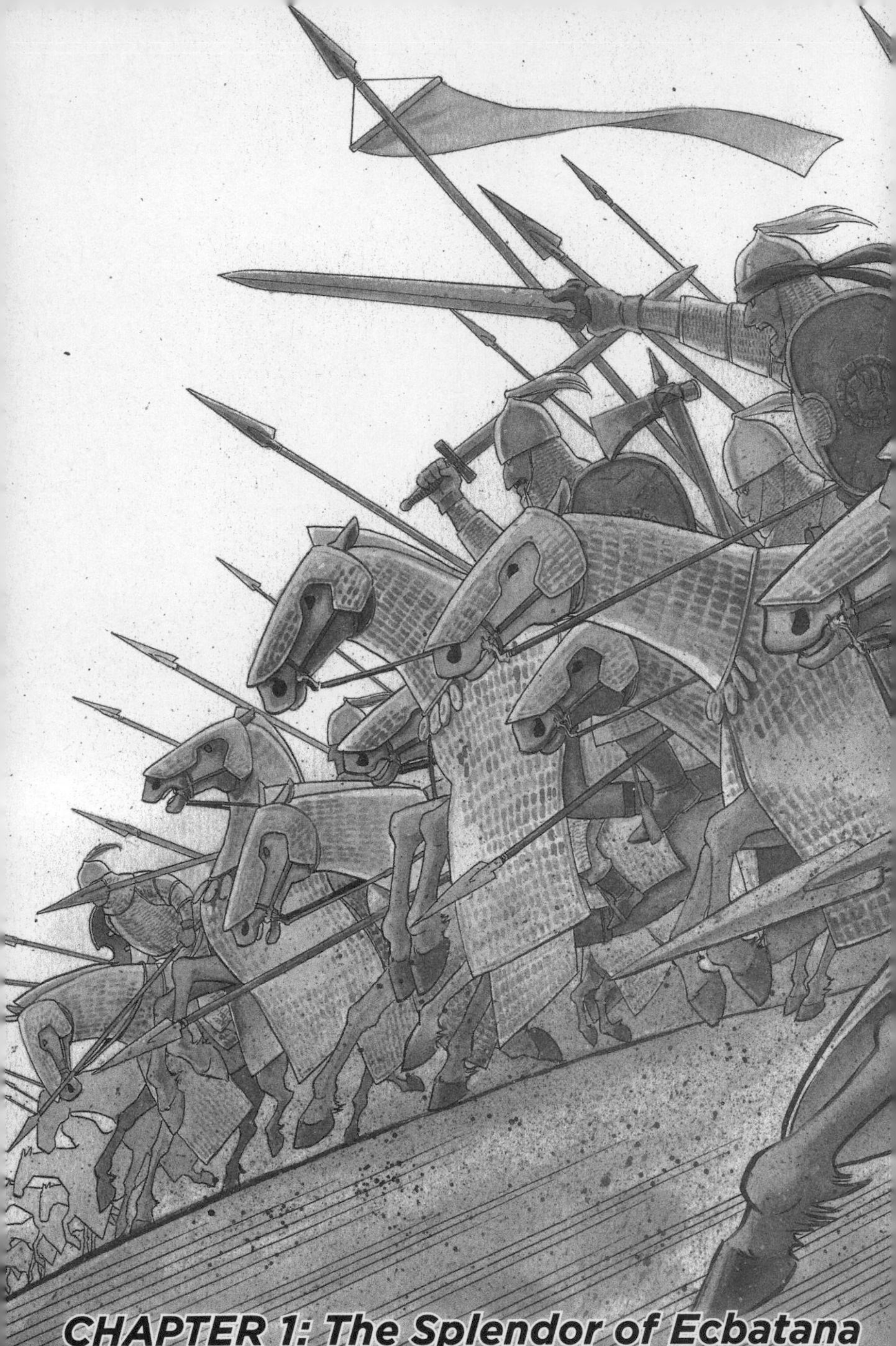

CHAPTER 1: The Splendor of Ecbatana

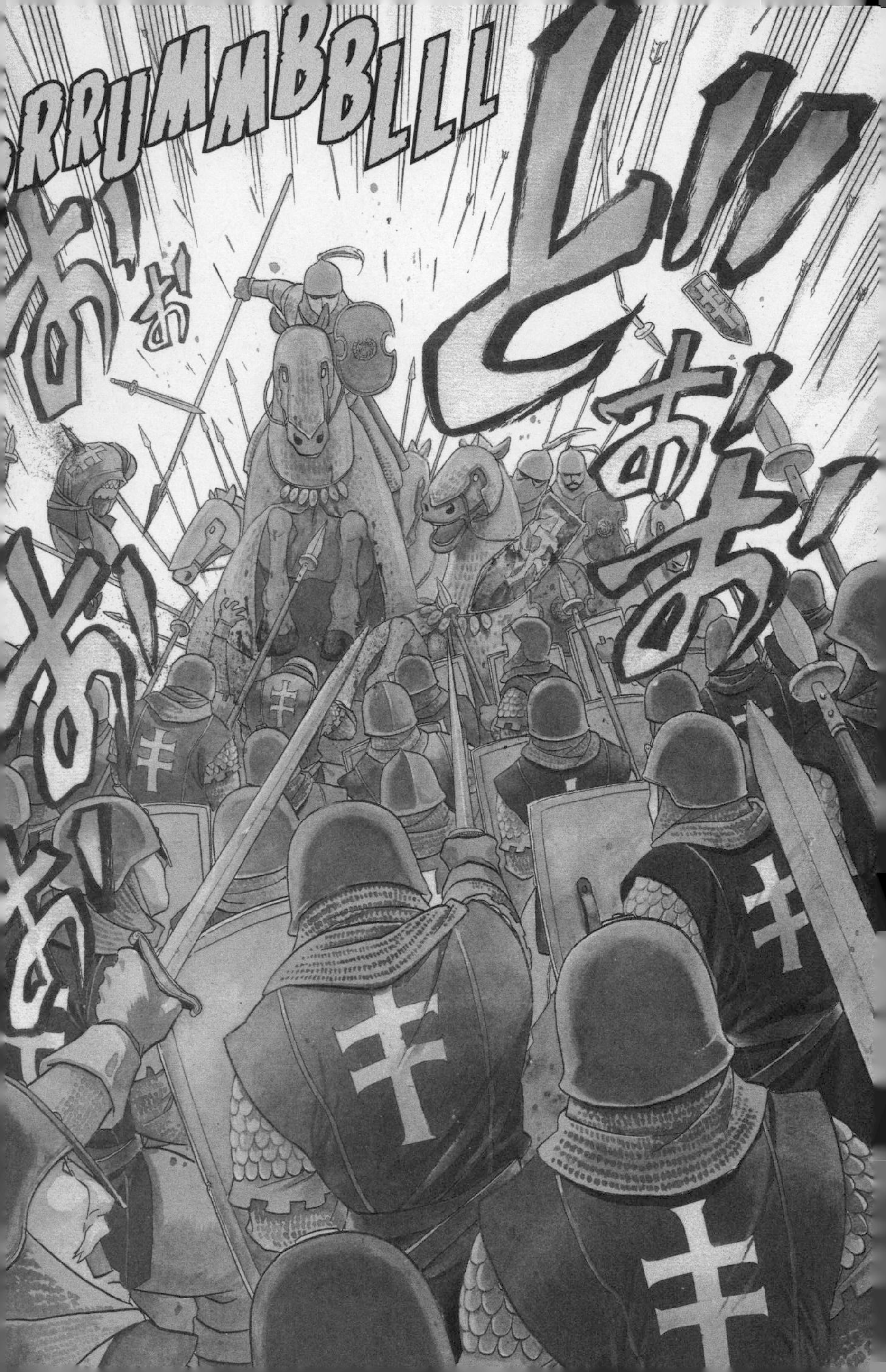
RRUMMBBLLL

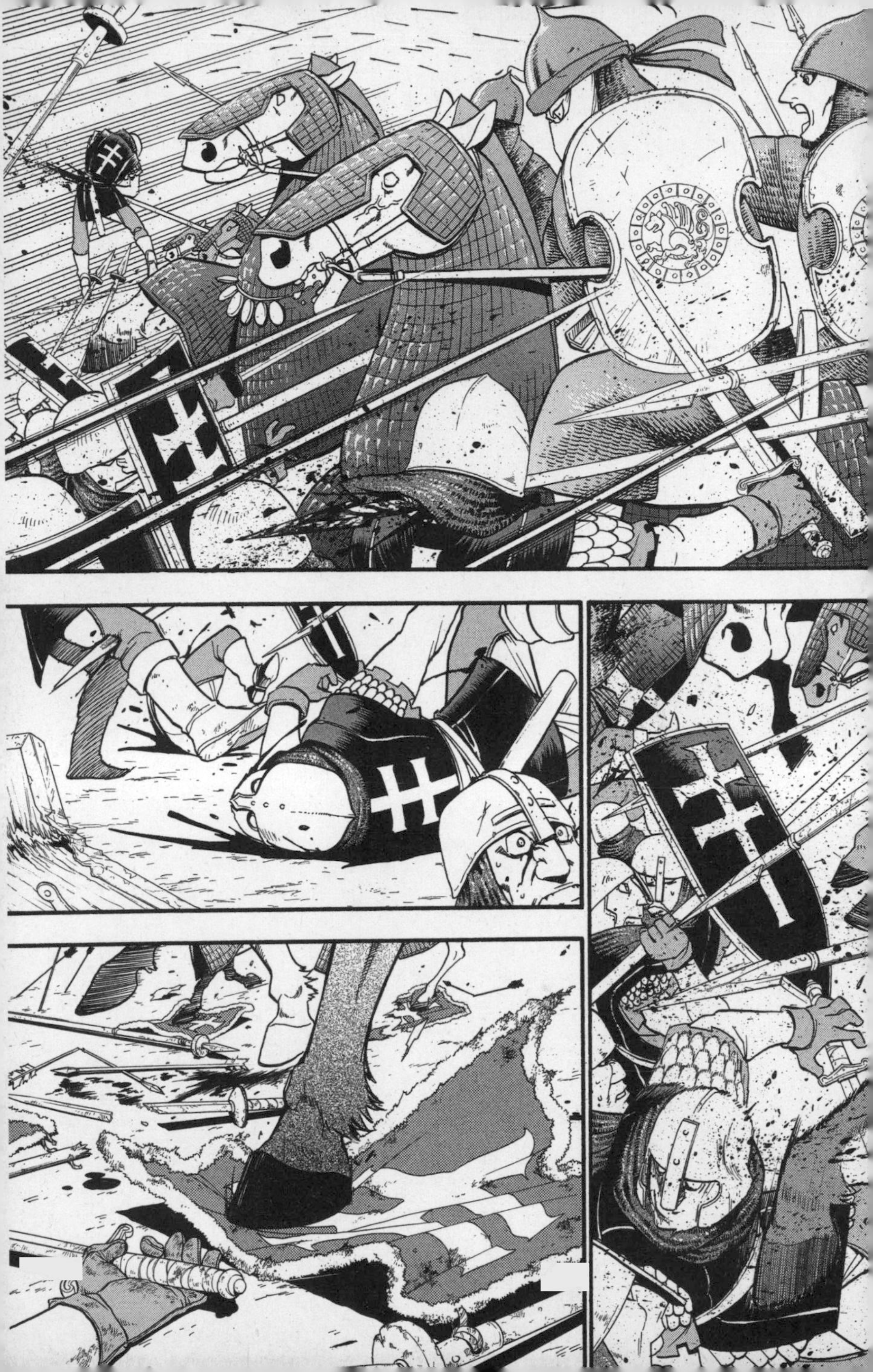

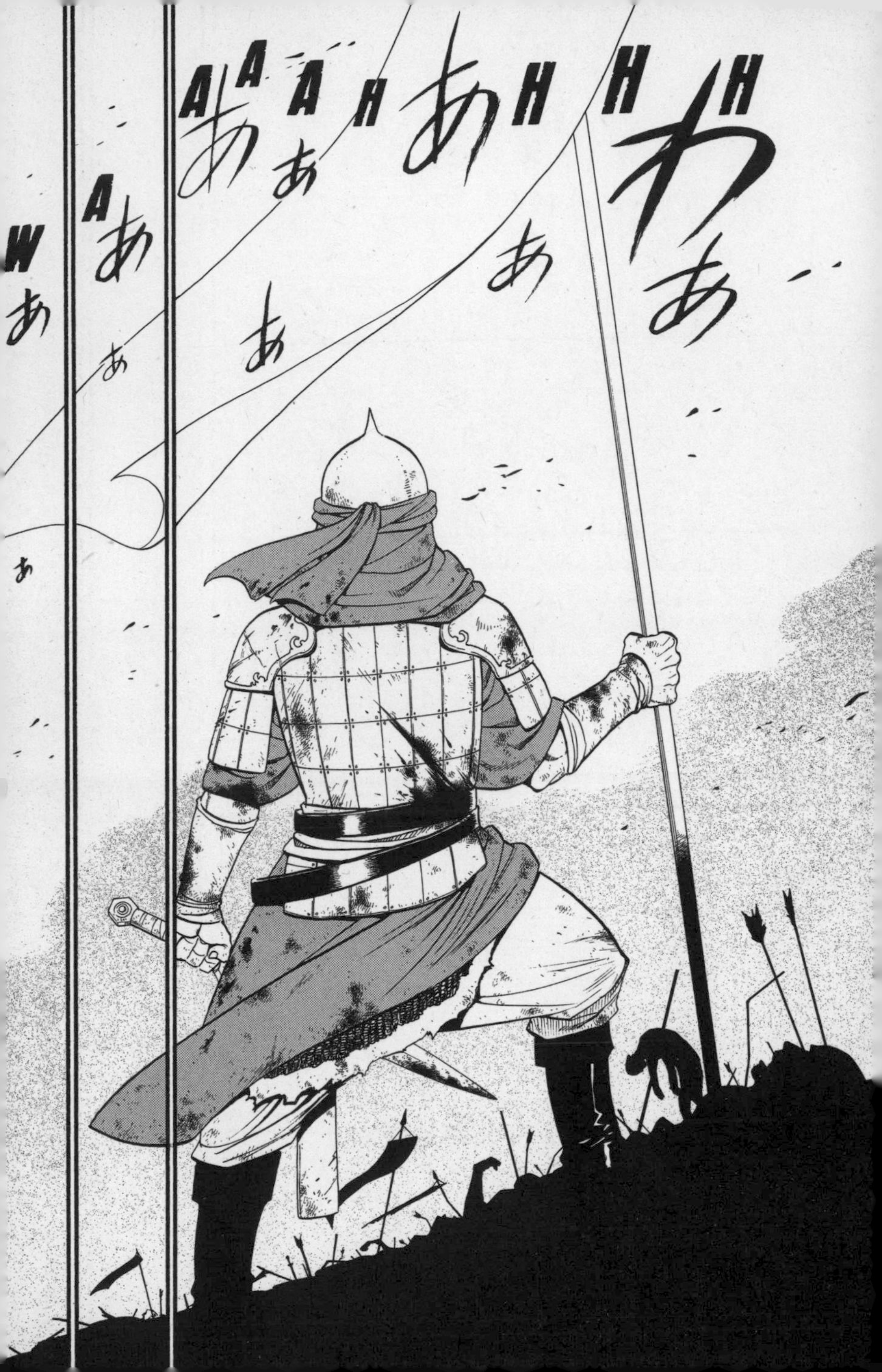

WAAAAHHHH
わああああああああああ

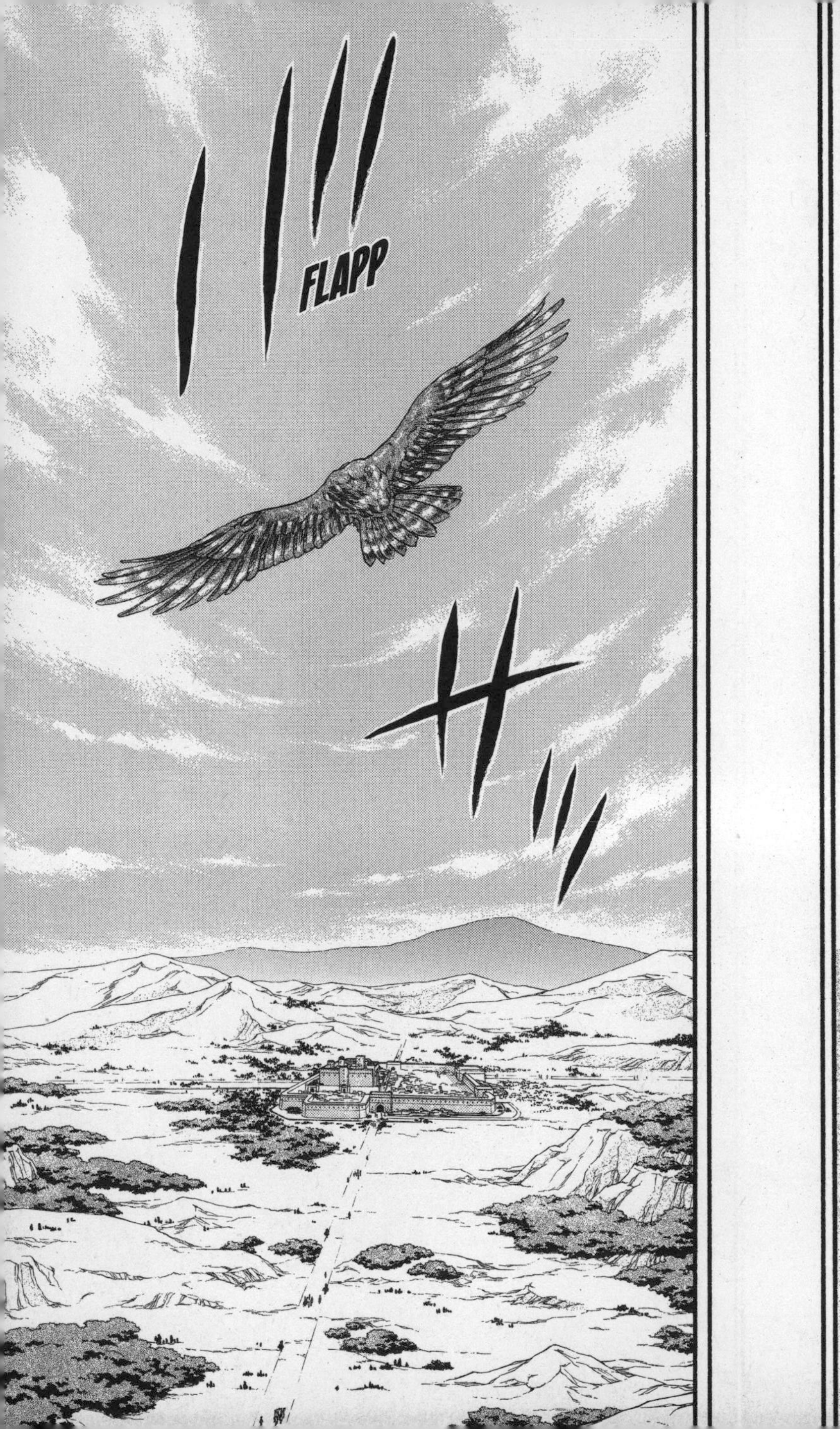
FLAPP

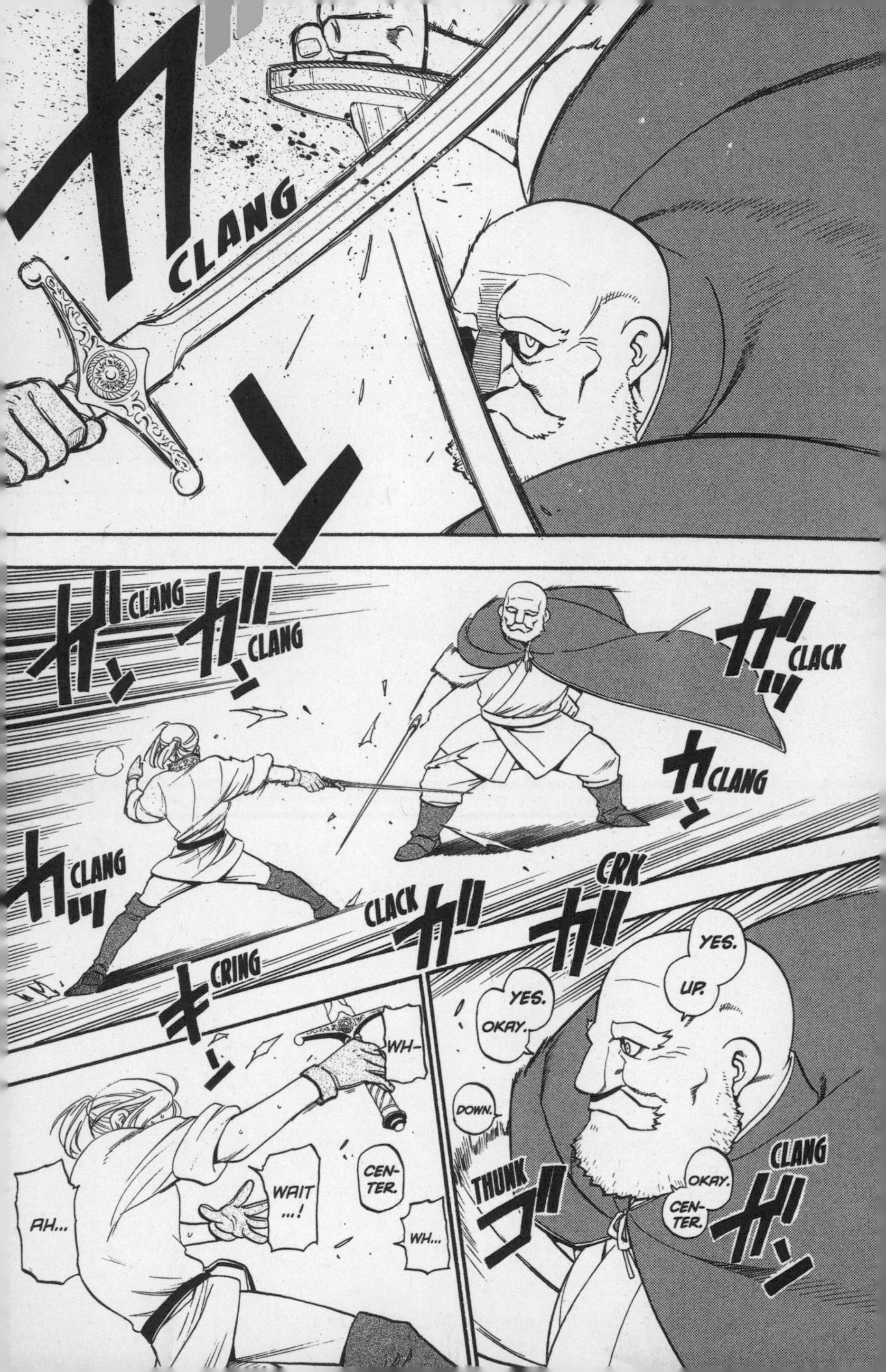
CLANG
CLACK
CLANG
CLANG
CLANG
CLANG
CRK
CLACK
YES.
UP.
YES.
OKAY.
DOWN.
CLANG
OKAY.
CEN-
TER.
THUNK
CRING
WH-
CEN-
TER.
WAIT
...!
WH...
AH...

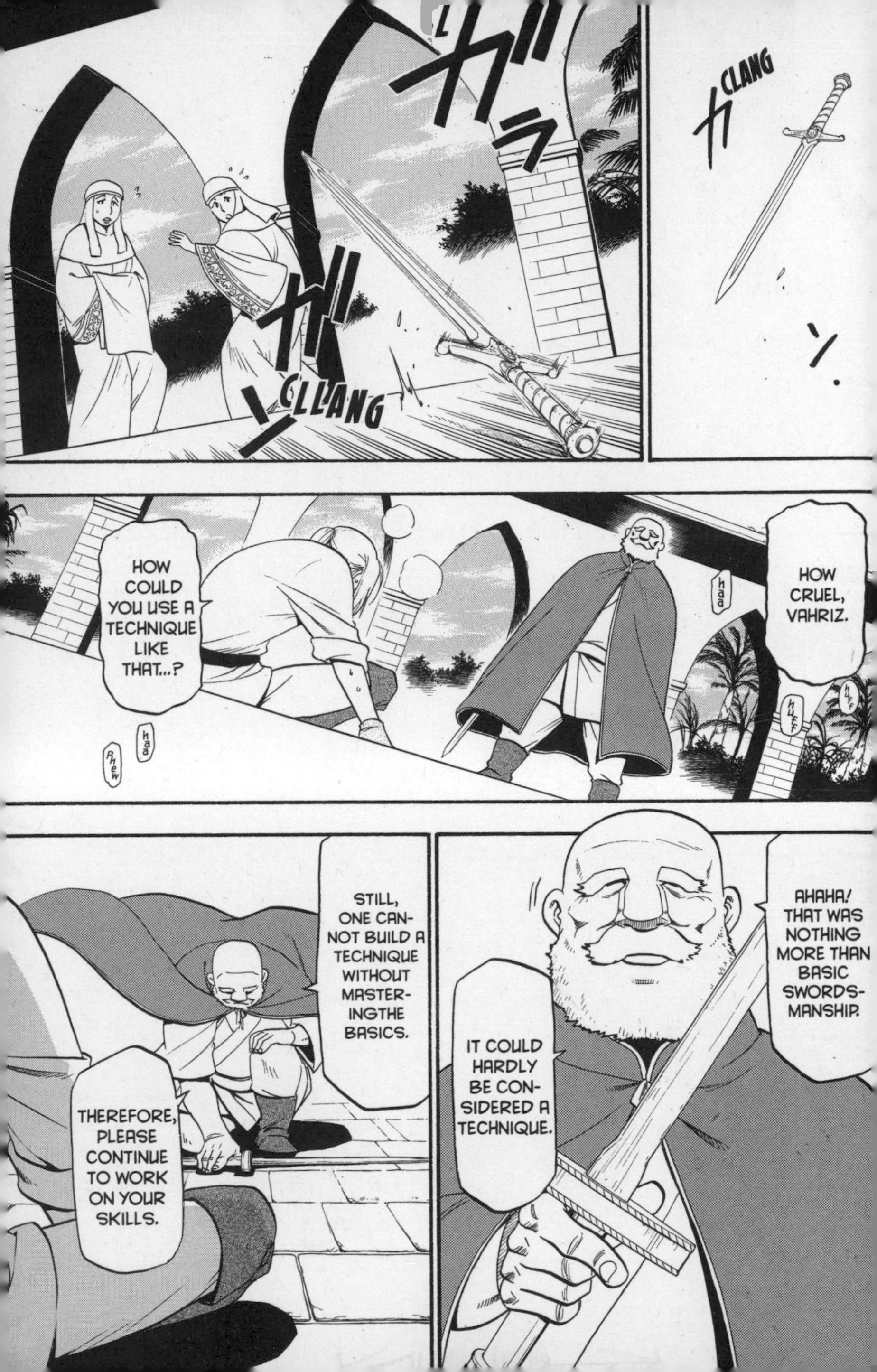

カ
CLANG
ン
ガラ
ガ
CLLANG
ン
HOW CRUEL, VAHRIZ.
huff
huff
haa
HOW COULD YOU USE A TECHNIQUE LIKE THAT...?
haa
Phew
AHAHA! THAT WAS NOTHING MORE THAN BASIC SWORDS-MANSHIP.
IT COULD HARDLY BE CON-SIDERED A TECHNIQUE.
STILL, ONE CAN-NOT BUILD A TECHNIQUE WITHOUT MASTER-INGTHE BASICS.
THEREFORE, PLEASE CONTINUE TO WORK ON YOUR SKILLS.

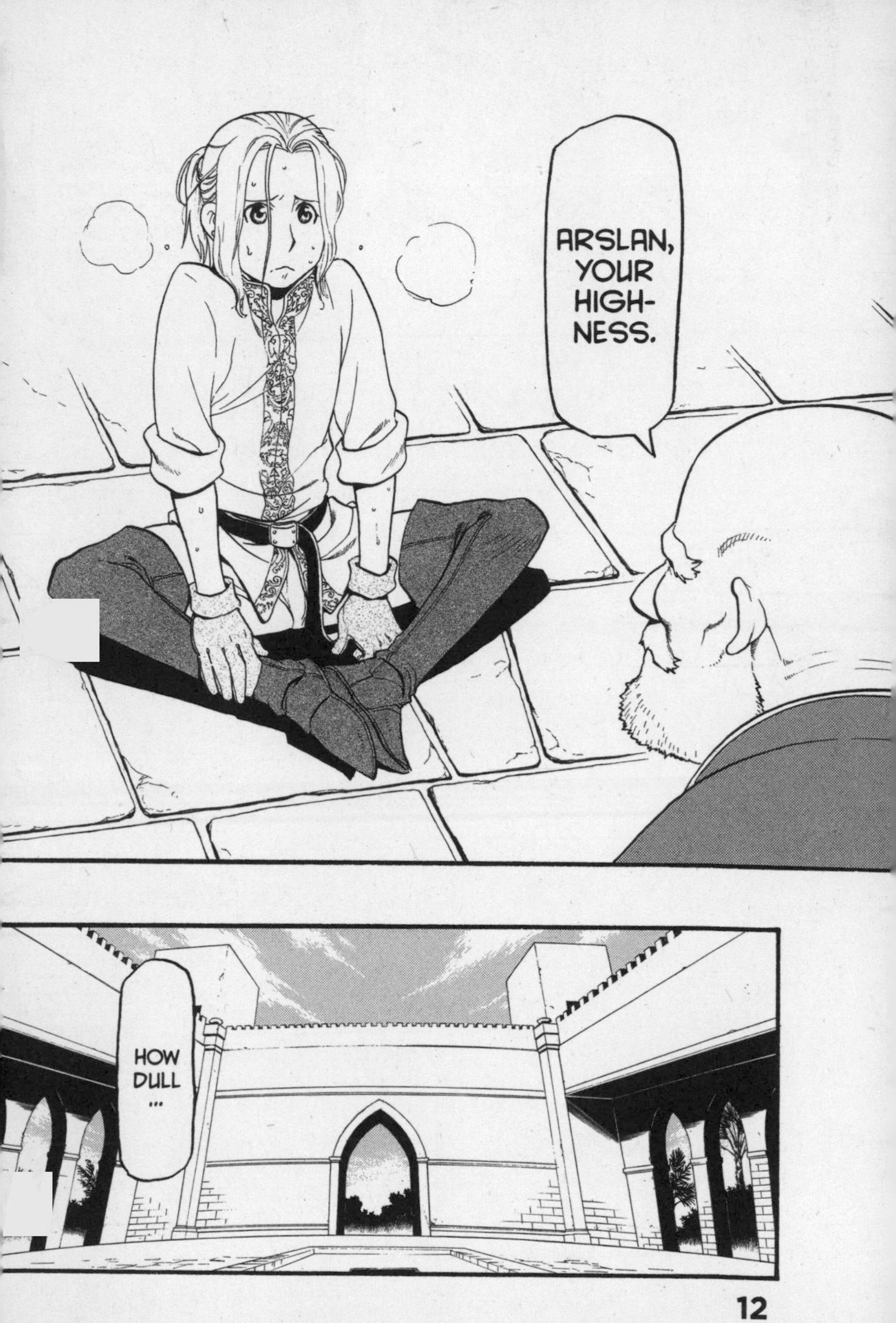
ARSLAN, YOUR HIGH-NESS.
HOW DULL ...

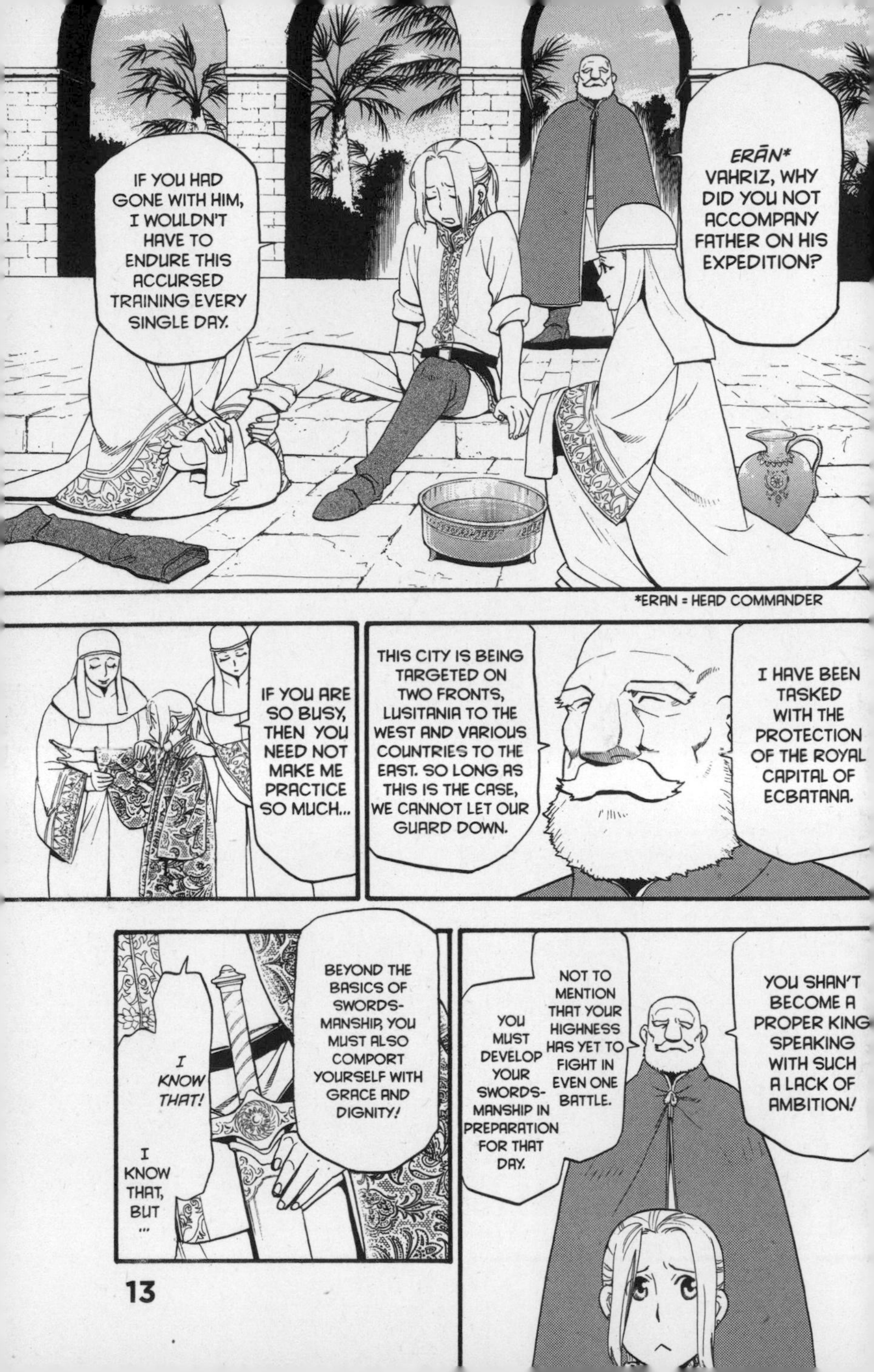
ERĀN* VAHRIZ, WHY DID YOU NOT ACCOMPANY FATHER ON HIS EXPEDITION?
IF YOU HAD GONE WITH HIM, I WOULDN'T HAVE TO ENDURE THIS ACCURSED TRAINING EVERY SINGLE DAY.
*ERAN = HEAD COMMANDER
I HAVE BEEN TASKED WITH THE PROTECTION OF THE ROYAL CAPITAL OF ECBATANA.
THIS CITY IS BEING TARGETED ON TWO FRONTS, LUSITANIA TO THE WEST AND VARIOUS COUNTRIES TO THE EAST. SO LONG AS THIS IS THE CASE, WE CANNOT LET OUR GUARD DOWN.
IF YOU ARE SO BUSY, THEN YOU NEED NOT MAKE ME PRACTICE SO MUCH...
YOU SHAN'T BECOME A PROPER KING SPEAKING WITH SUCH A LACK OF AMBITION!
NOT TO MENTION THAT YOUR HIGHNESS HAS YET TO FIGHT IN EVEN ONE BATTLE.
YOU MUST DEVELOP YOUR SWORDSMANSHIP IN PREPARATION FOR THAT DAY.
BEYOND THE BASICS OF SWORDSMANSHIP, YOU MUST ALSO COMPORT YOURSELF WITH GRACE AND DIGNITY!
I KNOW THAT!
I KNOW THAT, BUT ...

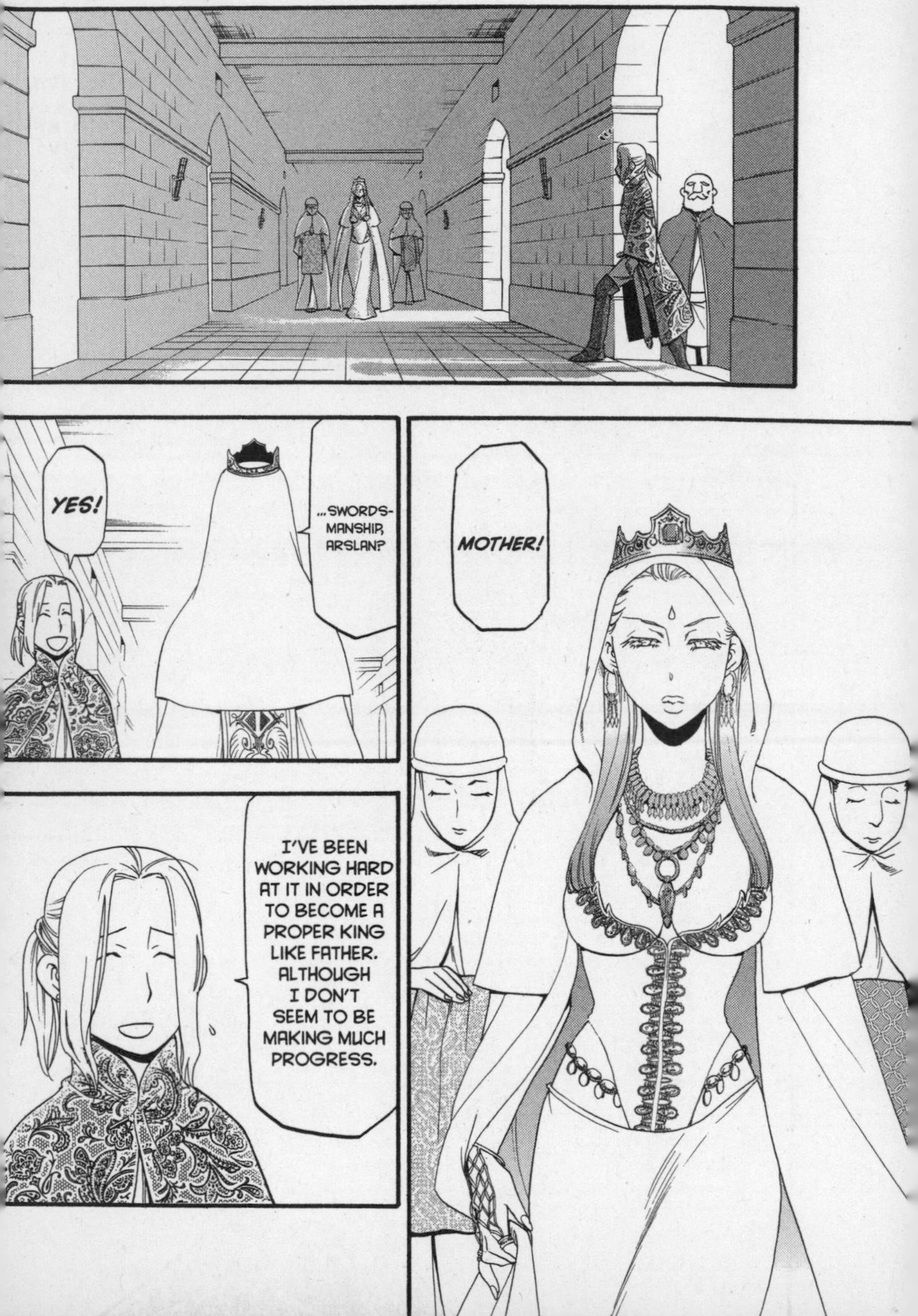
MOTHER!
...SWORDS-MANSHIP, ARSLAN?
YES!
I'VE BEEN WORKING HARD AT IT IN ORDER TO BECOME A PROPER KING LIKE FATHER. ALTHOUGH I DON'T SEEM TO BE MAKING MUCH PROGRESS.

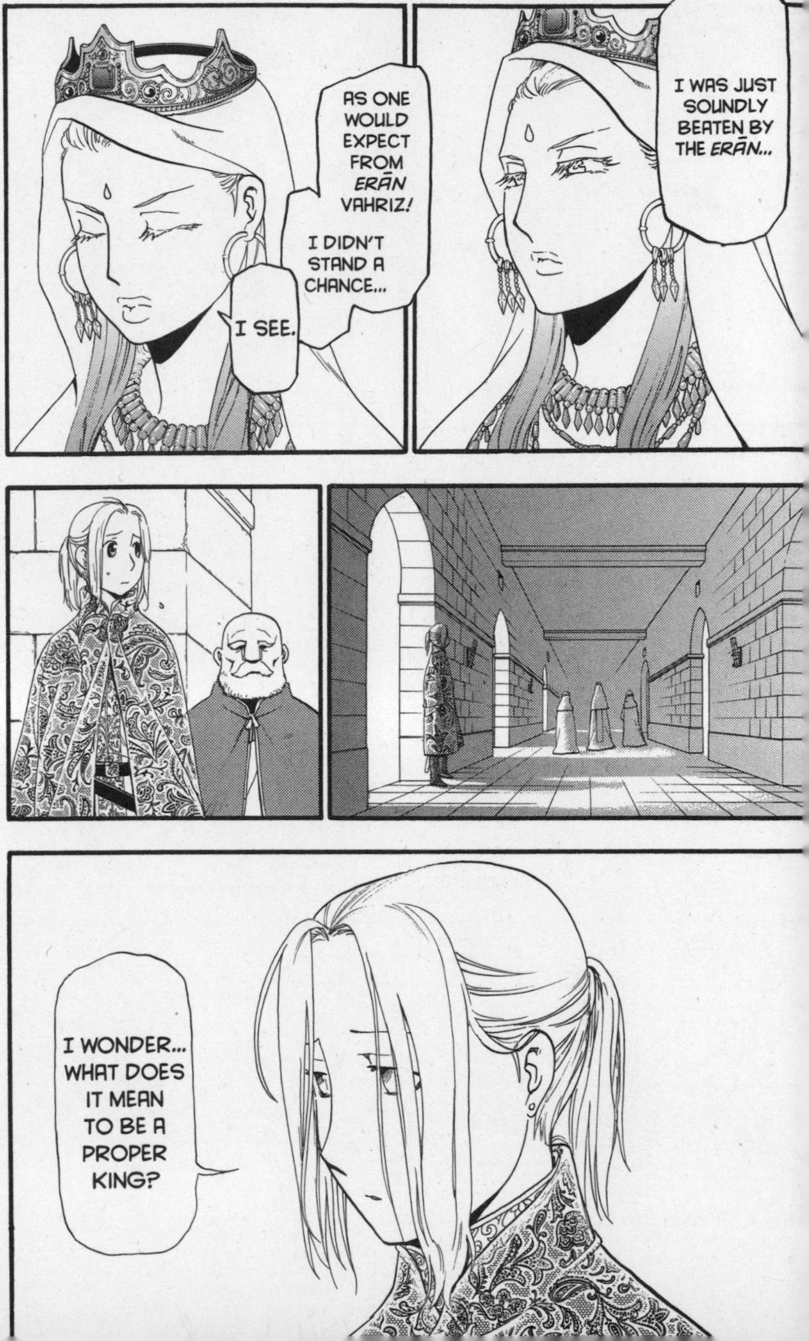
I WAS JUST SOUNDLY BEATEN BY THE *ERĀN*...
AS ONE WOULD EXPECT FROM *ERĀN* VAHRIZ!
I DIDN'T STAND A CHANCE...
I SEE.
I WONDER... WHAT DOES IT MEAN TO BE A PROPER KING?

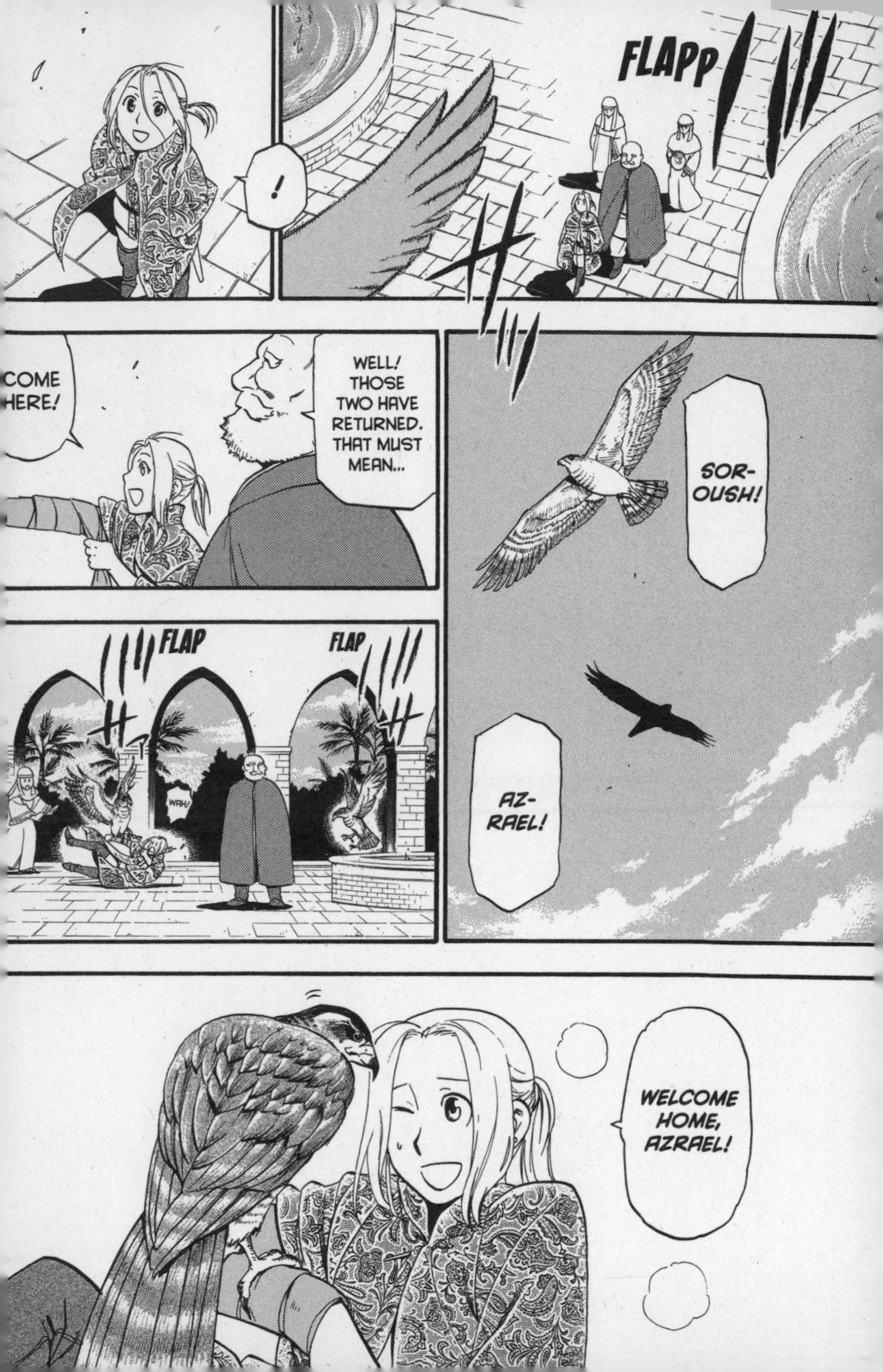
FLAPP
!
SOR-OUSH!
AZ-RAEL!
WELL! THOSE TWO HAVE RETURNED. THAT MUST MEAN...
COME HERE!
FLAP
FLAP
WAH!
WELCOME HOME, AZRAEL!

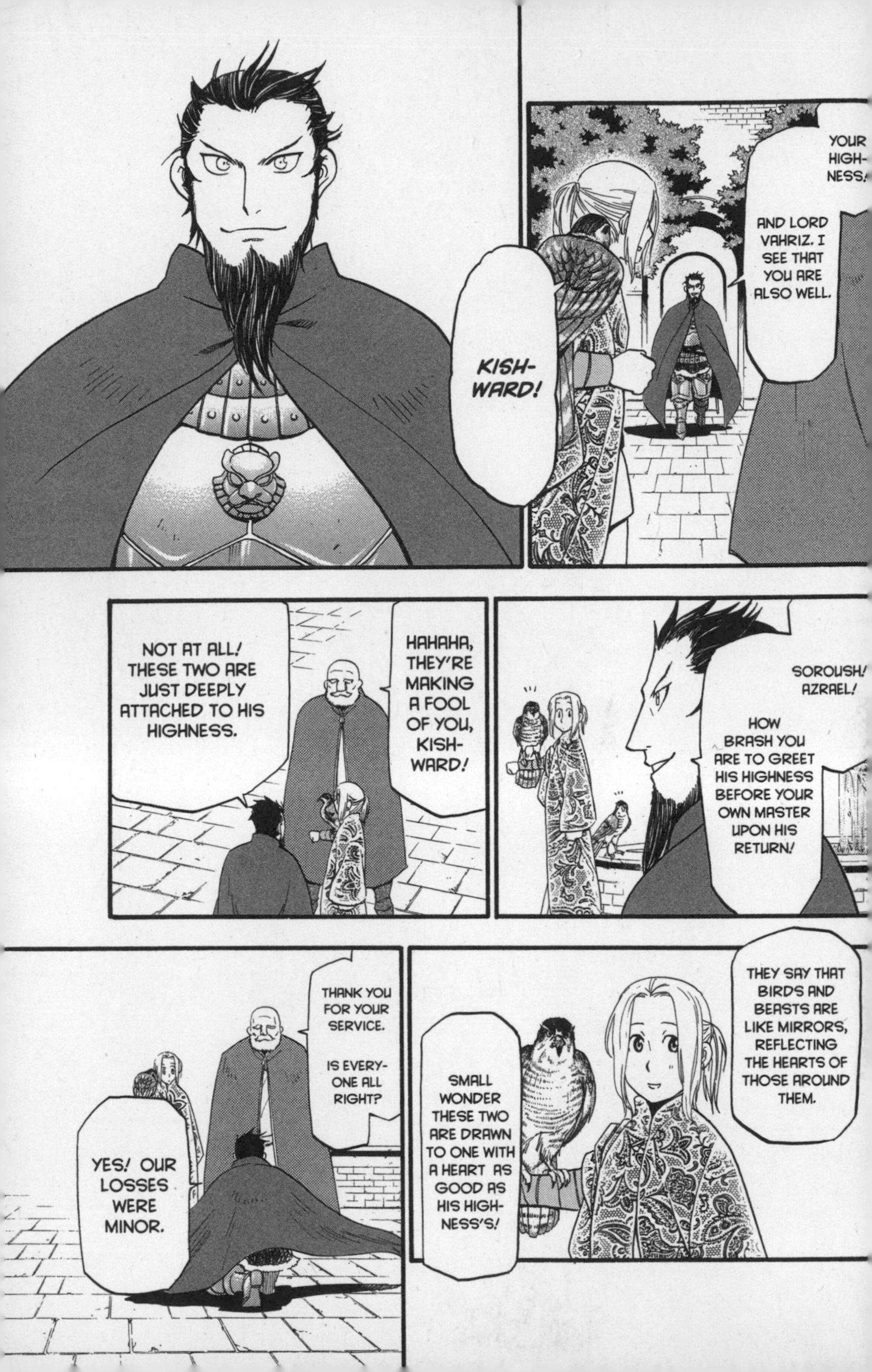
YOUR HIGHNESS!
AND LORD VAHRIZ. I SEE THAT YOU ARE ALSO WELL.
KISHWARD!
SOROUSH! AZRAEL!
HOW BRASH YOU ARE TO GREET HIS HIGHNESS BEFORE YOUR OWN MASTER UPON HIS RETURN!
HAHAHA, THEY'RE MAKING A FOOL OF YOU, KISHWARD!
NOT AT ALL! THESE TWO ARE JUST DEEPLY ATTACHED TO HIS HIGHNESS.
THEY SAY THAT BIRDS AND BEASTS ARE LIKE MIRRORS, REFLECTING THE HEARTS OF THOSE AROUND THEM.
SMALL WONDER THESE TWO ARE DRAWN TO ONE WITH A HEART AS GOOD AS HIS HIGHNESS'S!
THANK YOU FOR YOUR SERVICE.
IS EVERYONE ALL RIGHT?
YES! OUR LOSSES WERE MINOR.

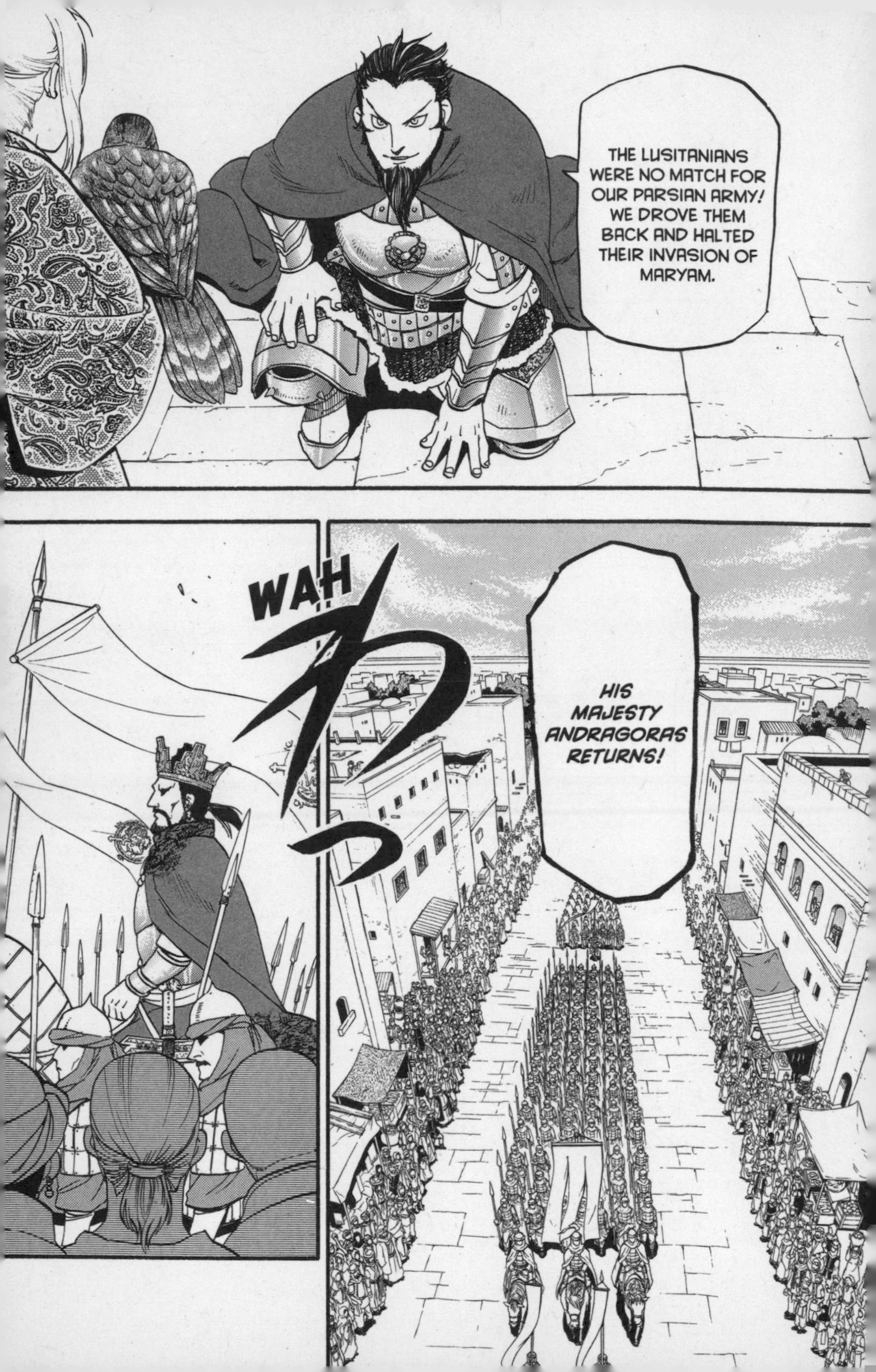
THE LUSITANIANS WERE NO MATCH FOR OUR PARSIAN ARMY! WE DROVE THEM BACK AND HALTED THEIR INVASION OF MARYAM.
HIS MAJESTY ANDRAGORAS RETURNS!
WAH

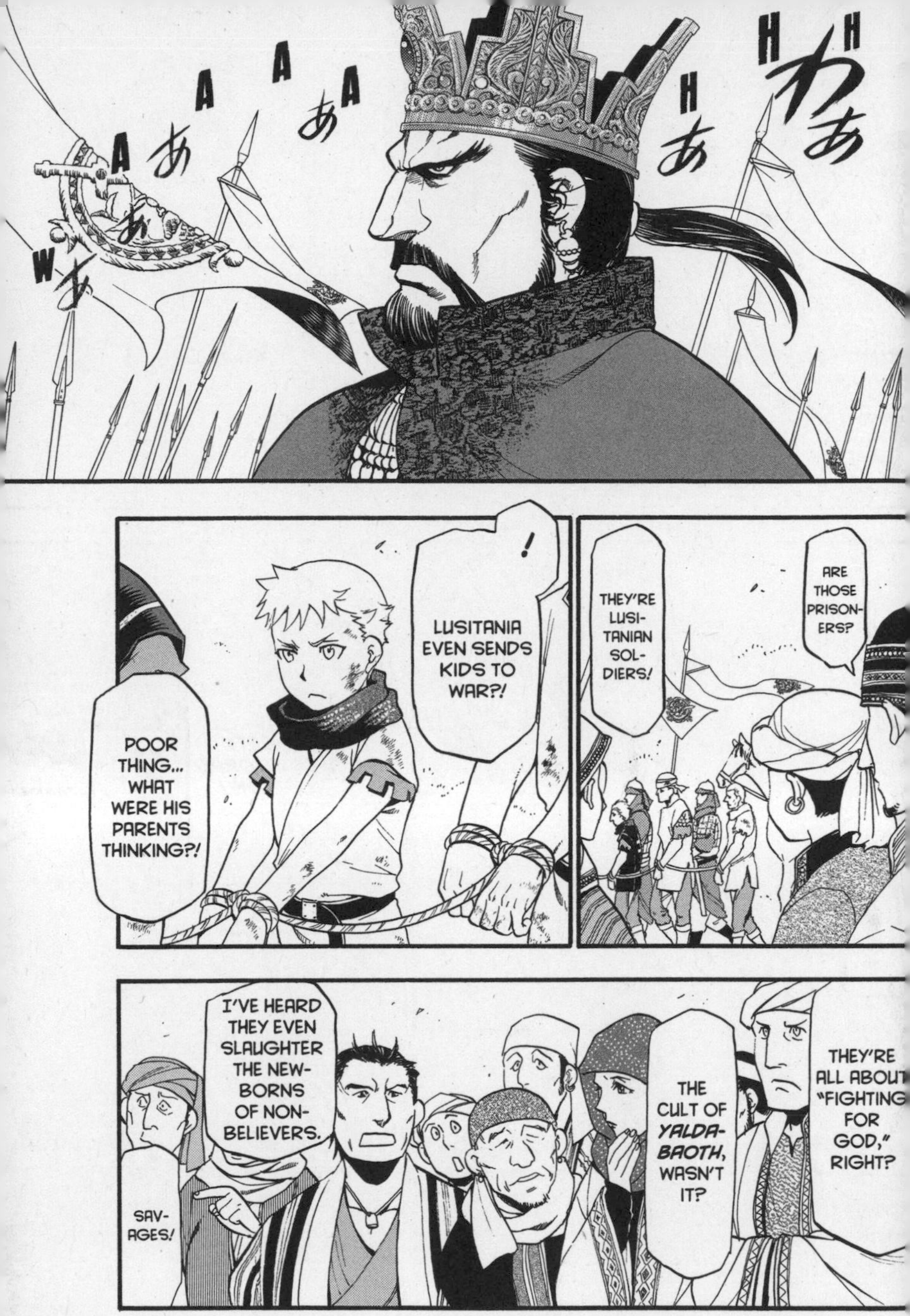
WAAAAAHHH
わああああああ
ARE THOSE PRISONERS?
THEY'RE LUSITANIAN SOLDIERS!
!
LUSITANIA EVEN SENDS KIDS TO WAR?!
POOR THING... WHAT WERE HIS PARENTS THINKING?!
THEY'RE ALL ABOUT "FIGHTING FOR GOD," RIGHT?
THE CULT OF *YALDABAOTH*, WASN'T IT?
I'VE HEARD THEY EVEN SLAUGHTER THE NEWBORNS OF NON-BELIEVERS.
SAVAGES!

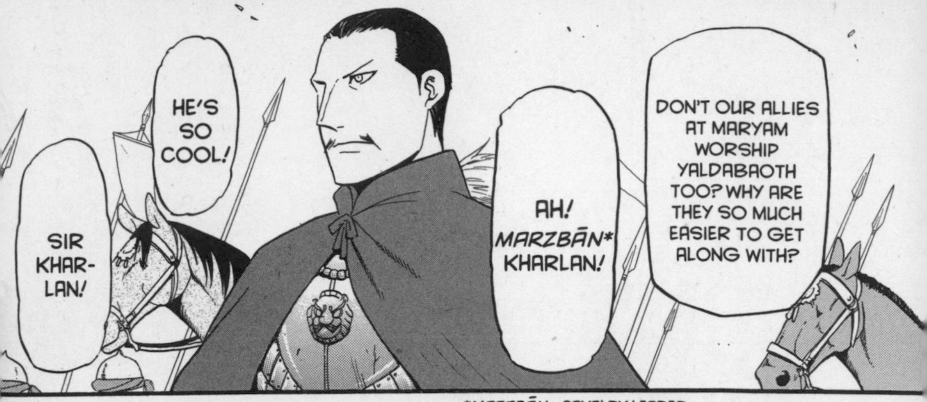
DON'T OUR ALLIES AT MARYAM WORSHIP YALDABAOTH TOO? WHY ARE THEY SO MUCH EASIER TO GET ALONG WITH?
AH! *MARZBĀN** KHARLAN!
HE'S SO COOL!
SIR KHARLAN!

**MARZBĀN* = CAVALRY LEADER

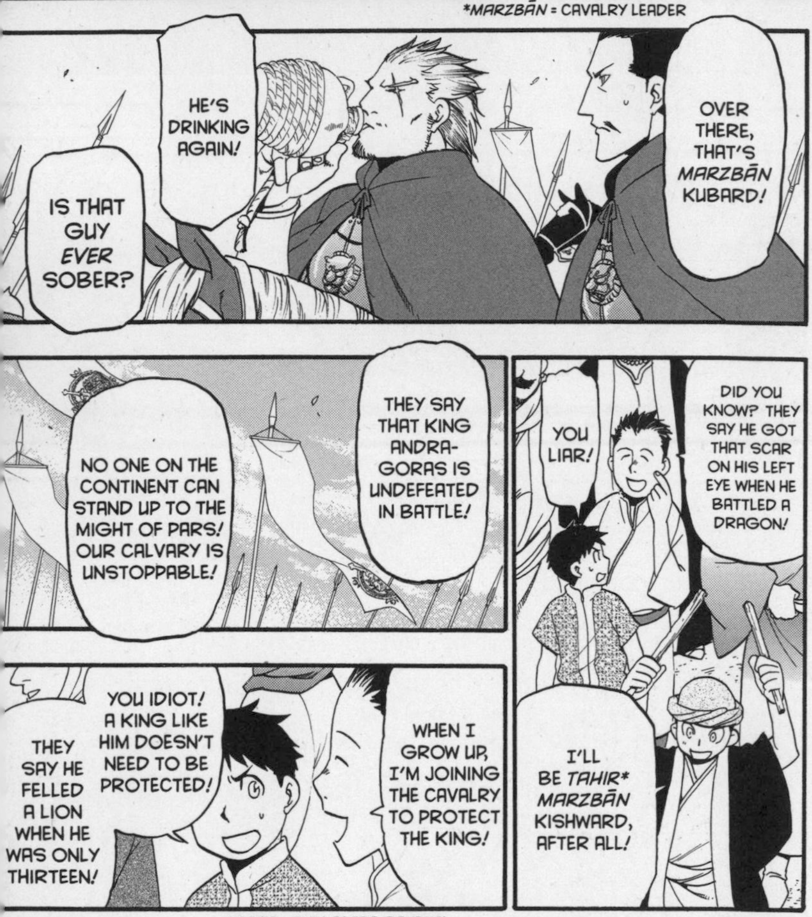
OVER THERE, THAT'S *MARZBĀN* KUBARD!
HE'S DRINKING AGAIN!
IS THAT GUY *EVER* SOBER?
DID YOU KNOW? THEY SAY HE GOT THAT SCAR ON HIS LEFT EYE WHEN HE BATTLED A DRAGON!
YOU LIAR!
I'LL BE *TAHIR** *MARZBĀN* KISHWARD, AFTER ALL!
THEY SAY THAT KING ANDRAGORAS IS UNDEFEATED IN BATTLE!
NO ONE ON THE CONTINENT CAN STAND UP TO THE MIGHT OF PARS! OUR CALVARY IS UNSTOPPABLE!
WHEN I GROW UP, I'M JOINING THE CAVALRY TO PROTECT THE KING!
YOU IDIOT! A KING LIKE HIM DOESN'T NEED TO BE PROTECTED!
THEY SAY HE FELLED A LION WHEN HE WAS ONLY THIRTEEN!

**TAHIR* = TWIN-BLADE GENERAL

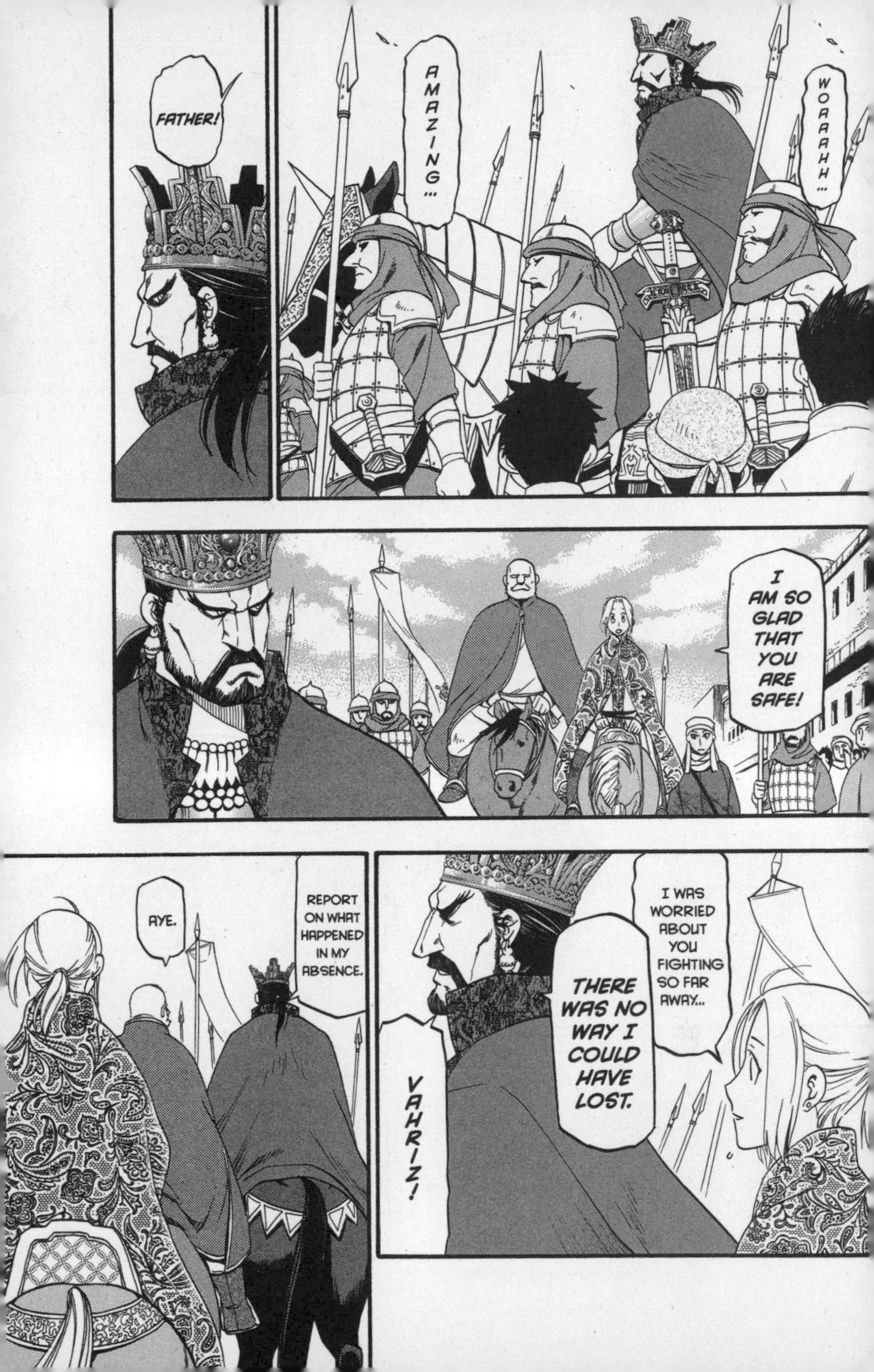
WOAAAAHH...
AMAZING...
FATHER!
I AM SO GLAD THAT YOU ARE SAFE!
I WAS WORRIED ABOUT YOU FIGHTING SO FAR AWAY...
THERE WAS NO WAY I COULD HAVE LOST.
VAHRIZ!
REPORT ON WHAT HAPPENED IN MY ABSENCE.
AYE.

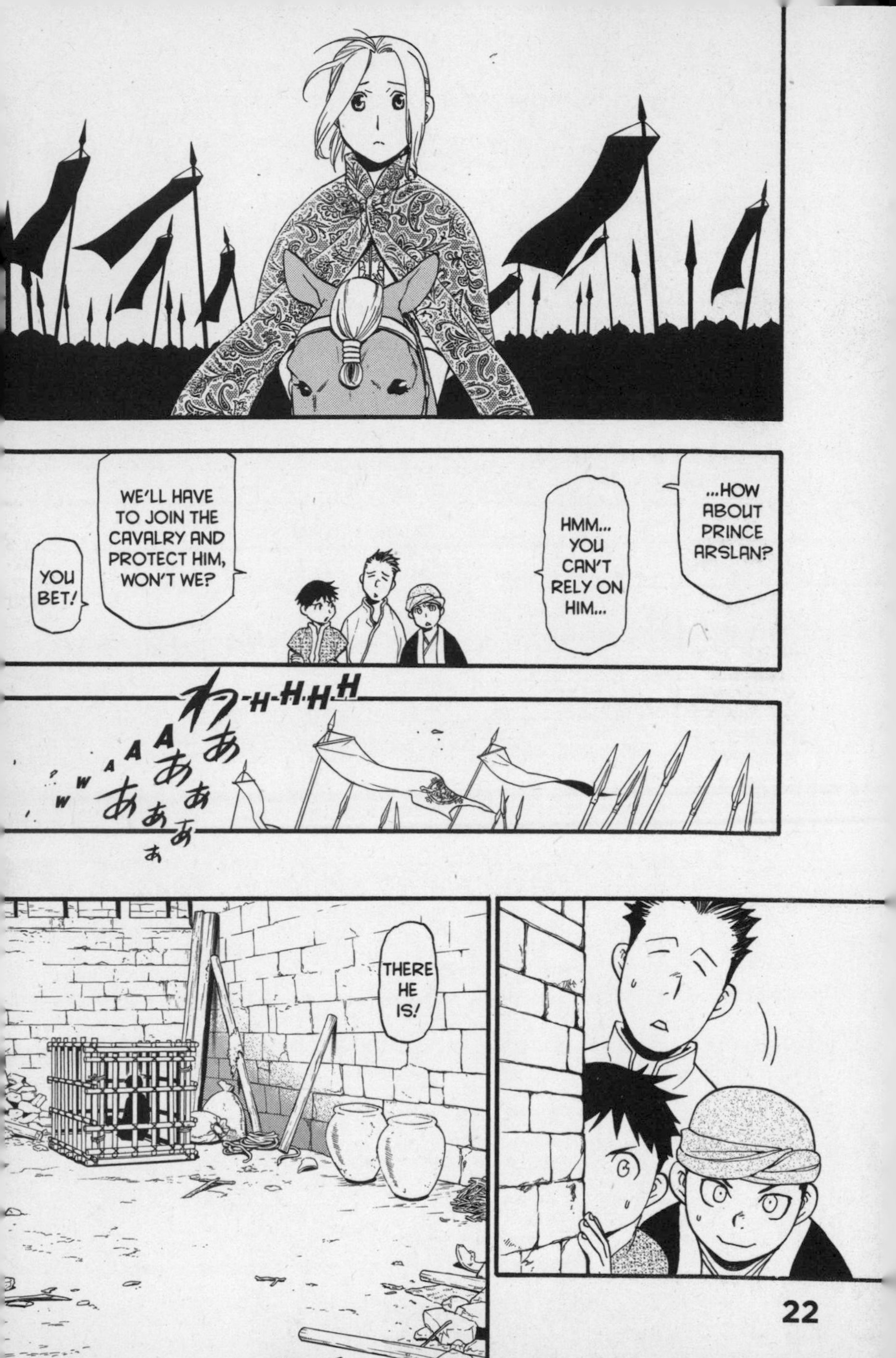
...HOW ABOUT PRINCE ARSLAN?
HMM... YOU CAN'T RELY ON HIM...
WE'LL HAVE TO JOIN THE CAVALRY AND PROTECT HIM, WON'T WE?
YOU BET!
わ-H-H-H-H
あああああああ
AAAWWW
THERE HE IS!

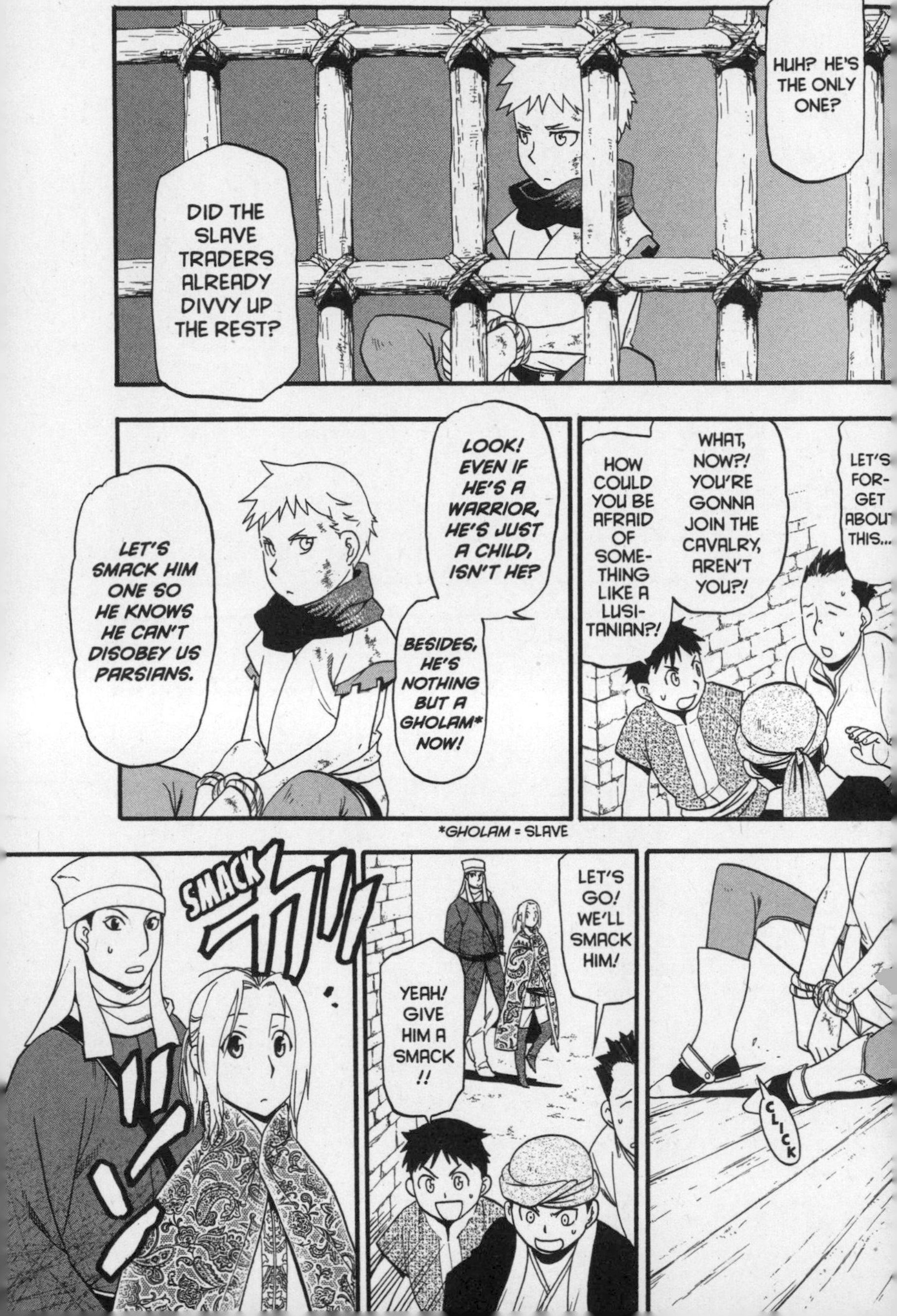
HUH? HE'S THE ONLY ONE?
DID THE SLAVE TRADERS ALREADY DIVVY UP THE REST?
LET'S FORGET ABOUT THIS...
WHAT, NOW?! YOU'RE GONNA JOIN THE CAVALRY, AREN'T YOU?!
HOW COULD YOU BE AFRAID OF SOMETHING LIKE A LUSITANIAN?!
LOOK! EVEN IF HE'S A WARRIOR, HE'S JUST A CHILD, ISN'T HE?
BESIDES, HE'S NOTHING BUT A GHOLAM* NOW!
LET'S SMACK HIM ONE SO HE KNOWS HE CAN'T DISOBEY US PARSIANS.
CLICK
LET'S GO! WE'LL SMACK HIM!
YEAH! GIVE HIM A SMACK!!
SMACK

*GHOLAM = SLAVE

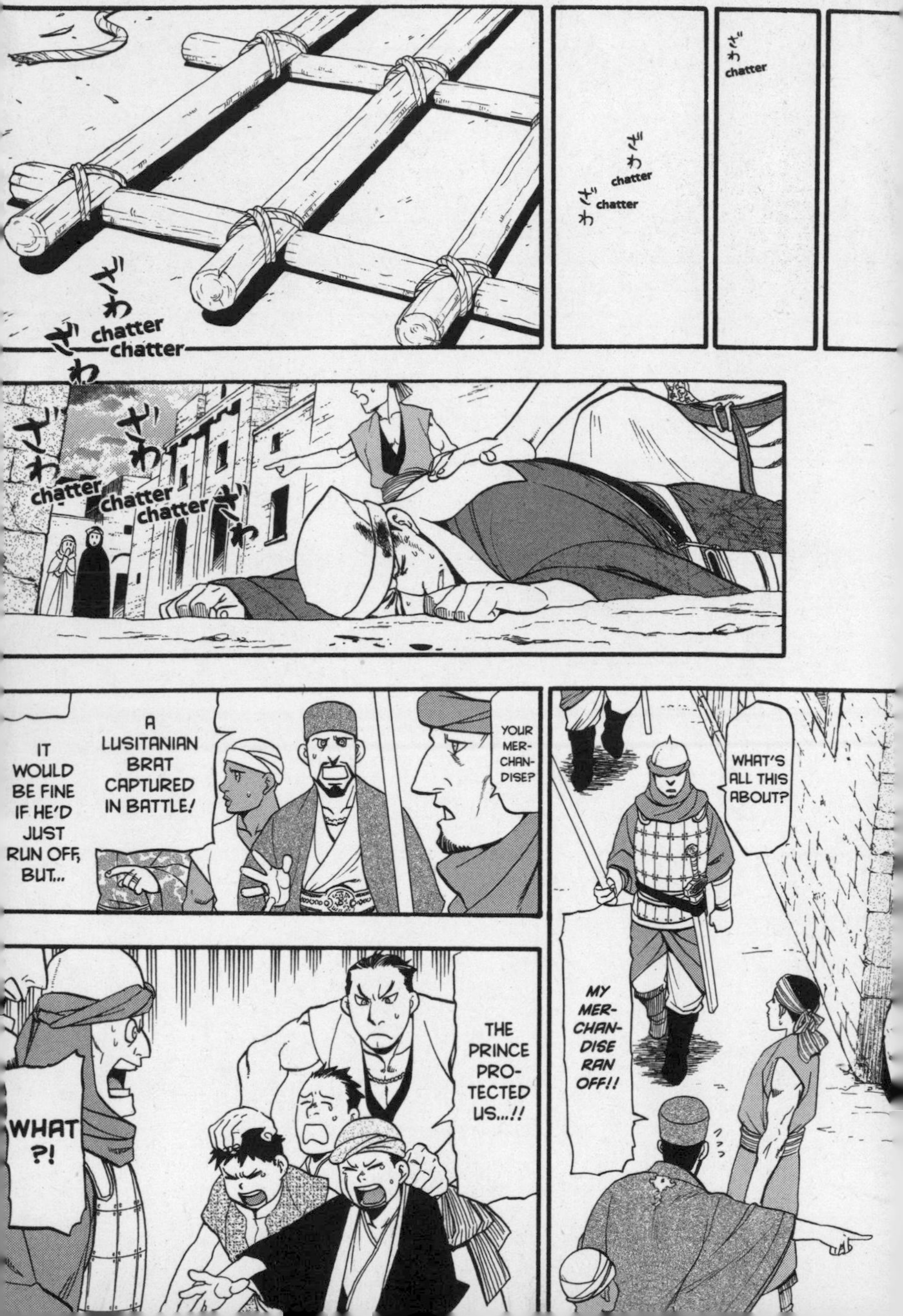
ざわ
chatter
ざわ ざわ
chatter chatter
ざわ ざわ
chatter chatter
ざわ ざわ ざわ
chatter chatter chatter
WHAT'S ALL THIS ABOUT?
MY MER-CHAN-DISE RAN OFF!!
YOUR MER-CHAN-DISE?
A LUSITANIAN BRAT CAPTURED IN BATTLE!
IT WOULD BE FINE IF HE'D JUST RUN OFF, BUT...
THE PRINCE PRO-TECTED US...!!
WHAT?!

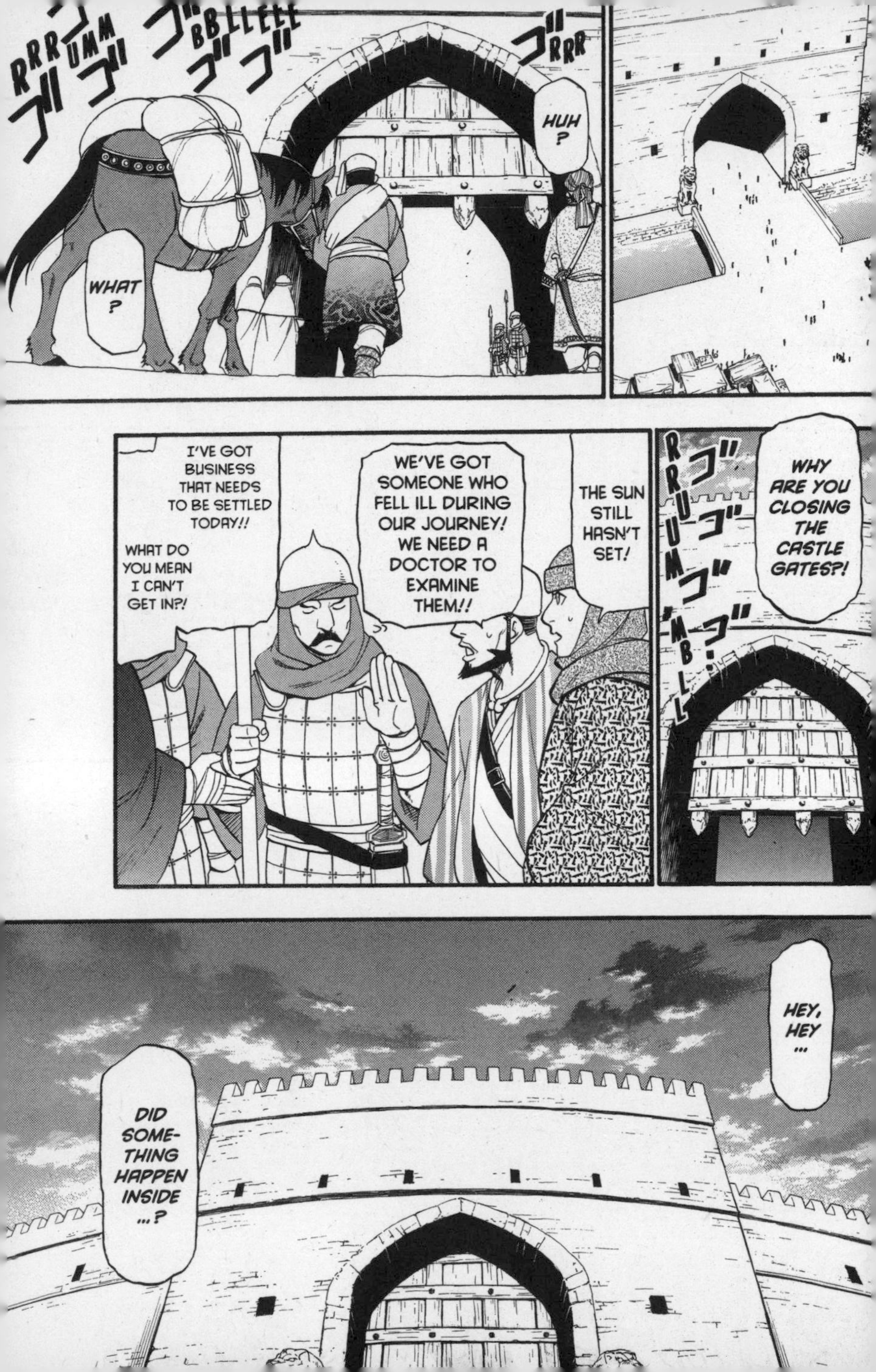
RRRUMM
BBLLEEE
RRR
HUH?
WHAT?
RRUMMBLL
WHY ARE YOU CLOSING THE CASTLE GATES?!
THE SUN STILL HASN'T SET!
WE'VE GOT SOMEONE WHO FELL ILL DURING OUR JOURNEY! WE NEED A DOCTOR TO EXAMINE THEM!!
I'VE GOT BUSINESS THAT NEEDS TO BE SETTLED TODAY!!
WHAT DO YOU MEAN I CAN'T GET IN?!
HEY, HEY ...
DID SOME-THING HAPPEN INSIDE ...?

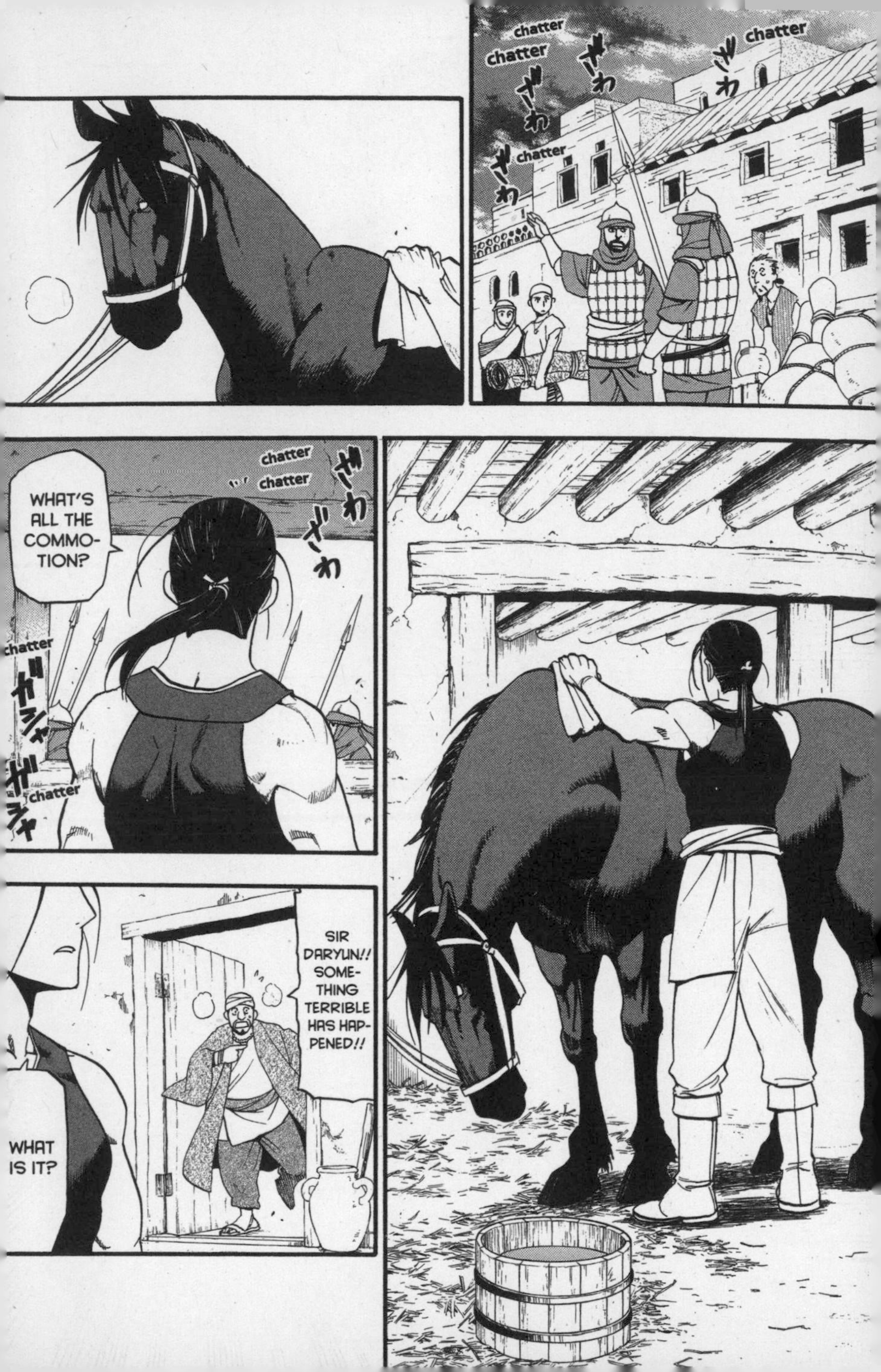
chatter
chatter
chatter
chatter
ざわ
ざわ
ざわ
ざわ
WHAT'S ALL THE COMMO-TION?
chatter
chatter
ざわ
ざわ
chatter
chatter
ガシャ
ガシャ
SIR DARYUN!! SOME-THING TERRIBLE HAS HAP-PENED!!
WHAT IS IT?

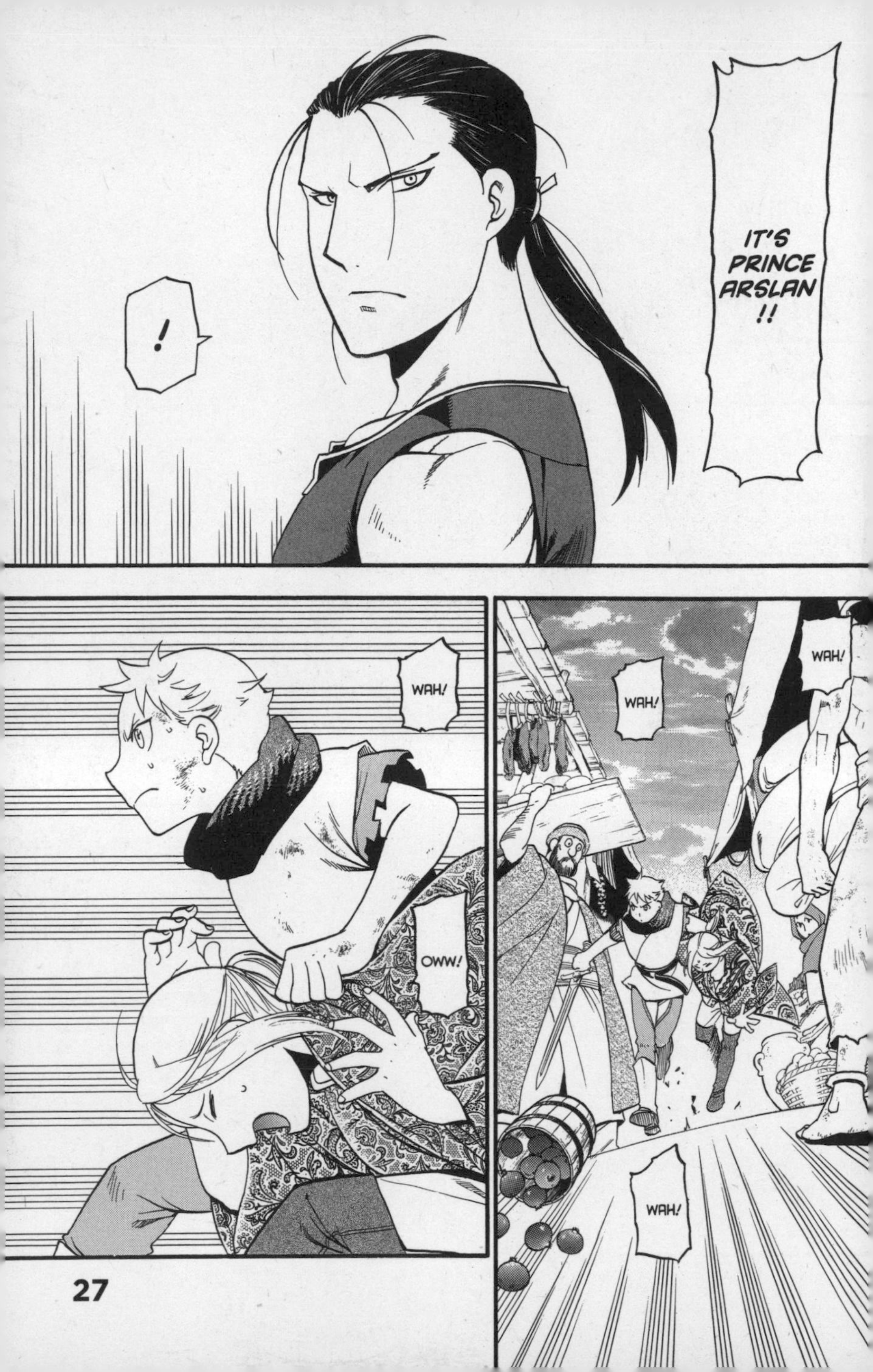
IT'S PRINCE ARSLAN!!
!
WAH!
WAH!
WAH!
WAH!
OWW!

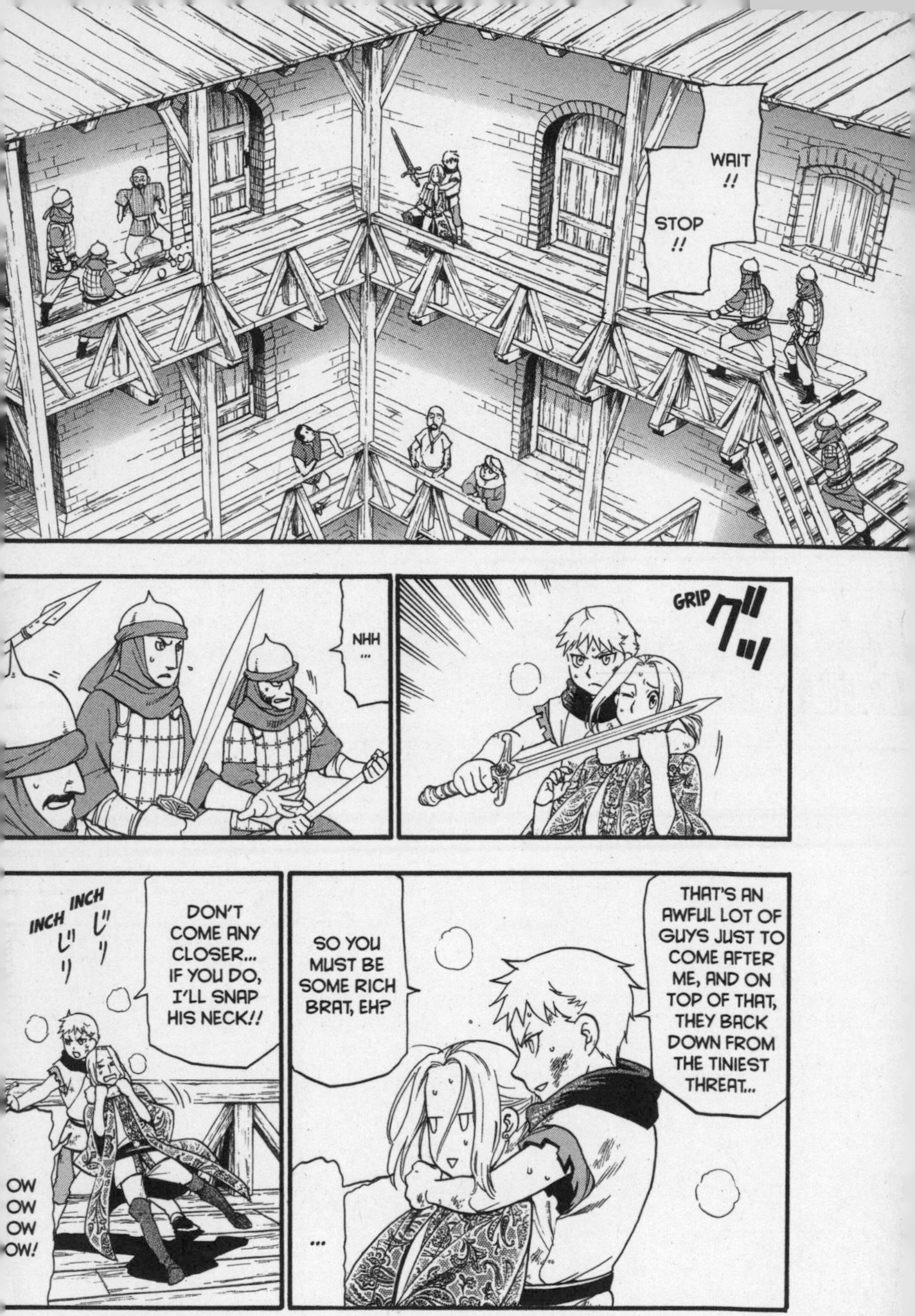
WAIT!!
STOP!!
GRIP グッ
NHH...
THAT'S AN AWFUL LOT OF GUYS JUST TO COME AFTER ME, AND ON TOP OF THAT, THEY BACK DOWN FROM THE TINIEST THREAT...
SO YOU MUST BE SOME RICH BRAT, EH?
...
INCH INCH じりじり
DON'T COME ANY CLOSER... IF YOU DO, I'LL SNAP HIS NECK!!
OW OW OW OW!

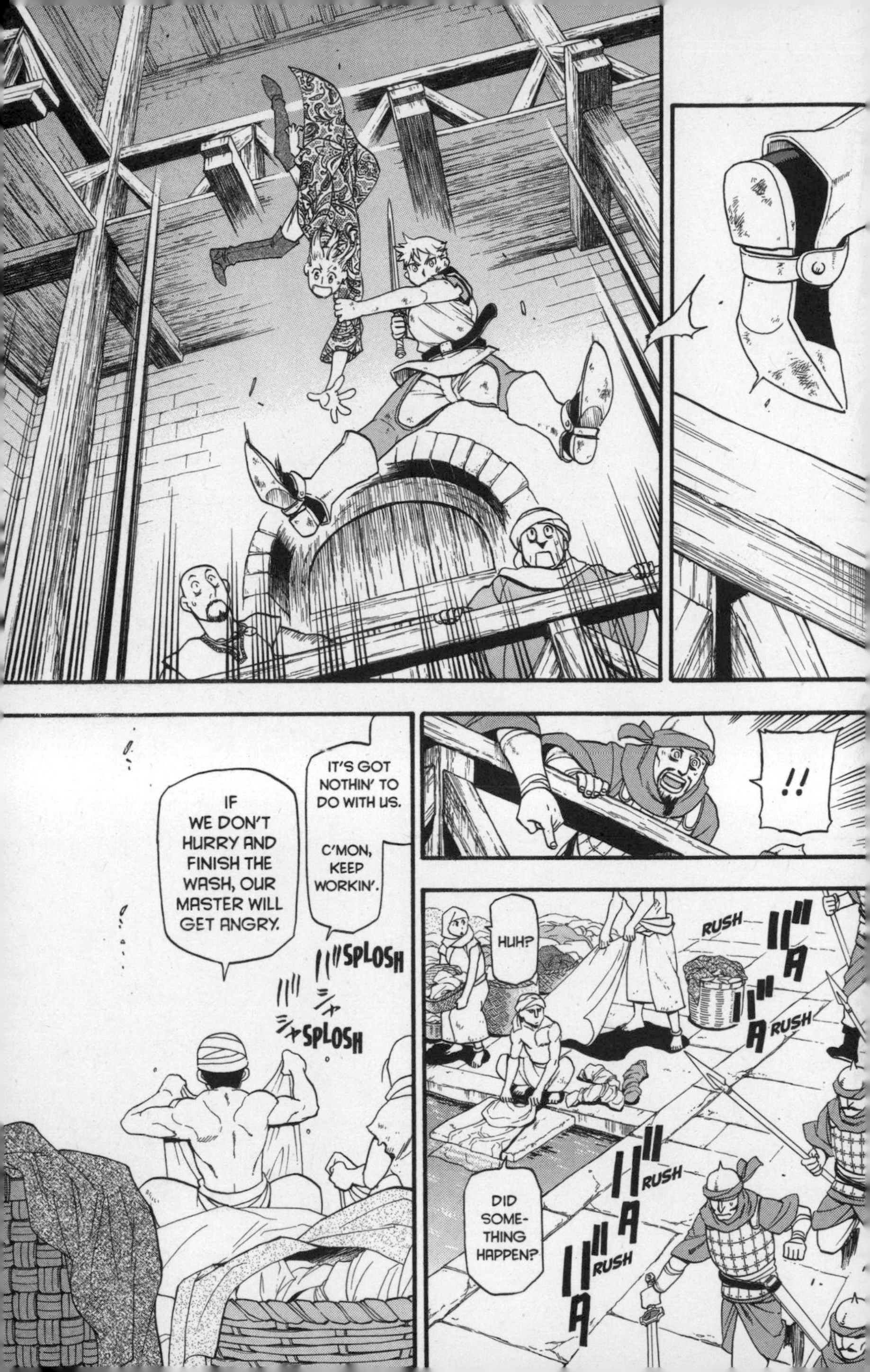
!!
HUH?
RUSH
RUSH
DID SOME-THING HAPPEN?
RUSH
RUSH
IT'S GOT NOTHIN' TO DO WITH US.
C'MON, KEEP WORKIN'.
IF WE DON'T HURRY AND FINISH THE WASH, OUR MASTER WILL GET ANGRY.
SPLOSH
シャ
シャ SPLOSH

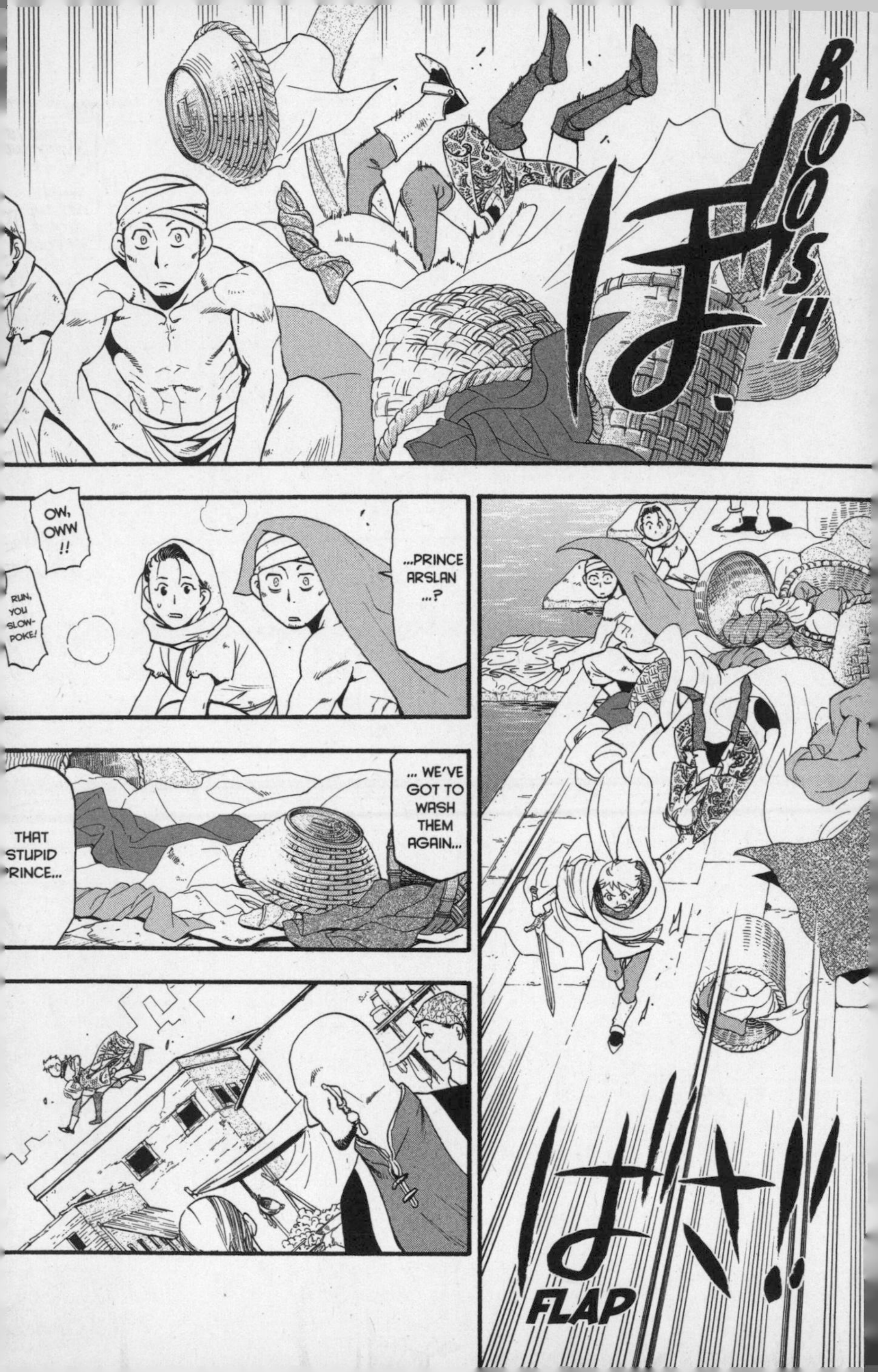
BOOSH
FLAP
...PRINCE ARSLAN ...?
OW, OWW !!
RUN, YOU SLOW-POKE!
... WE'VE GOT TO WASH THEM AGAIN...
THAT STUPID PRINCE...

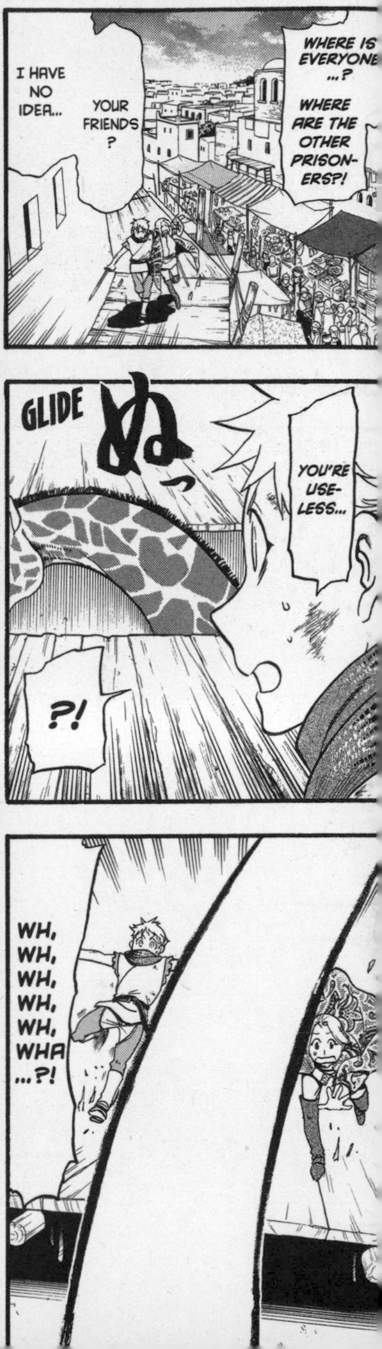
WHERE IS EVERYONE ...?
WHERE ARE THE OTHER PRISONERS?!
YOUR FRIENDS ?
I HAVE NO IDEA...
YOU'RE USELESS...
GLIDE
ぬっ
?!
WH, WH, WH, WH, WH, WHA ...?!

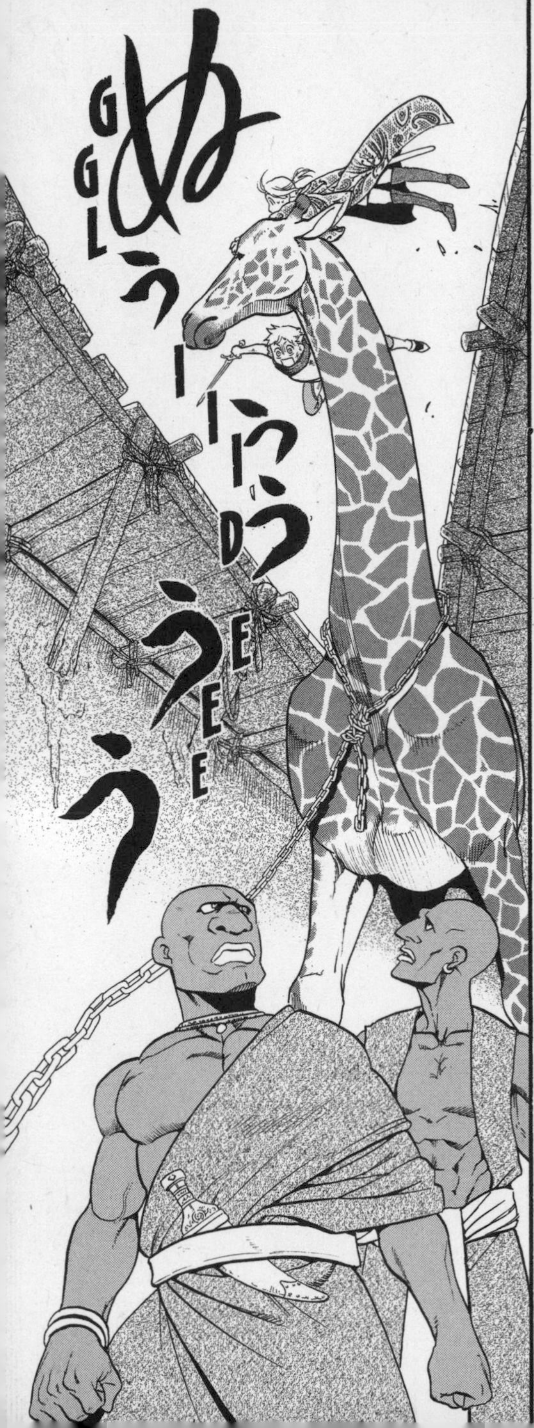
GGLIIDEEE

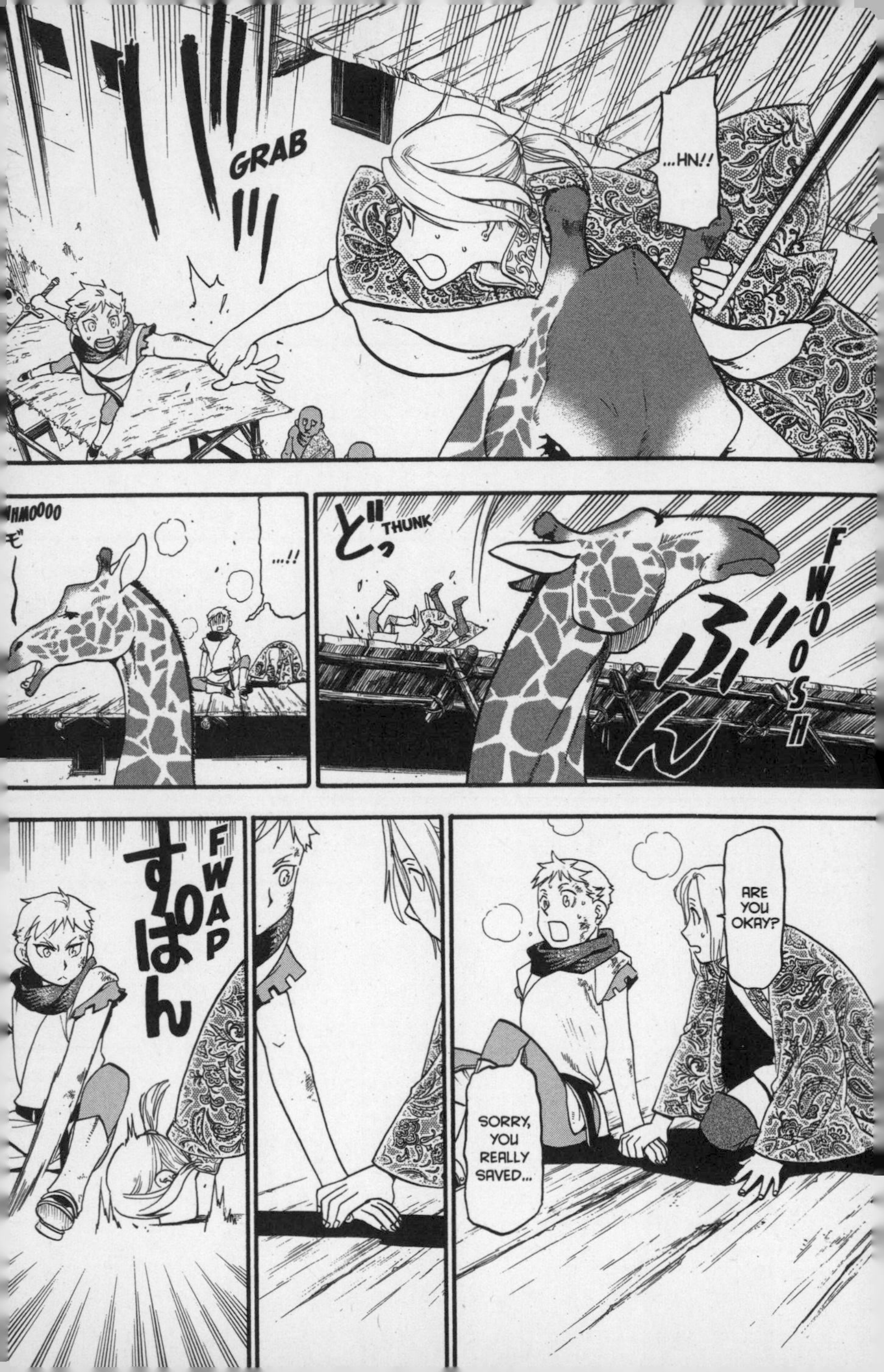
...HN!!
GRAB
FWOOSH
ぶぉん
どっ
THUNK
...!!
HMOOOO
モ~
ARE YOU OKAY?
SORRY, YOU REALLY SAVED...
FWAP
すぽん

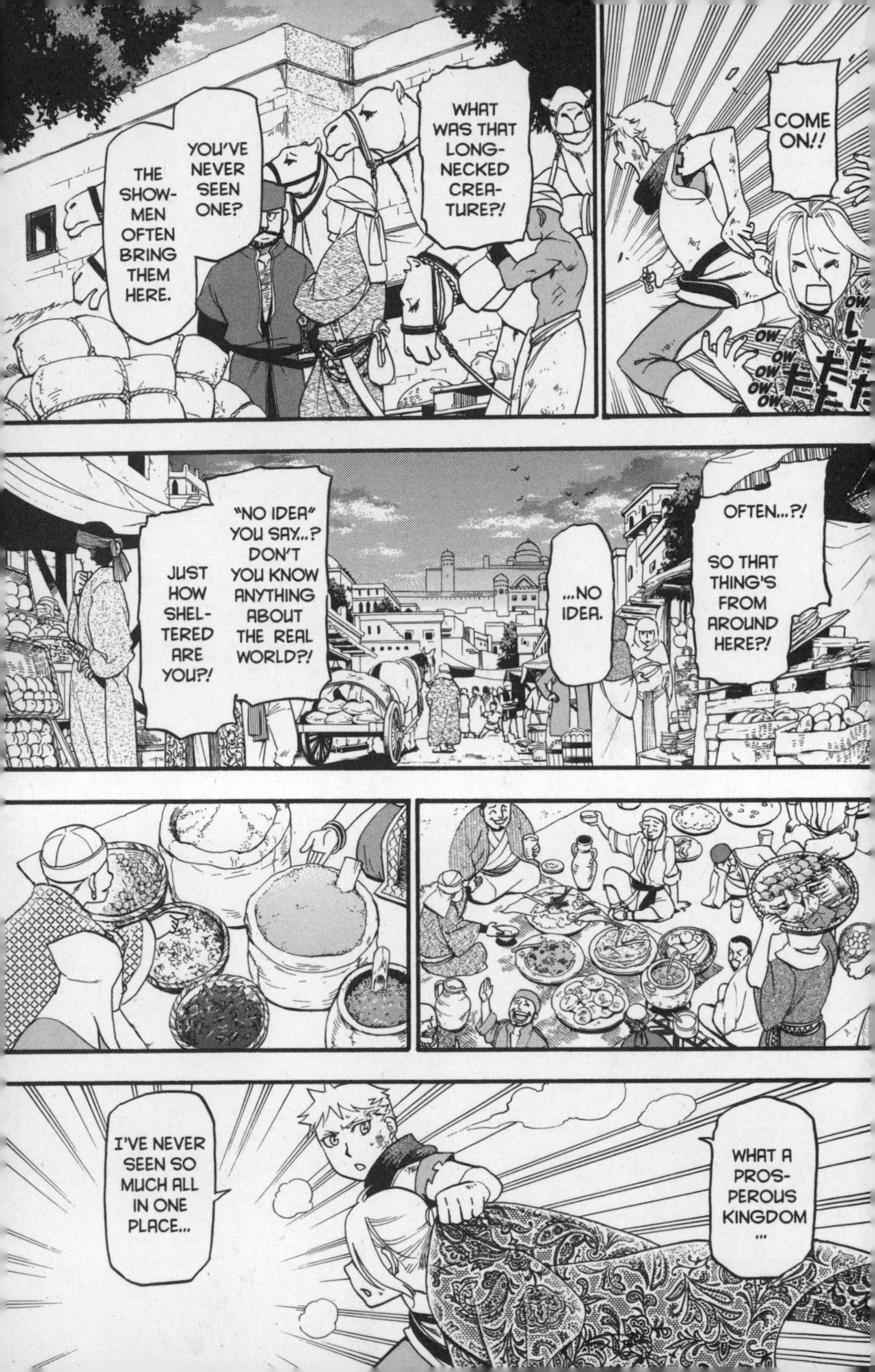
COME ON!!
OW OW OW OW OW
WHAT WAS THAT LONG-NECKED CREATURE?!
YOU'VE NEVER SEEN ONE?
THE SHOWMEN OFTEN BRING THEM HERE.
OFTEN...?!
SO THAT THING'S FROM AROUND HERE?!
...NO IDEA.
"NO IDEA" YOU SAY...? DON'T YOU KNOW ANYTHING ABOUT THE REAL WORLD?!
JUST HOW SHELTERED ARE YOU?!
WHAT A PROSPEROUS KINGDOM ...
I'VE NEVER SEEN SO MUCH ALL IN ONE PLACE...

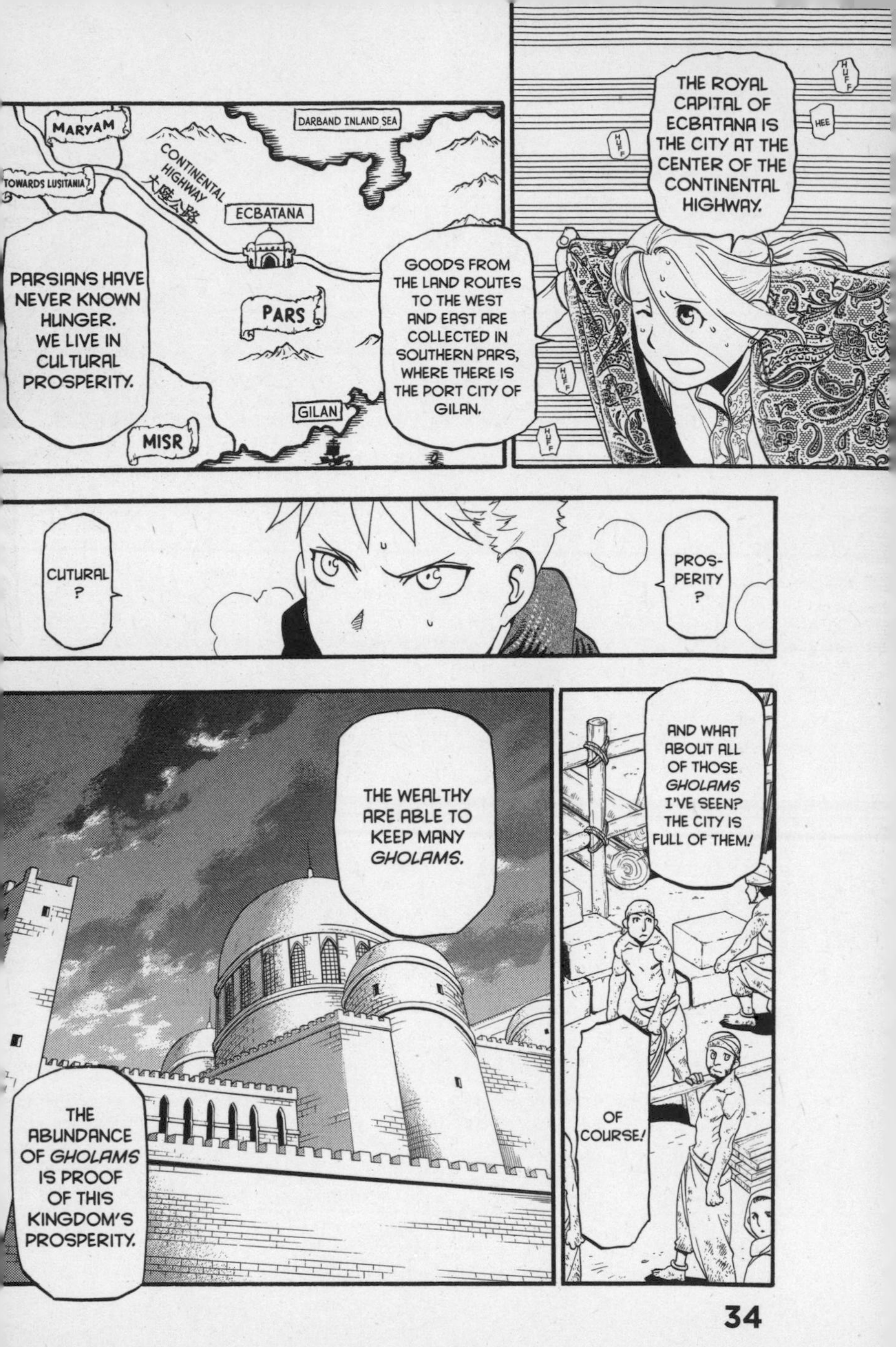
HUFF
HEE
HUFF
THE ROYAL CAPITAL OF ECBATANA IS THE CITY AT THE CENTER OF THE CONTINENTAL HIGHWAY.
HUFF
HUFF
DARBAND INLAND SEA
MARYAM
TOWARDS LUSITANIA
CONTINENTAL HIGHWAY
大陸公路
ECBATANA
PARS
GILAN
MISR
GOODS FROM THE LAND ROUTES TO THE WEST AND EAST ARE COLLECTED IN SOUTHERN PARS, WHERE THERE IS THE PORT CITY OF GILAN.
PARSIANS HAVE NEVER KNOWN HUNGER. WE LIVE IN CULTURAL PROSPERITY.
PROS-PERITY?
CUTURAL?
AND WHAT ABOUT ALL OF THOSE *GHOLAMS* I'VE SEEN? THE CITY IS FULL OF THEM!
OF COURSE!
THE WEALTHY ARE ABLE TO KEEP MANY *GHOLAMS.*
THE ABUNDANCE OF *GHOLAMS* IS PROOF OF THIS KINGDOM'S PROSPERITY.

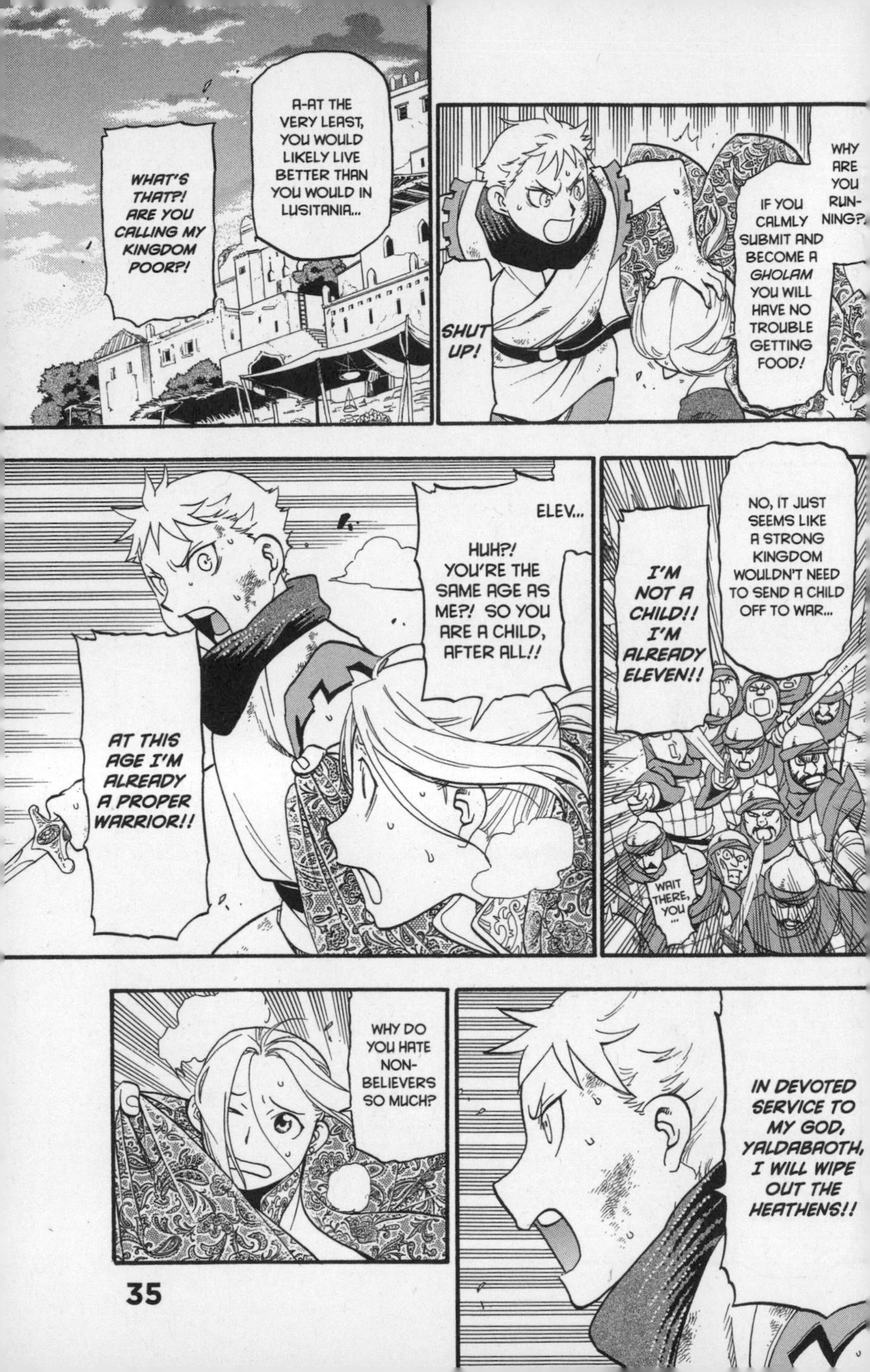
WHY ARE YOU RUN-NING?
IF YOU CALMLY SUBMIT AND BECOME A GHOLAM YOU WILL HAVE NO TROUBLE GETTING FOOD!
SHUT UP!
A-AT THE VERY LEAST, YOU WOULD LIKELY LIVE BETTER THAN YOU WOULD IN LUSITANIA...
WHAT'S THAT?! ARE YOU CALLING MY KINGDOM POOR?!
NO, IT JUST SEEMS LIKE A STRONG KINGDOM WOULDN'T NEED TO SEND A CHILD OFF TO WAR...
I'M NOT A CHILD!! I'M ALREADY ELEVEN!!
WAIT THERE, YOU...
ELEV...
HUH?! YOU'RE THE SAME AGE AS ME?! SO YOU ARE A CHILD, AFTER ALL!!
AT THIS AGE I'M ALREADY A PROPER WARRIOR!!
IN DEVOTED SERVICE TO MY GOD, YALDABAOTH, I WILL WIPE OUT THE HEATHENS!!
WHY DO YOU HATE NON-BELIEVERS SO MUCH?

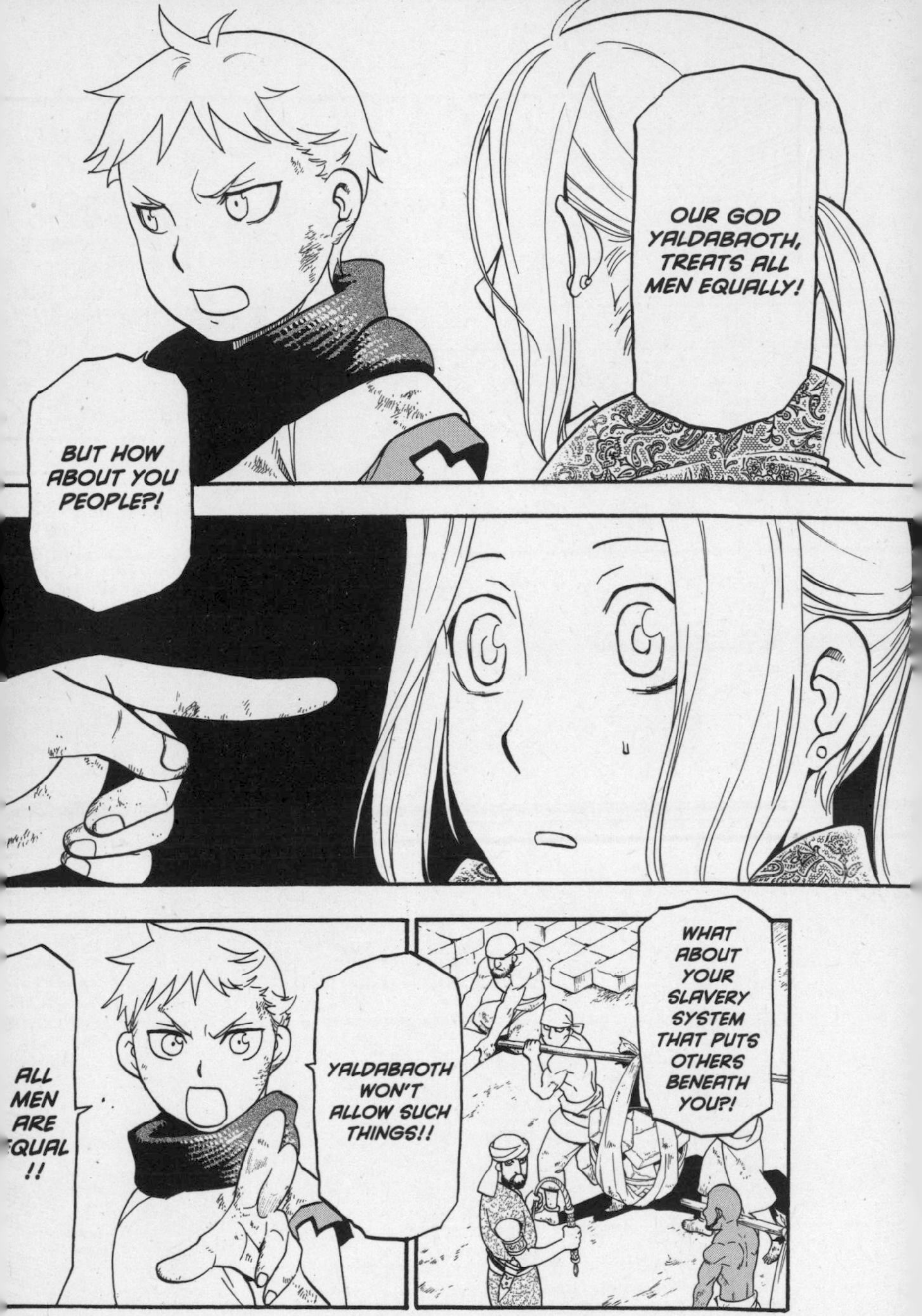
OUR GOD YALDABAOTH, TREATS ALL MEN EQUALLY!
BUT HOW ABOUT YOU PEOPLE?!
WHAT ABOUT YOUR SLAVERY SYSTEM THAT PUTS OTHERS BENEATH YOU?!
YALDABAOTH WON'T ALLOW SUCH THINGS!!
ALL MEN ARE EQUAL !!

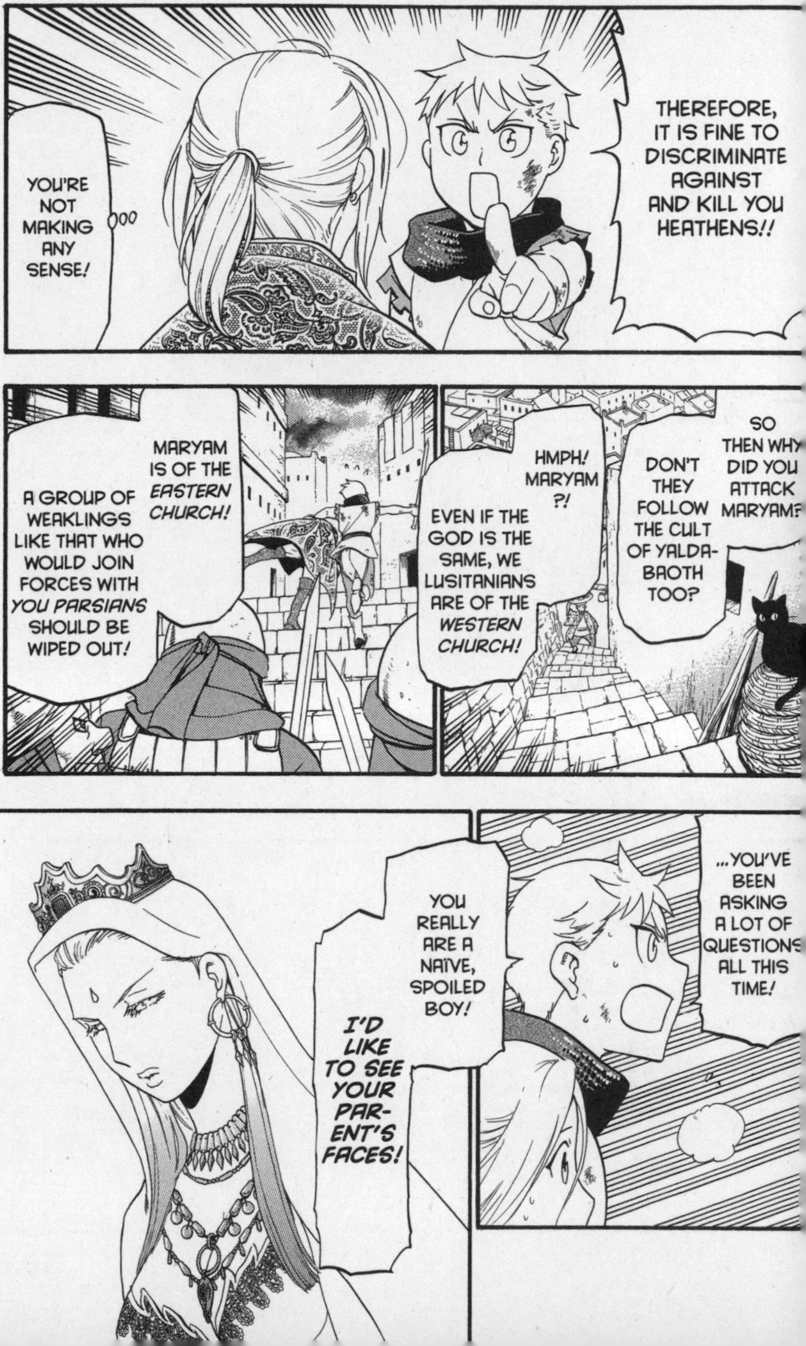
THEREFORE, IT IS FINE TO DISCRIMINATE AGAINST AND KILL YOU HEATHENS!!
YOU'RE NOT MAKING ANY SENSE!
SO THEN WHY DID YOU ATTACK MARYAM?
DON'T THEY FOLLOW THE CULT OF YALDA-BAOTH TOO?
HMPH! MARYAM?!
EVEN IF THE GOD IS THE SAME, WE LUSITANIANS ARE OF THE *WESTERN CHURCH!*
MARYAM IS OF THE *EASTERN CHURCH!*
A GROUP OF WEAKLINGS LIKE THAT WHO WOULD JOIN FORCES WITH *YOU PARSIANS* SHOULD BE WIPED OUT!
...YOU'VE BEEN ASKING A LOT OF QUESTIONS ALL THIS TIME!
YOU REALLY ARE A NAÏVE, SPOILED BOY!
I'D LIKE TO SEE YOUR PAR-ENT'S FACES!

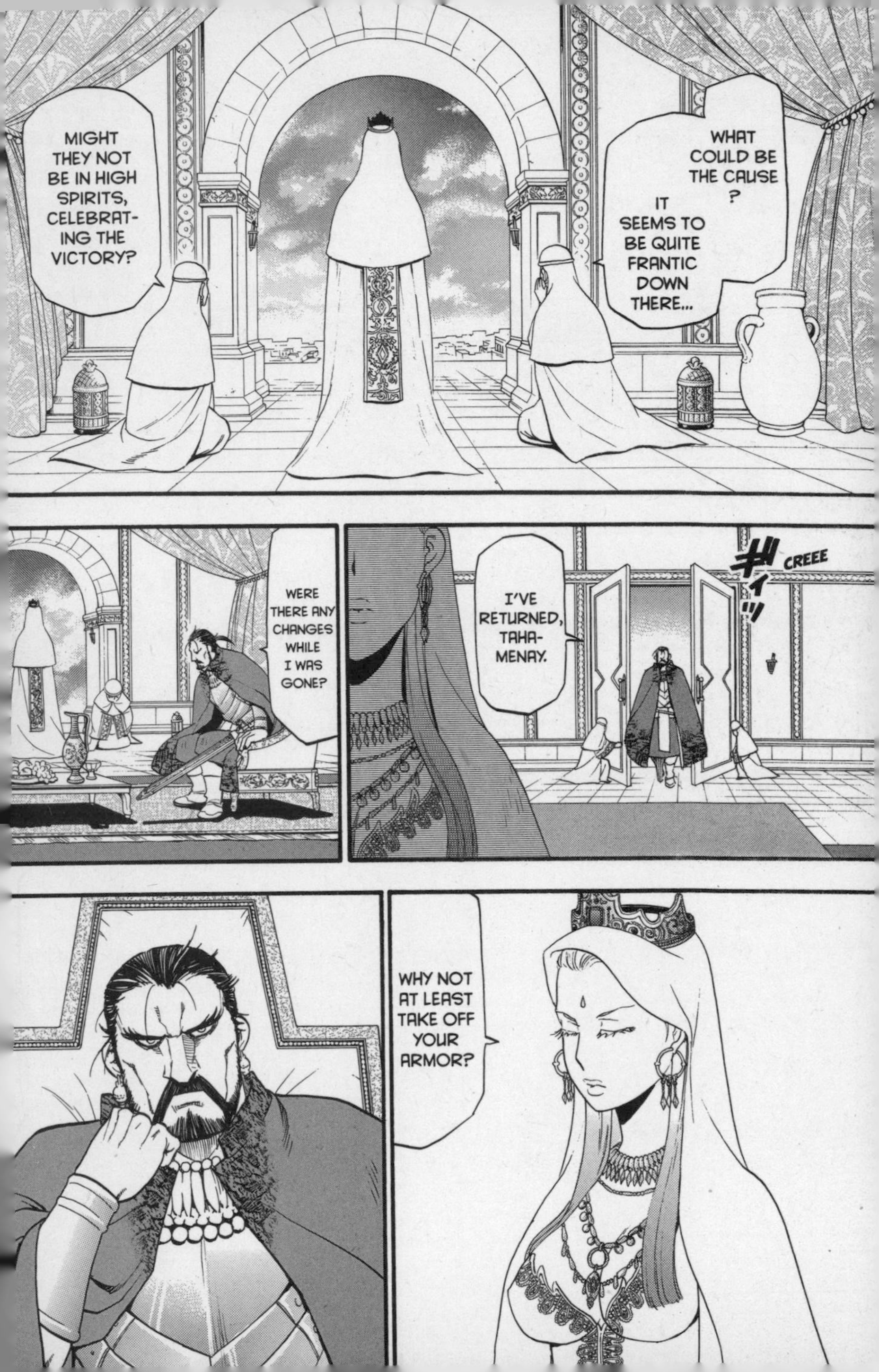
WHAT COULD BE THE CAUSE?
IT SEEMS TO BE QUITE FRANTIC DOWN THERE...
MIGHT THEY NOT BE IN HIGH SPIRITS, CELEBRATING THE VICTORY?
CREEE
I'VE RETURNED, TAHAMENAY.
WERE THERE ANY CHANGES WHILE I WAS GONE?
WHY NOT AT LEAST TAKE OFF YOUR ARMOR?

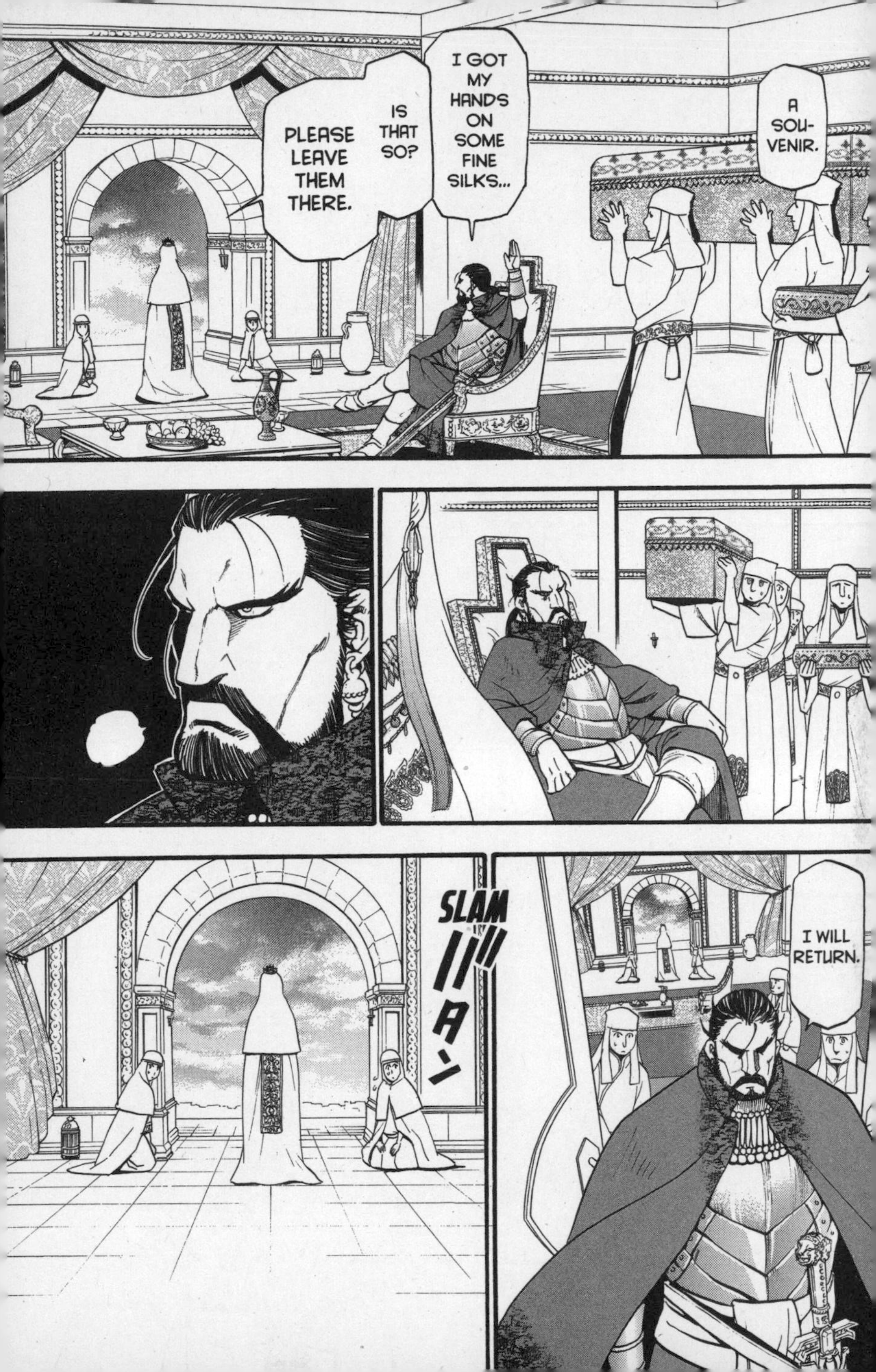
A SOUVENIR.
I GOT MY HANDS ON SOME FINE SILKS...
IS THAT SO?
PLEASE LEAVE THEM THERE.
I WILL RETURN.
SLAM

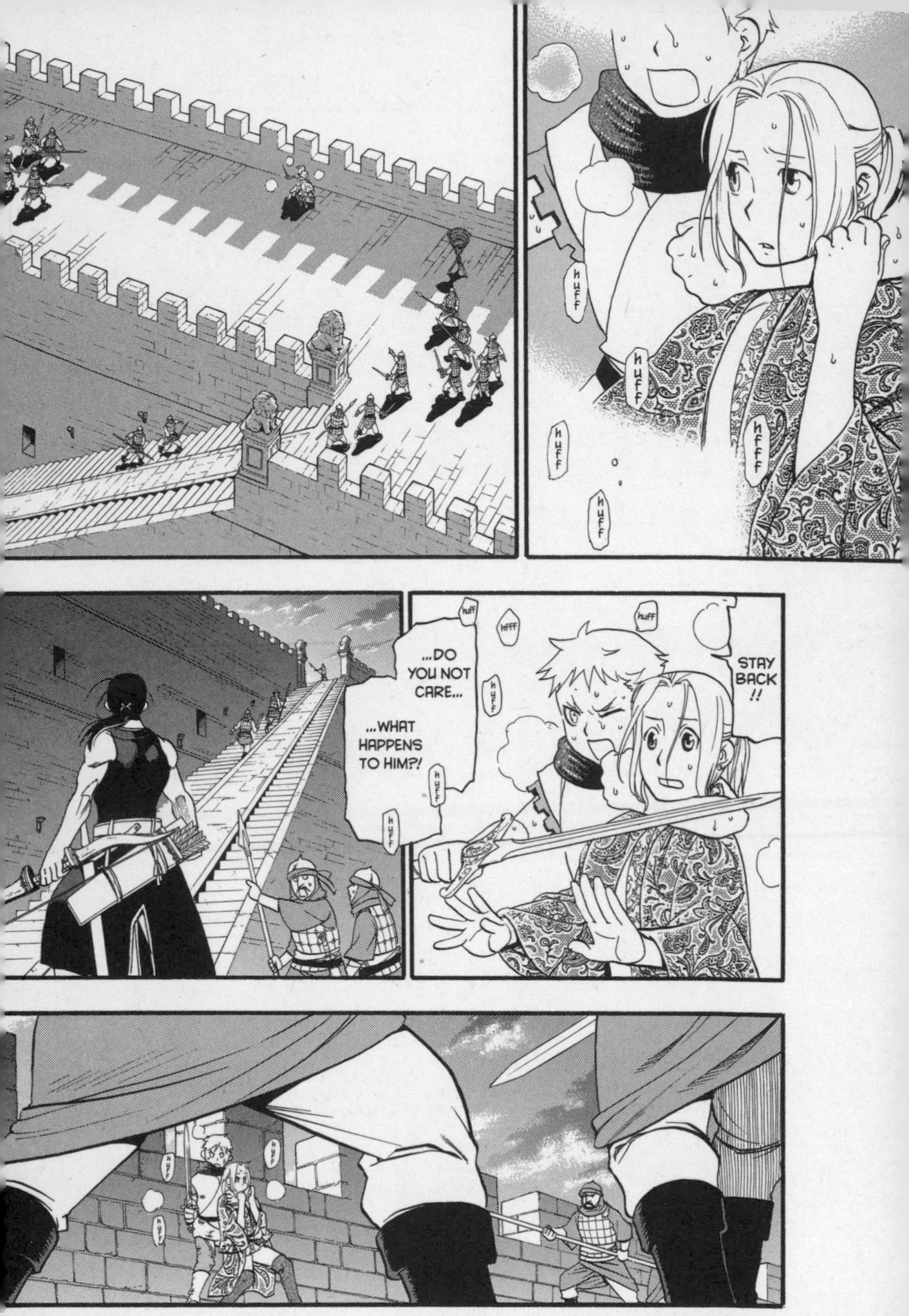
huff
huff
huff
hfff
huff
huff
huff
hfff
huff
STAY BACK!!
...DO YOU NOT CARE...
...WHAT HAPPENS TO HIM?!
huff
huff
huff
huff
huff

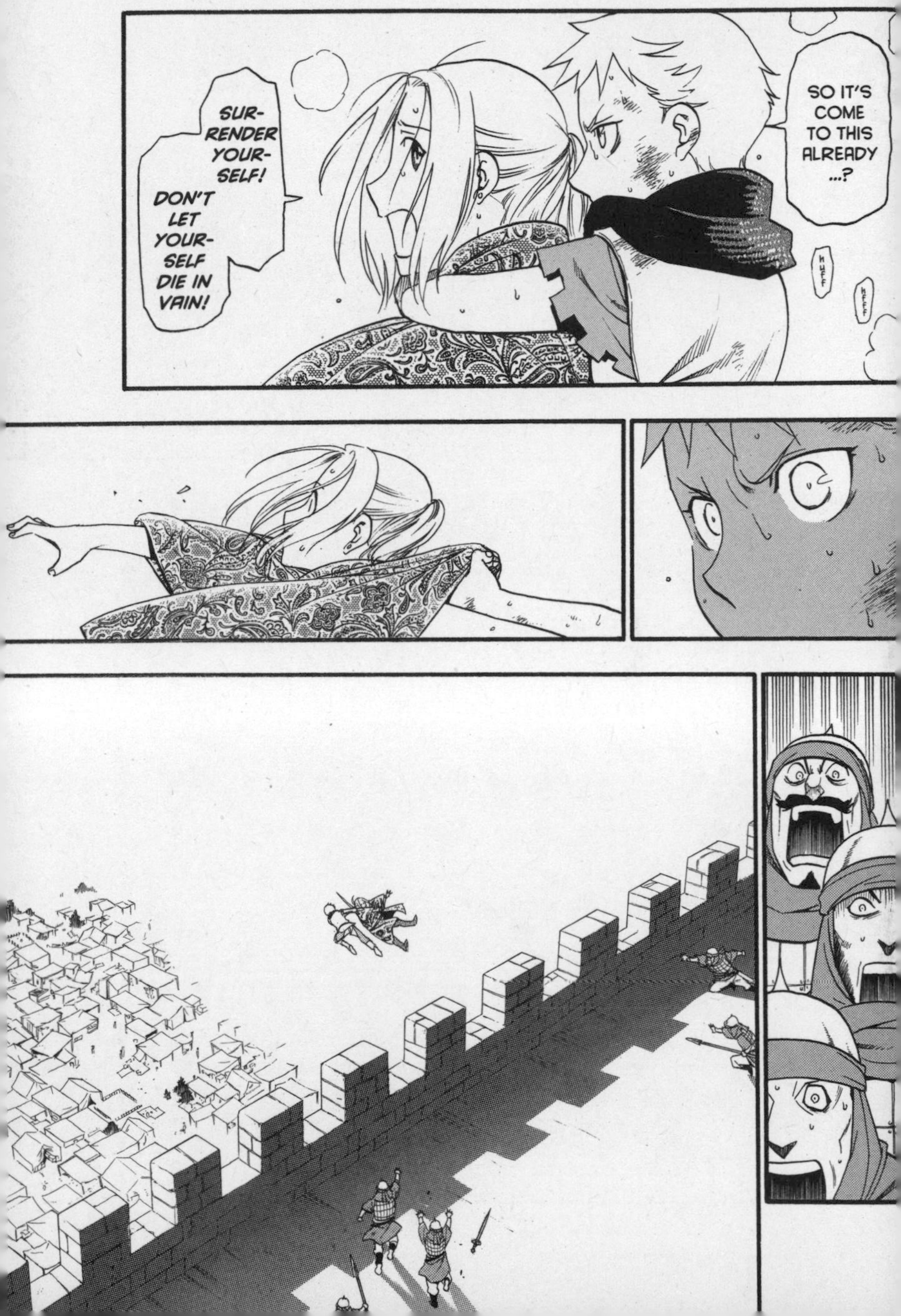
SO IT'S COME TO THIS ALREADY ...?
HUFF
HUFF
SUR-RENDER YOUR-SELF! DON'T LET YOUR-SELF DIE IN VAIN!

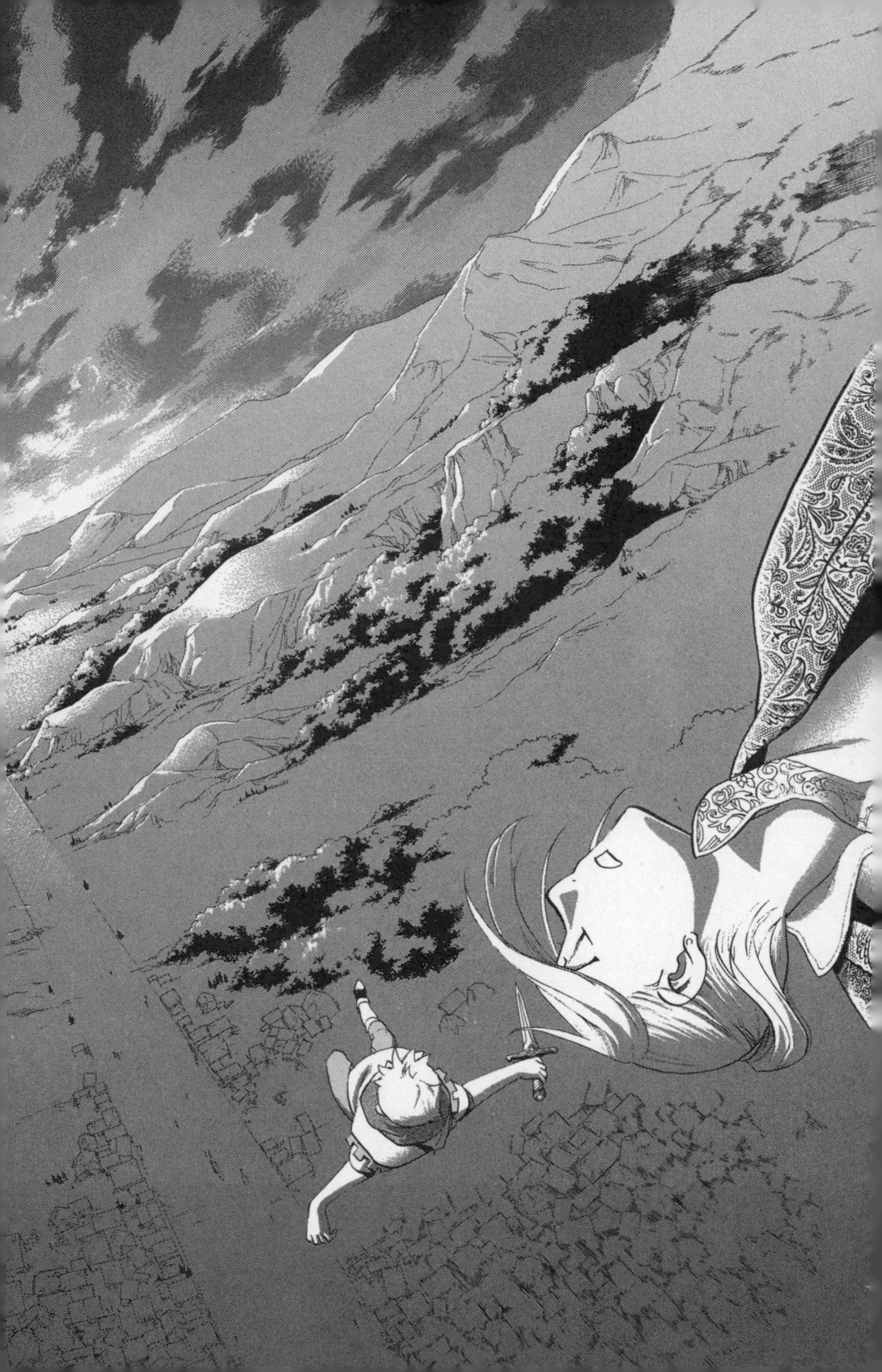

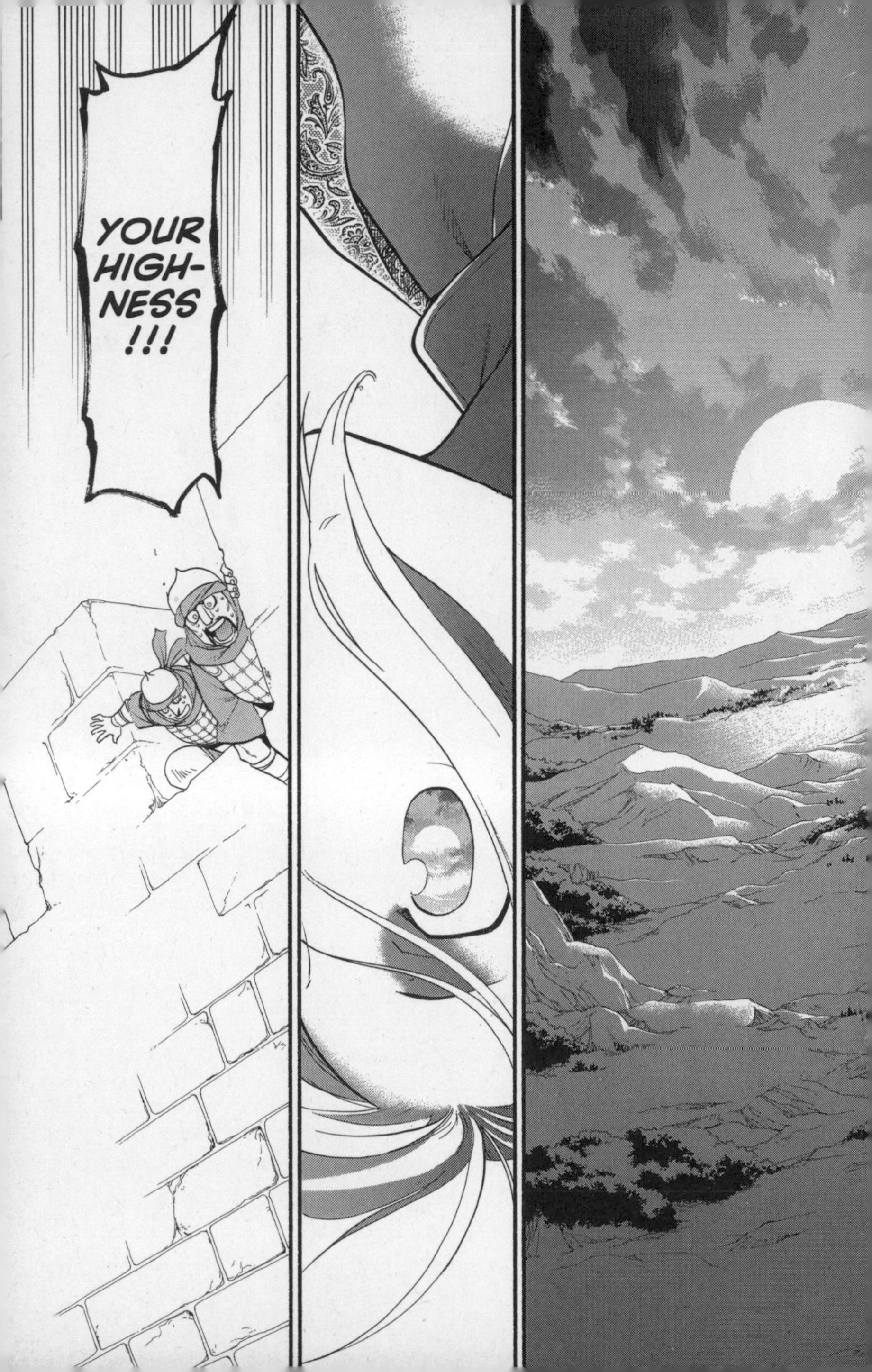
YOUR HIGH-NESS !!!

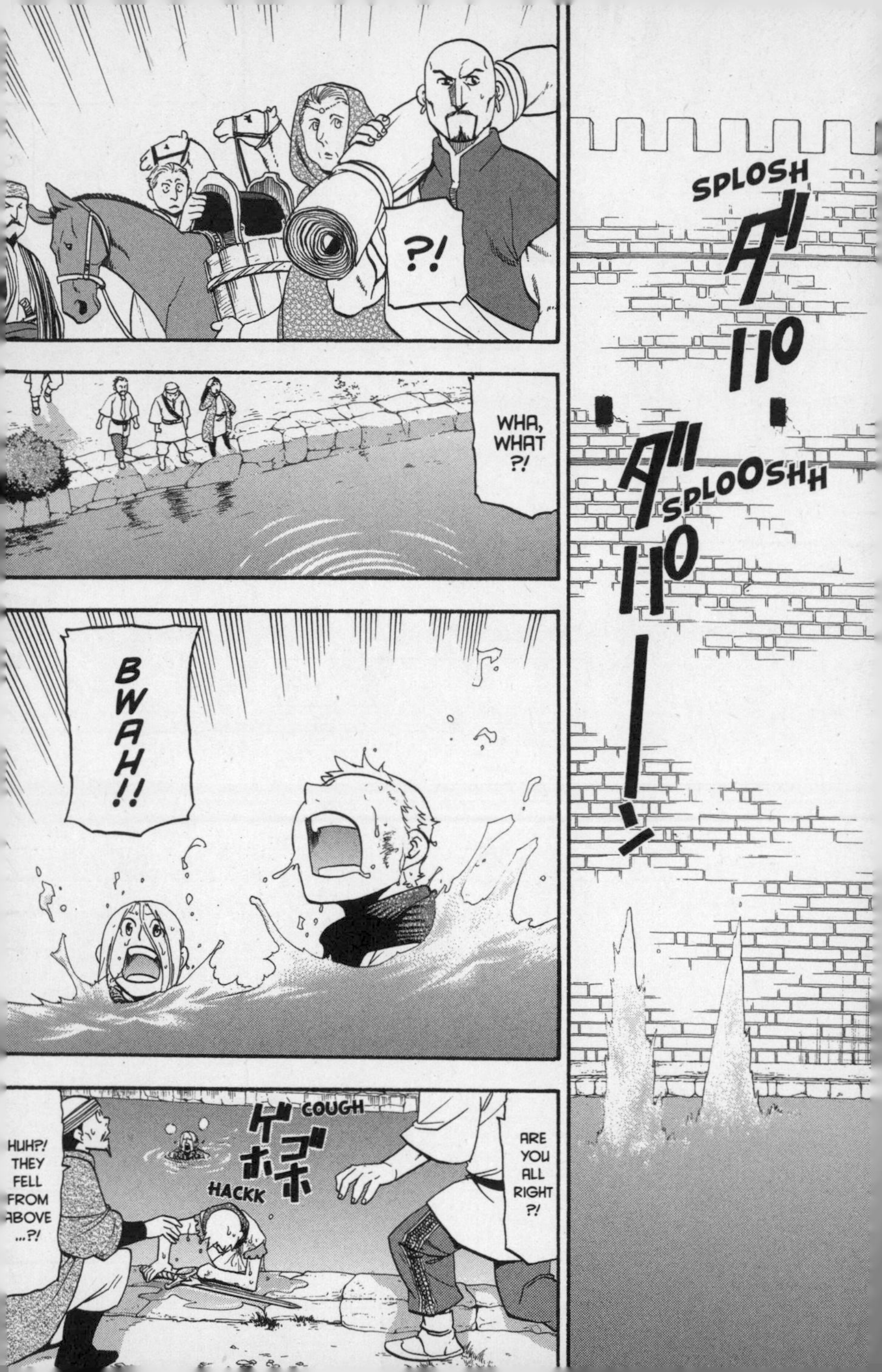
SPLOSH
ダパ
SPLOOSHH
ダパーーッ
?!
WHA, WHAT ?!
BWAH!!
ARE YOU ALL RIGHT ?!
COUGH
ゲホゴホ
HACKK
HUH?! THEY FELL FROM ABOVE ...?!

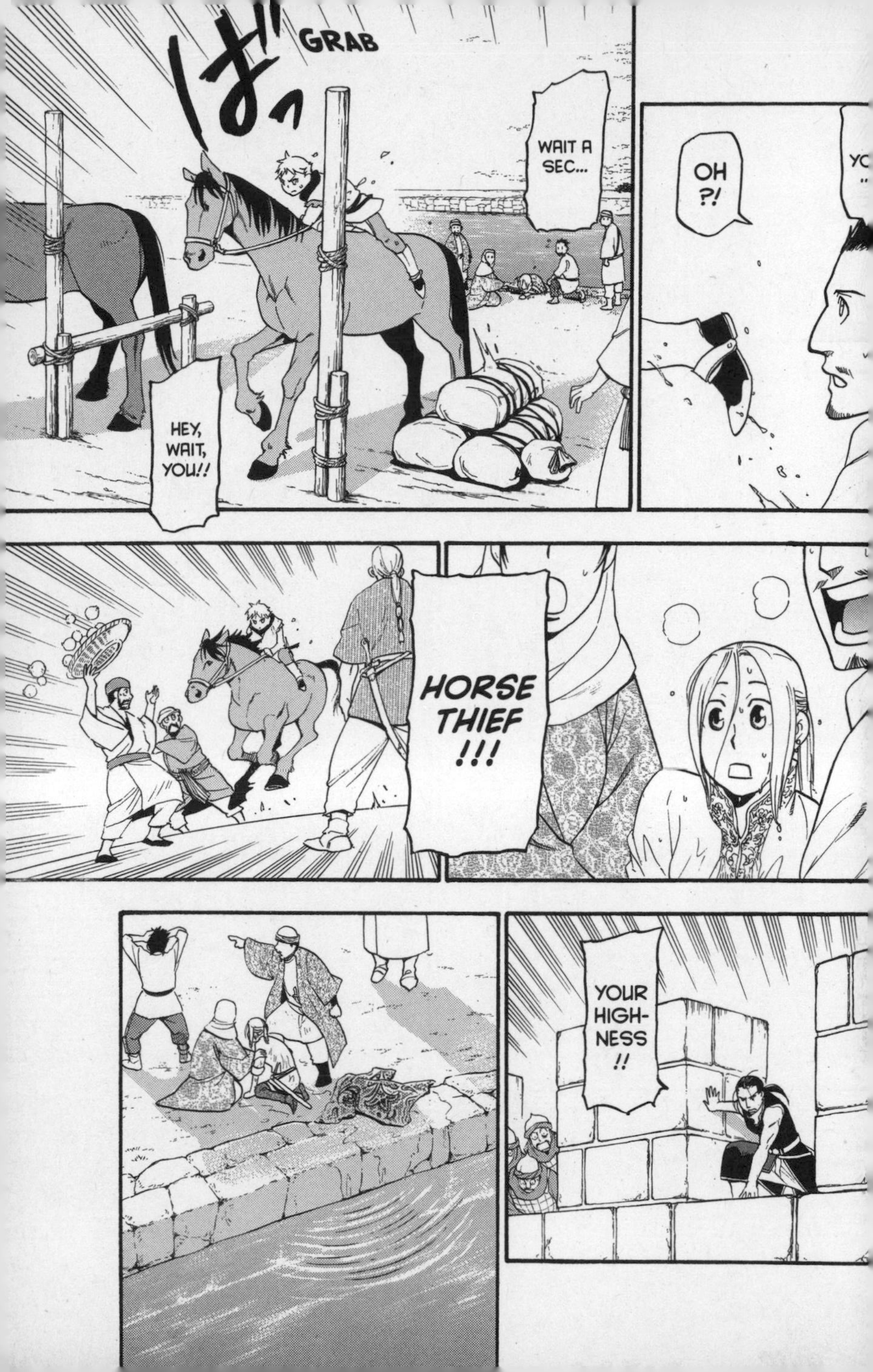
OH ?!
WAIT A SEC...
GRAB
HEY, WAIT, YOU!!
HORSE THIEF !!!
YOUR HIGH-NESS !!

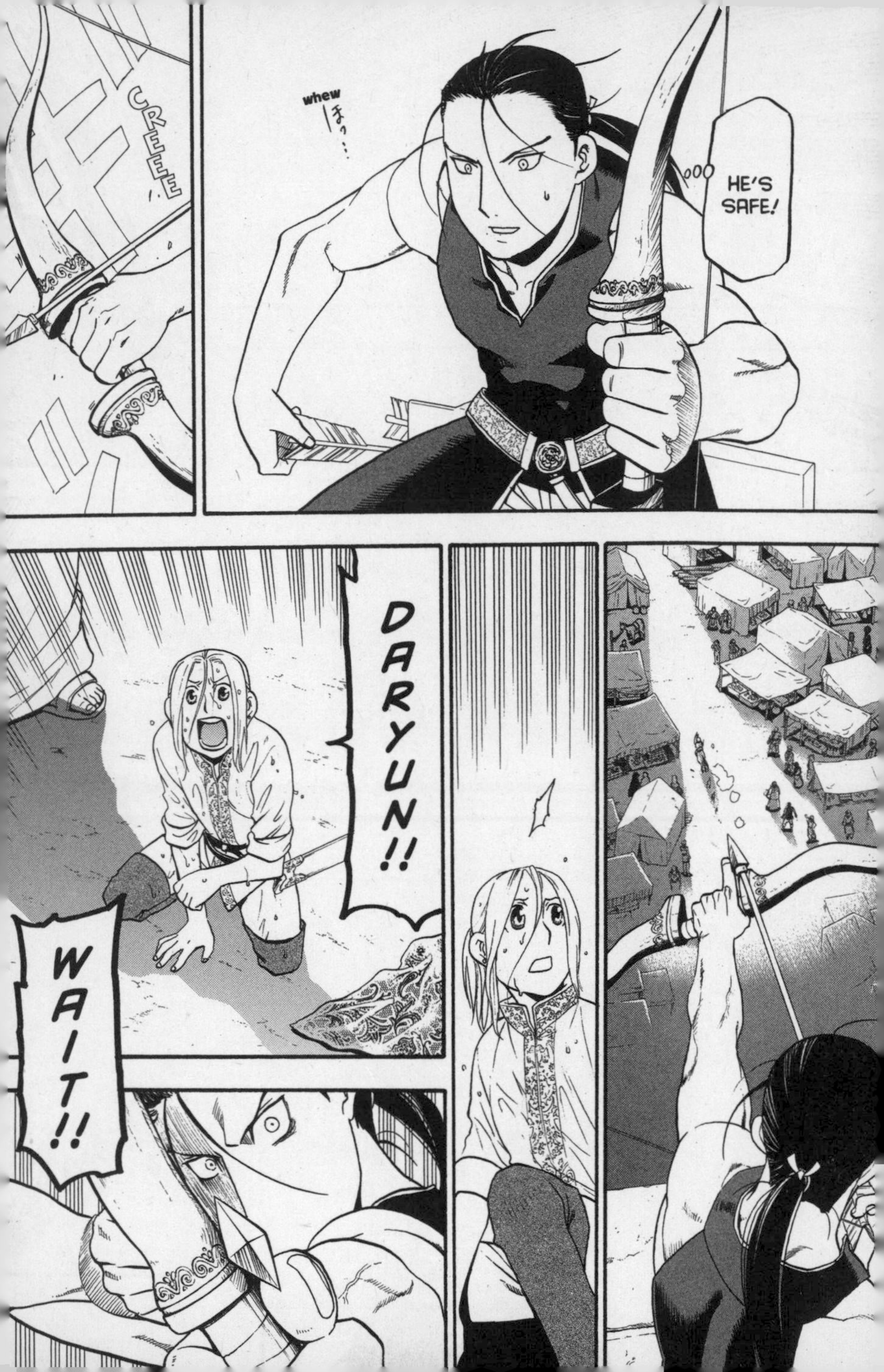

whew
ほっ…
HE'S SAFE!
CREEE
DARYUN!!
WAIT!!

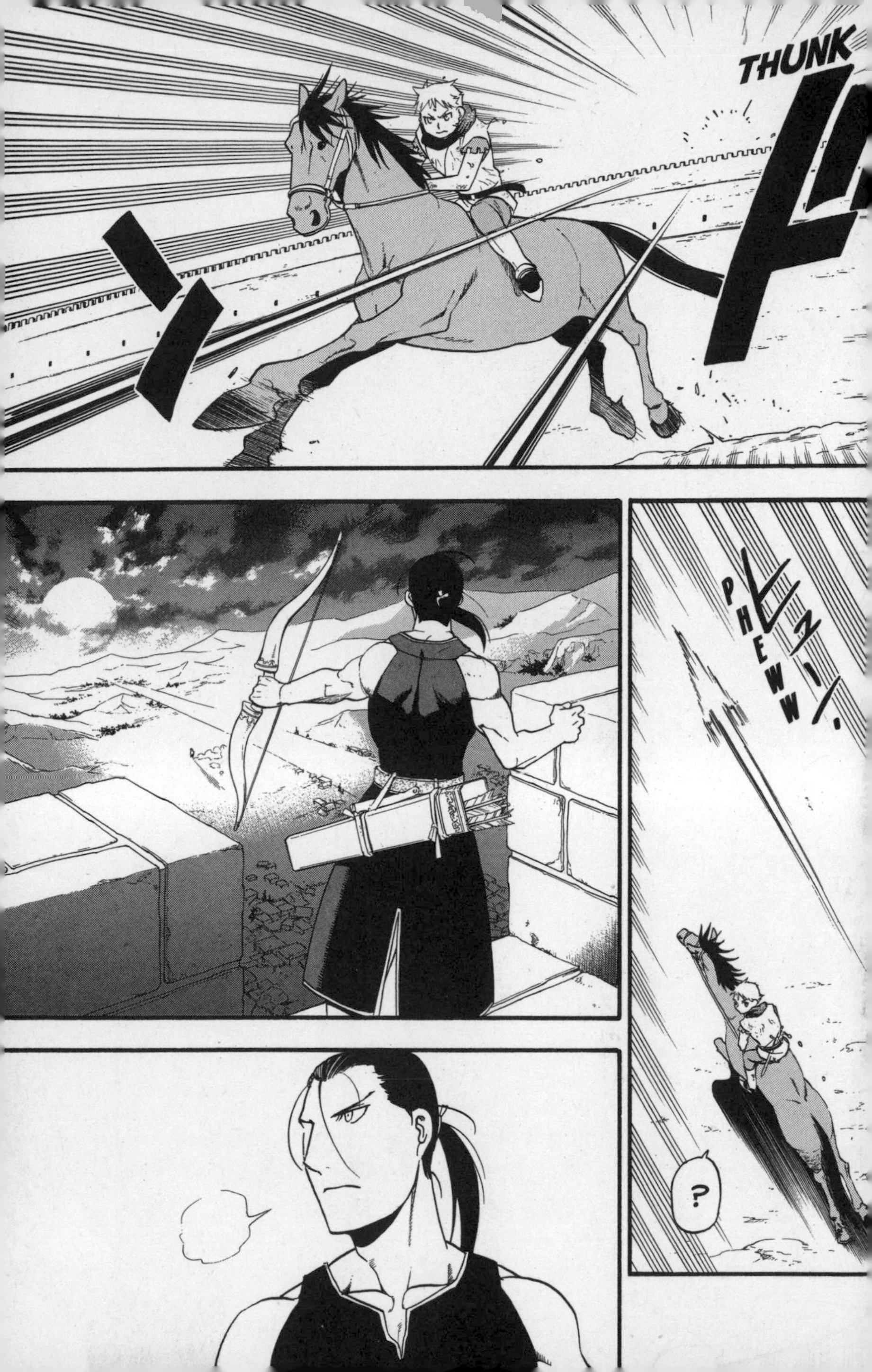
THUNK
PHEWW
?

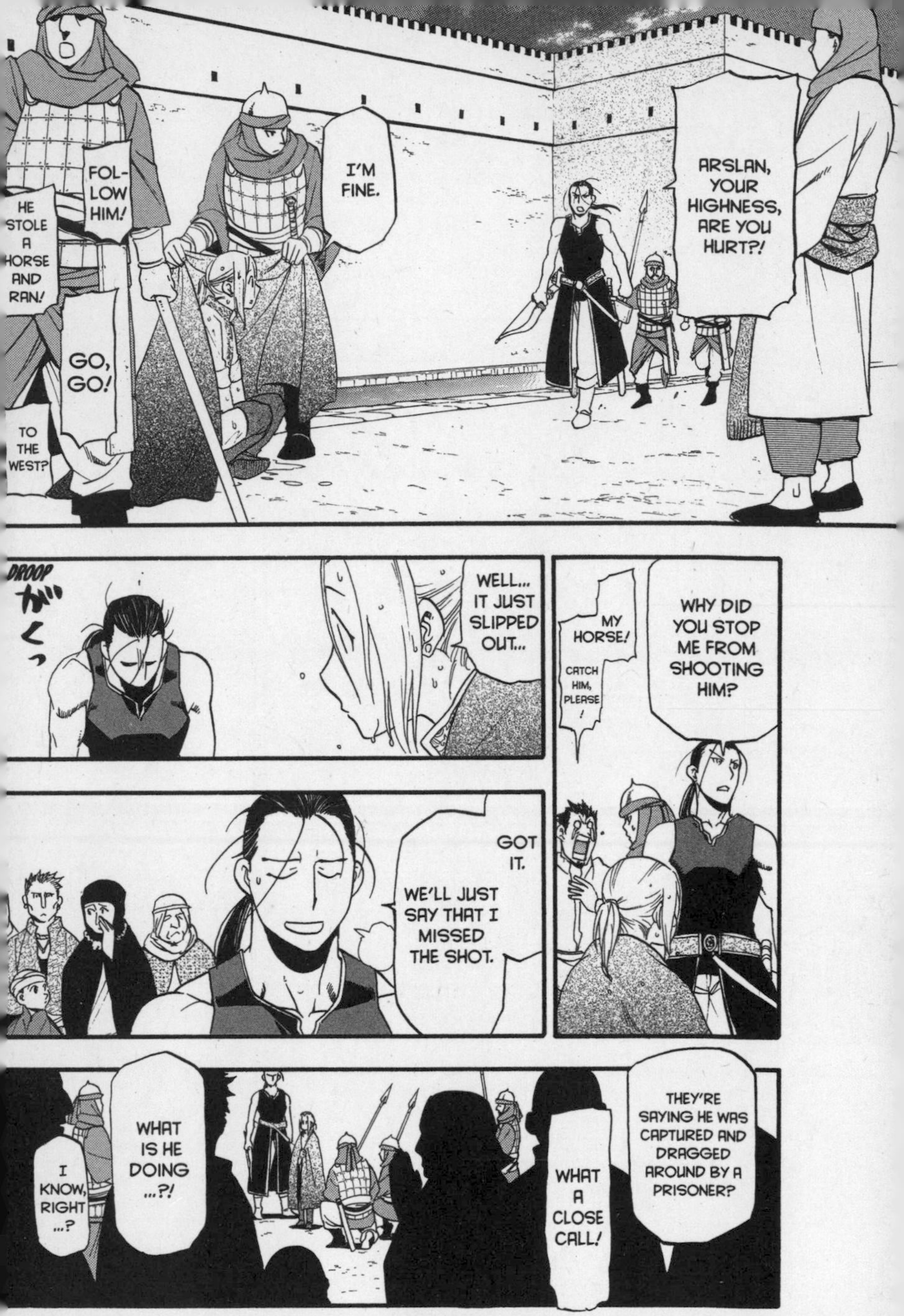
ARSLAN, YOUR HIGHNESS, ARE YOU HURT?!
I'M FINE.
FOL-LOW HIM!
HE STOLE A HORSE AND RAN!
GO, GO!
TO THE WEST?
WHY DID YOU STOP ME FROM SHOOTING HIM?
MY HORSE!
CATCH HIM, PLEASE!
WELL... IT JUST SLIPPED OUT...
DROOP
がくっ
GOT IT.
WE'LL JUST SAY THAT I MISSED THE SHOT.
THEY'RE SAYING HE WAS CAPTURED AND DRAGGED AROUND BY A PRISONER?
WHAT A CLOSE CALL!
WHAT IS HE DOING ...?!
I KNOW, RIGHT ...?

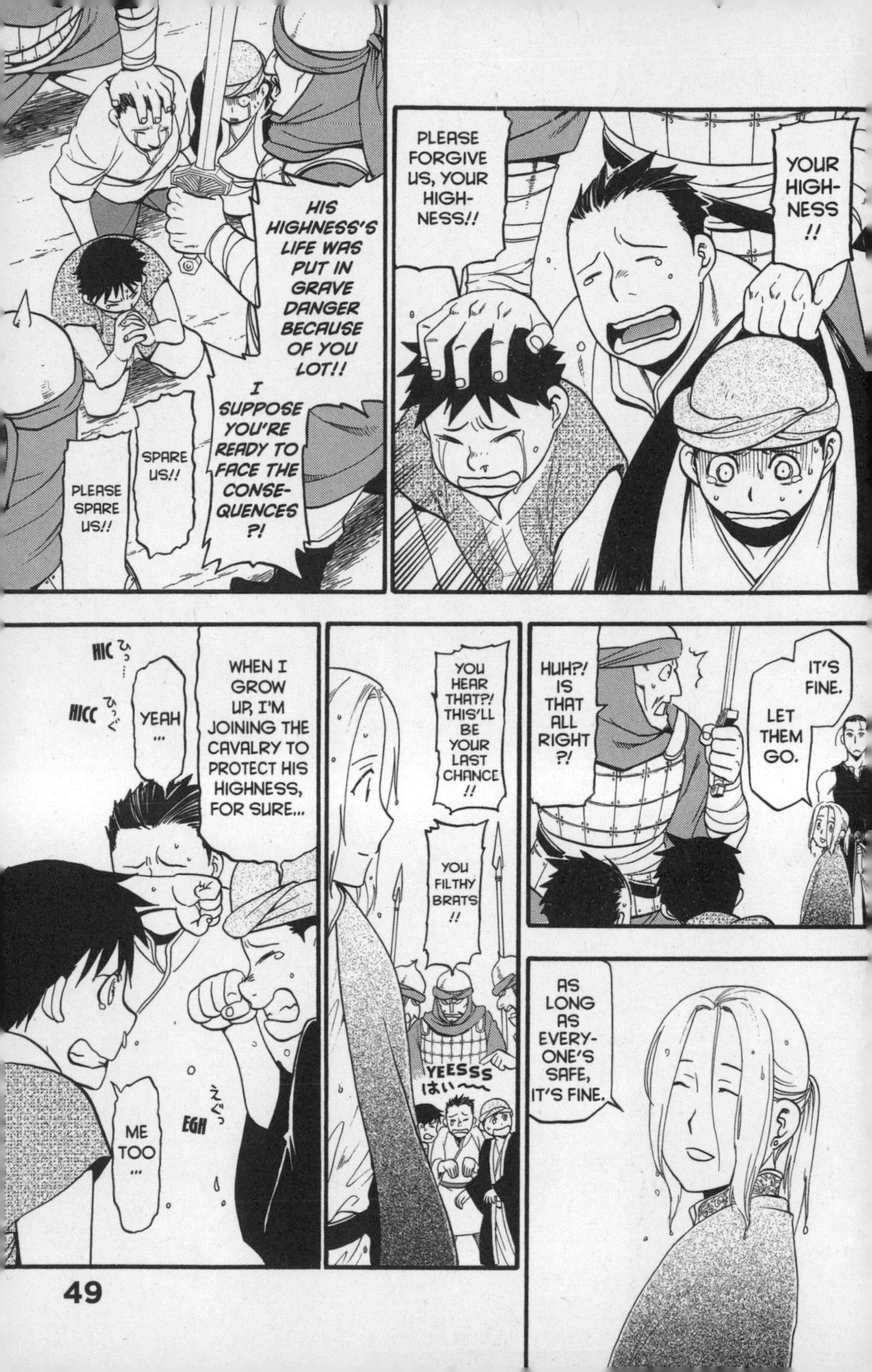
YOUR HIGHNESS!!
PLEASE FORGIVE US, YOUR HIGHNESS!!
HIS HIGHNESS'S LIFE WAS PUT IN GRAVE DANGER BECAUSE OF YOU LOT!!
I SUPPOSE YOU'RE READY TO FACE THE CONSEQUENCES?!
SPARE US!!
PLEASE SPARE US!!
IT'S FINE.
LET THEM GO.
HUH?! IS THAT ALL RIGHT?!
AS LONG AS EVERYONE'S SAFE, IT'S FINE.
YOU HEAR THAT?! THIS'LL BE YOUR LAST CHANCE!!
YOU FILTHY BRATS!!
YEESSS はい～～
WHEN I GROW UP, I'M JOINING THE CAVALRY TO PROTECT HIS HIGHNESS, FOR SURE...
HIC ひっ…
HICC ひっく
YEAH...
EGH えぐっ
ME TOO...

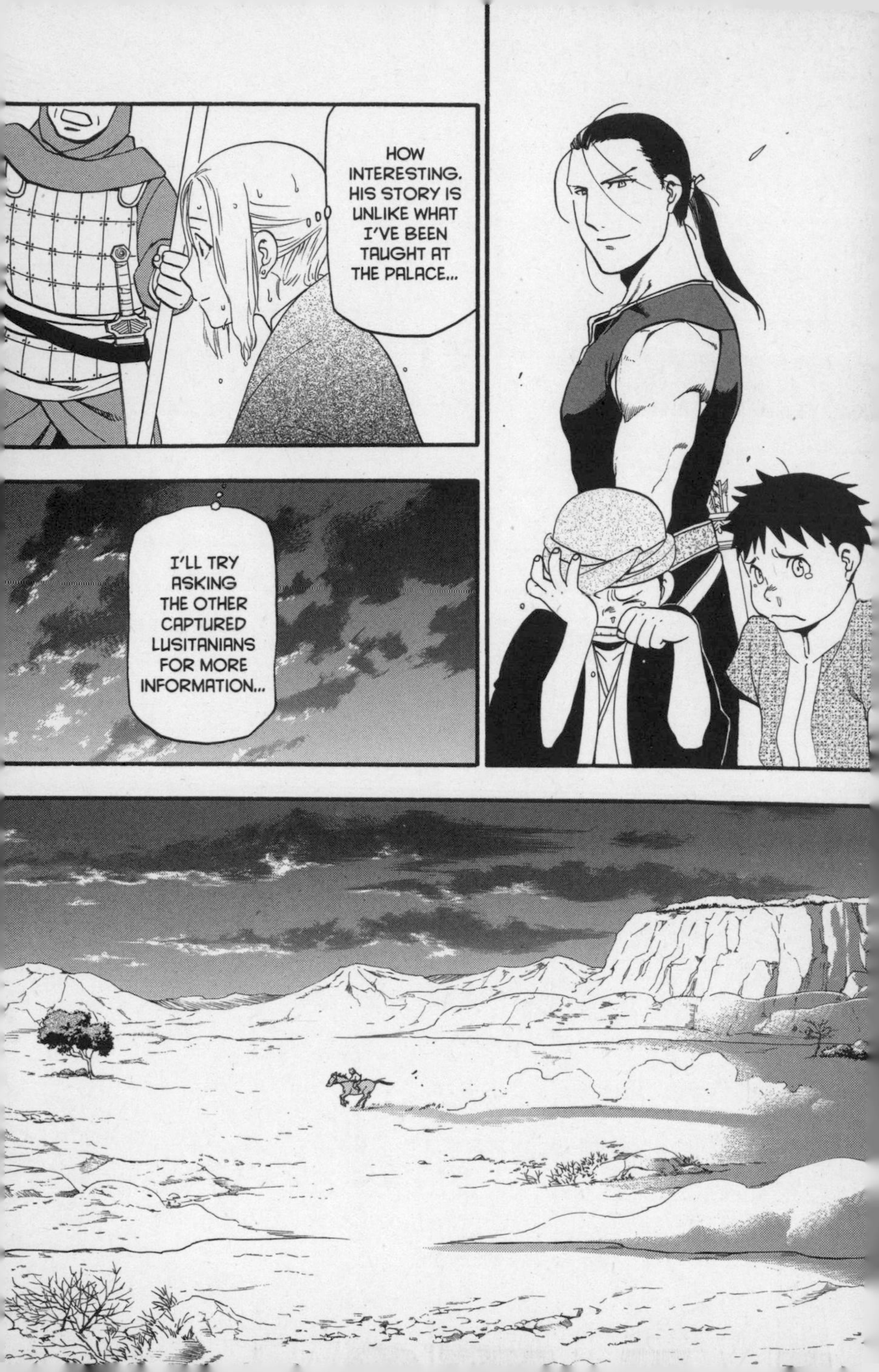
HOW INTERESTING. HIS STORY IS UNLIKE WHAT I'VE BEEN TAUGHT AT THE PALACE...
I'LL TRY ASKING THE OTHER CAPTURED LUSITANIANS FOR MORE INFORMATION...

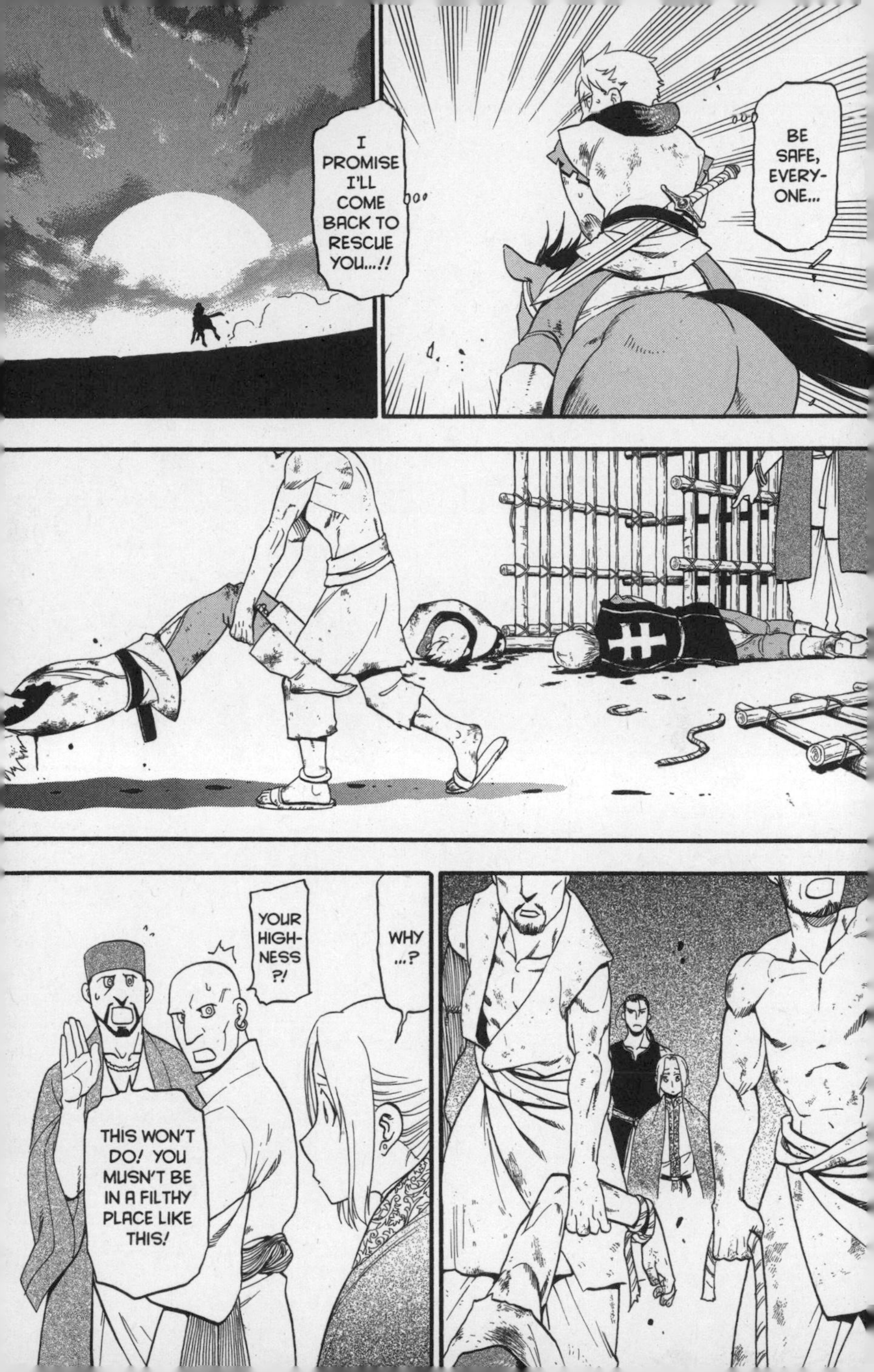
BE SAFE, EVERY-ONE...
I PROMISE I'LL COME BACK TO RESCUE YOU...!!
WHY ...?
YOUR HIGH-NESS ?!
THIS WON'T DO! YOU MUSN'T BE IN A FILTHY PLACE LIKE THIS!

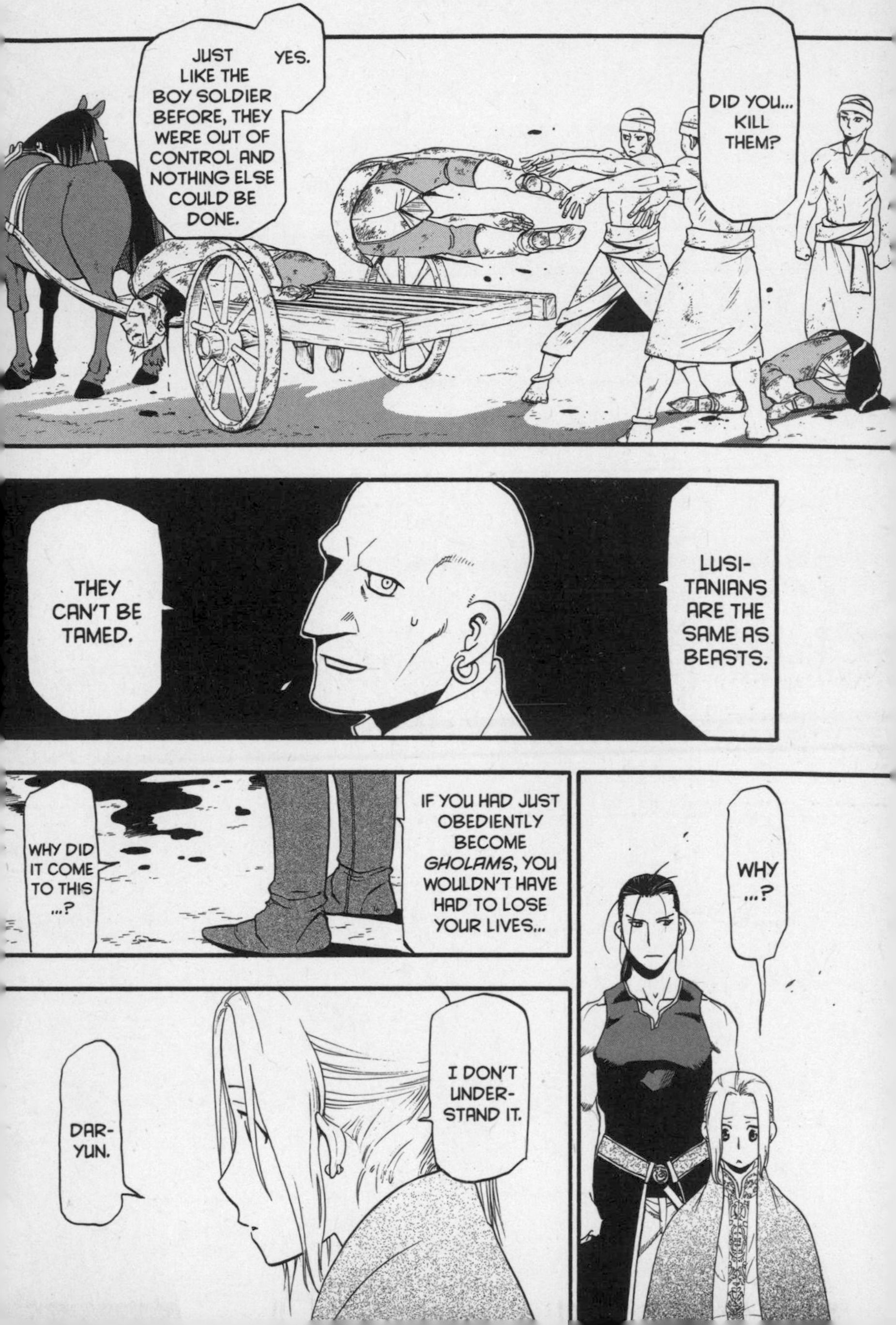
DID YOU... KILL THEM?
YES.
JUST LIKE THE BOY SOLDIER BEFORE, THEY WERE OUT OF CONTROL AND NOTHING ELSE COULD BE DONE.
LUSI-TANIANS ARE THE SAME AS BEASTS.
THEY CAN'T BE TAMED.
WHY ...?
IF YOU HAD JUST OBEDIENTLY BECOME *GHOLAMS*, YOU WOULDN'T HAVE HAD TO LOSE YOUR LIVES...
WHY DID IT COME TO THIS ...?
I DON'T UNDER-STAND IT.
DAR-YUN.

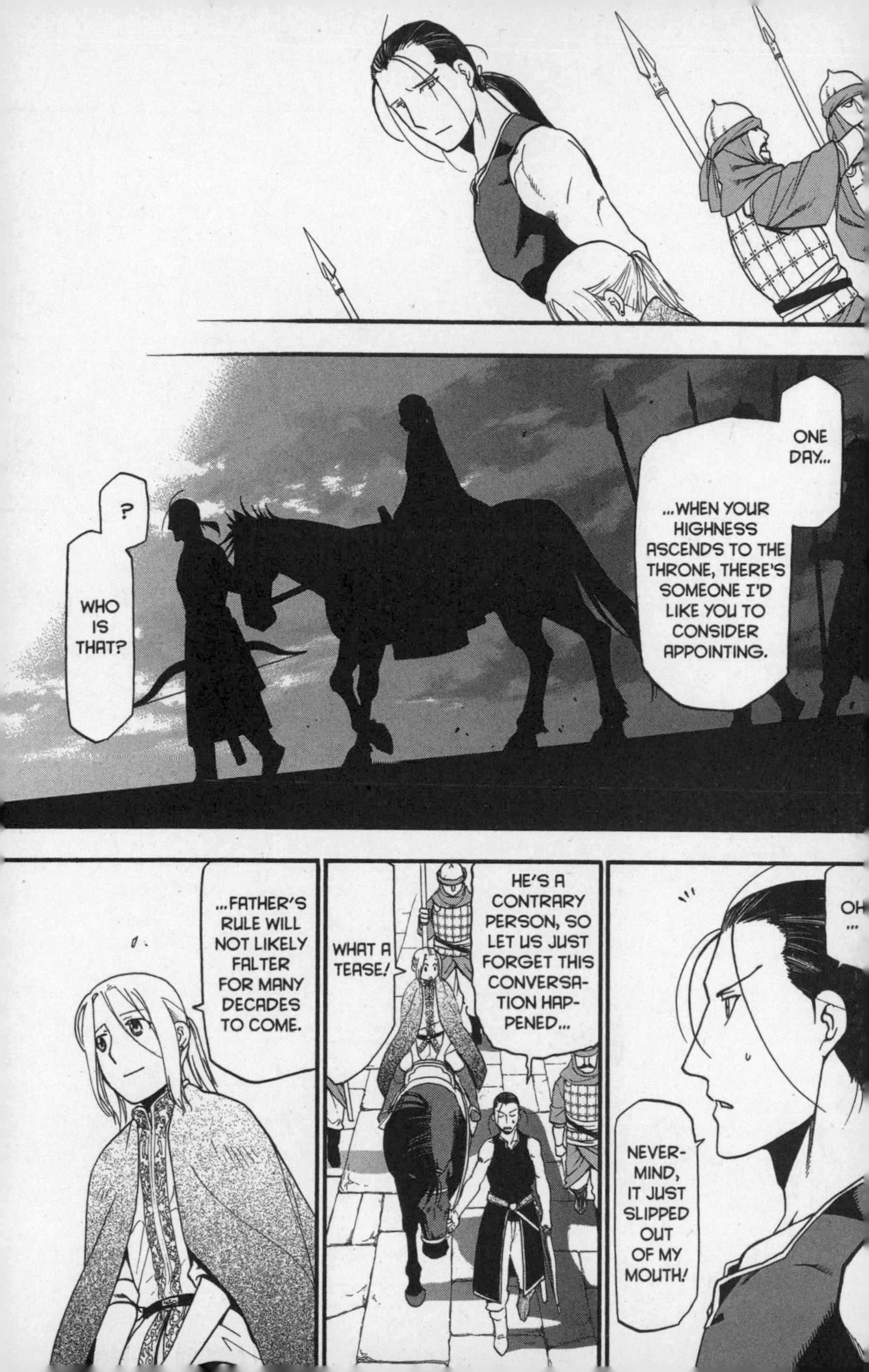
ONE DAY...
...WHEN YOUR HIGHNESS ASCENDS TO THE THRONE, THERE'S SOMEONE I'D LIKE YOU TO CONSIDER APPOINTING.
?
WHO IS THAT?
OH ...
NEVER-MIND, IT JUST SLIPPED OUT OF MY MOUTH!
HE'S A CONTRARY PERSON, SO LET US JUST FORGET THIS CONVERSATION HAPPENED...
WHAT A TEASE!
...FATHER'S RULE WILL NOT LIKELY FALTER FOR MANY DECADES TO COME.

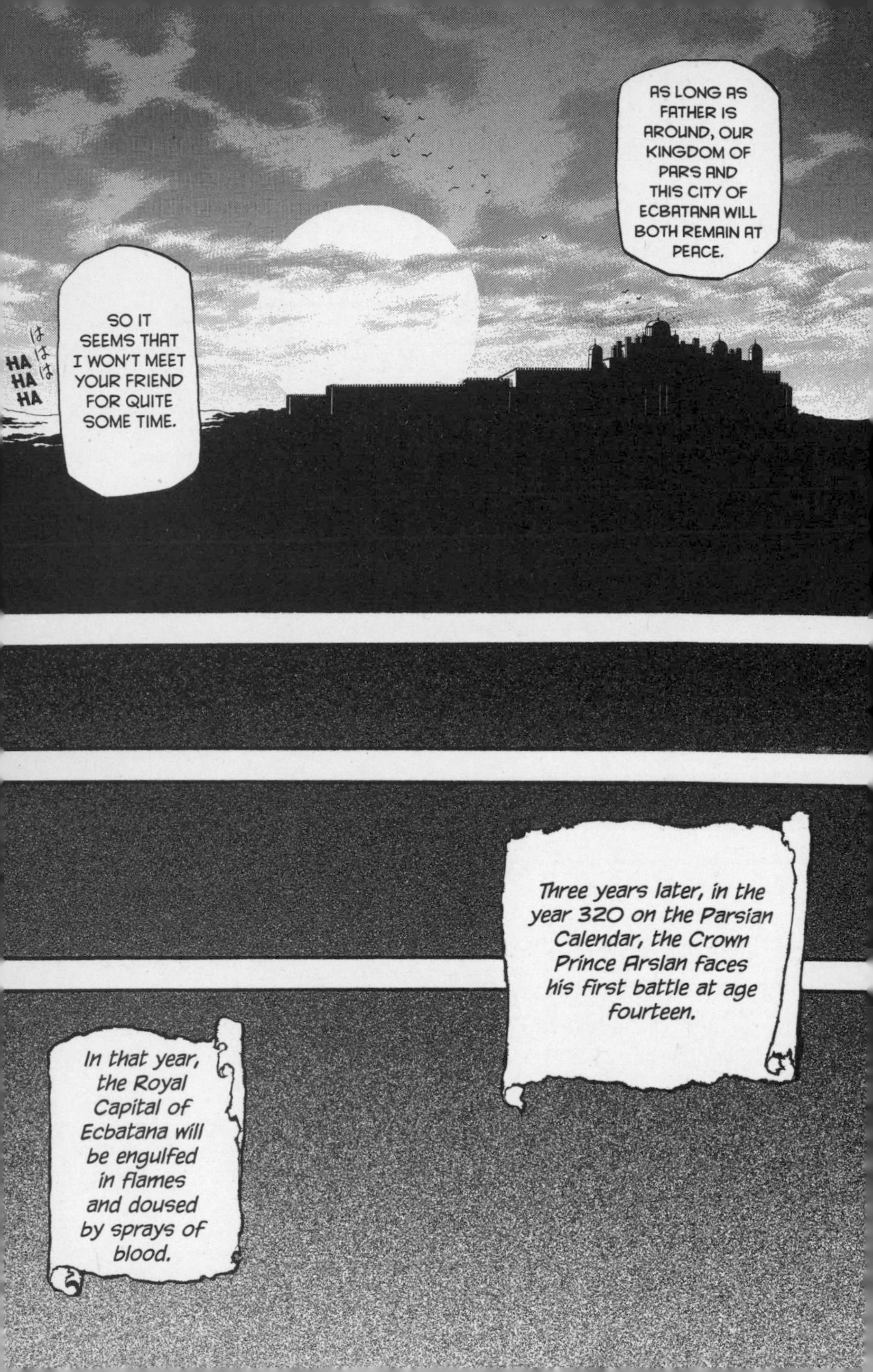
AS LONG AS FATHER IS AROUND, OUR KINGDOM OF PARS AND THIS CITY OF ECBATANA WILL BOTH REMAIN AT PEACE.
SO IT SEEMS THAT I WON'T MEET YOUR FRIEND FOR QUITE SOME TIME.
ははは
HA HA HA
Three years later, in the year 320 on the Parsian Calendar, the Crown Prince Arslan faces his first battle at age fourteen.
In that year, the Royal Capital of Ecbatana will be engulfed in flames and doused by sprays of blood.

CRING

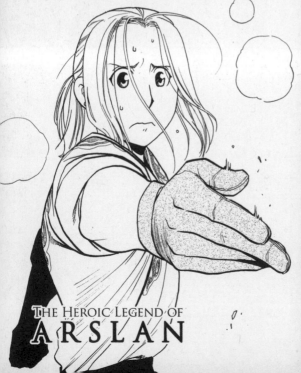

THE HEROIC LEGEND OF
ARSLAN

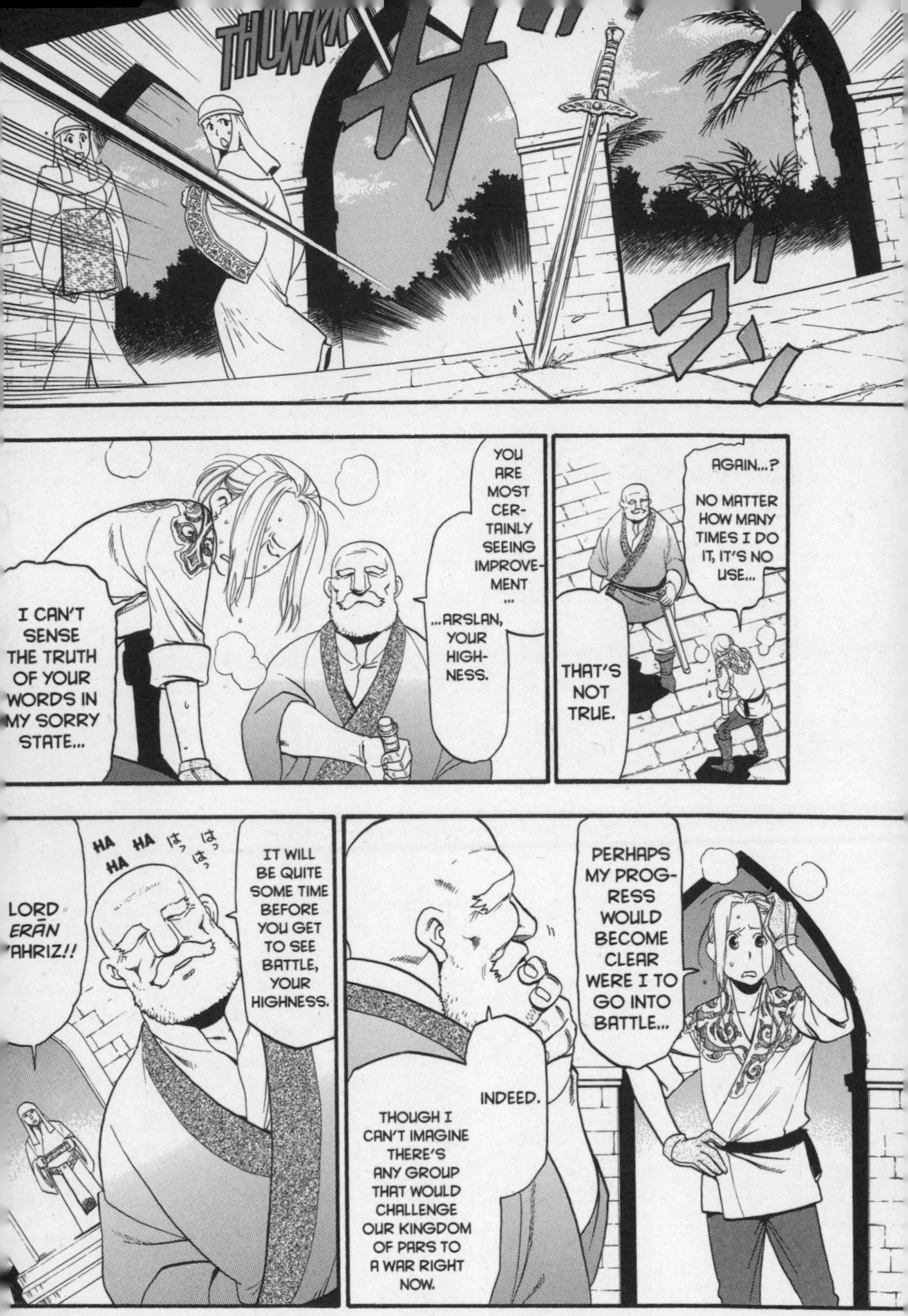
THUNKK
AGAIN...? NO MATTER HOW MANY TIMES I DO IT, IT'S NO USE...
THAT'S NOT TRUE.
YOU ARE MOST CERTAINLY SEEING IMPROVEMENT ...
...ARSLAN, YOUR HIGHNESS.
I CAN'T SENSE THE TRUTH OF YOUR WORDS IN MY SORRY STATE...
PERHAPS MY PROGRESS WOULD BECOME CLEAR WERE I TO GO INTO BATTLE...
INDEED.
THOUGH I CAN'T IMAGINE THERE'S ANY GROUP THAT WOULD CHALLENGE OUR KINGDOM OF PARS TO A WAR RIGHT NOW.
HA HA HA HA はっはっ
IT WILL BE QUITE SOME TIME BEFORE YOU GET TO SEE BATTLE, YOUR HIGHNESS.
LORD ERĀN AHRIZ!!

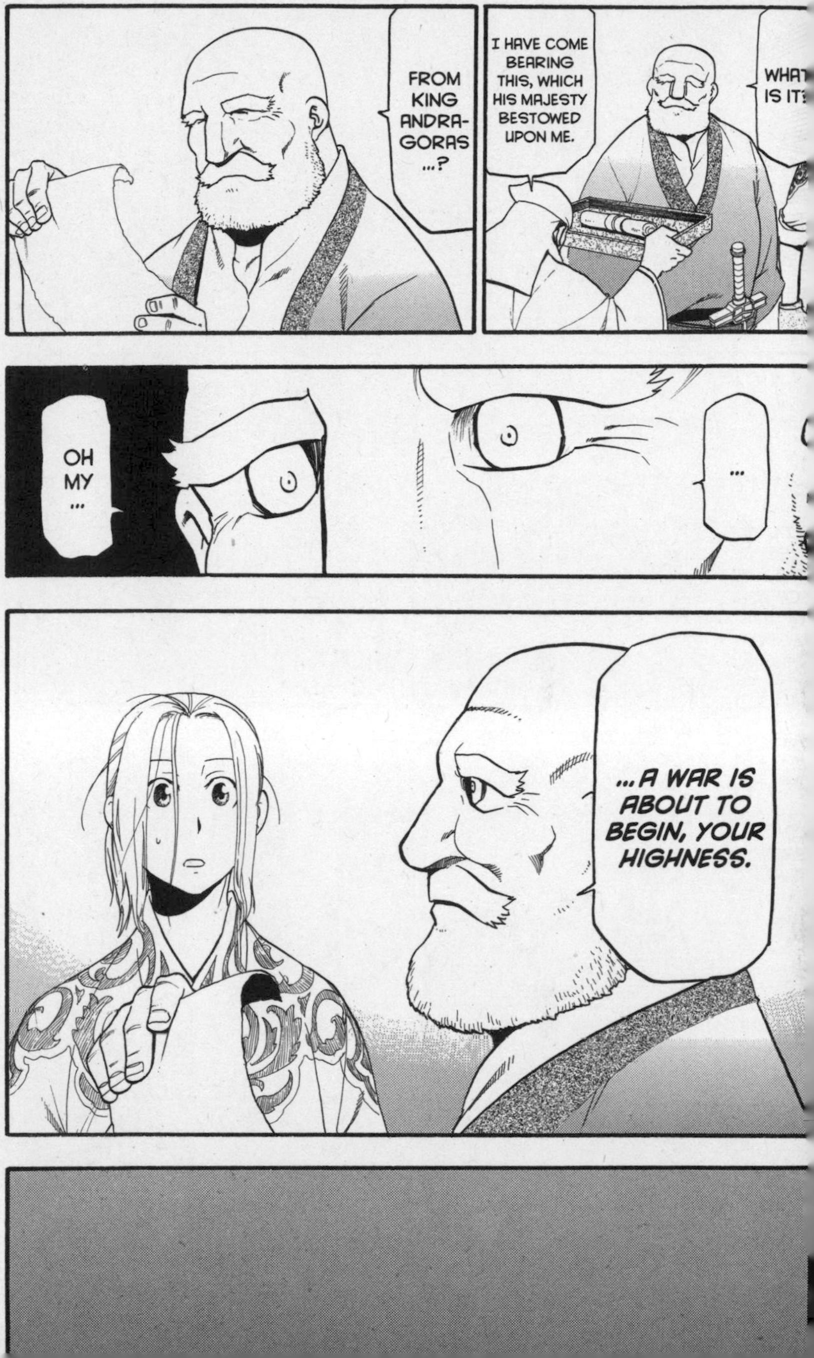
WHAT IS IT?
I HAVE COME BEARING THIS, WHICH HIS MAJESTY BESTOWED UPON ME.
FROM KING ANDRA-GORAS ...?
...
OH MY ...
...A WAR IS ABOUT TO BEGIN, YOUR HIGHNESS.

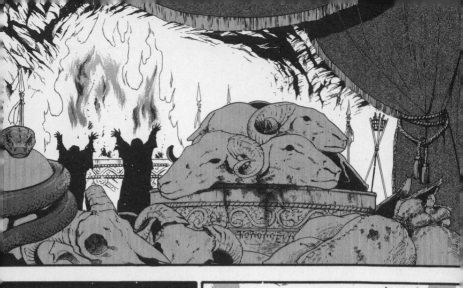

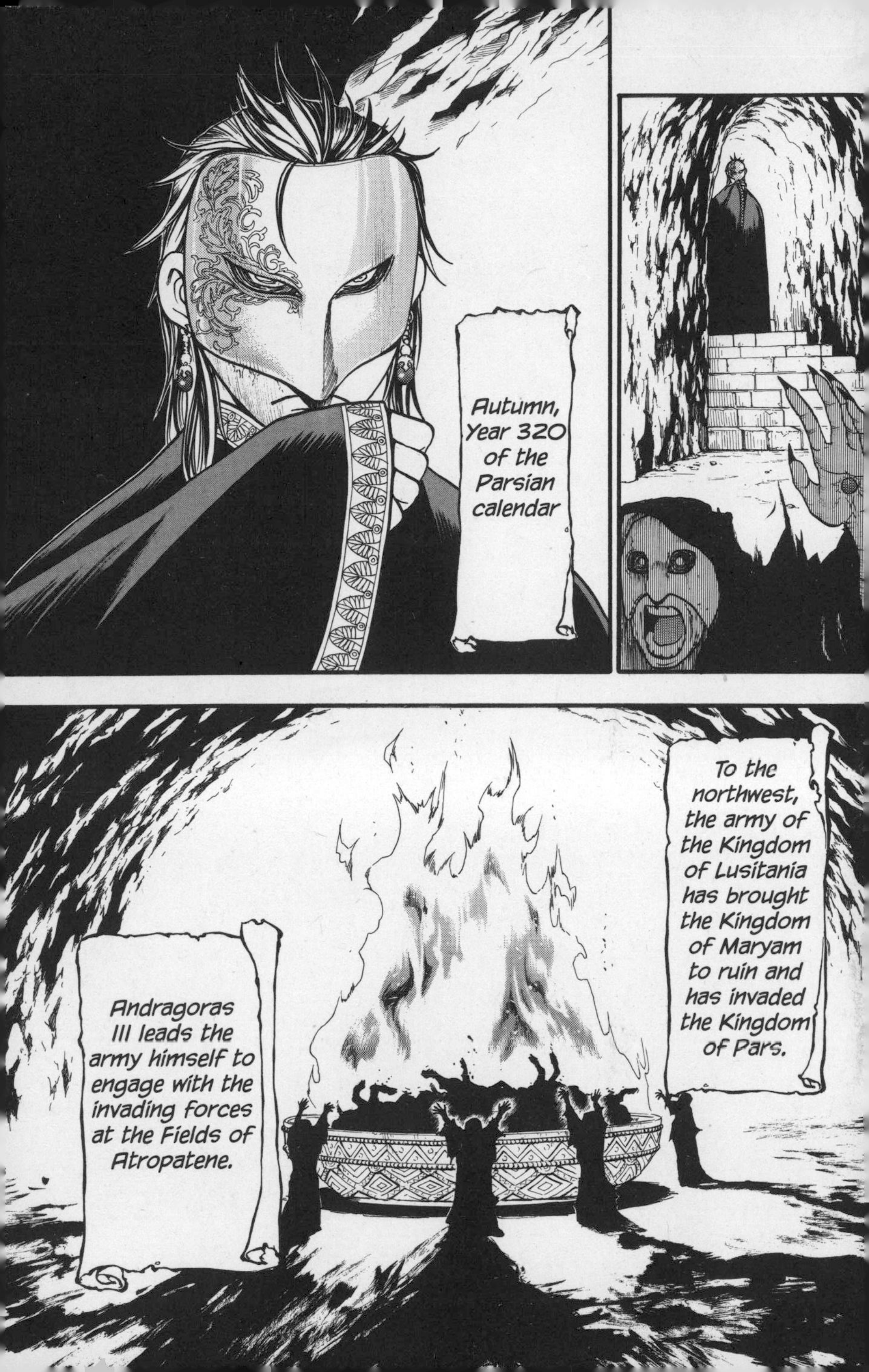
Autumn, Year 320 of the Parsian calendar
To the northwest, the army of the Kingdom of Lusitania has brought the Kingdom of Maryam to ruin and has invaded the Kingdom of Pars.
Andragoras III leads the army himself to engage with the invading forces at the Fields of Atropatene.

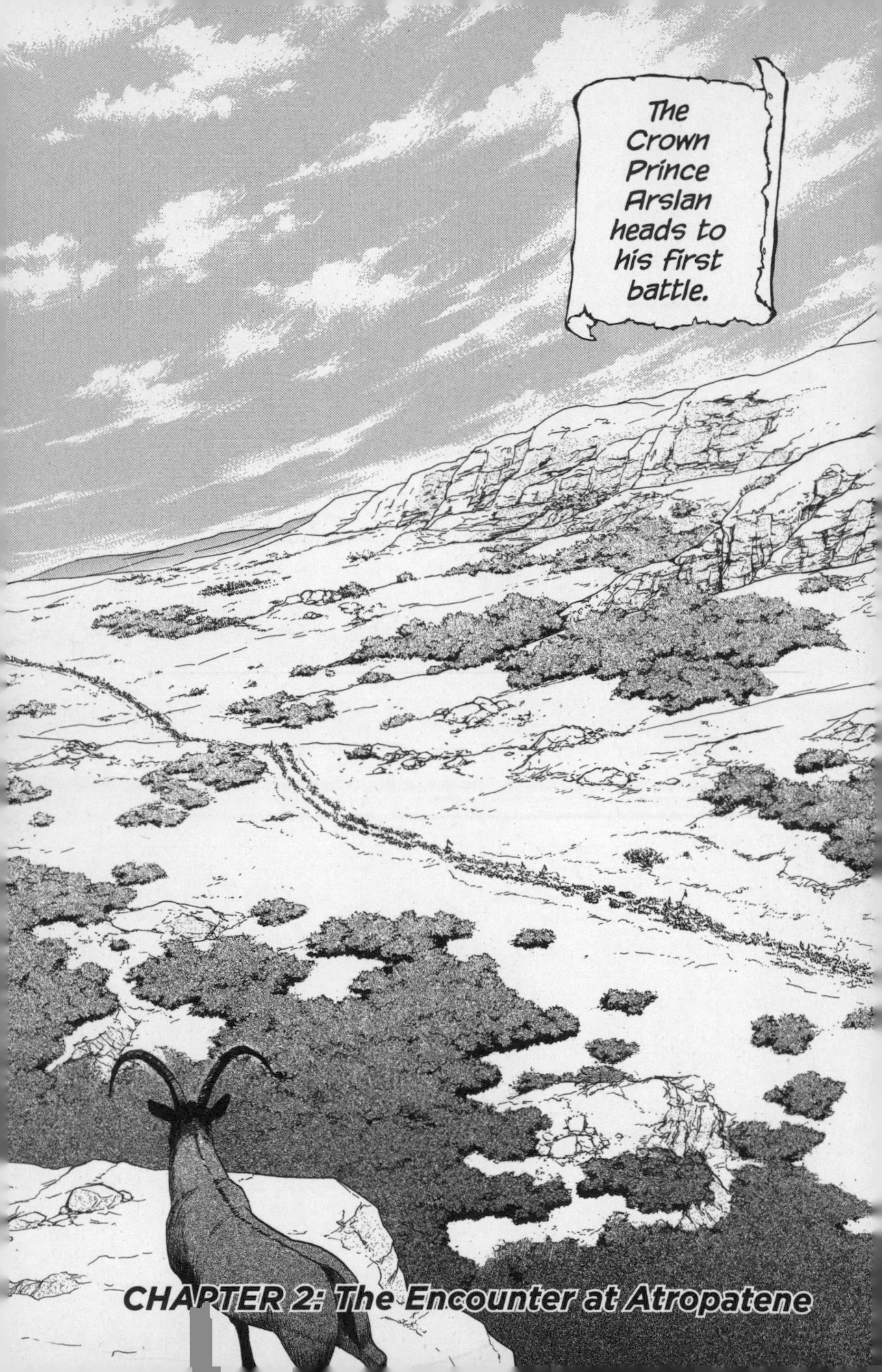
The Crown Prince Arslan heads to his first battle.
CHAPTER 2: The Encounter at Atropatene

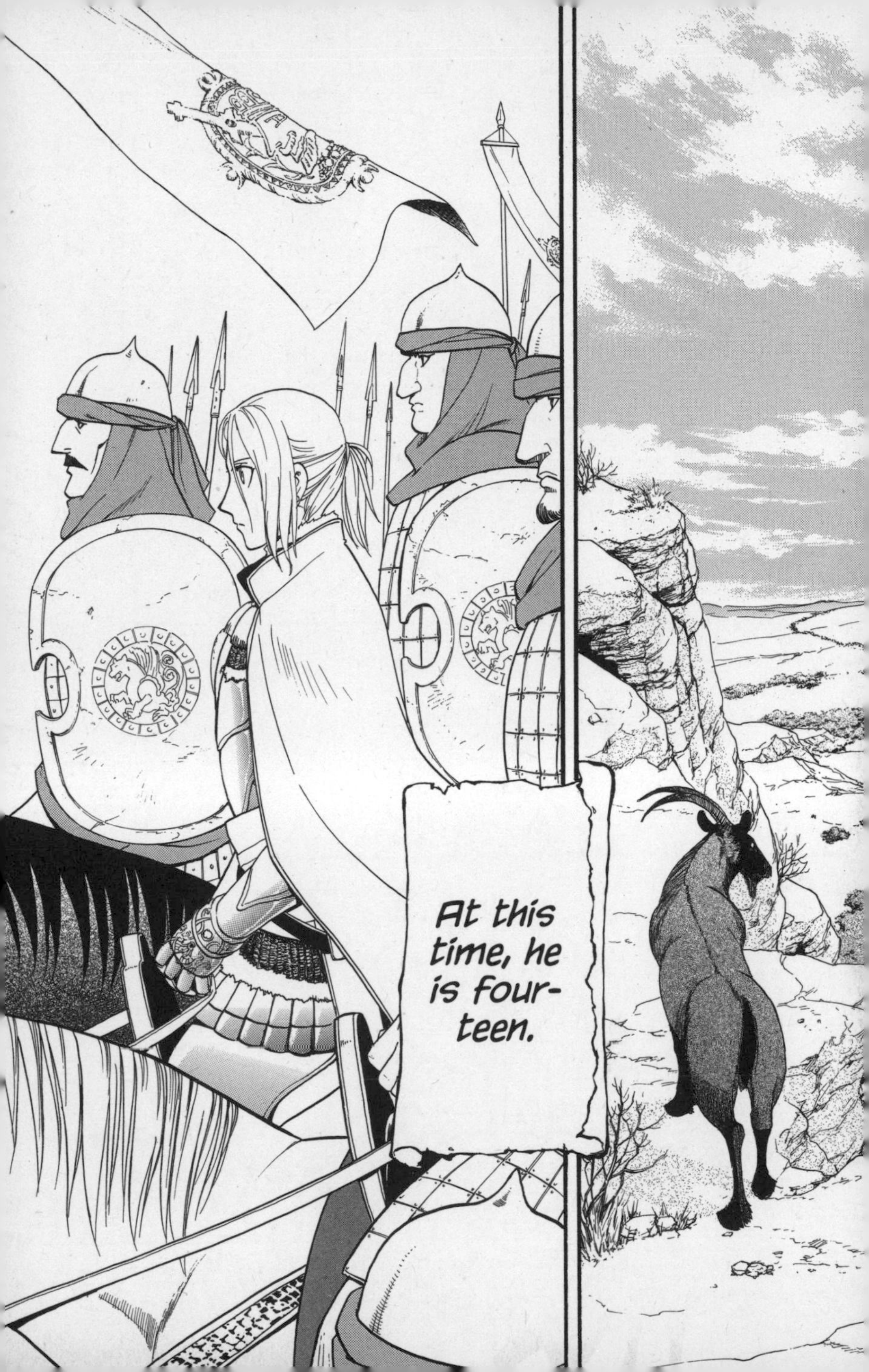
At this time, he is four-teen.

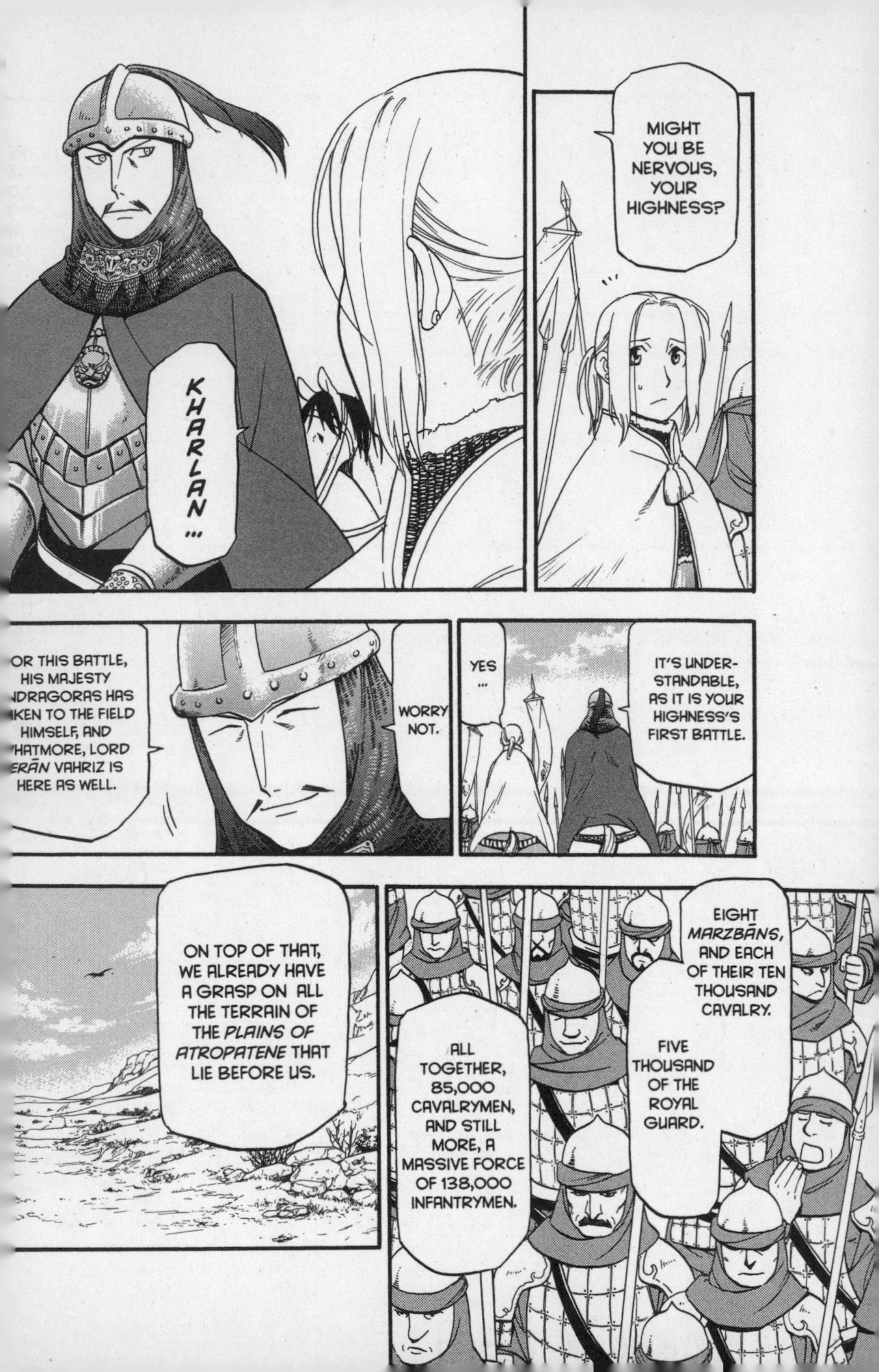
MIGHT YOU BE NERVOUS, YOUR HIGHNESS?
KHARLAN...
IT'S UNDER-STANDABLE, AS IT IS YOUR HIGHNESS'S FIRST BATTLE.
YES...
WORRY NOT.
OR THIS BATTLE, HIS MAJESTY NDRAGORAS HAS IKEN TO THE FIELD HIMSELF, AND VHATMORE, LORD ERĀN VAHRIZ IS HERE AS WELL.
EIGHT *MARZBĀNS*, AND EACH OF THEIR TEN THOUSAND CAVALRY.
FIVE THOUSAND OF THE ROYAL GUARD.
ALL TOGETHER, 85,000 CAVALRYMEN, AND STILL MORE, A MASSIVE FORCE OF 138,000 INFANTRYMEN.
ON TOP OF THAT, WE ALREADY HAVE A GRASP ON ALL THE TERRAIN OF THE *PLAINS OF ATROPATENE* THAT LIE BEFORE US.

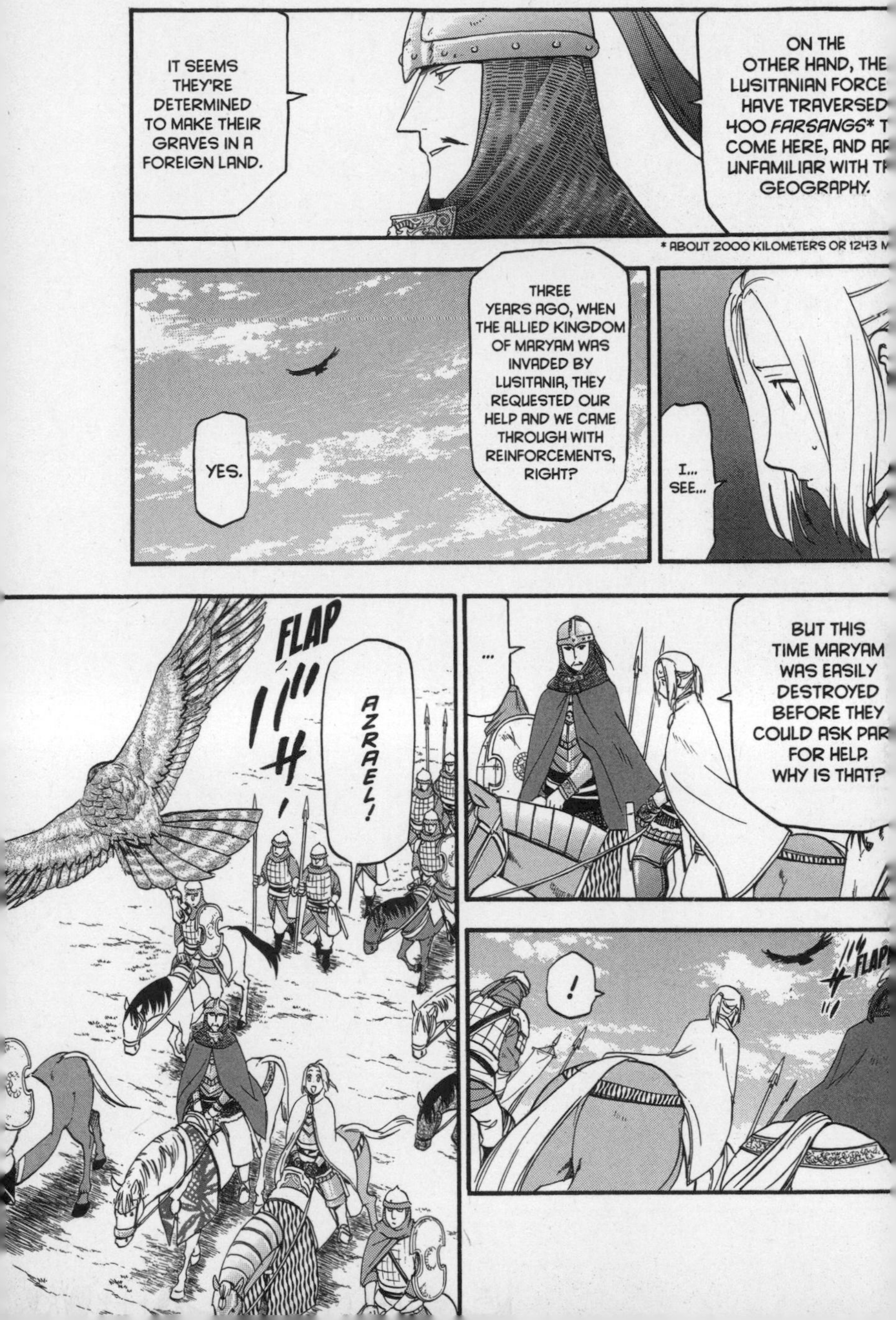
ON THE OTHER HAND, THE LUSITANIAN FORCE HAVE TRAVERSED 400 *FARSANGS** T COME HERE, AND AF UNFAMILIAR WITH TH GEOGRAPHY.
IT SEEMS THEY'RE DETERMINED TO MAKE THEIR GRAVES IN A FOREIGN LAND.
I... SEE...
THREE YEARS AGO, WHEN THE ALLIED KINGDOM OF MARYAM WAS INVADED BY LUSITANIA, THEY REQUESTED OUR HELP AND WE CAME THROUGH WITH REINFORCEMENTS, RIGHT?
YES.
BUT THIS TIME MARYAM WAS EASILY DESTROYED BEFORE THEY COULD ASK PAR FOR HELP. WHY IS THAT?
...
FLAP
!
AZRAEL!
FLAP

* ABOUT 2000 KILOMETERS OR 1243 M

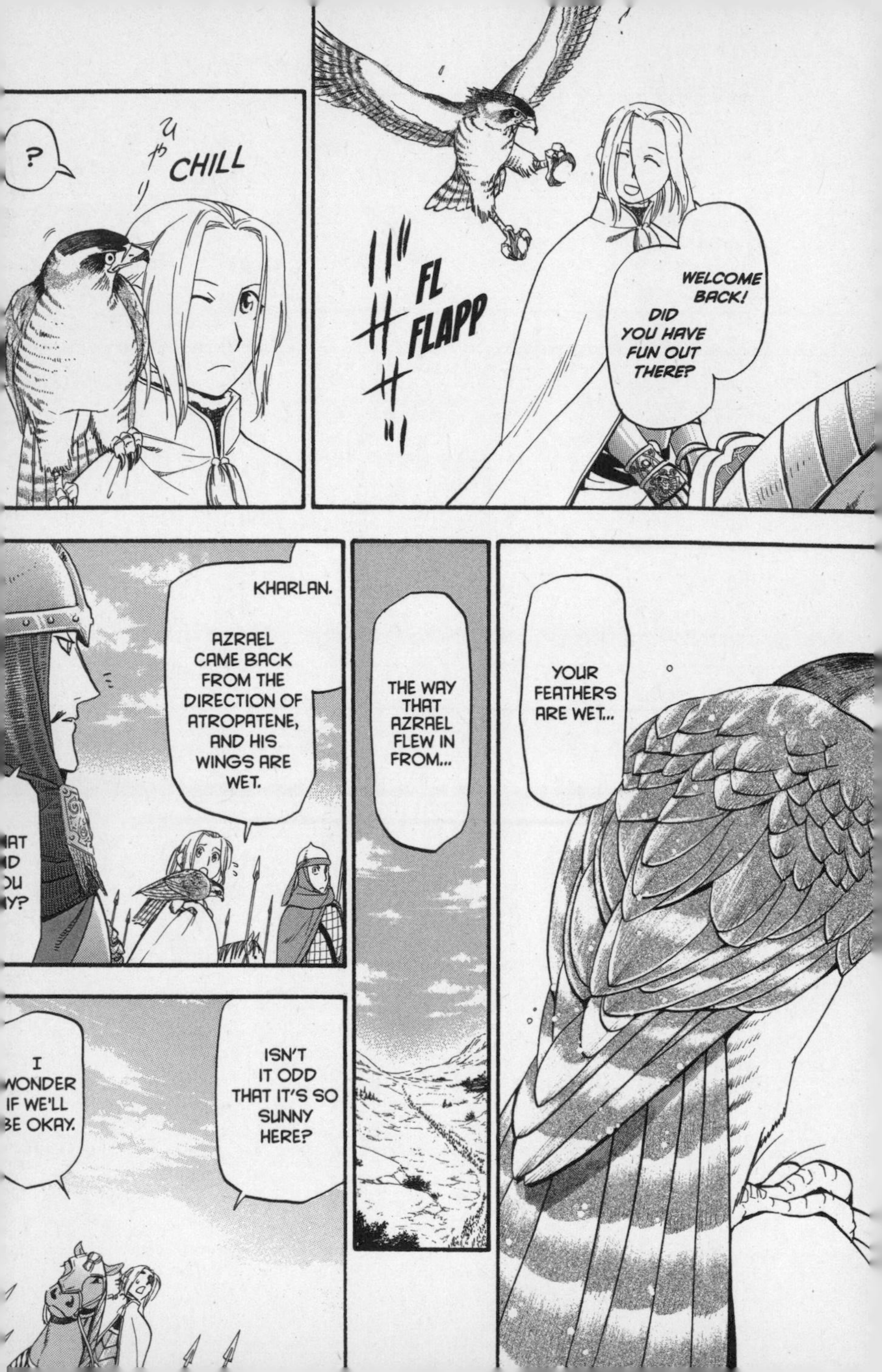
FL
FLAPP
WELCOME BACK!
DID YOU HAVE FUN OUT THERE?
?
ひやり
CHILL
YOUR FEATHERS ARE WET...
THE WAY THAT AZRAEL FLEW IN FROM...
KHARLAN.
AZRAEL CAME BACK FROM THE DIRECTION OF ATROPATENE, AND HIS WINGS ARE WET.
ISN'T IT ODD THAT IT'S SO SUNNY HERE?
I WONDER IF WE'LL BE OKAY.

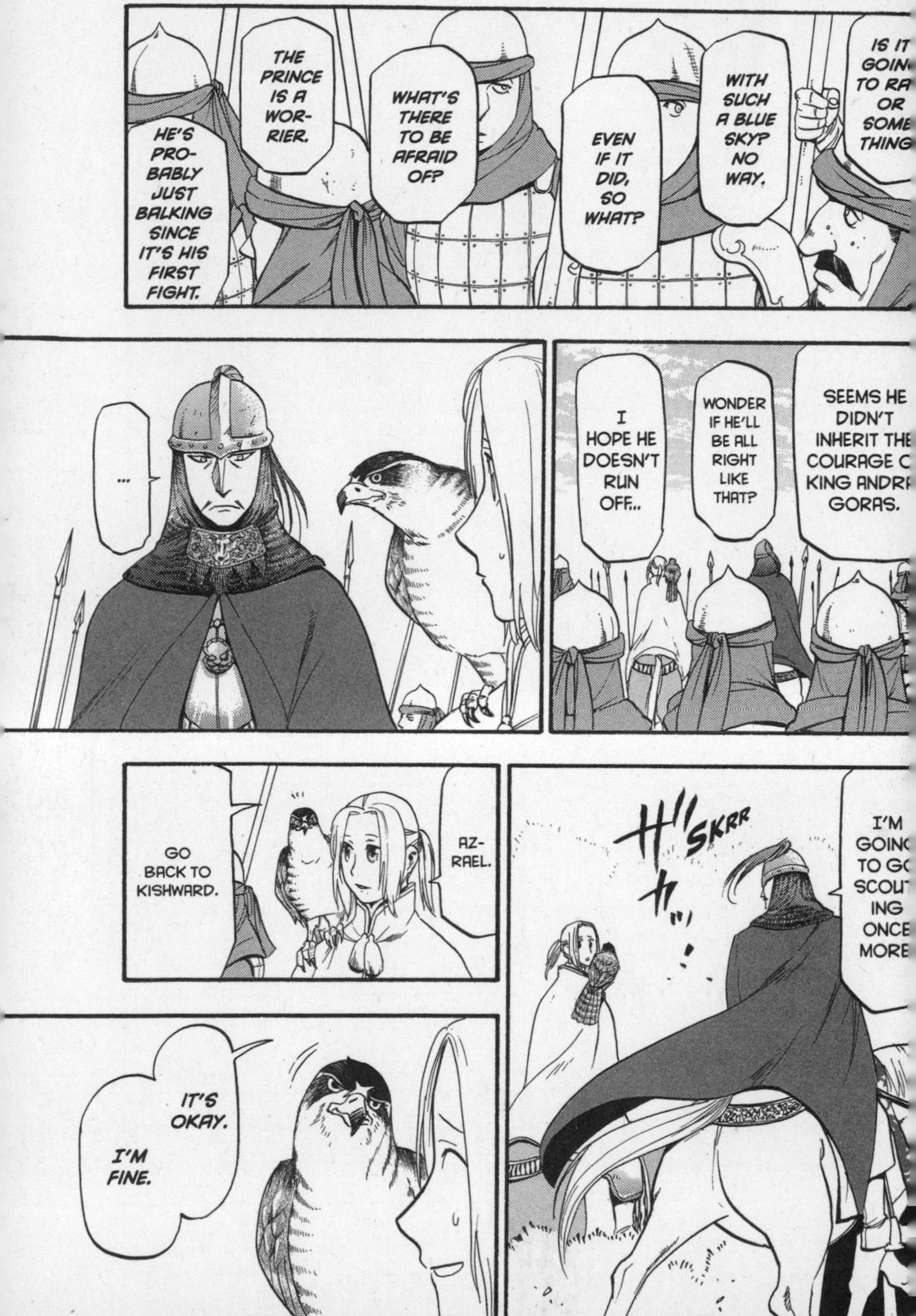
IS IT GOIN TO RA OR SOME THING
WITH SUCH A BLUE SKY? NO WAY.
EVEN IF IT DID, SO WHAT?
WHAT'S THERE TO BE AFRAID OF?
THE PRINCE IS A WOR-RIER.
HE'S PRO-BABLY JUST BALKING SINCE IT'S HIS FIRST FIGHT.
SEEMS HE DIDN'T INHERIT THE COURAGE O KING ANDRA GORAS.
WONDER IF HE'LL BE ALL RIGHT LIKE THAT?
I HOPE HE DOESN'T RUN OFF...
...
I'M GOING TO GO SCOUT ING ONCE MORE
SKRR
AZ-RAEL.
GO BACK TO KISHWARD.
IT'S OKAY.
I'M FINE.

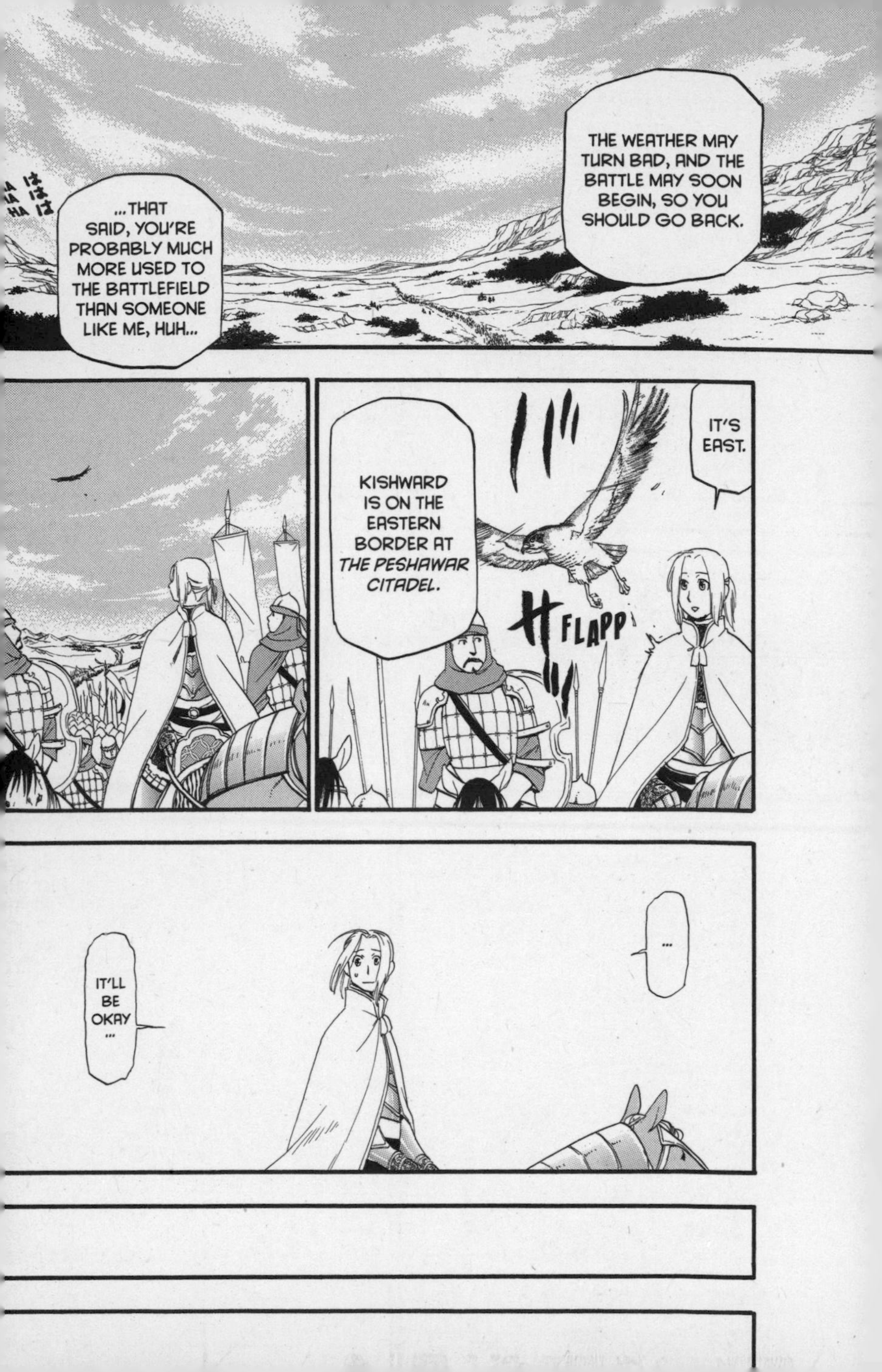
THE WEATHER MAY TURN BAD, AND THE BATTLE MAY SOON BEGIN, SO YOU SHOULD GO BACK.
...THAT SAID, YOU'RE PROBABLY MUCH MORE USED TO THE BATTLEFIELD THAN SOMEONE LIKE ME, HUH...
ははは
HA HA HA
IT'S EAST.
KISHWARD IS ON THE EASTERN BORDER AT *THE PESHAWAR CITADEL.*
FLAPP
...
IT'LL BE OKAY...

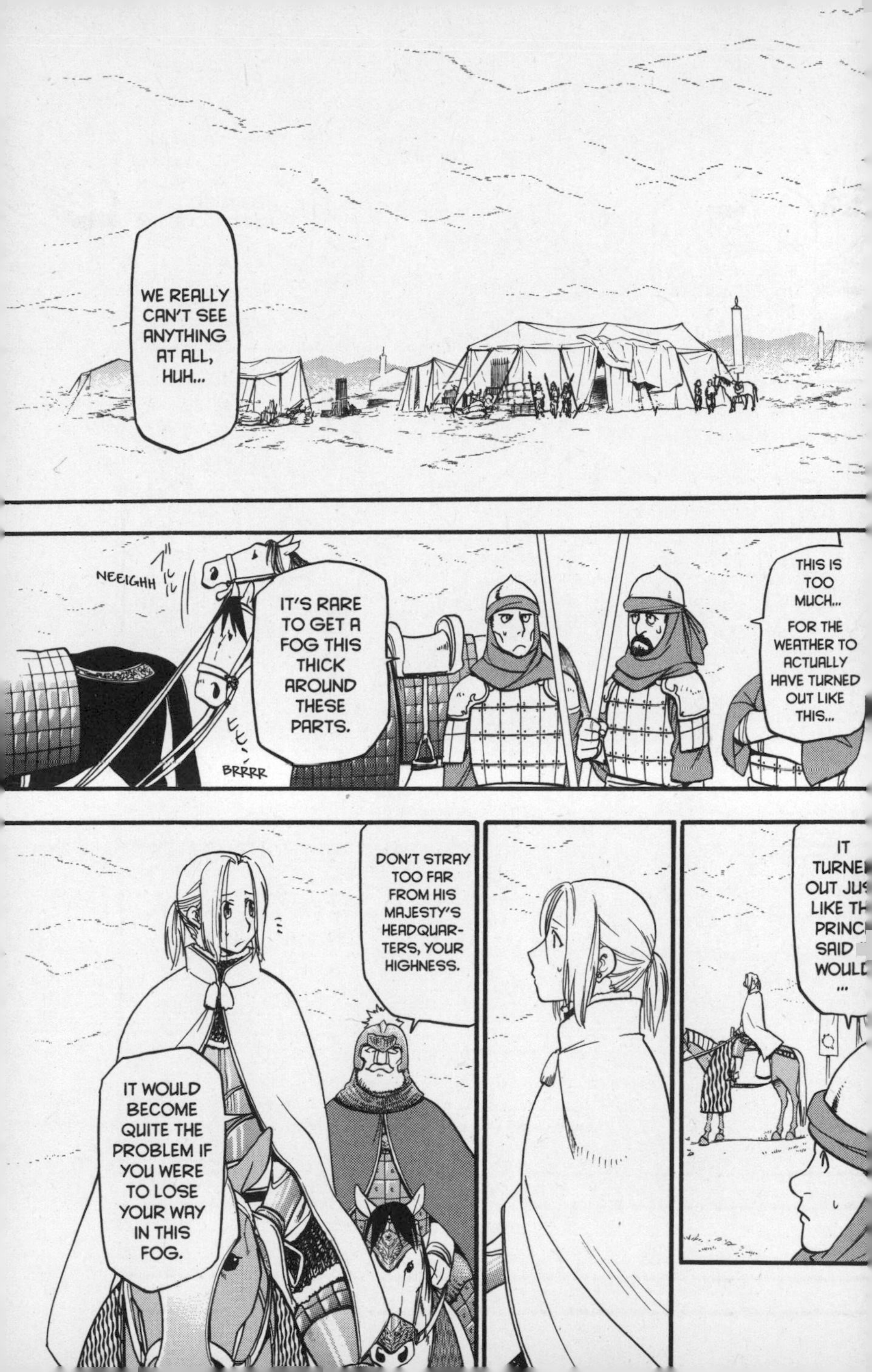
WE REALLY CAN'T SEE ANYTHING AT ALL, HUH...
THIS IS TOO MUCH... FOR THE WEATHER TO ACTUALLY HAVE TURNED OUT LIKE THIS...
IT'S RARE TO GET A FOG THIS THICK AROUND THESE PARTS.
NEEIGHH
BRRRR
IT TURNE OUT JUS LIKE TH PRINC SAID WOULD ...
DON'T STRAY TOO FAR FROM HIS MAJESTY'S HEADQUAR-TERS, YOUR HIGHNESS.
IT WOULD BECOME QUITE THE PROBLEM IF YOU WERE TO LOSE YOUR WAY IN THIS FOG.

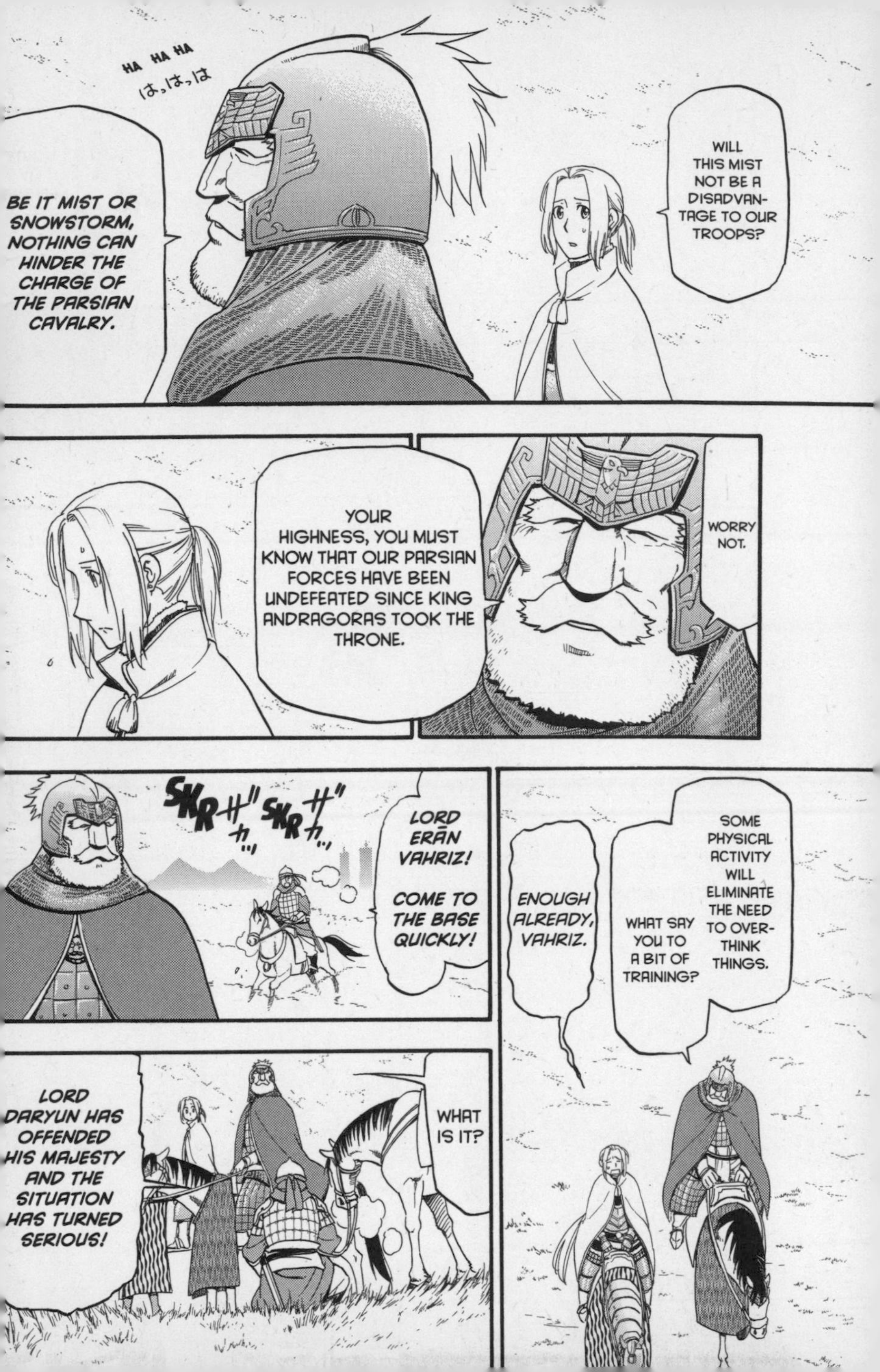
WILL THIS MIST NOT BE A DISADVANTAGE TO OUR TROOPS?
HA HA HA
はっはっは
BE IT MIST OR SNOWSTORM, NOTHING CAN HINDER THE CHARGE OF THE PARSIAN CAVALRY.
WORRY NOT.
YOUR HIGHNESS, YOU MUST KNOW THAT OUR PARSIAN FORCES HAVE BEEN UNDEFEATED SINCE KING ANDRAGORAS TOOK THE THRONE.
SOME PHYSICAL ACTIVITY WILL ELIMINATE THE NEED TO OVER-THINK THINGS.
WHAT SAY YOU TO A BIT OF TRAINING?
ENOUGH ALREADY, VAHRIZ.
LORD ERĀN VAHRIZ!
COME TO THE BASE QUICKLY!
SKR SKR
WHAT IS IT?
LORD DARYUN HAS OFFENDED HIS MAJESTY AND THE SITUATION HAS TURNED SERIOUS!

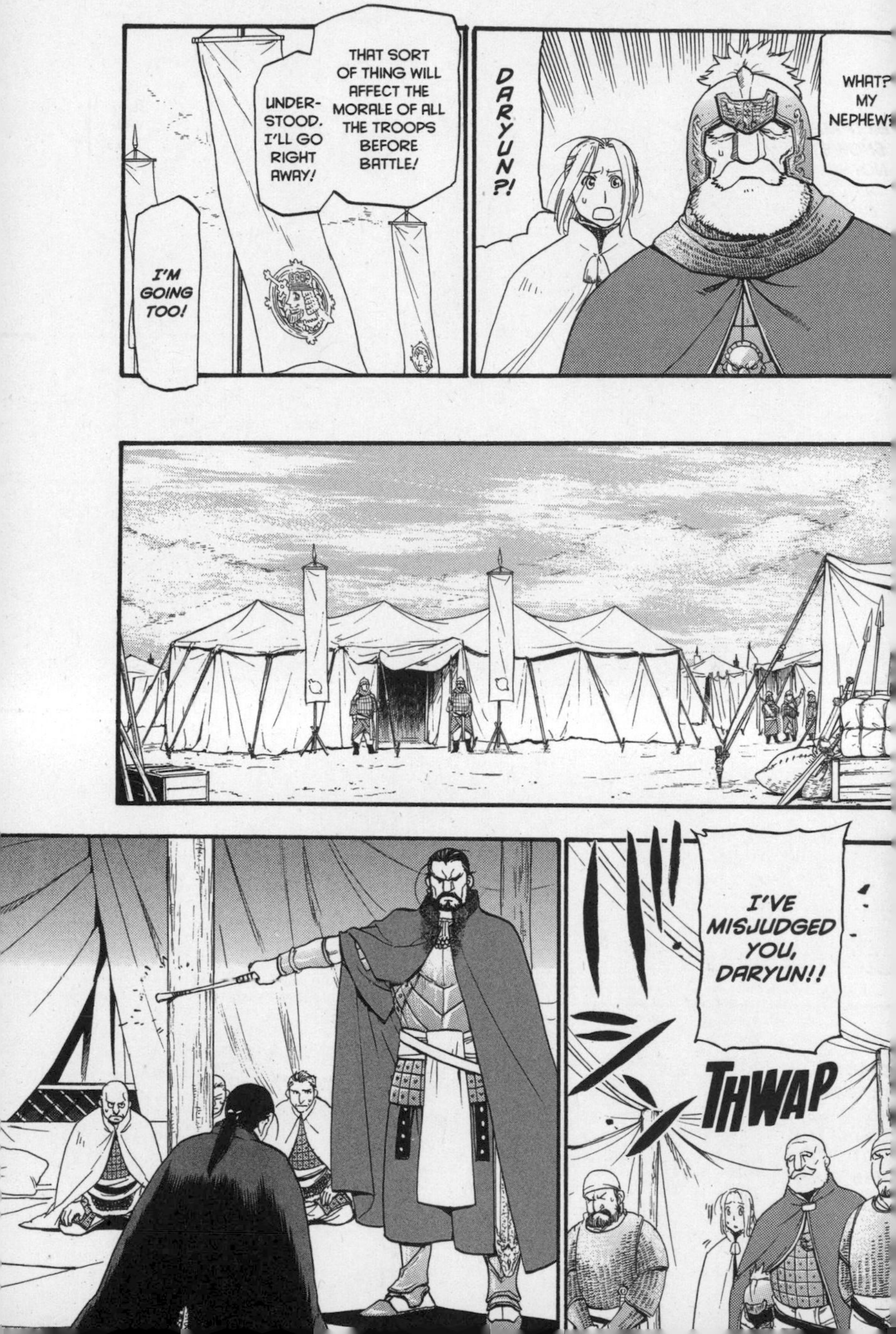
WHAT? MY NEPHEW?
DARYUN?!
THAT SORT OF THING WILL AFFECT THE MORALE OF ALL THE TROOPS BEFORE BATTLE!
UNDER-STOOD. I'LL GO RIGHT AWAY!
I'M GOING TOO!
I'VE MISJUDGED YOU, DARYUN!!
THWAP

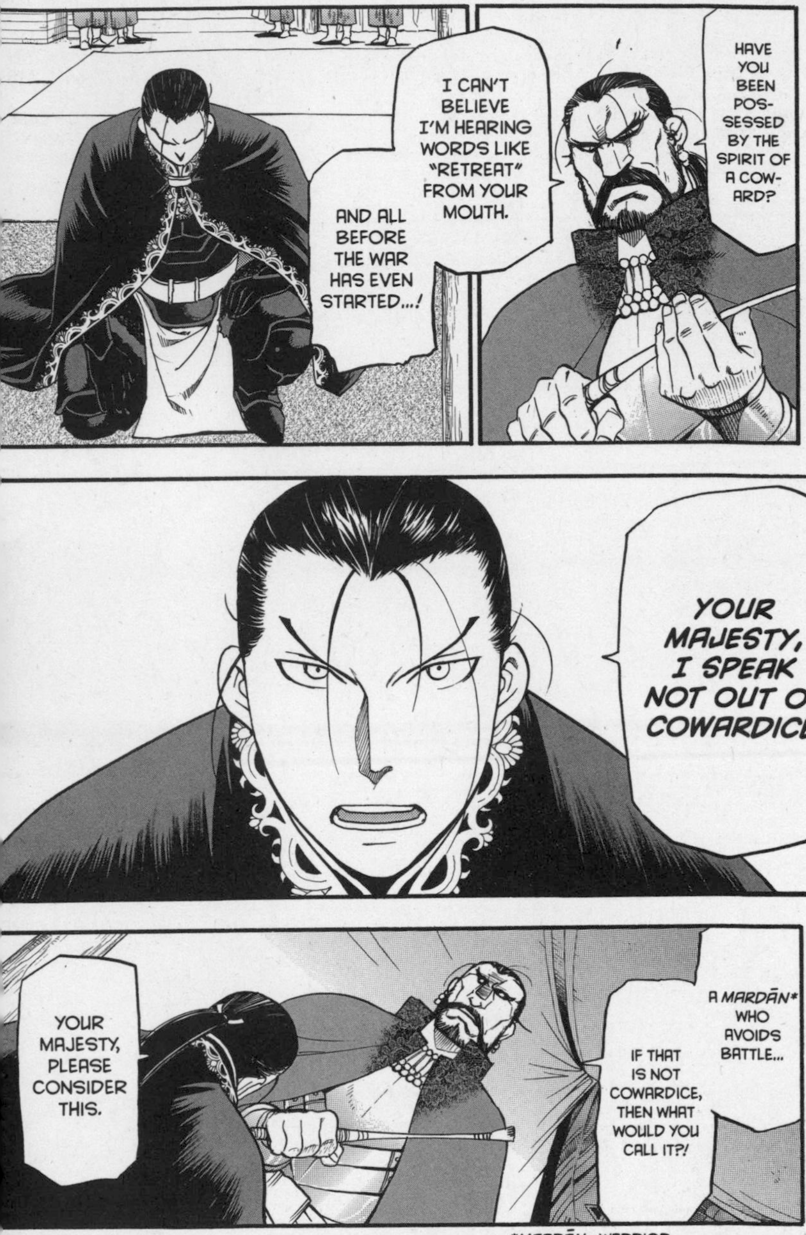
HAVE YOU BEEN POSSESSED BY THE SPIRIT OF A COWARD?
I CAN'T BELIEVE I'M HEARING WORDS LIKE "RETREAT" FROM YOUR MOUTH.
AND ALL BEFORE THE WAR HAS EVEN STARTED...!
YOUR MAJESTY, I SPEAK NOT OUT OF COWARDICE.
A *MARDĀN** WHO AVOIDS BATTLE...
IF THAT IS NOT COWARDICE, THEN WHAT WOULD YOU CALL IT?!
YOUR MAJESTY, PLEASE CONSIDER THIS.

**MARDĀN* = WARRIOR

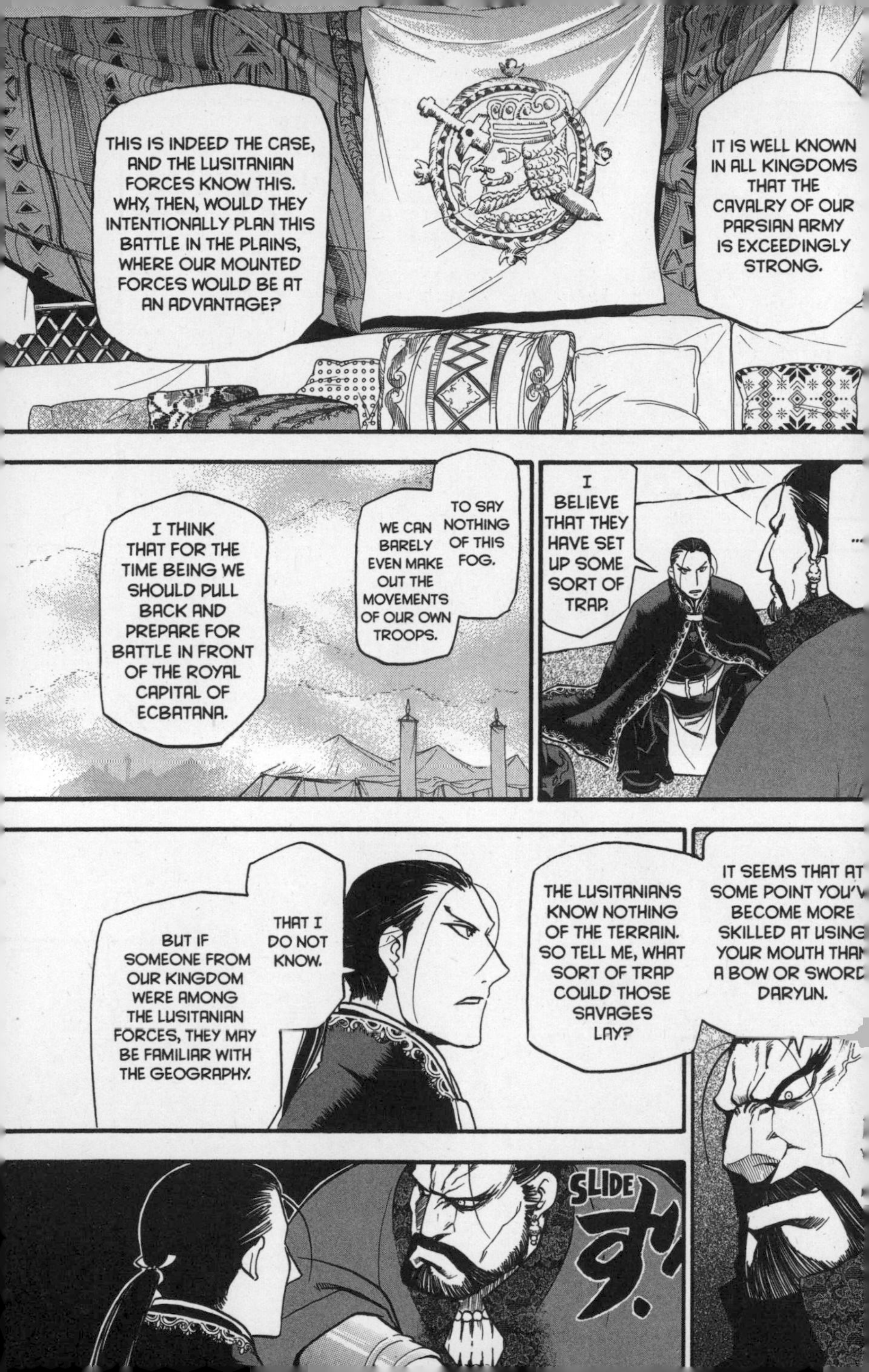
IT IS WELL KNOWN IN ALL KINGDOMS THAT THE CAVALRY OF OUR PARSIAN ARMY IS EXCEEDINGLY STRONG.
THIS IS INDEED THE CASE, AND THE LUSITANIAN FORCES KNOW THIS. WHY, THEN, WOULD THEY INTENTIONALLY PLAN THIS BATTLE IN THE PLAINS, WHERE OUR MOUNTED FORCES WOULD BE AT AN ADVANTAGE?
...
I BELIEVE THAT THEY HAVE SET UP SOME SORT OF TRAP.
TO SAY NOTHING OF THIS FOG.
WE CAN BARELY EVEN MAKE OUT THE MOVEMENTS OF OUR OWN TROOPS.
I THINK THAT FOR THE TIME BEING WE SHOULD PULL BACK AND PREPARE FOR BATTLE IN FRONT OF THE ROYAL CAPITAL OF ECBATANA.
IT SEEMS THAT AT SOME POINT YOU'V BECOME MORE SKILLED AT USING YOUR MOUTH THAN A BOW OR SWORD DARYUN.
THE LUSITANIANS KNOW NOTHING OF THE TERRAIN. SO TELL ME, WHAT SORT OF TRAP COULD THOSE SAVAGES LAY?
THAT I DO NOT KNOW.
BUT IF SOMEONE FROM OUR KINGDOM WERE AMONG THE LUSITANIAN FORCES, THEY MAY BE FAMILIAR WITH THE GEOGRAPHY.
SLIDE

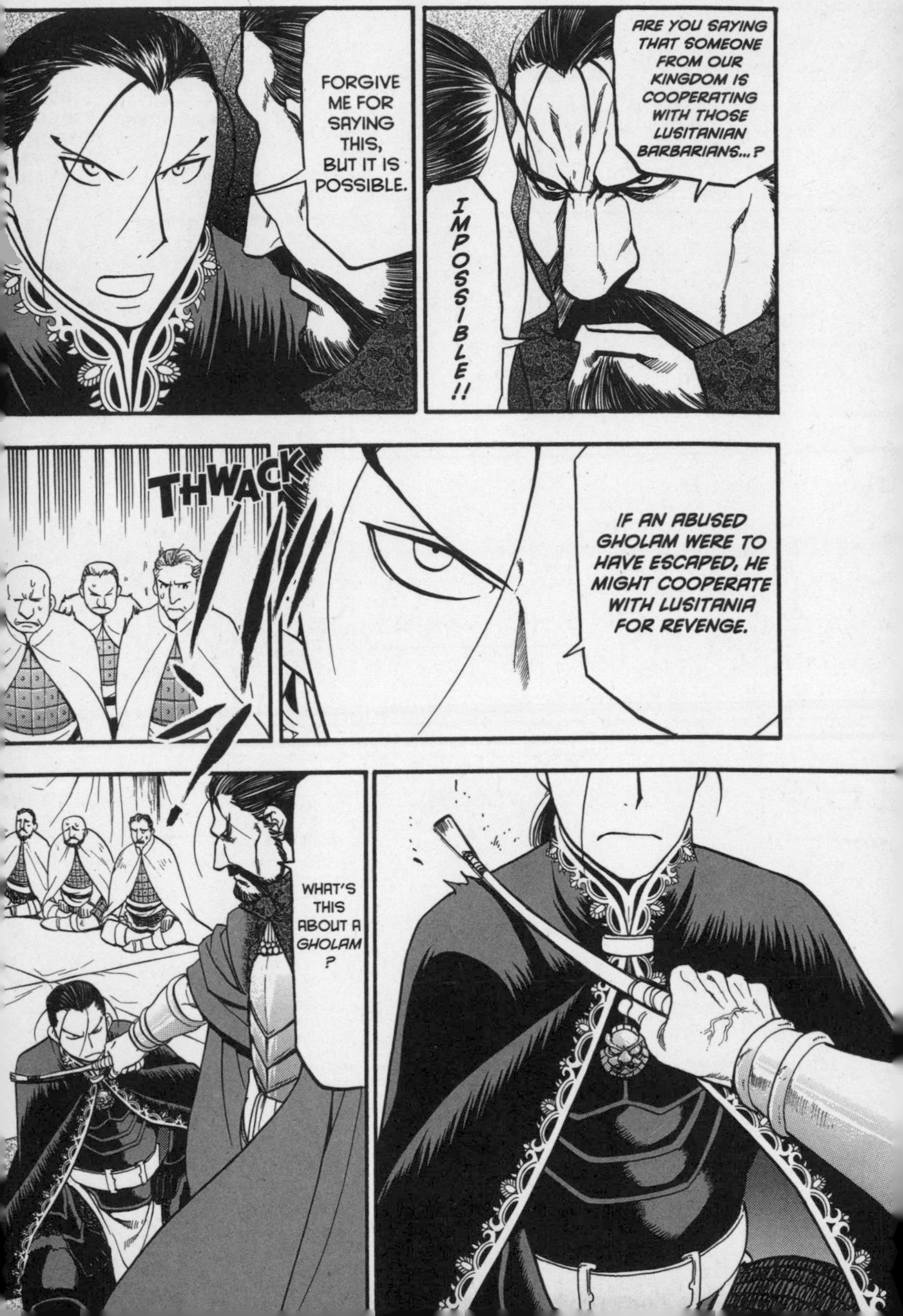
ARE YOU SAYING THAT SOMEONE FROM OUR KINGDOM IS COOPERATING WITH THOSE LUSITANIAN BARBARIANS...?
IMPOSSIBLE!!
FORGIVE ME FOR SAYING THIS, BUT IT IS POSSIBLE.
IF AN ABUSED GHOLAM WERE TO HAVE ESCAPED, HE MIGHT COOPERATE WITH LUSITANIA FOR REVENGE.
THWACK
WHAT'S THIS ABOUT A GHOLAM?

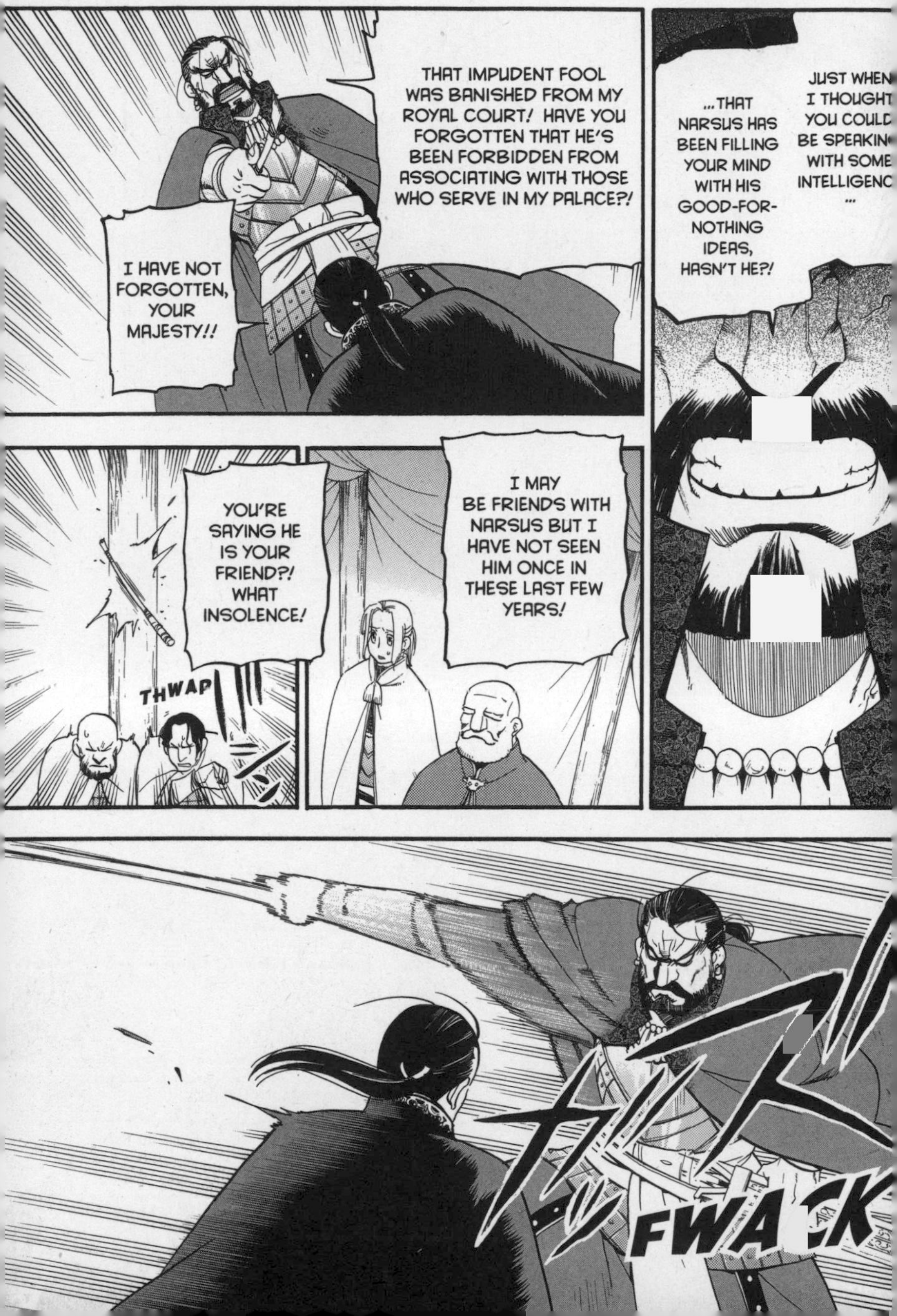
JUST WHEN I THOUGHT YOU COULD BE SPEAKIN WITH SOME INTELLIGENC ...
...THAT NARSUS HAS BEEN FILLING YOUR MIND WITH HIS GOOD-FOR-NOTHING IDEAS, HASN'T HE?!
THAT IMPUDENT FOOL WAS BANISHED FROM MY ROYAL COURT! HAVE YOU FORGOTTEN THAT HE'S BEEN FORBIDDEN FROM ASSOCIATING WITH THOSE WHO SERVE IN MY PALACE?!
I HAVE NOT FORGOTTEN, YOUR MAJESTY!!
I MAY BE FRIENDS WITH NARSUS BUT I HAVE NOT SEEN HIM ONCE IN THESE LAST FEW YEARS!
YOU'RE SAYING HE IS YOUR FRIEND?! WHAT INSOLENCE!
THWAP
FWA CK

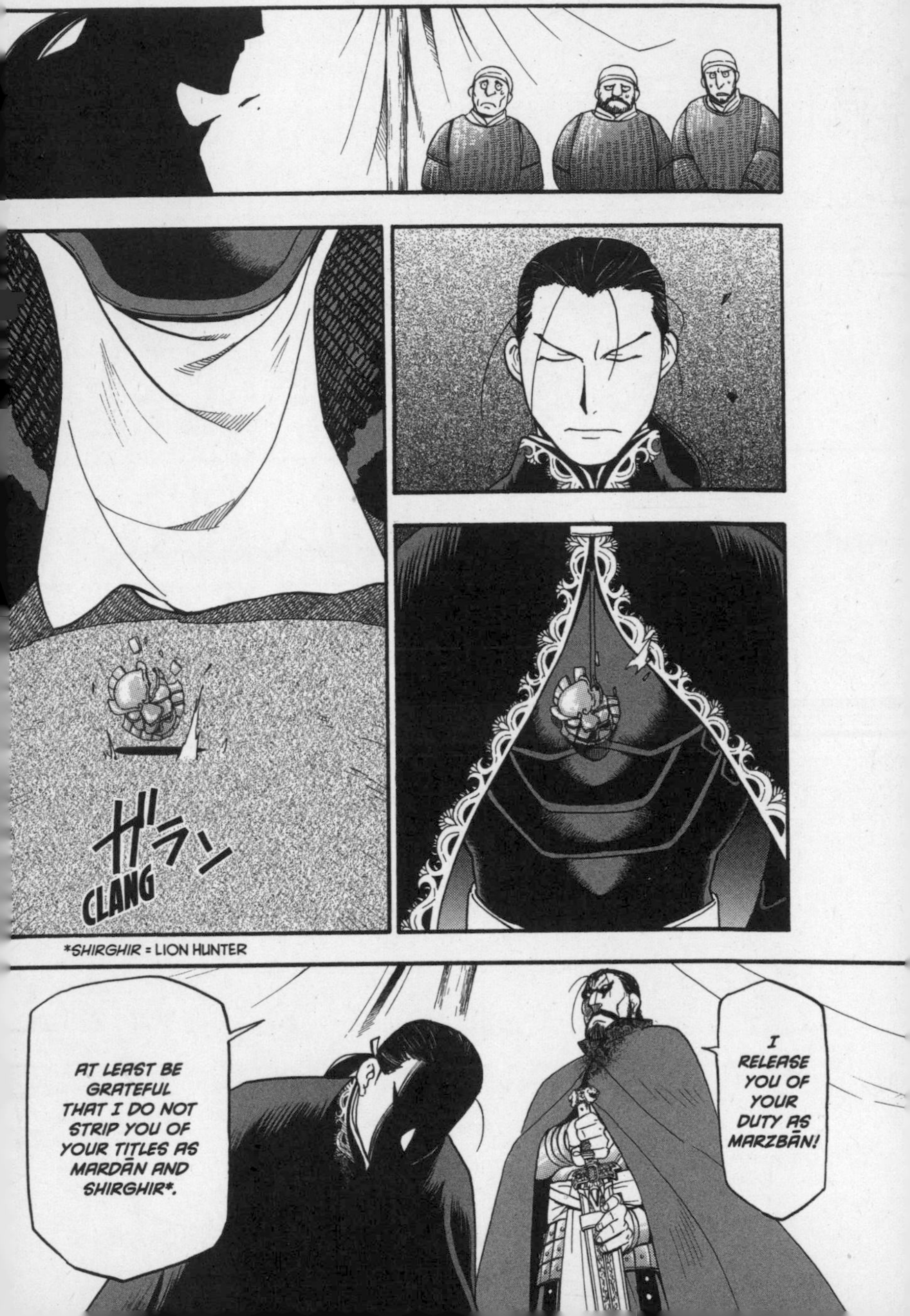
ガラン
CLANG
I RELEASE YOU OF YOUR DUTY AS MARZBĀN!
AT LEAST BE GRATEFUL THAT I DO NOT STRIP YOU OF YOUR TITLES AS MARDĀN AND SHIRGHIR*.

*SHIRGHIR = LION HUNTER

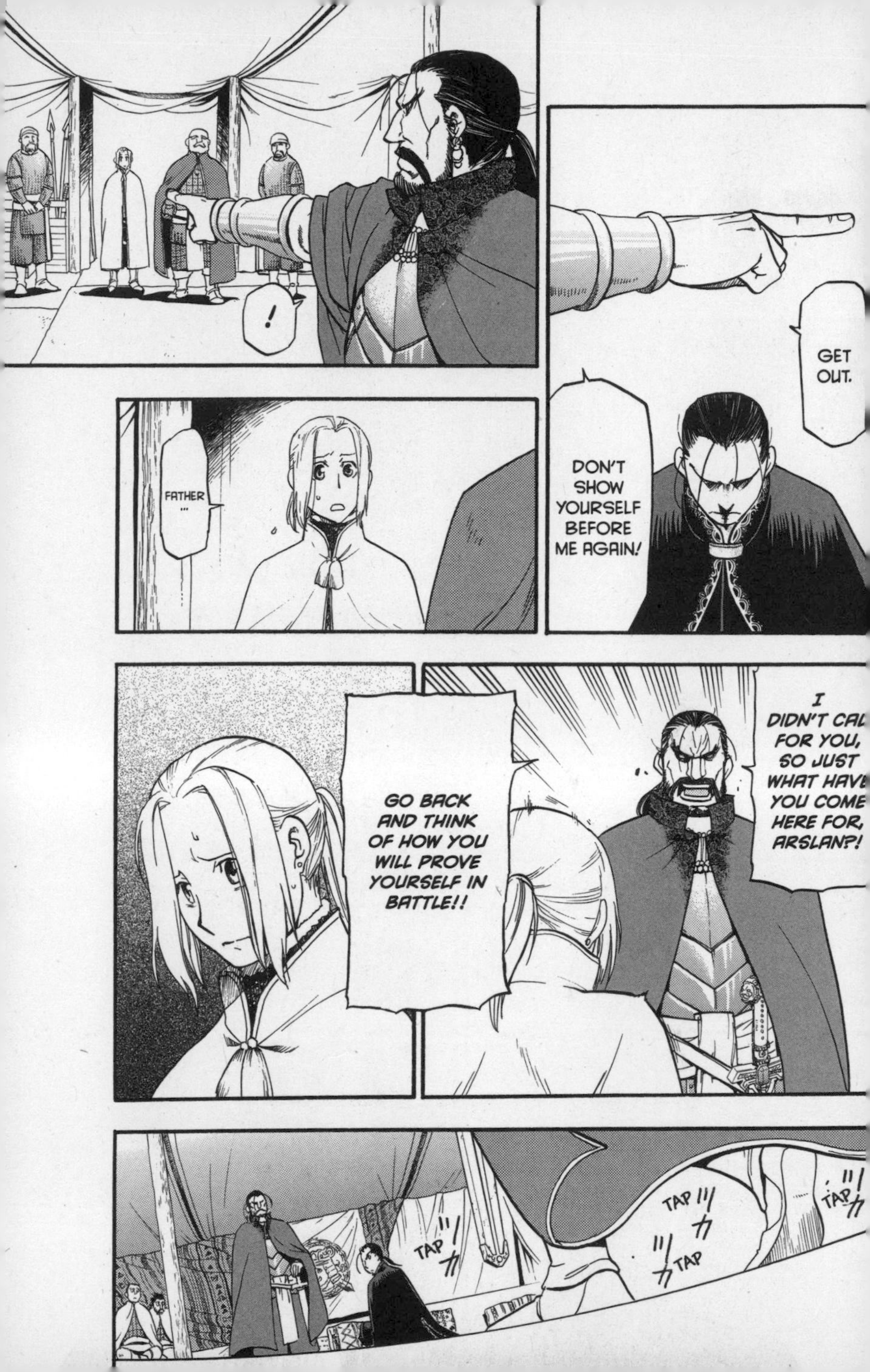
GET OUT.
DON'T SHOW YOURSELF BEFORE ME AGAIN!
!
FATHER ...
I DIDN'T CAL FOR YOU, SO JUST WHAT HAVE YOU COME HERE FOR, ARSLAN?!
GO BACK AND THINK OF HOW YOU WILL PROVE YOURSELF IN BATTLE!!
TAP
TAP
TAP
TAP

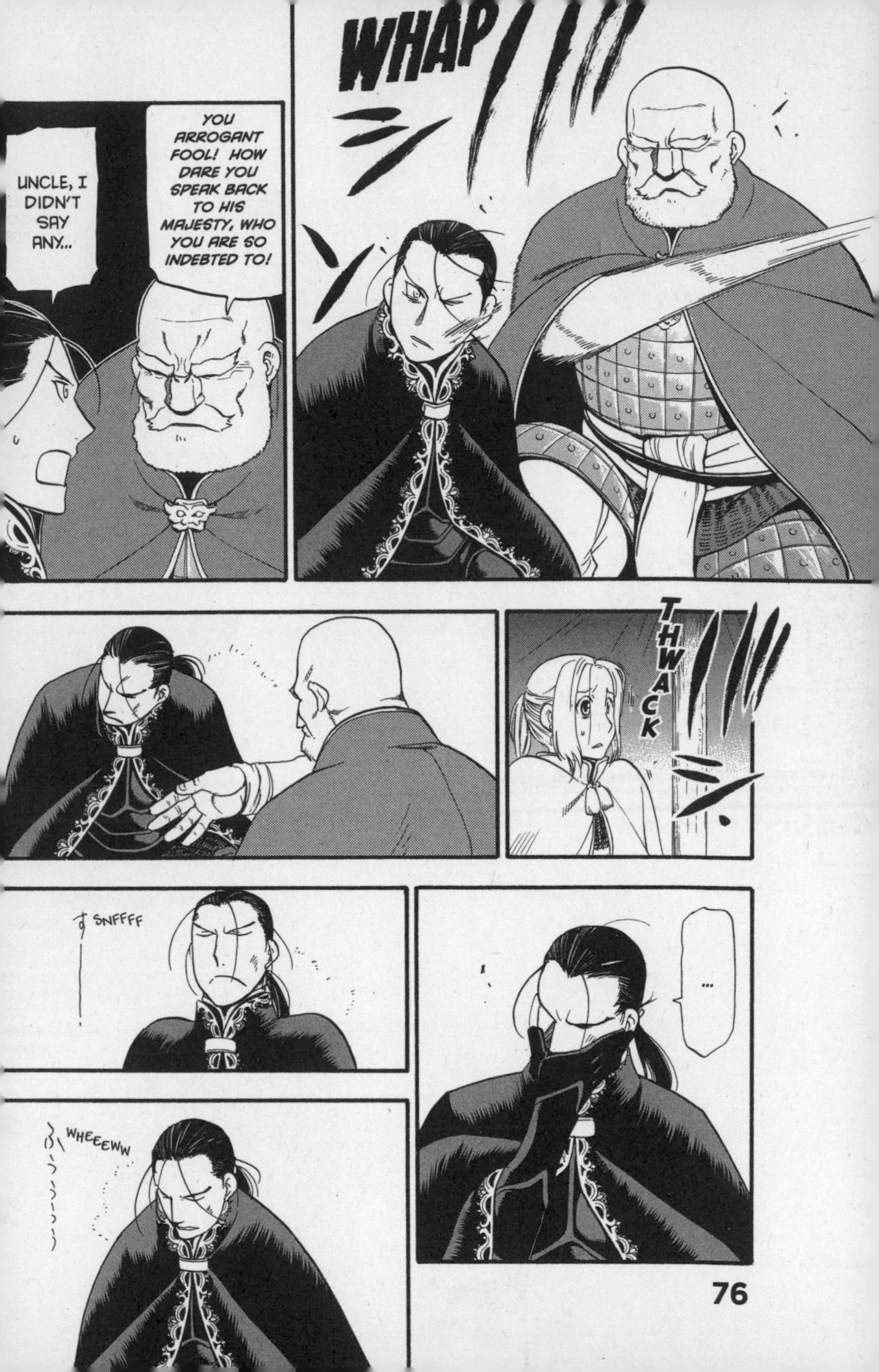
WHAP
YOU ARROGANT FOOL! HOW DARE YOU SPEAK BACK TO HIS MAJESTY, WHO YOU ARE SO INDEBTED TO!
UNCLE, I DIDN'T SAY ANY...
THWACK
...
す SNFFFF
WHEEEWW

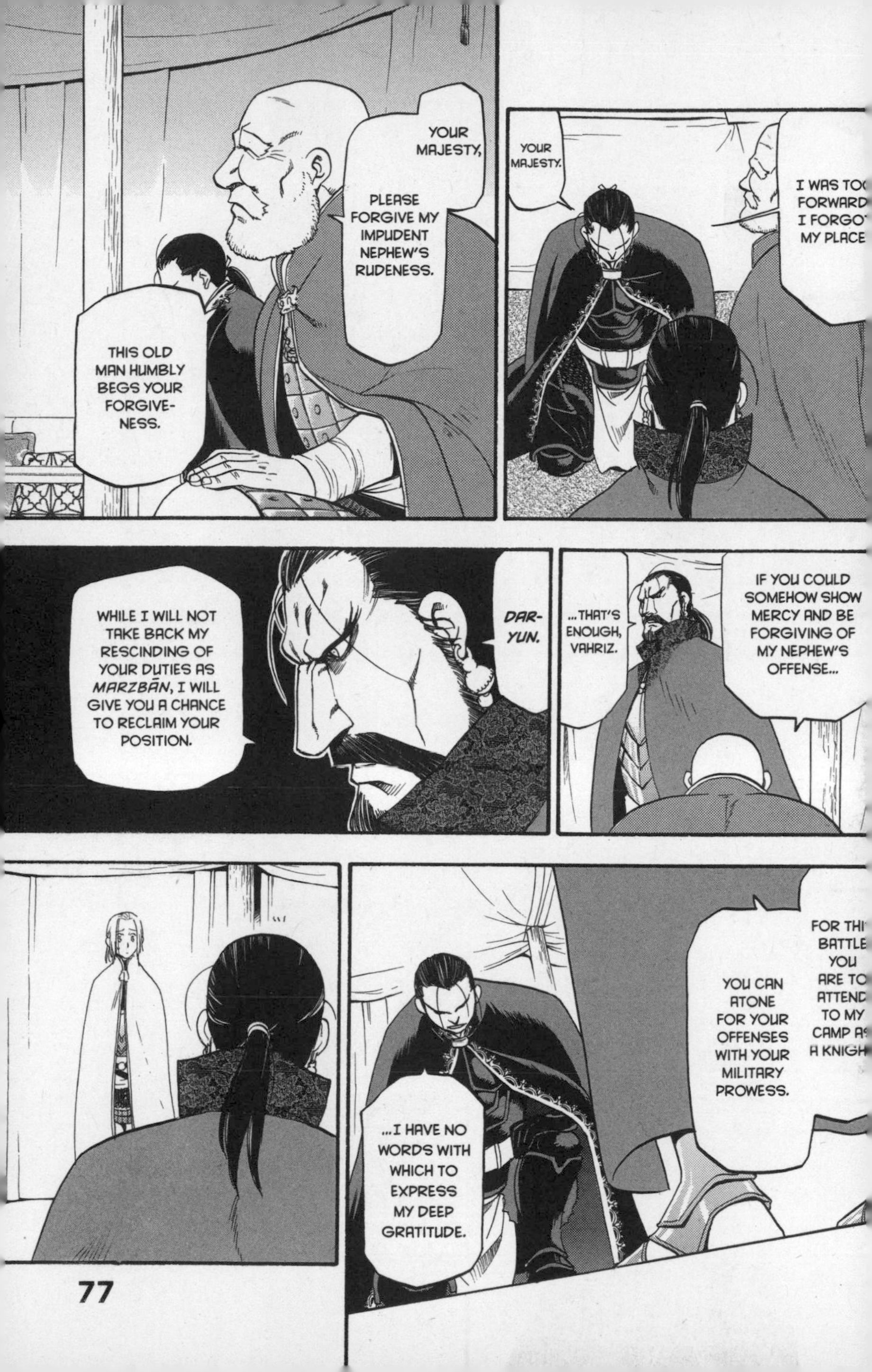
YOUR MAJESTY.
I WAS TOO FORWARD I FORGOT MY PLACE
YOUR MAJESTY, PLEASE FORGIVE MY IMPUDENT NEPHEW'S RUDENESS.
THIS OLD MAN HUMBLY BEGS YOUR FORGIVE-NESS.
IF YOU COULD SOMEHOW SHOW MERCY AND BE FORGIVING OF MY NEPHEW'S OFFENSE...
...THAT'S ENOUGH, VAHRIZ.
DAR-YUN.
WHILE I WILL NOT TAKE BACK MY RESCINDING OF YOUR DUTIES AS *MARZBĀN*, I WILL GIVE YOU A CHANCE TO RECLAIM YOUR POSITION.
FOR THI BATTLE YOU ARE TO ATTEND TO MY CAMP AS A KNIGH
YOU CAN ATONE FOR YOUR OFFENSES WITH YOUR MILITARY PROWESS.
...I HAVE NO WORDS WITH WHICH TO EXPRESS MY DEEP GRATITUDE.

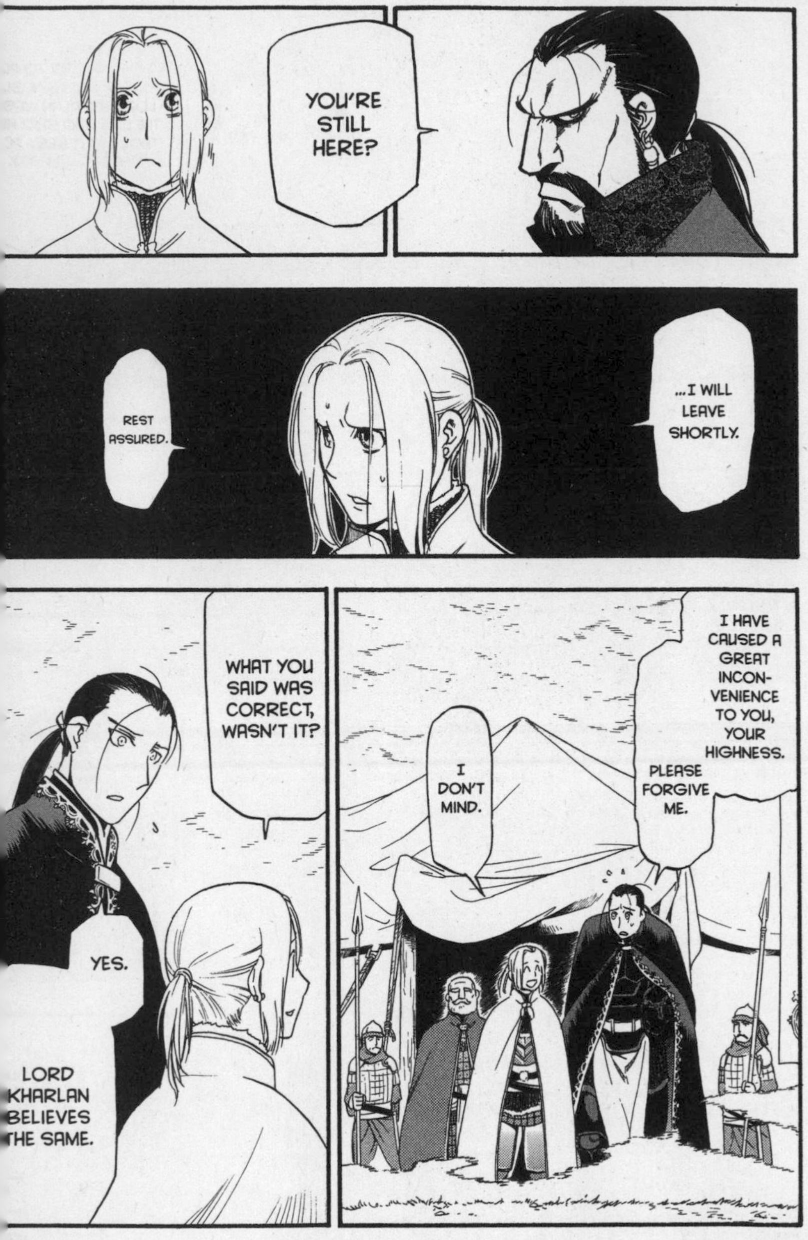
YOU'RE STILL HERE?
...I WILL LEAVE SHORTLY.
REST ASSURED.
I HAVE CAUSED A GREAT INCONVENIENCE TO YOU, YOUR HIGHNESS.
PLEASE FORGIVE ME.
I DON'T MIND.
WHAT YOU SAID WAS CORRECT, WASN'T IT?
YES.
LORD KHARLAN BELIEVES THE SAME.

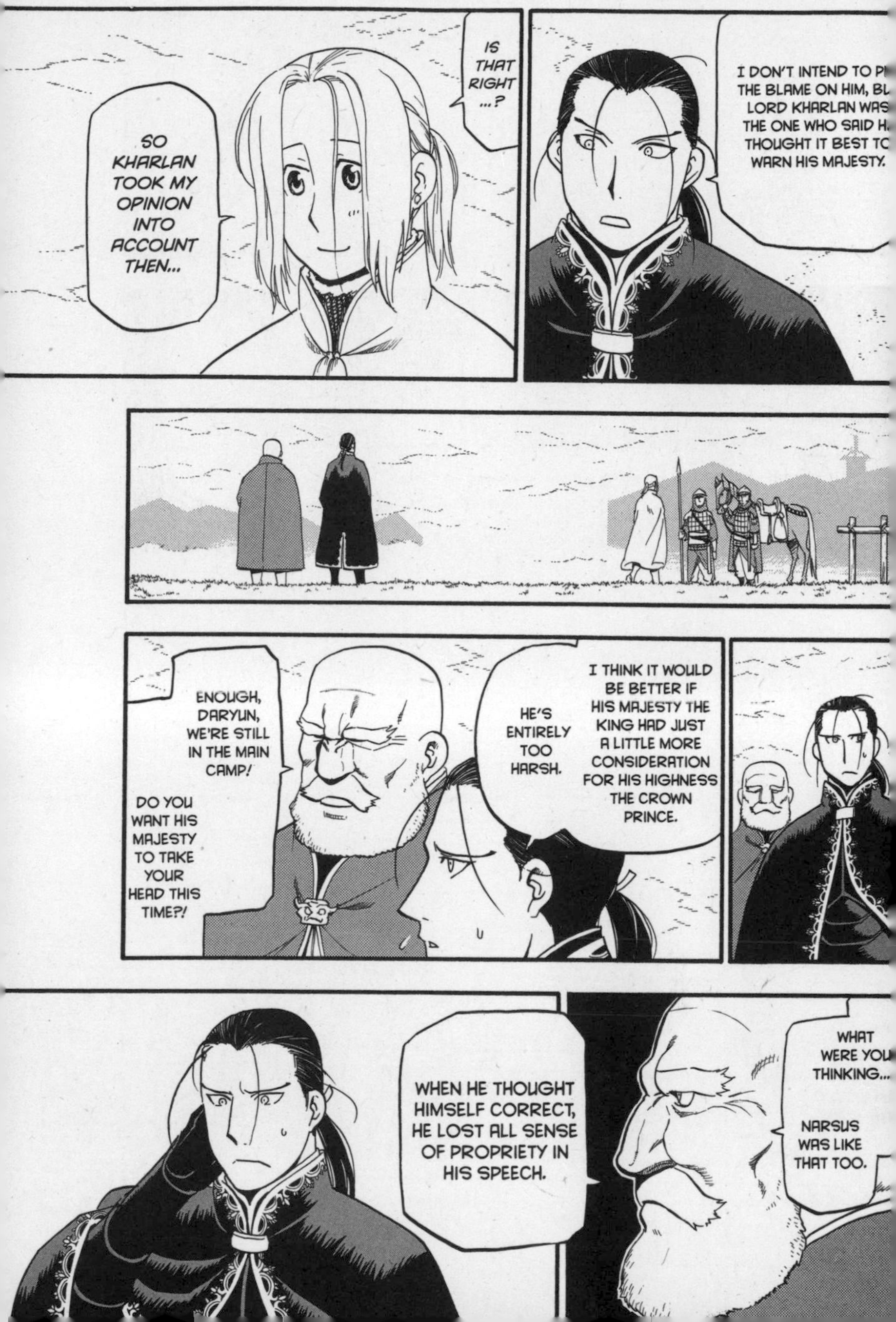
I DON'T INTEND TO P THE BLAME ON HIM, BL LORD KHARLAN WAS THE ONE WHO SAID H THOUGHT IT BEST TO WARN HIS MAJESTY.
IS THAT RIGHT ...?
SO KHARLAN TOOK MY OPINION INTO ACCOUNT THEN...
I THINK IT WOULD BE BETTER IF HIS MAJESTY THE KING HAD JUST A LITTLE MORE CONSIDERATION FOR HIS HIGHNESS THE CROWN PRINCE.
HE'S ENTIRELY TOO HARSH.
ENOUGH, DARYUN, WE'RE STILL IN THE MAIN CAMP!
DO YOU WANT HIS MAJESTY TO TAKE YOUR HEAD THIS TIME?!
WHAT WERE YOU THINKING...
NARSUS WAS LIKE THAT TOO.
WHEN HE THOUGHT HIMSELF CORRECT, HE LOST ALL SENSE OF PROPRIETY IN HIS SPEECH.

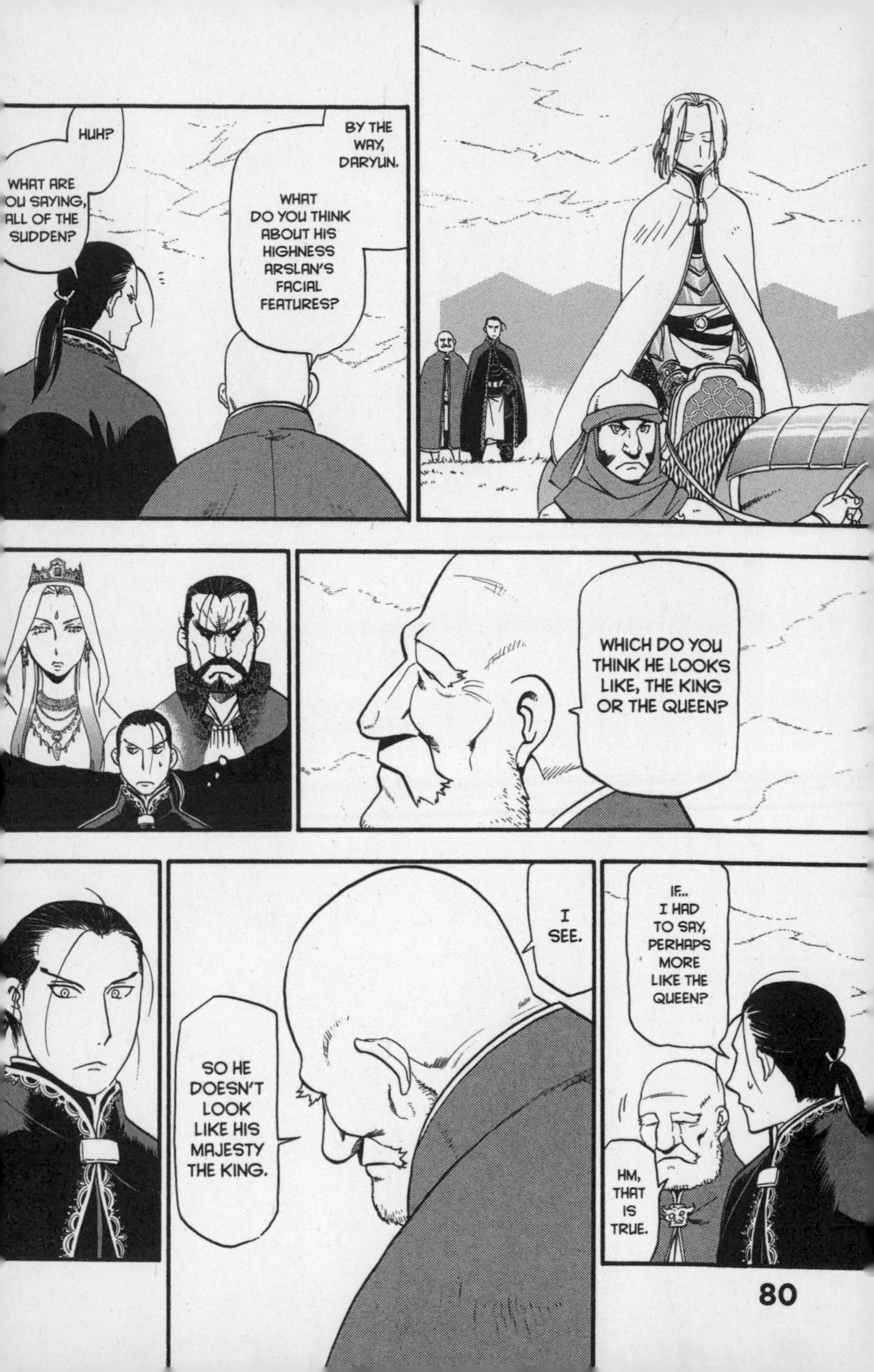
BY THE WAY, DARYUN.
WHAT DO YOU THINK ABOUT HIS HIGHNESS ARSLAN'S FACIAL FEATURES?
HUH?
WHAT ARE OU SAYING, ALL OF THE SUDDEN?
WHICH DO YOU THINK HE LOOKS LIKE, THE KING OR THE QUEEN?
IF... I HAD TO SAY, PERHAPS MORE LIKE THE QUEEN?
HM, THAT IS TRUE.
I SEE.
SO HE DOESN'T LOOK LIKE HIS MAJESTY THE KING.

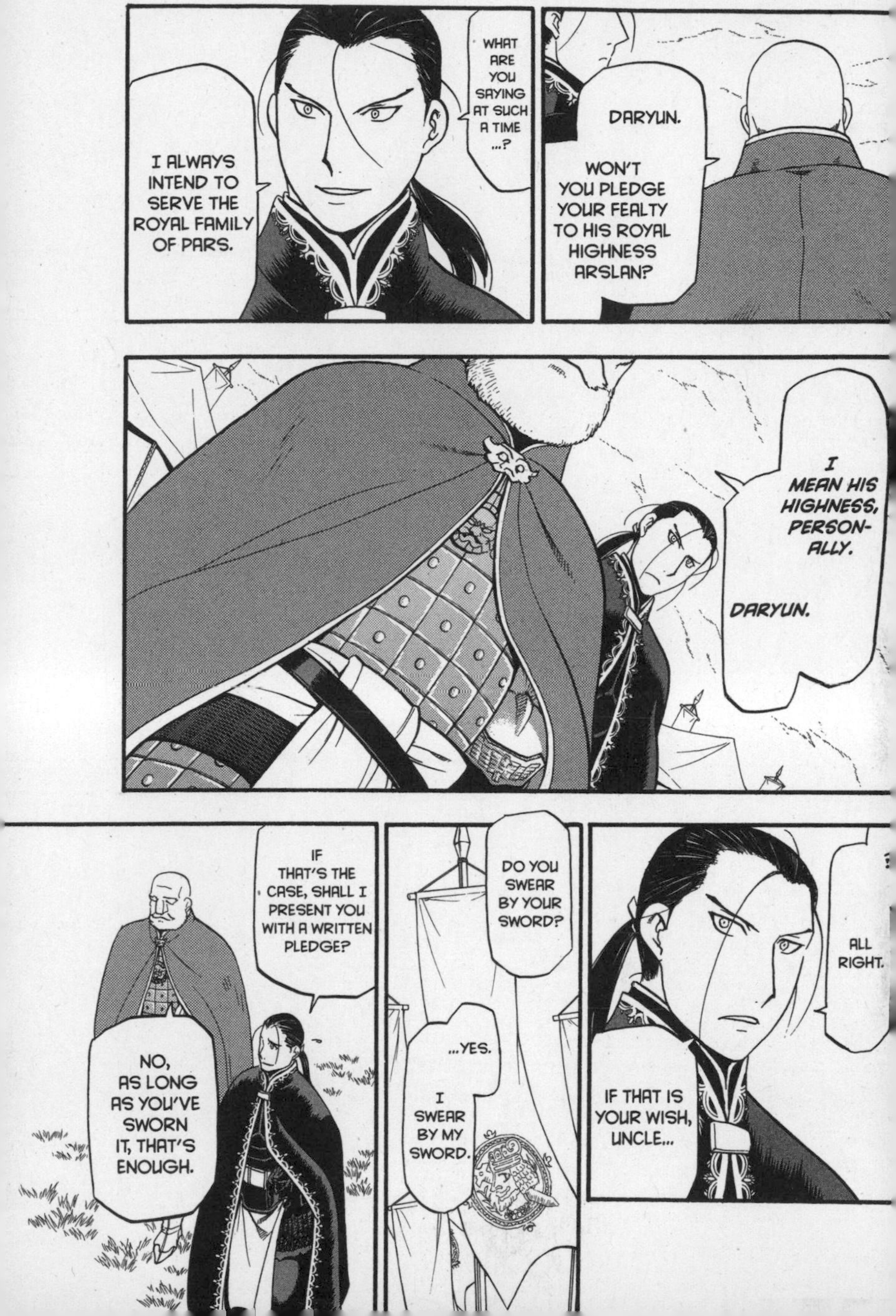
DARYUN.
WON'T YOU PLEDGE YOUR FEALTY TO HIS ROYAL HIGHNESS ARSLAN?
WHAT ARE YOU SAYING AT SUCH A TIME ...?
I ALWAYS INTEND TO SERVE THE ROYAL FAMILY OF PARS.
I MEAN HIS HIGHNESS, PERSON-ALLY.
DARYUN.
ALL RIGHT.
IF THAT IS YOUR WISH, UNCLE...
DO YOU SWEAR BY YOUR SWORD?
...YES.
I SWEAR BY MY SWORD.
IF THAT'S THE CASE, SHALL I PRESENT YOU WITH A WRITTEN PLEDGE?
NO, AS LONG AS YOU'VE SWORN IT, THAT'S ENOUGH.

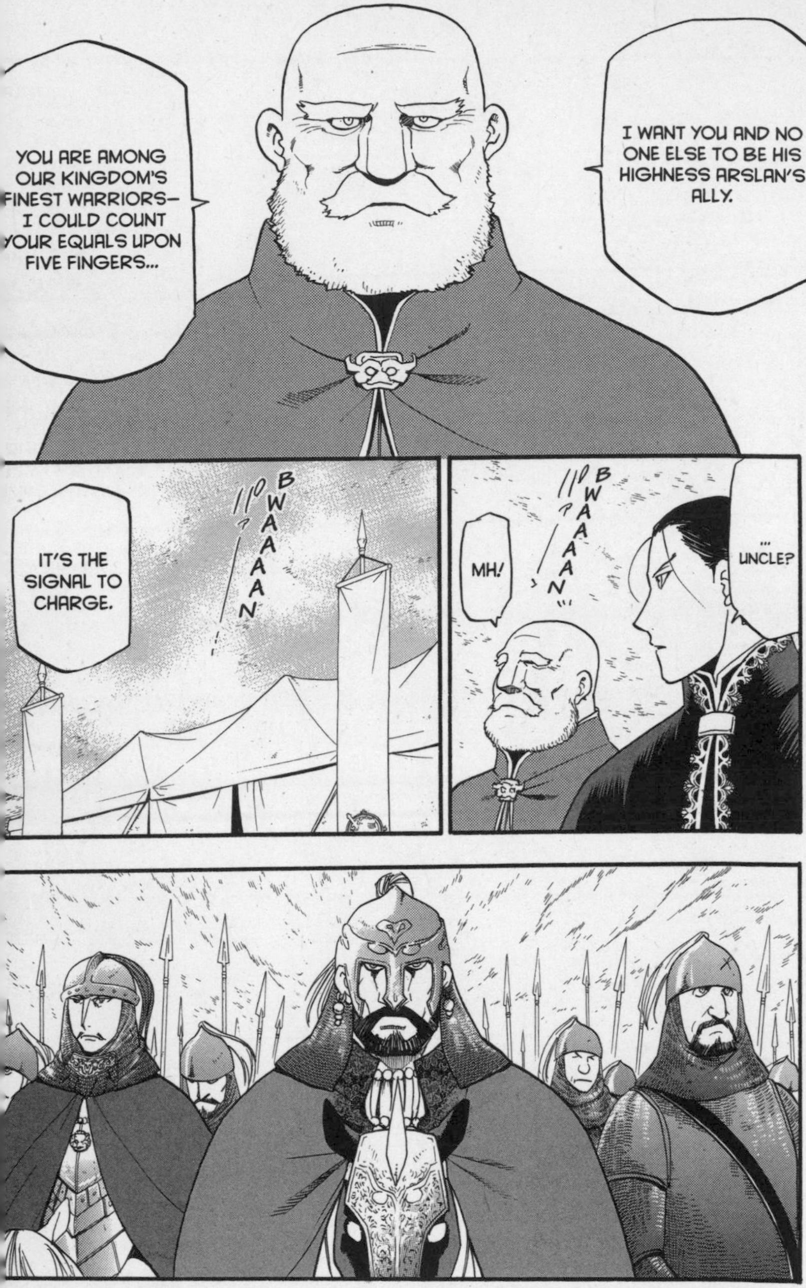
I WANT YOU AND NO ONE ELSE TO BE HIS HIGHNESS ARSLAN'S ALLY.
YOU ARE AMONG OUR KINGDOM'S FINEST WARRIORS—I COULD COUNT YOUR EQUALS UPON FIVE FINGERS...
... UNCLE?
BWAAAAN
MH!
BWAAAAN
IT'S THE SIGNAL TO CHARGE.

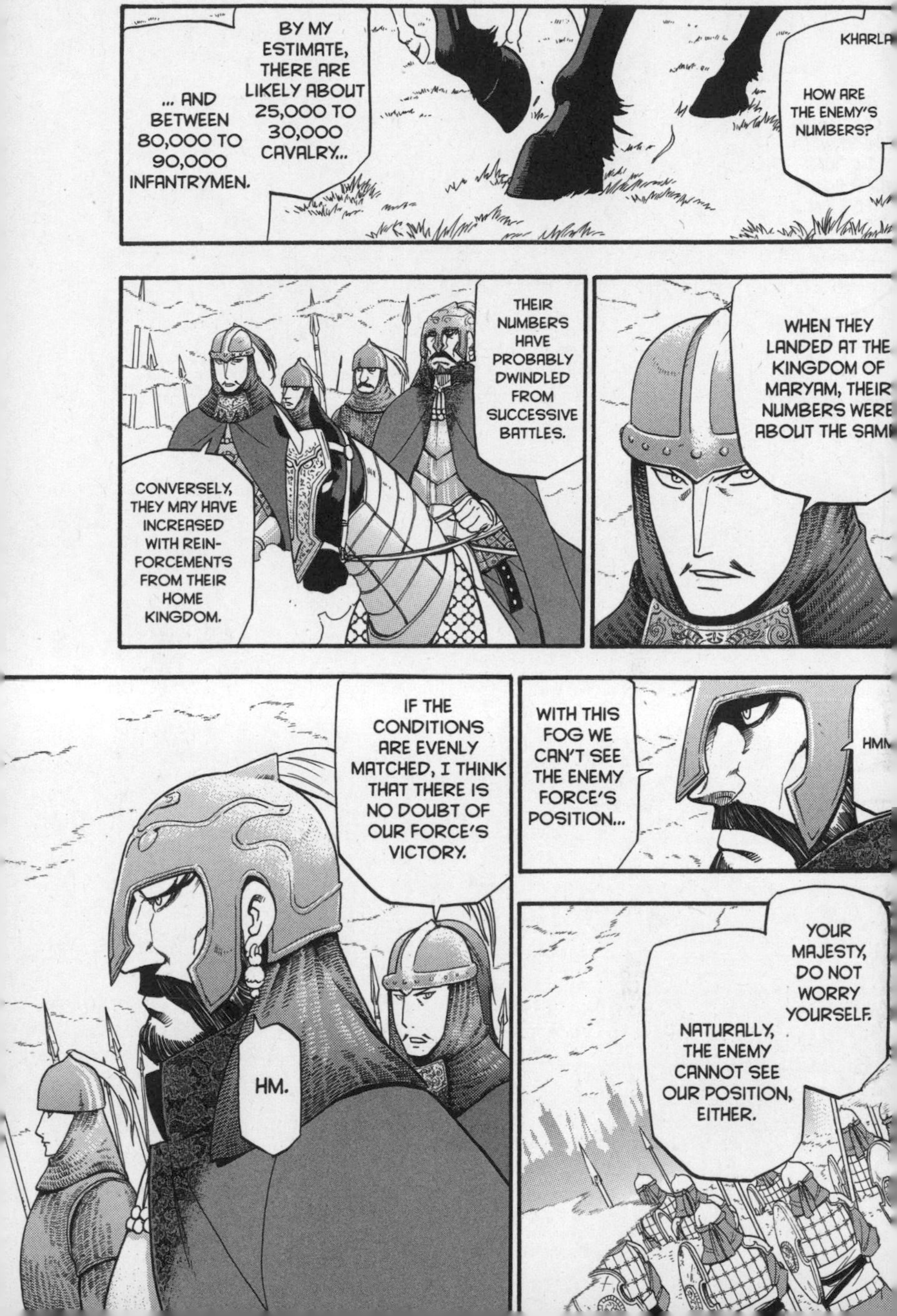
KHARLA
HOW ARE THE ENEMY'S NUMBERS?
BY MY ESTIMATE, THERE ARE LIKELY ABOUT 25,000 TO 30,000 CAVALRY...
... AND BETWEEN 80,000 TO 90,000 INFANTRYMEN.
WHEN THEY LANDED AT THE KINGDOM OF MARYAM, THEIR NUMBERS WERE ABOUT THE SAM
THEIR NUMBERS HAVE PROBABLY DWINDLED FROM SUCCESSIVE BATTLES.
CONVERSELY, THEY MAY HAVE INCREASED WITH REIN-FORCEMENTS FROM THEIR HOME KINGDOM.
HMM
WITH THIS FOG WE CAN'T SEE THE ENEMY FORCE'S POSITION...
YOUR MAJESTY, DO NOT WORRY YOURSELF.
NATURALLY, THE ENEMY CANNOT SEE OUR POSITION, EITHER.
IF THE CONDITIONS ARE EVENLY MATCHED, I THINK THAT THERE IS NO DOUBT OF OUR FORCE'S VICTORY.
HM.

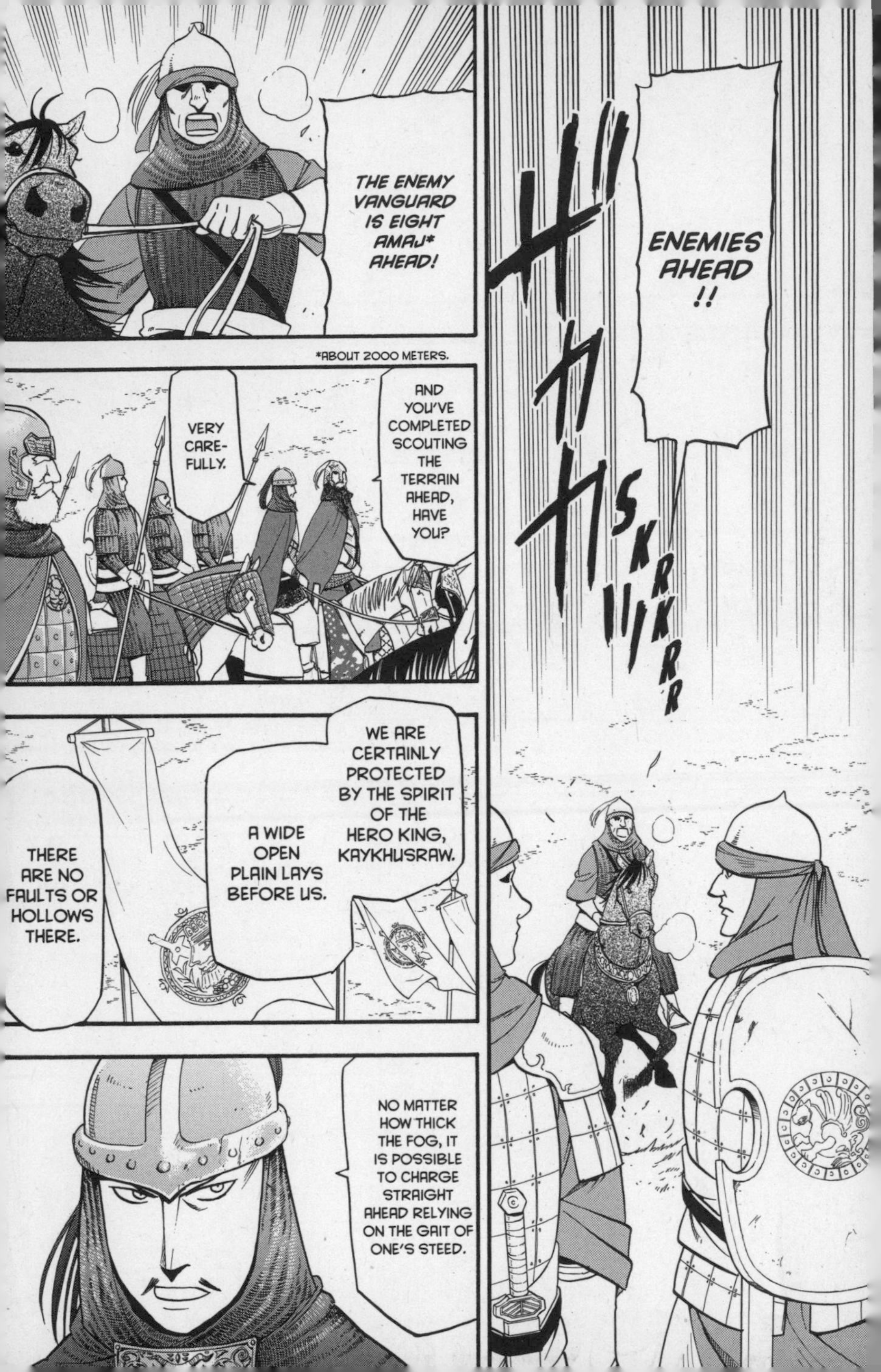
ENEMIES AHEAD !!
SKRRRR
THE ENEMY VANGUARD IS EIGHT AMAJ* AHEAD!
*ABOUT 2000 METERS.
AND YOU'VE COMPLETED SCOUTING THE TERRAIN AHEAD, HAVE YOU?
VERY CARE-FULLY.
WE ARE CERTAINLY PROTECTED BY THE SPIRIT OF THE HERO KING, KAYKHUSRAW.
A WIDE OPEN PLAIN LAYS BEFORE US.
THERE ARE NO FAULTS OR HOLLOWS THERE.
NO MATTER HOW THICK THE FOG, IT IS POSSIBLE TO CHARGE STRAIGHT AHEAD RELYING ON THE GAIT OF ONE'S STEED.

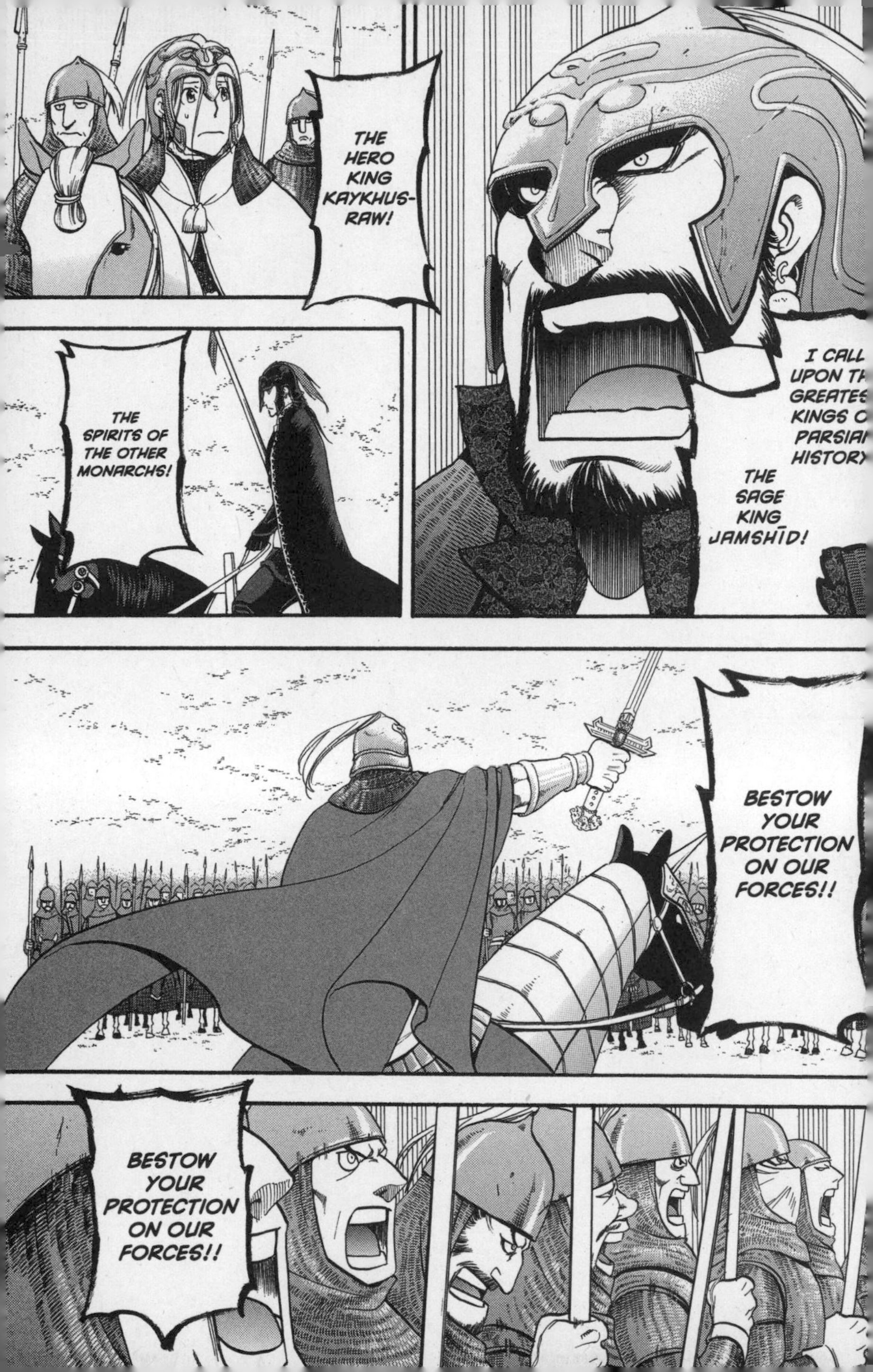

I CALL UPON TH GREATES KINGS O PARSIAI HISTORY
THE SAGE KING JAMSHĪD!
THE HERO KING KAYKHUS-RAW!
THE SPIRITS OF THE OTHER MONARCHS!
BESTOW YOUR PROTECTION ON OUR FORCES!!
BESTOW YOUR PROTECTION ON OUR FORCES!!

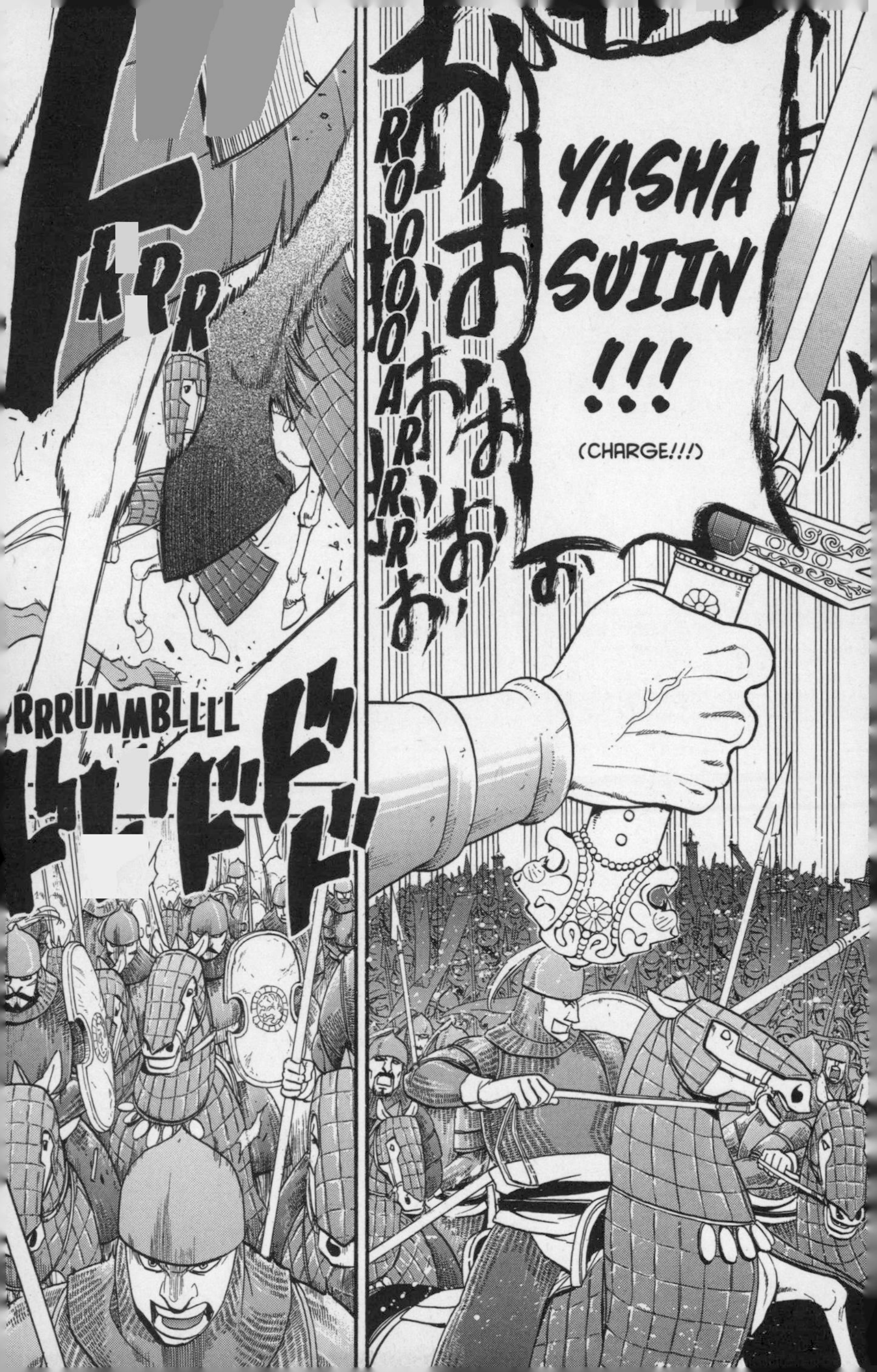
ROOOOARRR
YASHA SUIIN !!!
(CHARGE!!!)
KRR
RRRUMMBLLLL

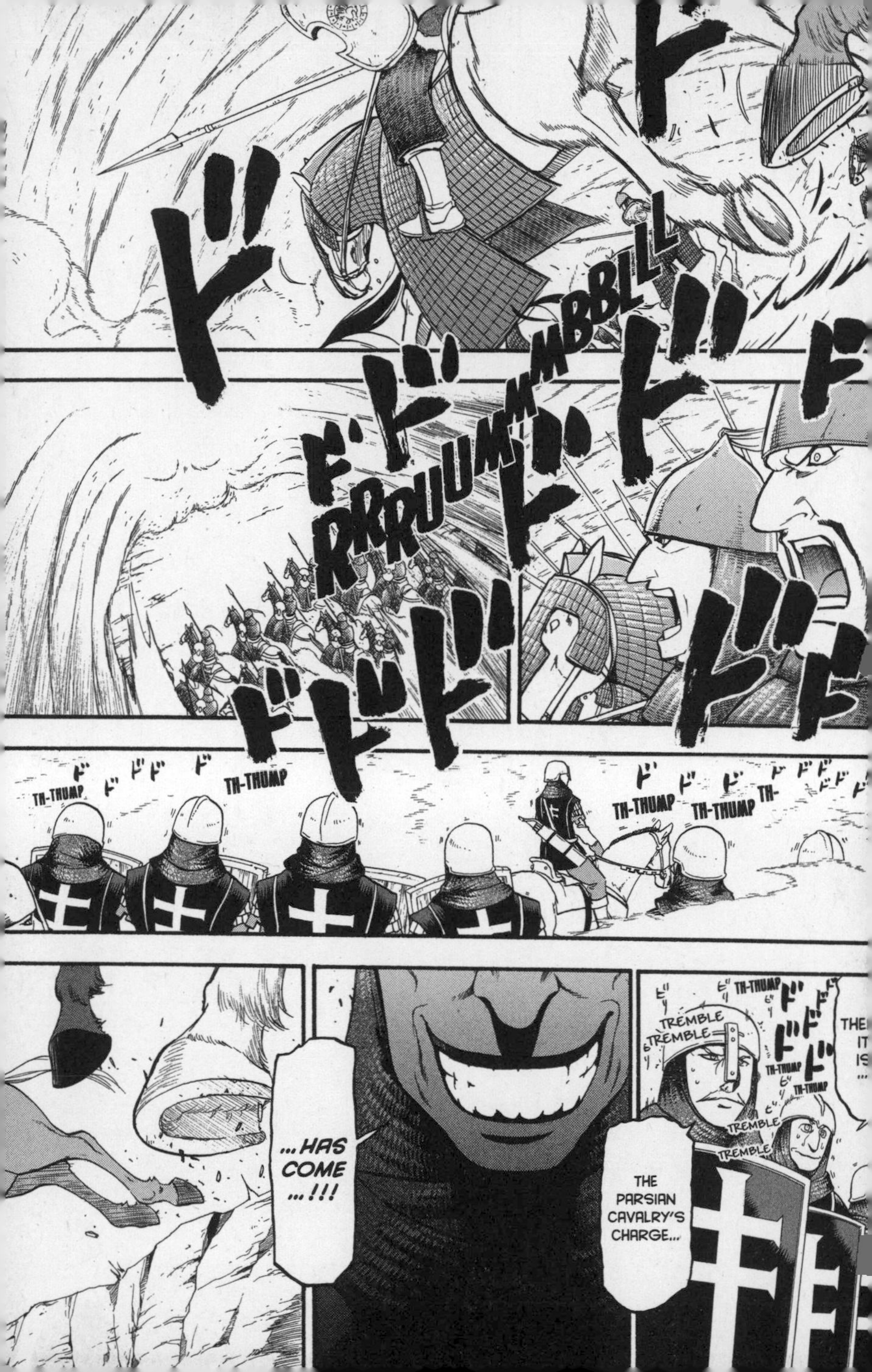
ドドド
RRRUUUMMMBBLLL
ドドドドド
TH-THUMP TH-THUMP TH-THUMP TH-
TH-THUMP TH-THUMP
THE IT IS ...
TH-THUMP TH-THUMP TH-THUMP
TREMBLE TREMBLE
TREMBLE TREMBLE
THE PARSIAN CAVALRY'S CHARGE...
...HAS COME ...!!!

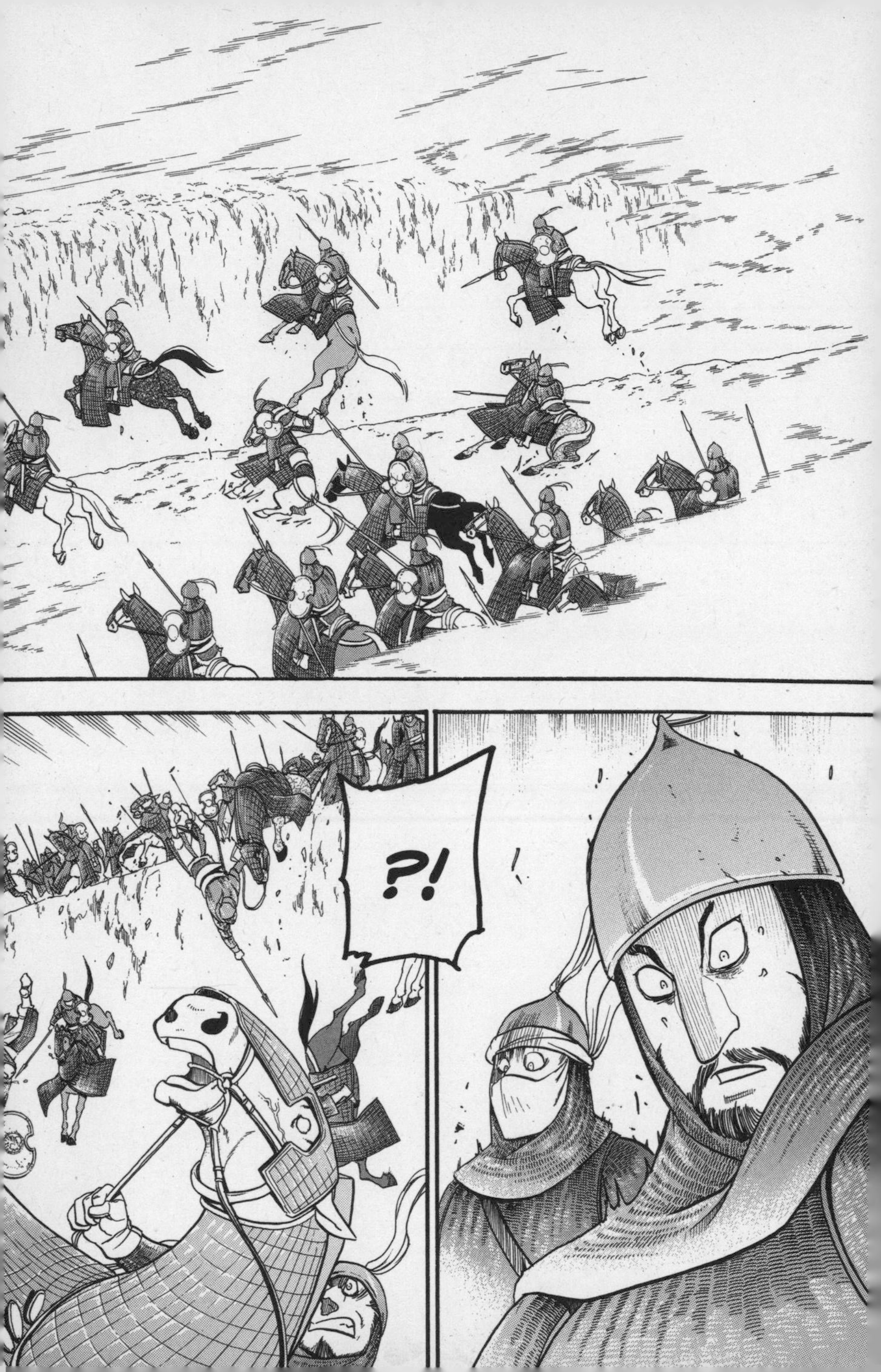
?!

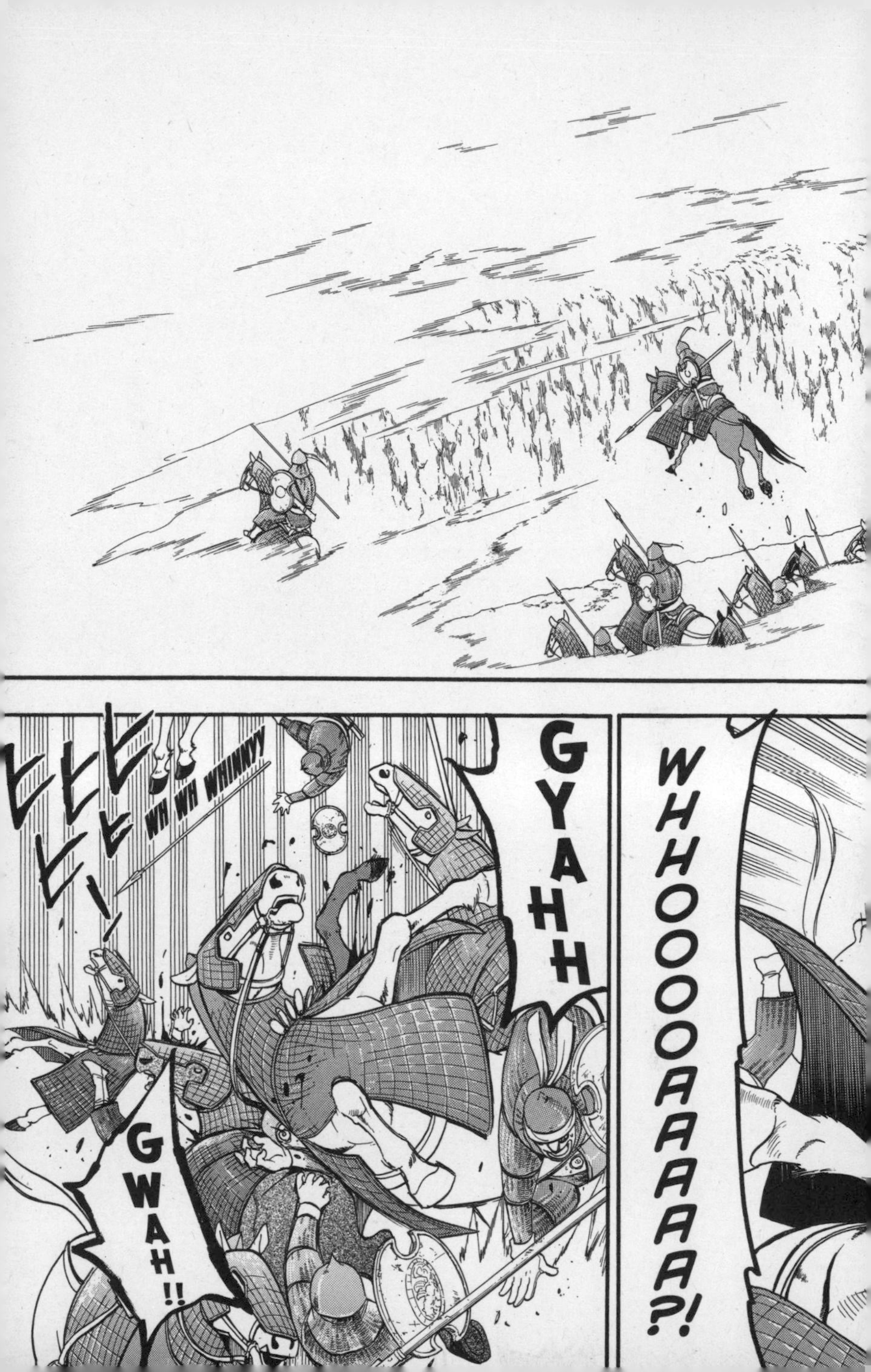
WHHOOOOAAAAAAA?!
GYAHH
WH WH WHINNYY
GWAH!!

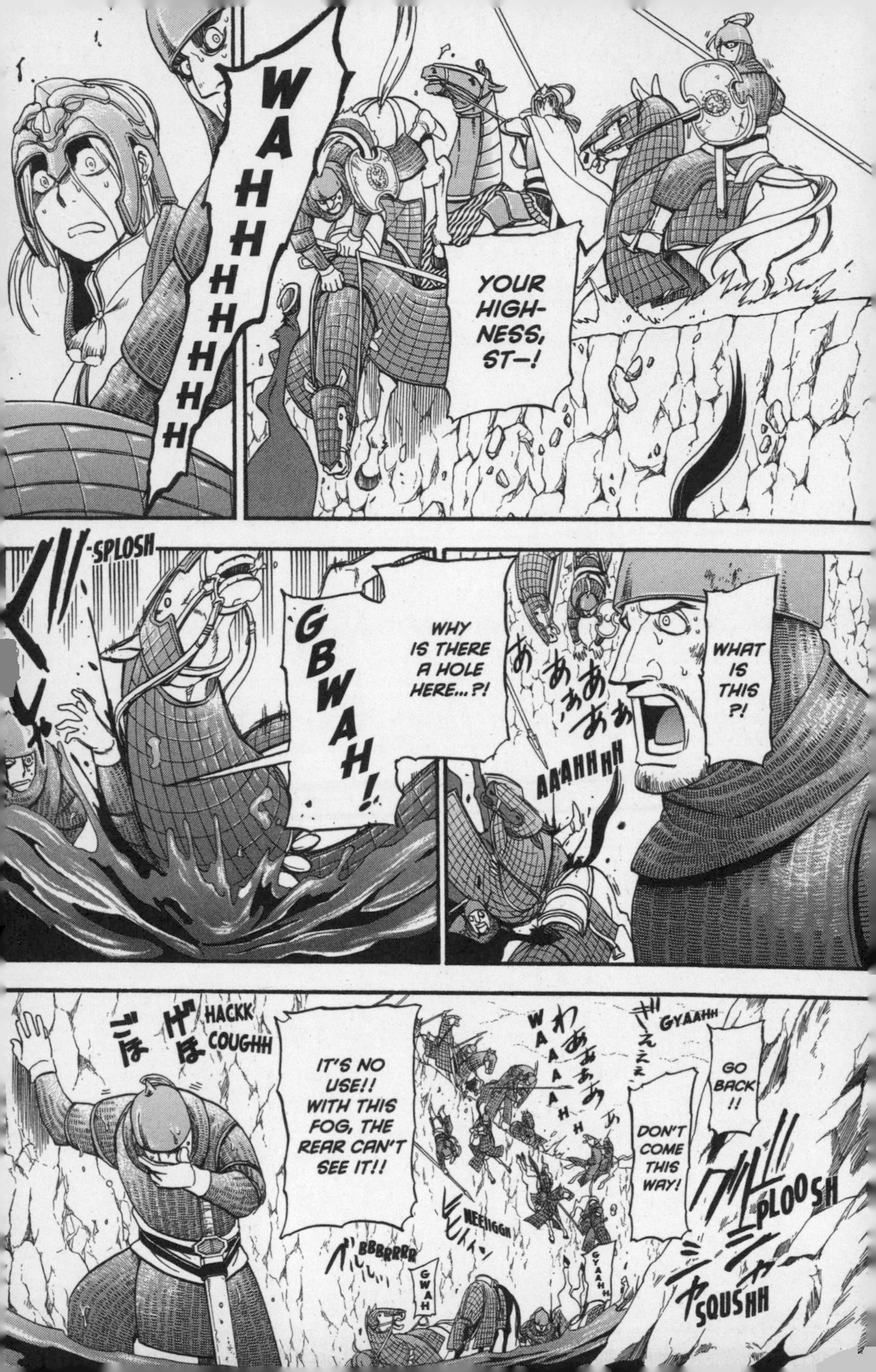
YOUR HIGH-NESS, ST—!
WAHHHHHHHHH
WHAT IS THIS ?!
AAAHHHH
WHY IS THERE A HOLE HERE...?!
GBWAH!
SPLOSH
GO BACK!!
DON'T COME THIS WAY!
GYAAHH
WAAAAHH
PLOOSH
SQUSHH
GYAAHH
NEEIIGGH
GWAH
BBBRRRRR
IT'S NO USE!! WITH THIS FOG, THE REAR CAN'T SEE IT!!
HACKK COUGHH

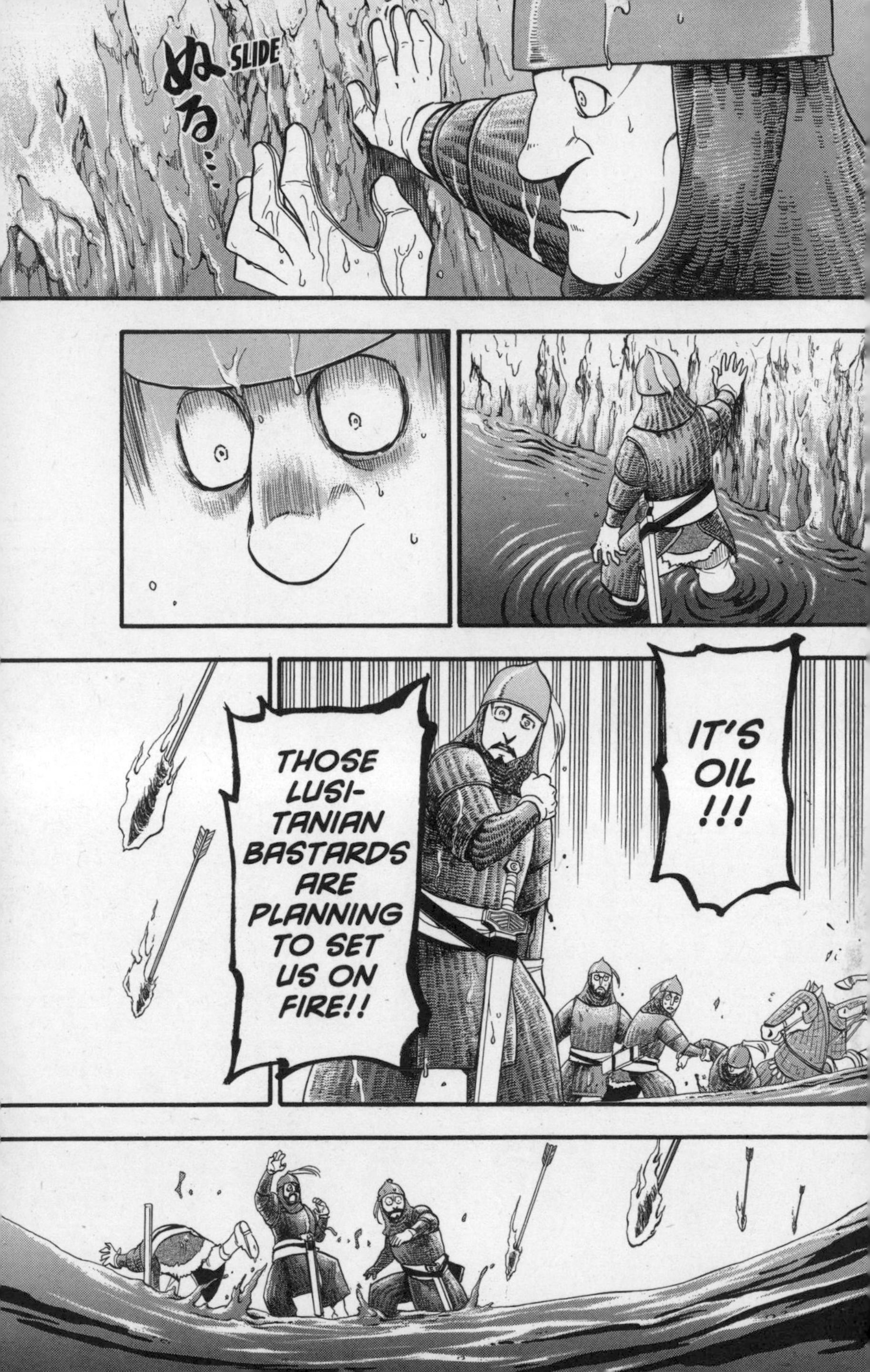
ぬる…
SLIDE
IT'S OIL!!!
THOSE LUSI-TANIAN BASTARDS ARE PLANNING TO SET US ON FIRE!!

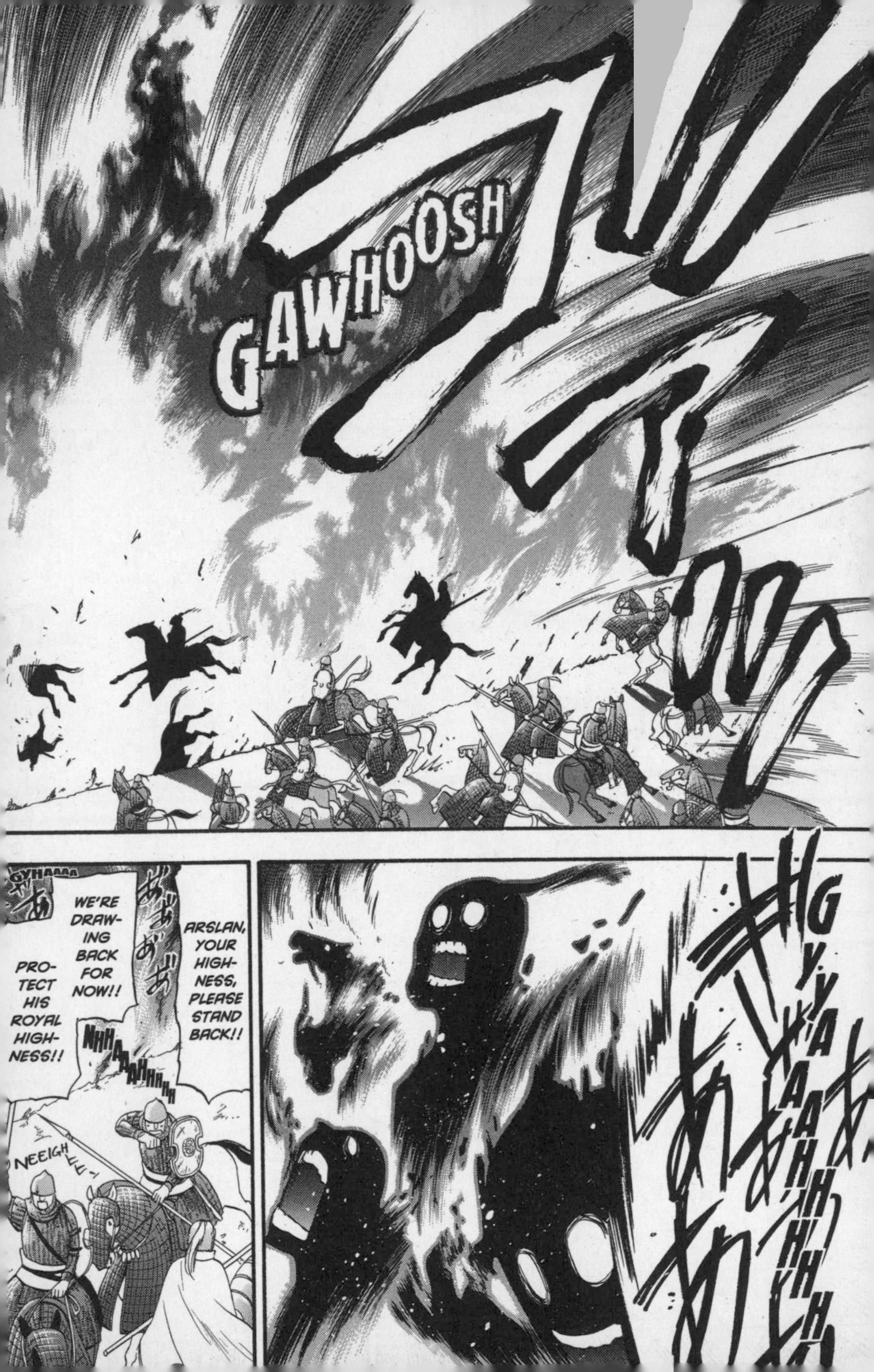
GAWHOOSH
GYYAAAAHHHHHH
ARSLAN, YOUR HIGHNESS, PLEASE STAND BACK!!
WE'RE DRAWING BACK FOR NOW!!
GYHAAAA
PROTECT HIS ROYAL HIGHNESS!!
NHHAAAHHHHH
NEEIGH

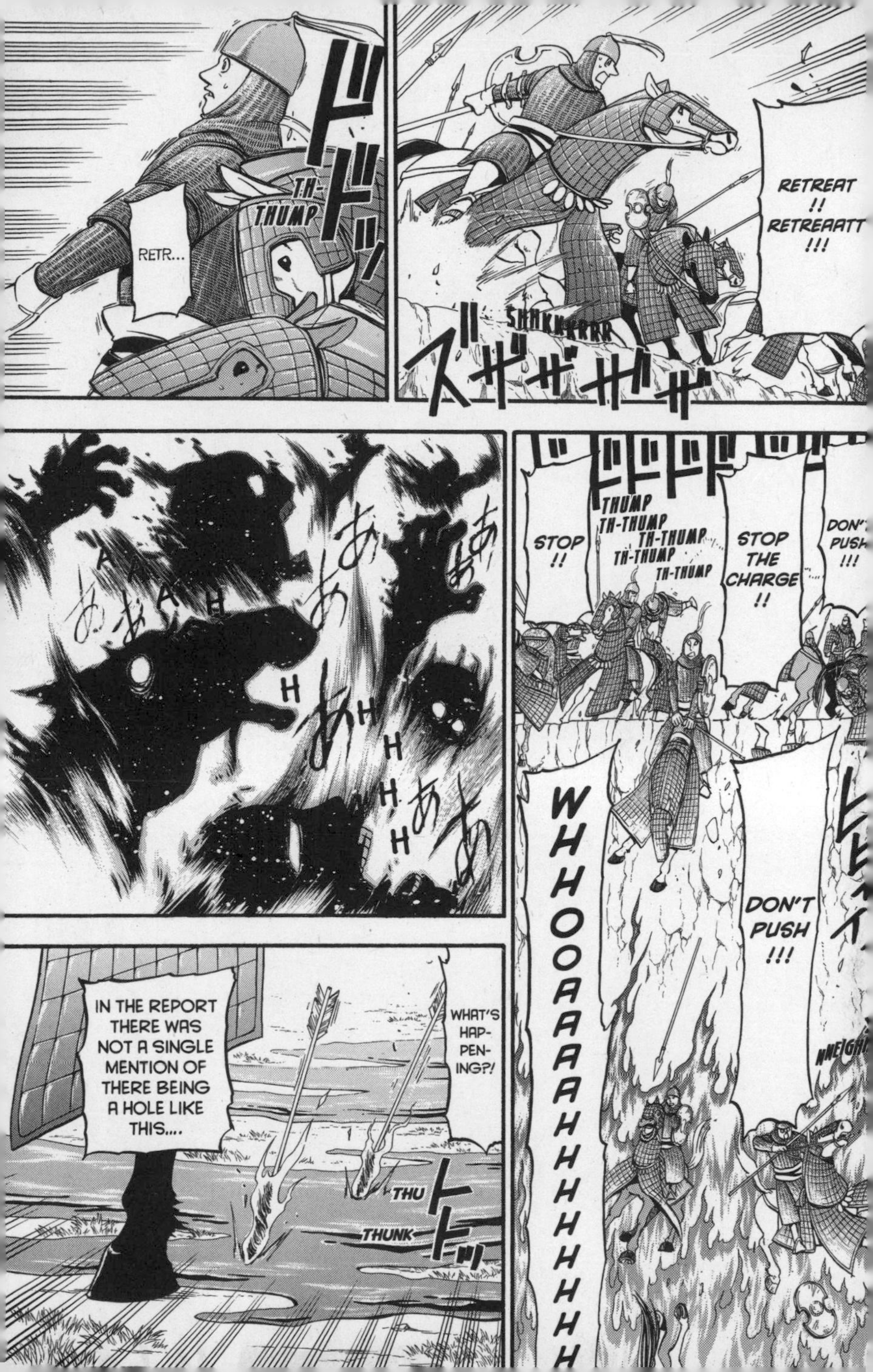
RETREAT !! RETREAATT !!!
SHHKKKRRR
TH-THUMP
RETR...
DON'T PUSH !!!
STOP THE CHARGE !!
THUMP TH-THUMP TH-THUMP TH-THUMP TH-THUMP
STOP !!
WHHOOOAAAAAHHHHHHHHH
DON'T PUSH !!!
NNEIGH
AAHHHHH
WHAT'S HAP-PEN-ING?!
IN THE REPORT THERE WAS NOT A SINGLE MENTION OF THERE BEING A HOLE LIKE THIS....
THU
THUNK

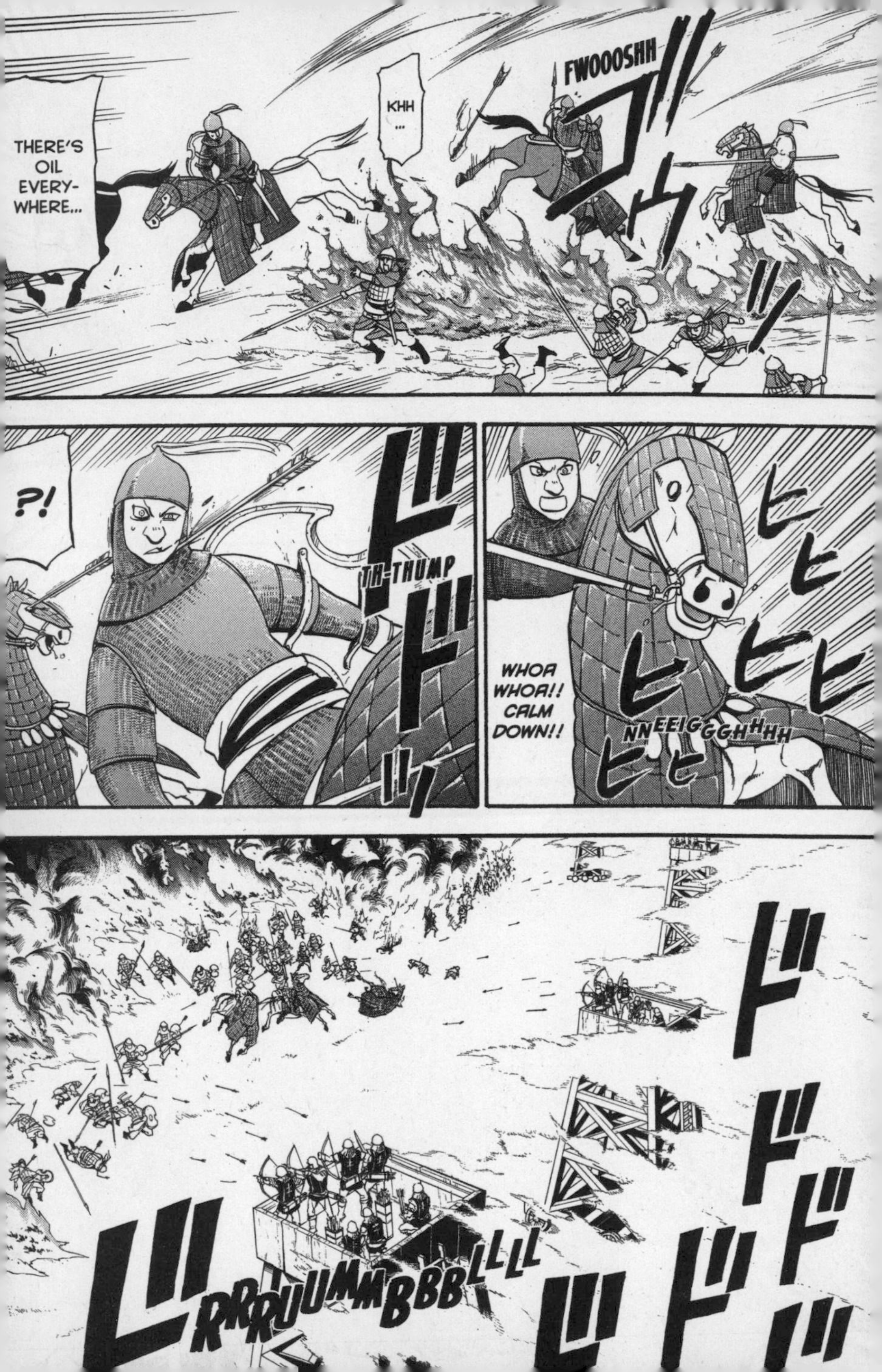
FWOOOSHH
KHH ...
THERE'S OIL EVERY-WHERE...
NNEEIGGGHHHH
WHOA WHOA!! CALM DOWN!!
TH-THUMP
?!
RRRRUUMMBBBLLLL

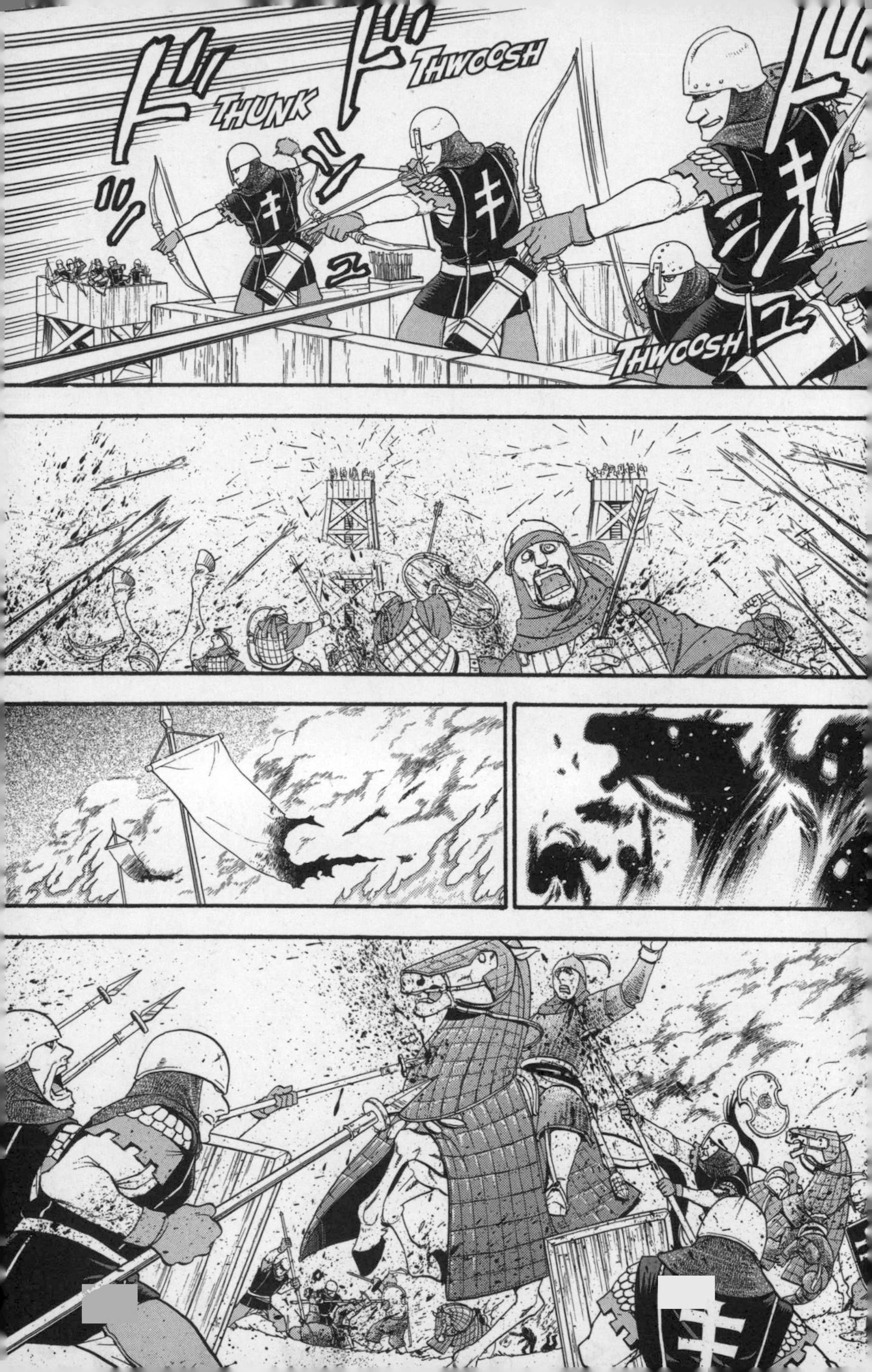
THWOOSH
THWOOSH
THUNK

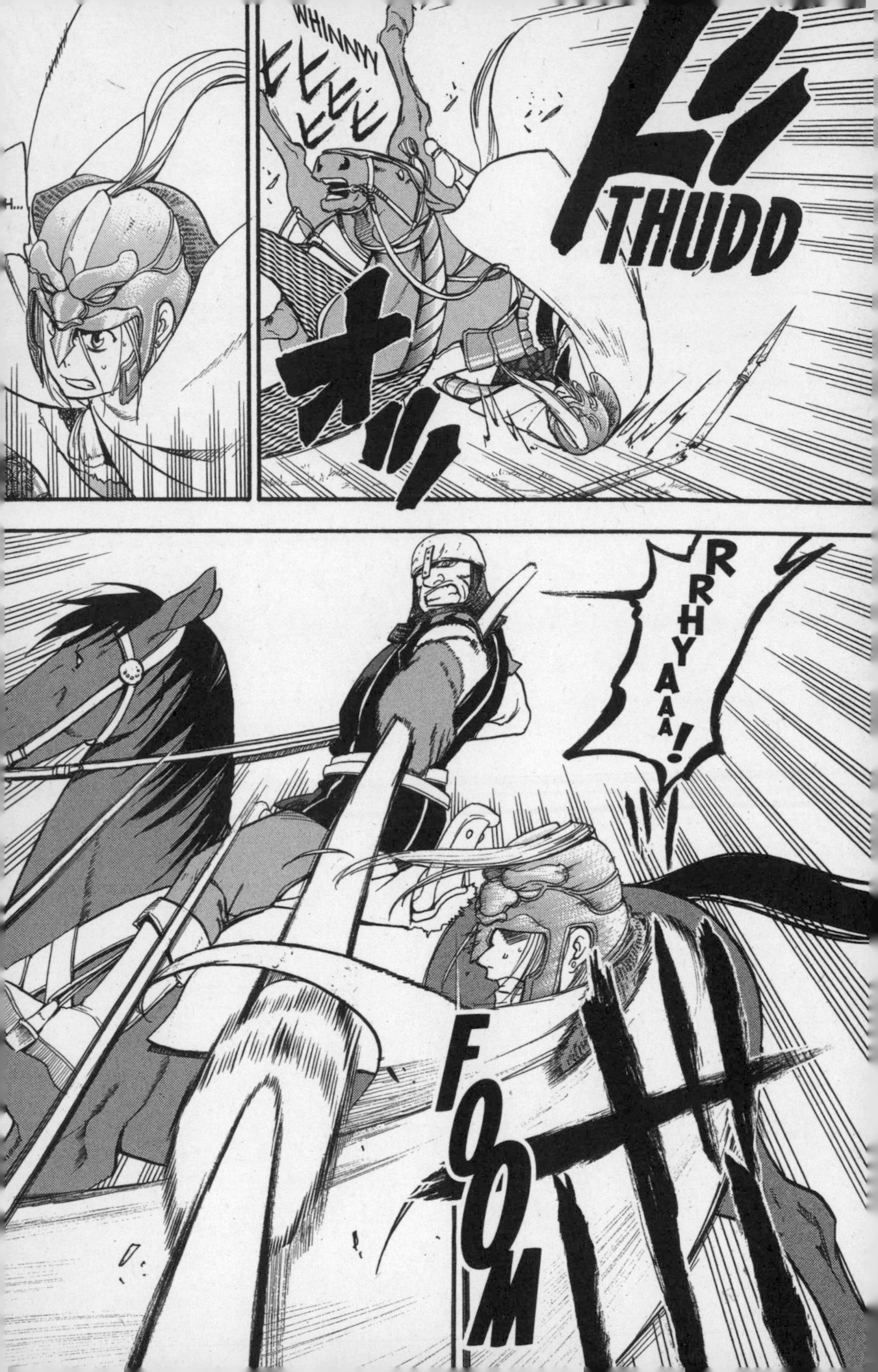
WHINNNYYY
THUDD
RRHYAAA!
FOOM

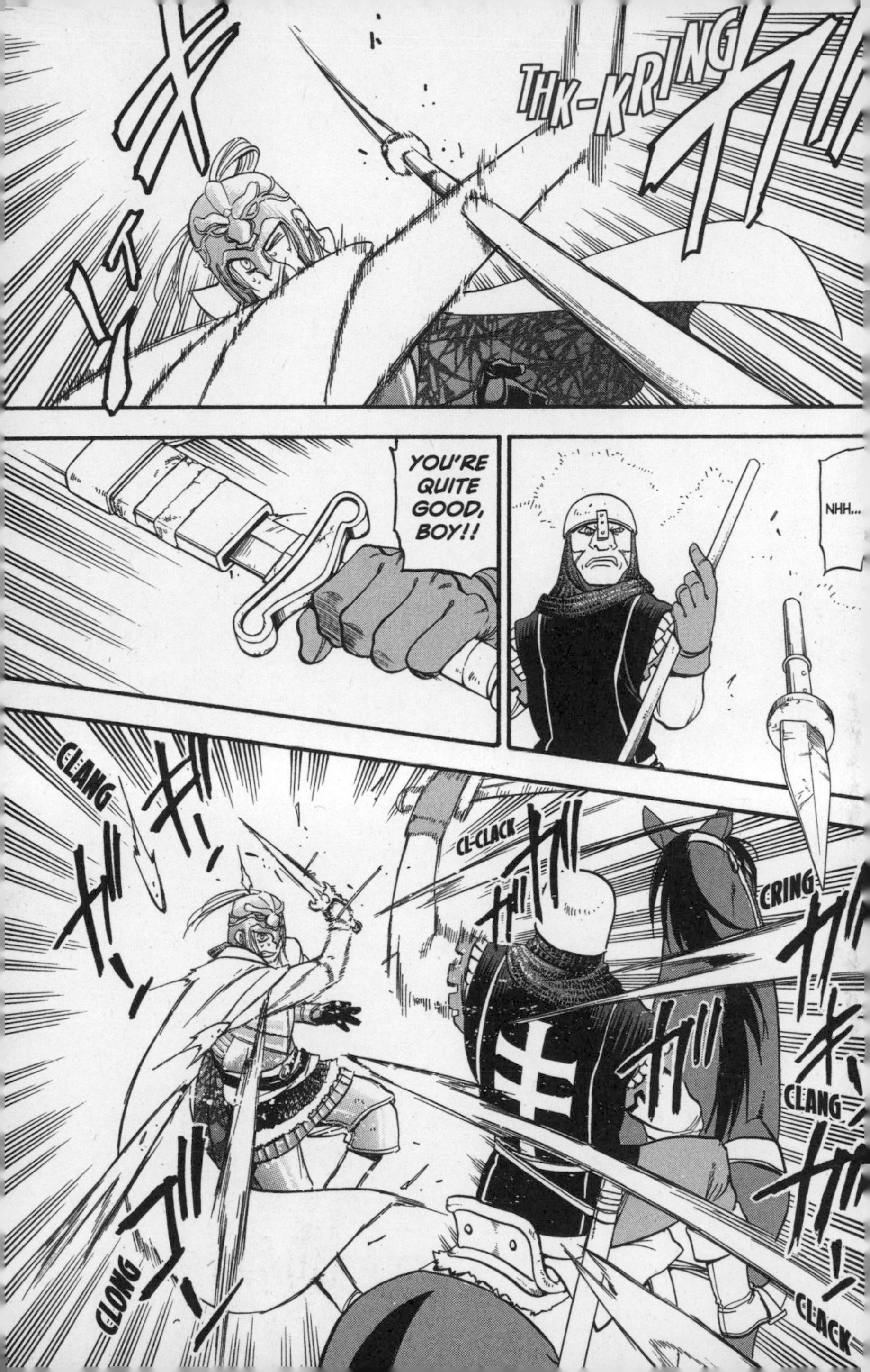
THK-KRING
NHH...
YOU'RE QUITE GOOD, BOY!!
CRING
CL-CLACK
CLANG
CLANG
CLACK
CLONG

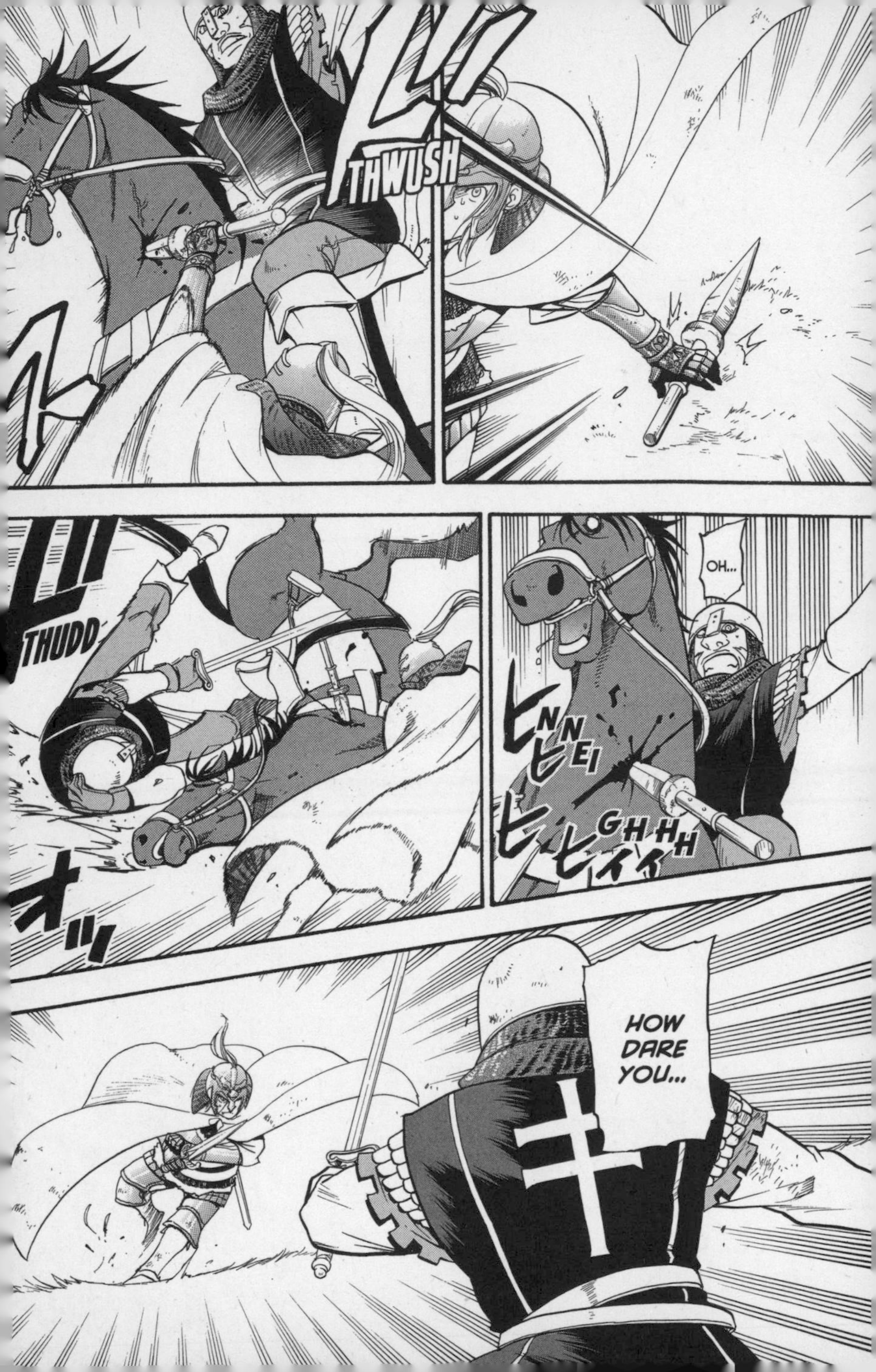
THWUSH
OH...
NNEI
GHHHH
THUDD
HOW DARE YOU...

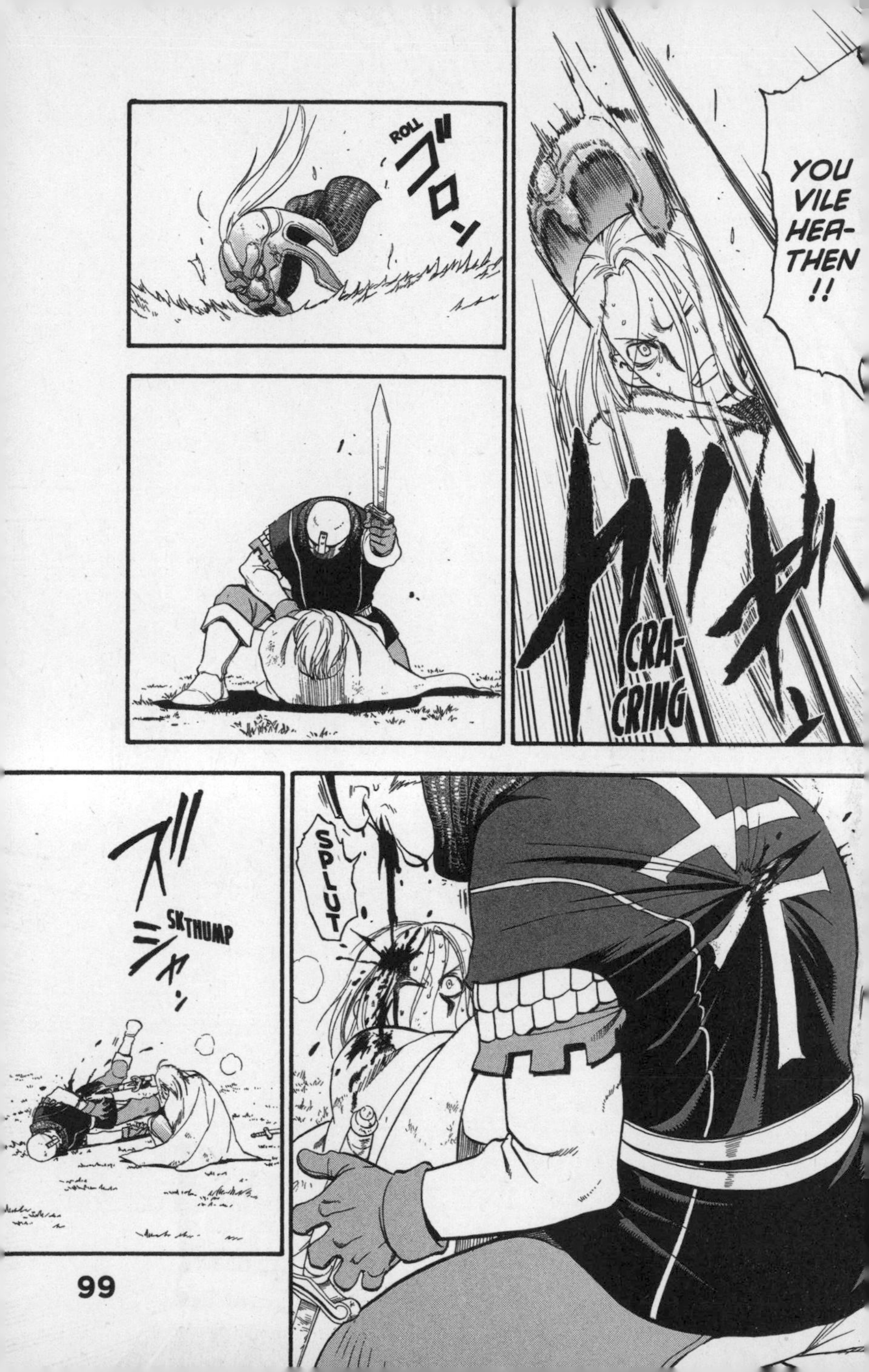
YOU VILE HEA-THEN!!
CRA-CRING
ROLL
ゴロン
SPLUT
SKTHUMP
ズシャン

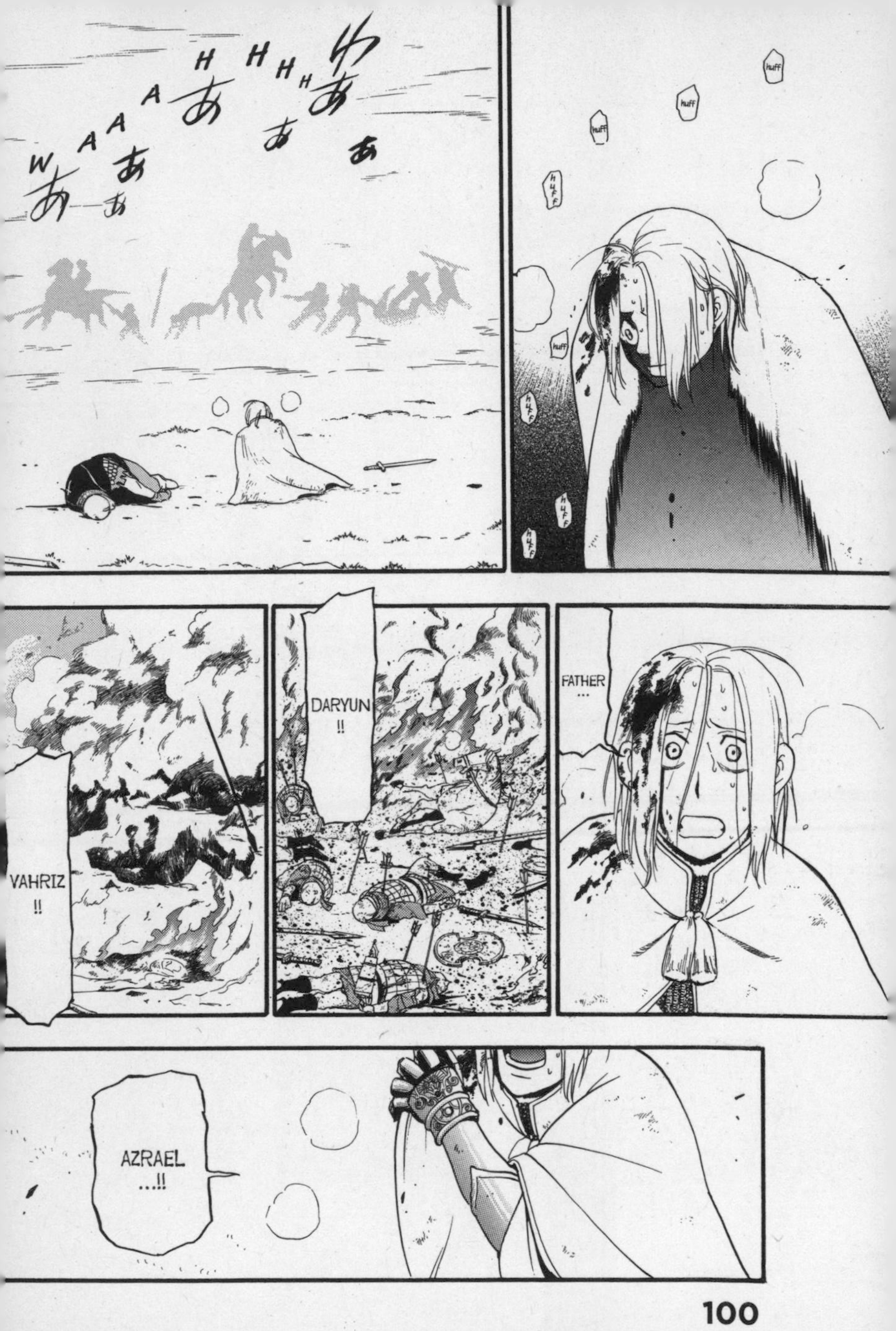
huff
huff
huff
huff
huff
huff
huff
huff
WAAAHHHH
FATHER ...
DARYUN !!
VAHRIZ !!
AZRAEL ...!!

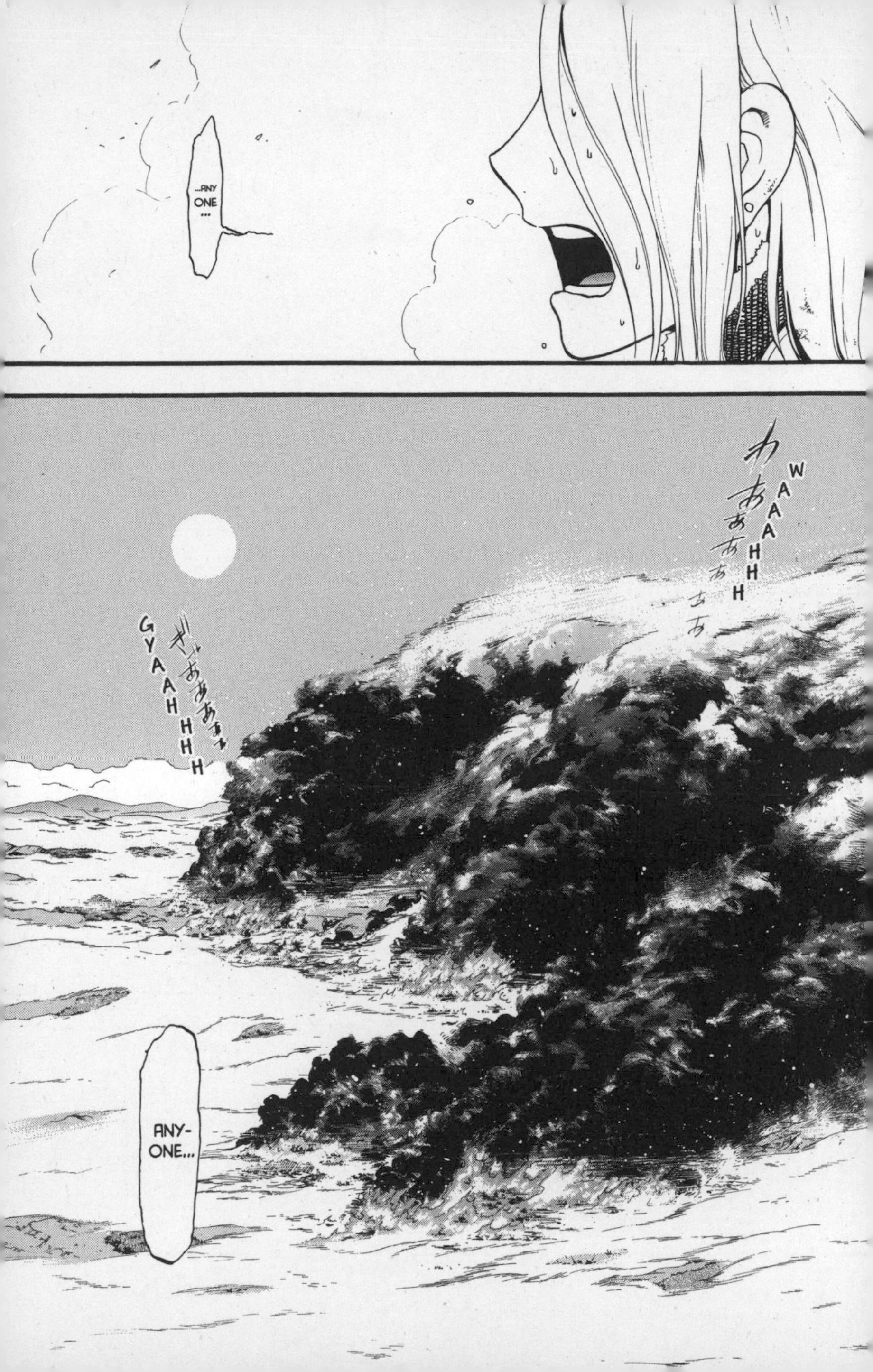
...ANY ONE...
WAAAAHHH
GYAAHHHH
ANY-ONE...

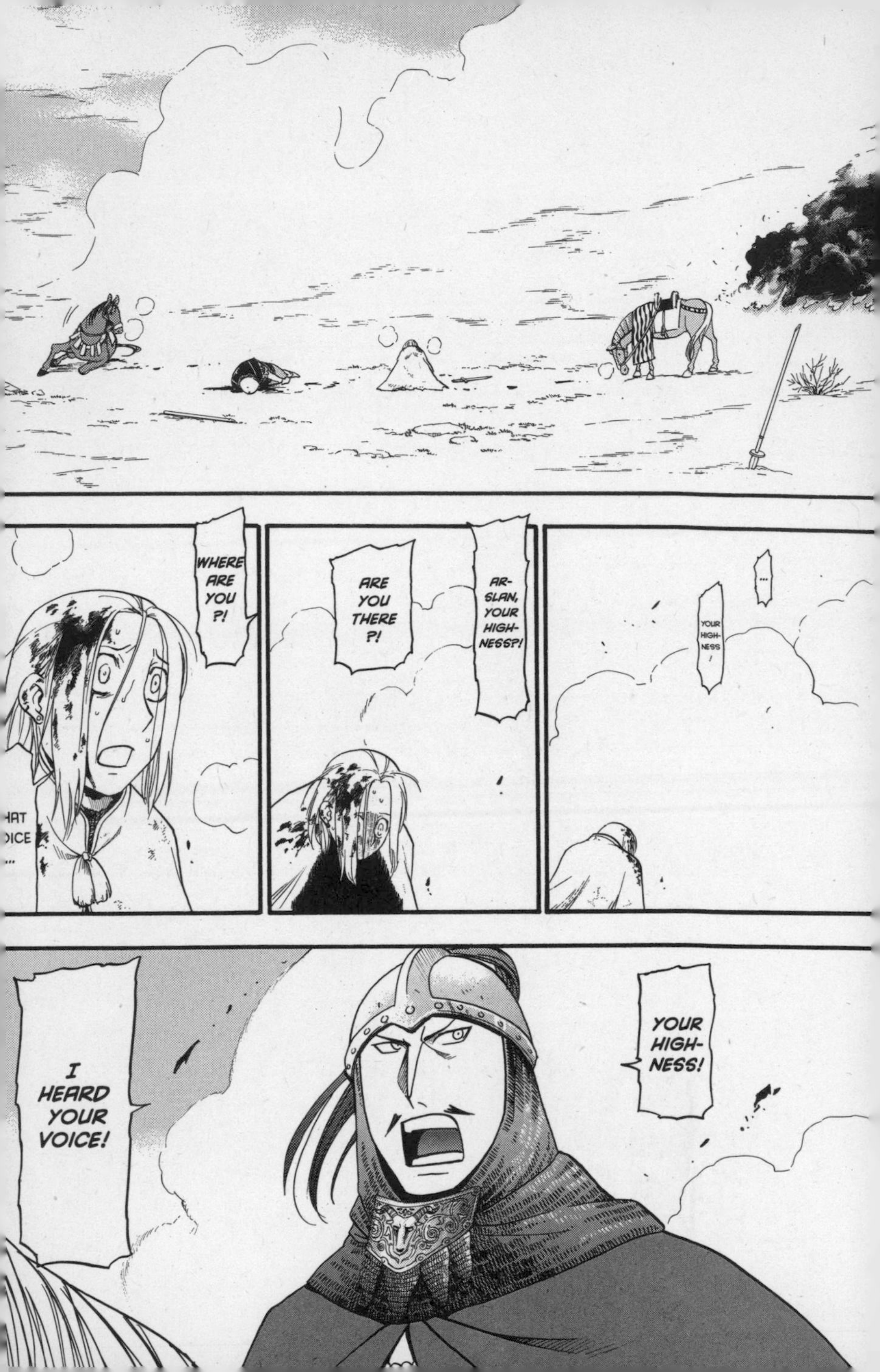

...
YOUR HIGHNESS!
AR-SLAN, YOUR HIGH-NESS?!
ARE YOU THERE?!
WHERE ARE YOU?!
HAT OICE ...
YOUR HIGH-NESS!
I HEARD YOUR VOICE!

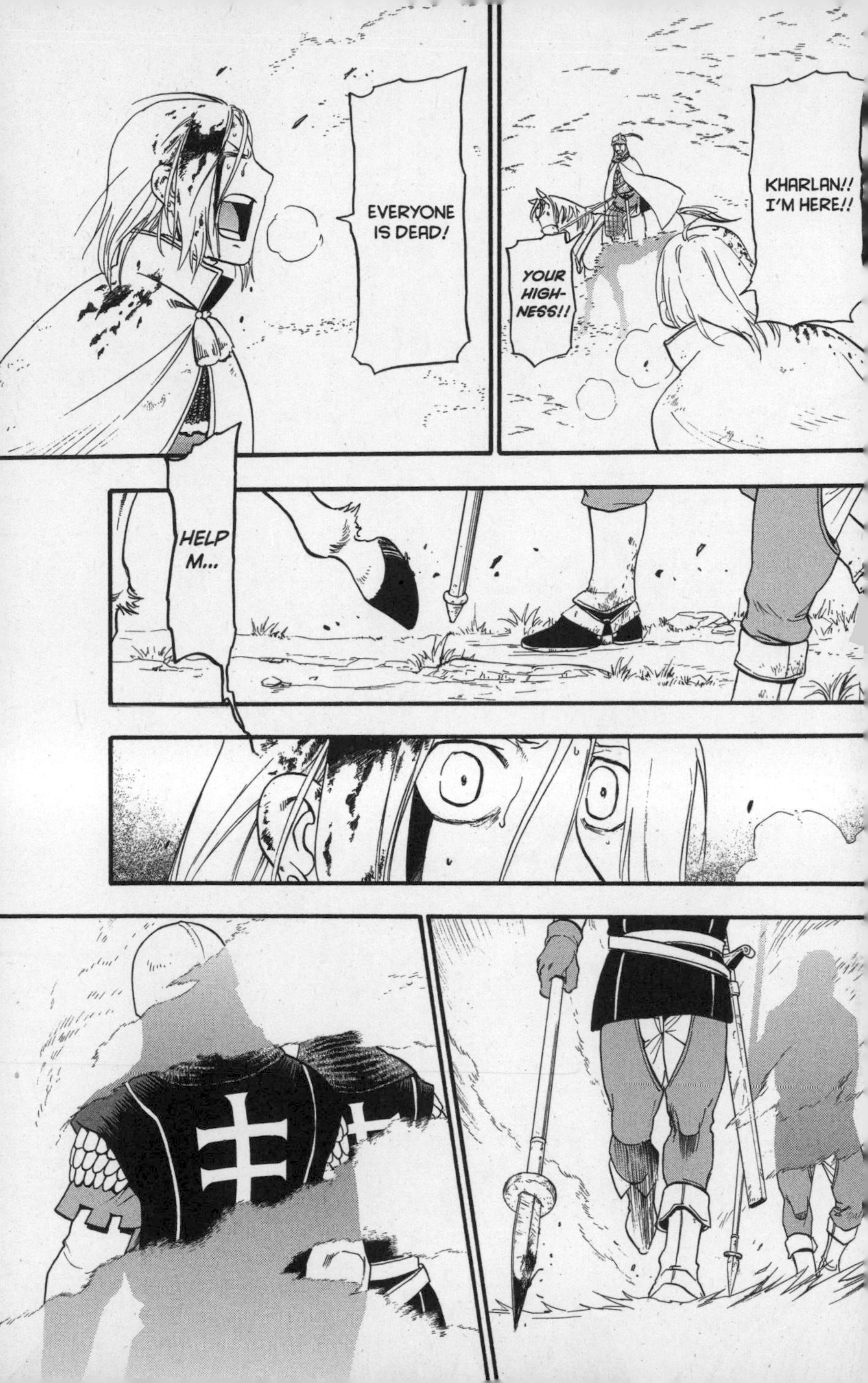
KHARLAN!! I'M HERE!!
YOUR HIGH-NESS!!
EVERYONE IS DEAD!
HELP M...

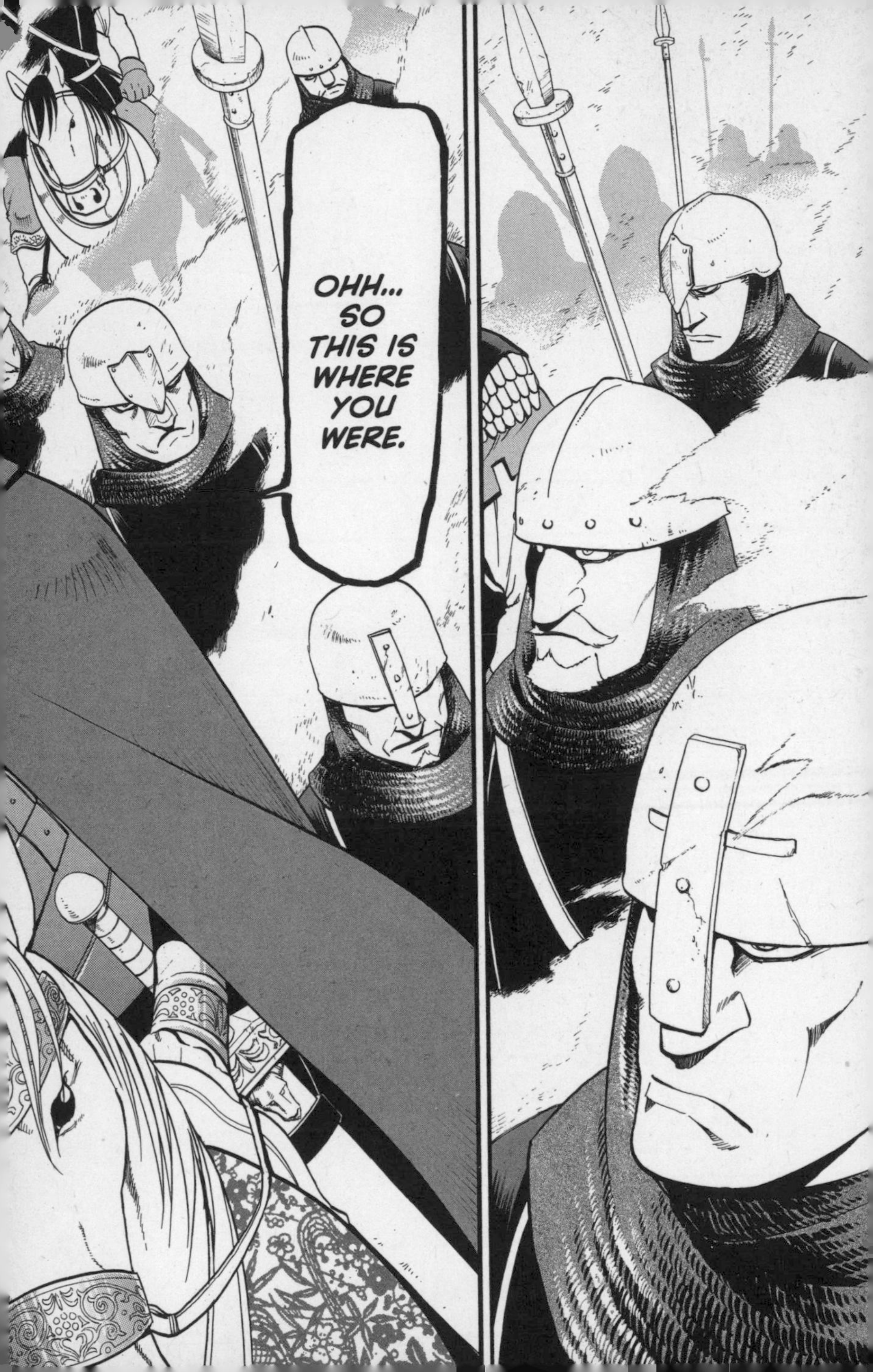
OHH... SO THIS IS WHERE YOU WERE.

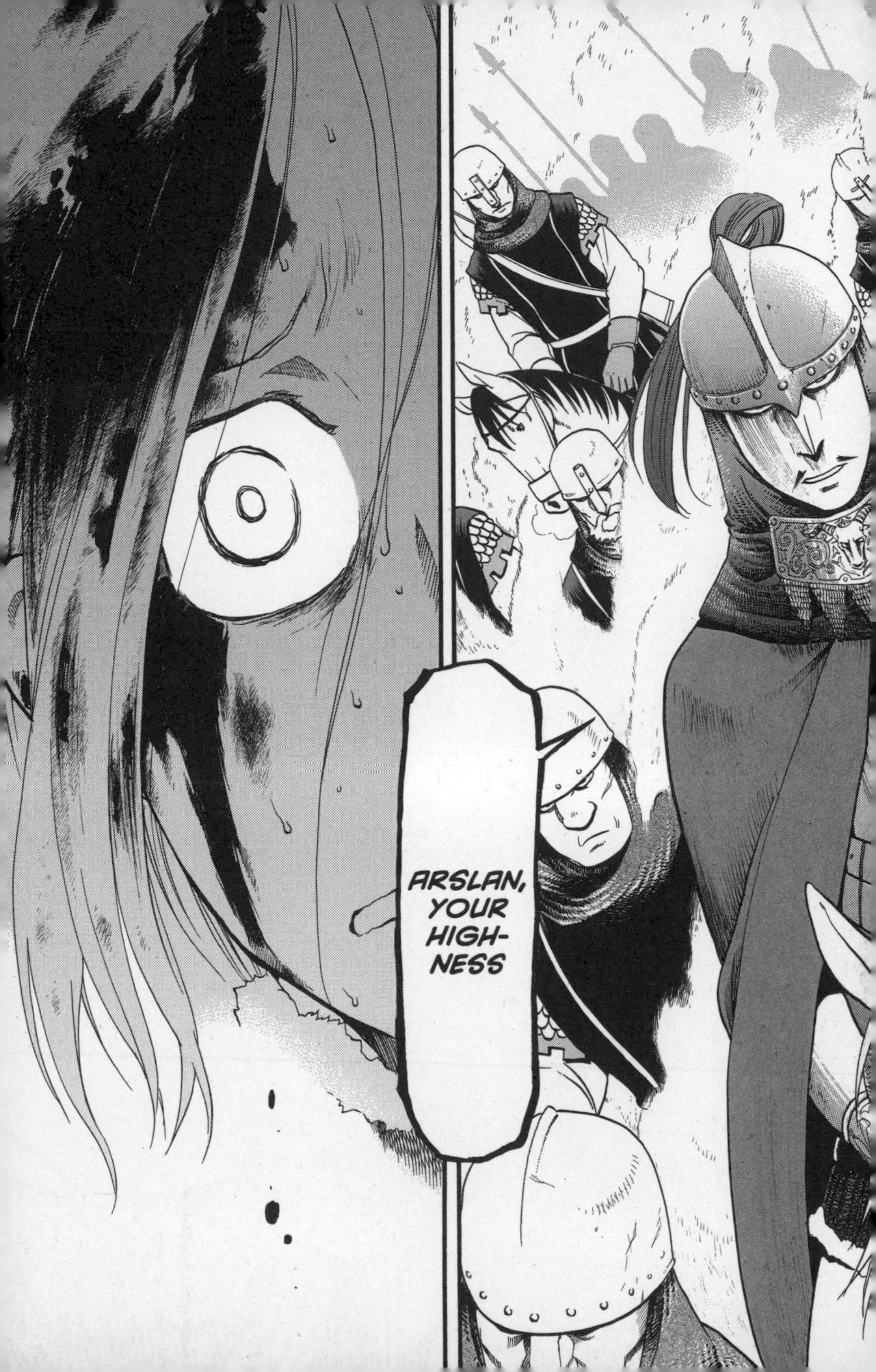
ARSLAN, YOUR HIGH-NESS

THE HEROIC LEGEND OF
ARSLAN

CHAPTER 3: The Knight in Black

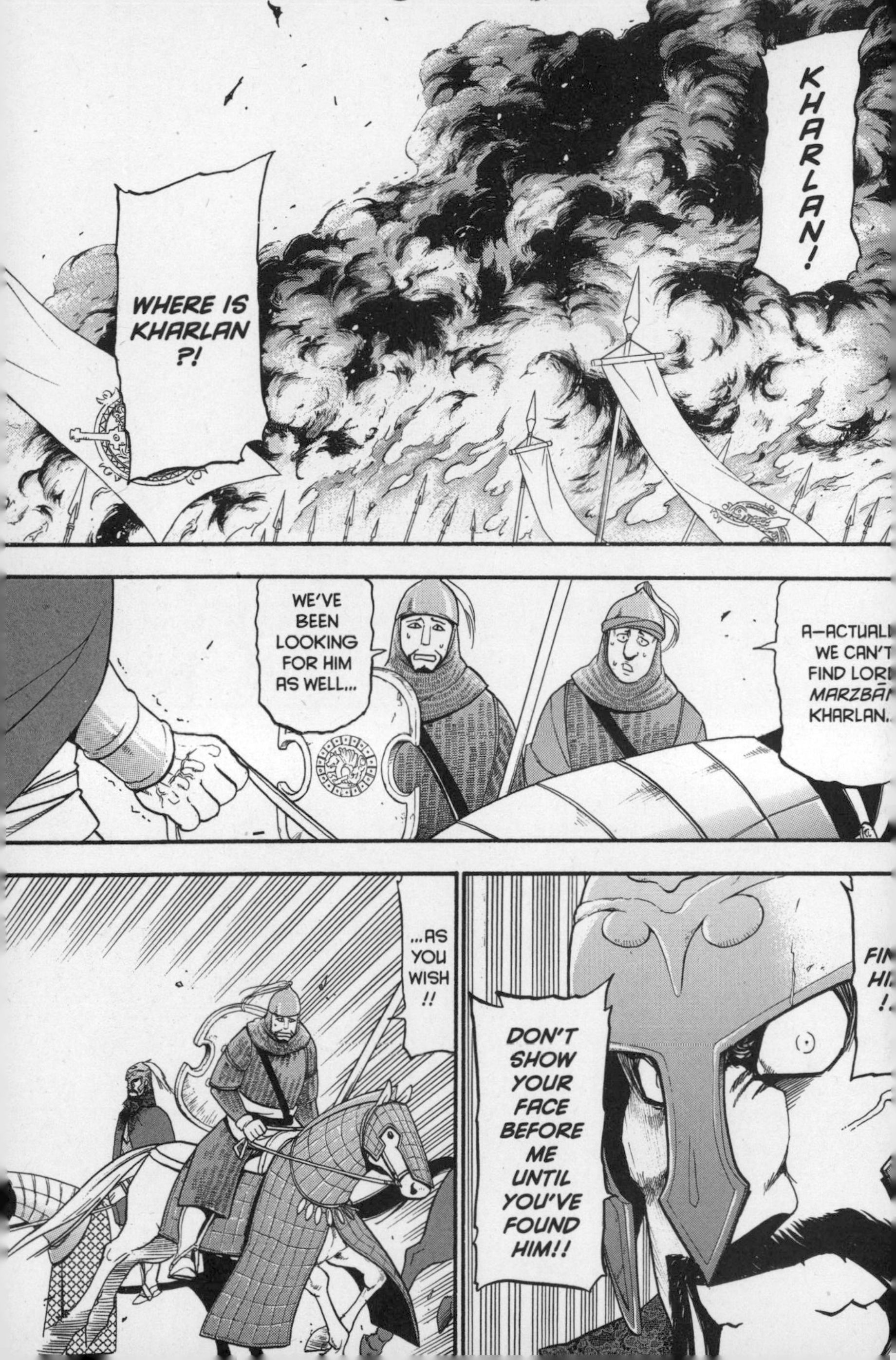

KHARLAN!
WHERE IS KHARLAN?!
A—ACTUAL WE CAN'T FIND LOR MARZBĀ KHARLAN...
WE'VE BEEN LOOKING FOR HIM AS WELL...
FIN HI !
DON'T SHOW YOUR FACE BEFORE ME UNTIL YOU'VE FOUND HIM!!
...AS YOU WISH!!

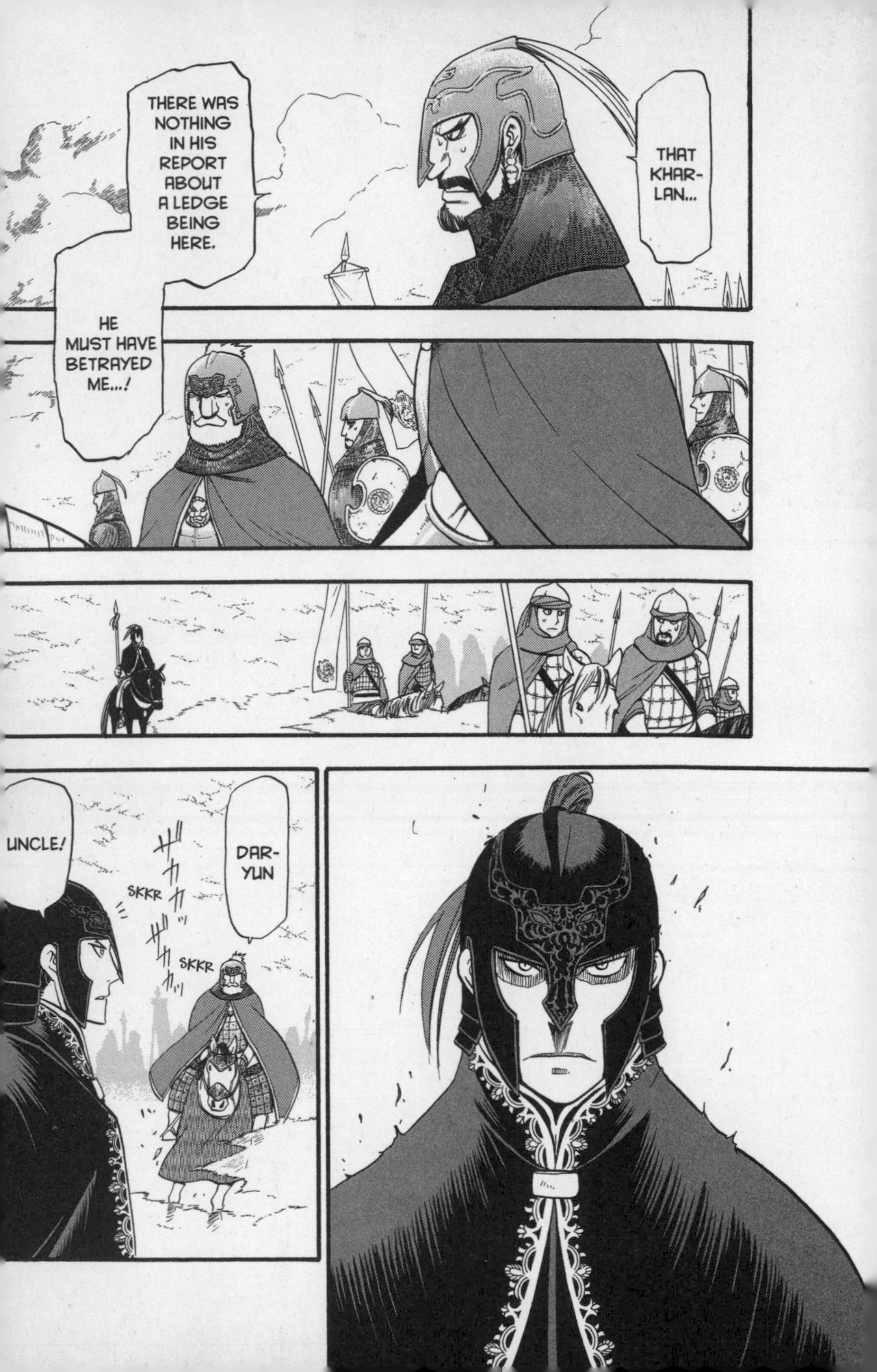

THAT KHAR-LAN...
THERE WAS NOTHING IN HIS REPORT ABOUT A LEDGE BEING HERE.
HE MUST HAVE BETRAYED ME...!
DAR-YUN
SKKR
SKKR
UNCLE!

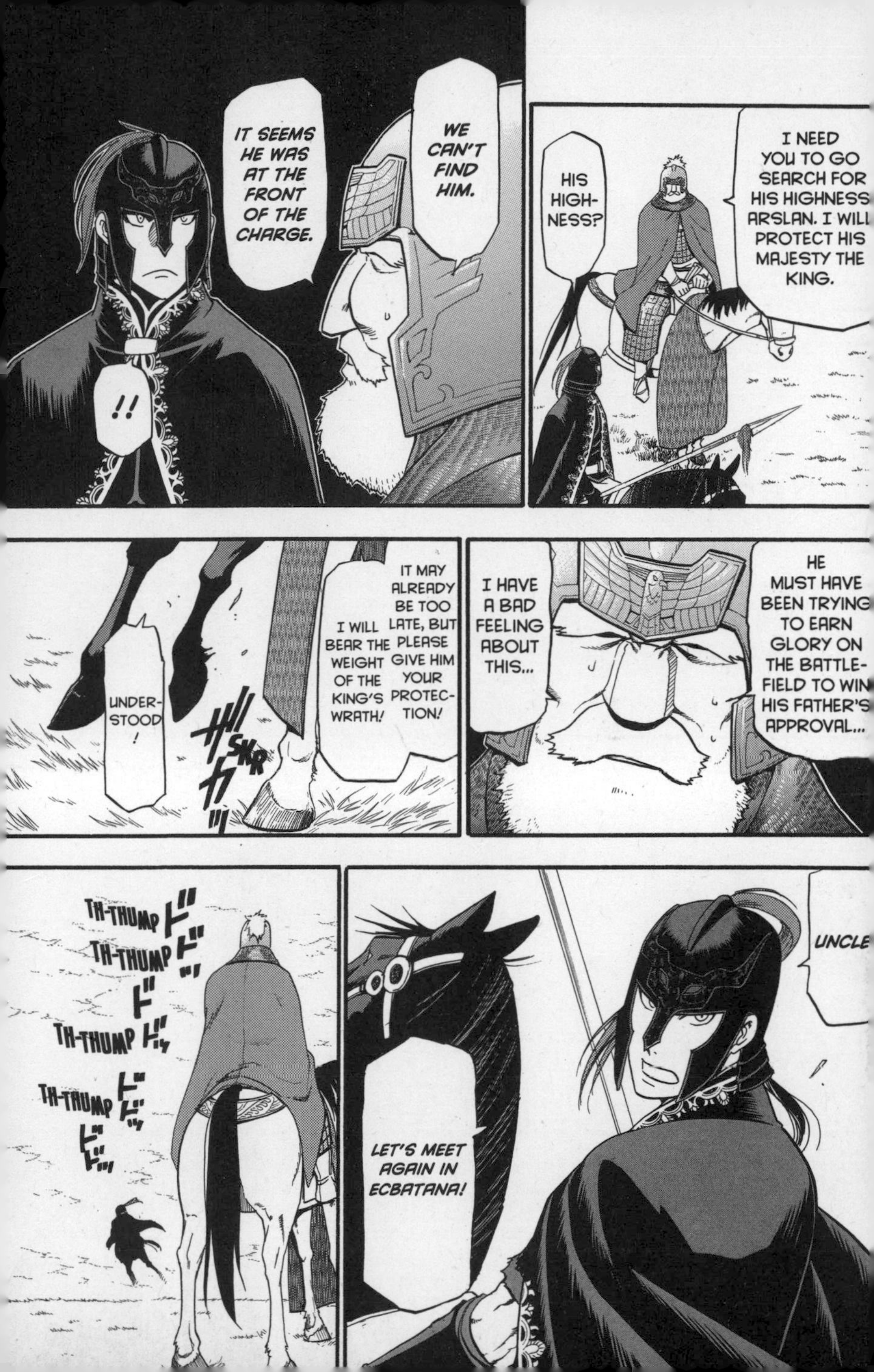
I NEED YOU TO GO SEARCH FOR HIS HIGHNESS ARSLAN. I WILL PROTECT HIS MAJESTY THE KING.
HIS HIGHNESS?
WE CAN'T FIND HIM.
IT SEEMS HE WAS AT THE FRONT OF THE CHARGE.
!!
HE MUST HAVE BEEN TRYING TO EARN GLORY ON THE BATTLEFIELD TO WIN HIS FATHER'S APPROVAL...
I HAVE A BAD FEELING ABOUT THIS...
IT MAY ALREADY BE TOO LATE, BUT PLEASE GIVE HIM YOUR PROTECTION!
I WILL BEAR THE WEIGHT OF THE KING'S WRATH!
UNDERSTOOD!
SKR
UNCLE
LET'S MEET AGAIN IN ECBATANA!
TH-THUMP
TH-THUMP
TH-THUMP
TH-THUMP

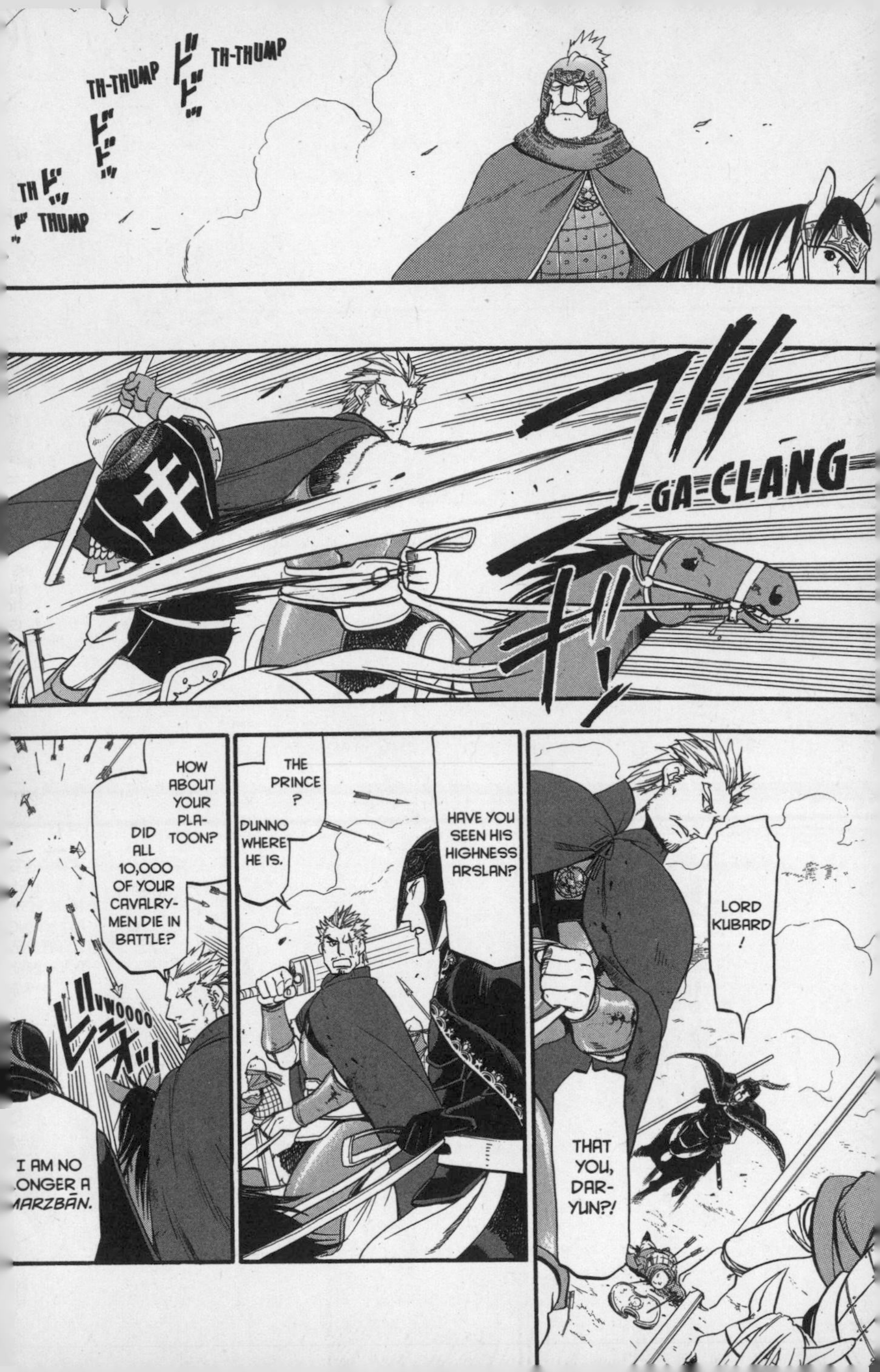

TH-THUMP
TH-THUMP
TH THUMP
GA-CLANG
LORD KUBARD!
THAT YOU, DAR-YUN?!
HAVE YOU SEEN HIS HIGHNESS ARSLAN?
THE PRINCE?
DUNNO WHERE HE IS.
HOW ABOUT YOUR PLA-TOON?
DID ALL 10,000 OF YOUR CAVALRY-MEN DIE IN BATTLE?
HWOOOO
I AM NO LONGER A MARZBĀN.

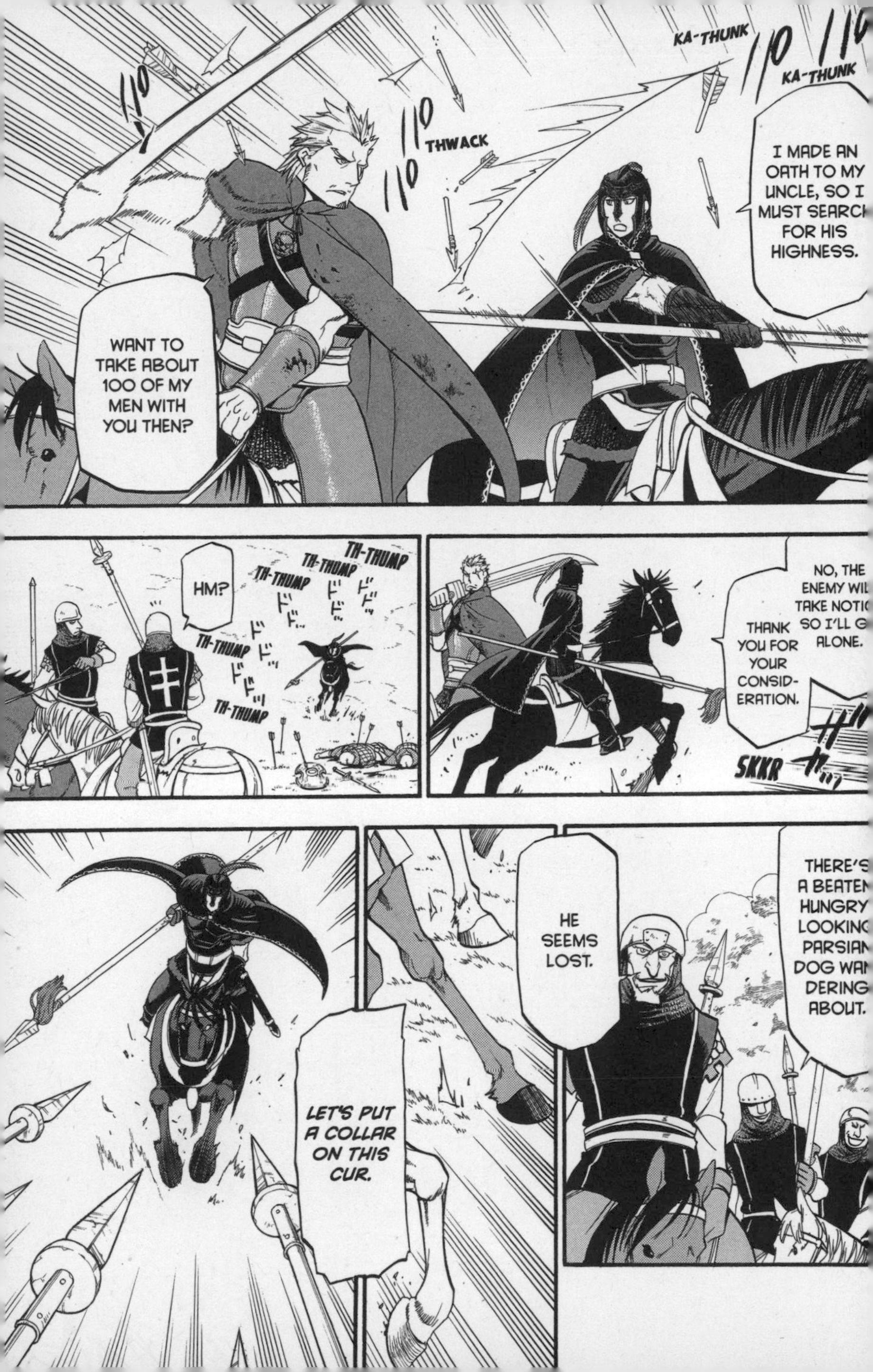
KA-THUNK
KA-THUNK
THWACK
I MADE AN OATH TO MY UNCLE, SO I MUST SEARC FOR HIS HIGHNESS.
WANT TO TAKE ABOUT 100 OF MY MEN WITH YOU THEN?
NO, THE ENEMY WIL TAKE NOTIC SO I'LL G ALONE.
THANK YOU FOR YOUR CONSID-ERATION.
SKKR
TH-THUMP
TH-THUMP
TH-THUMP
TH-THUMP
TH-THUMP
HM?
THERE'S A BEATEN HUNGRY LOOKING PARSIAN DOG WAN DERING ABOUT.
HE SEEMS LOST.
LET'S PUT A COLLAR ON THIS CUR.

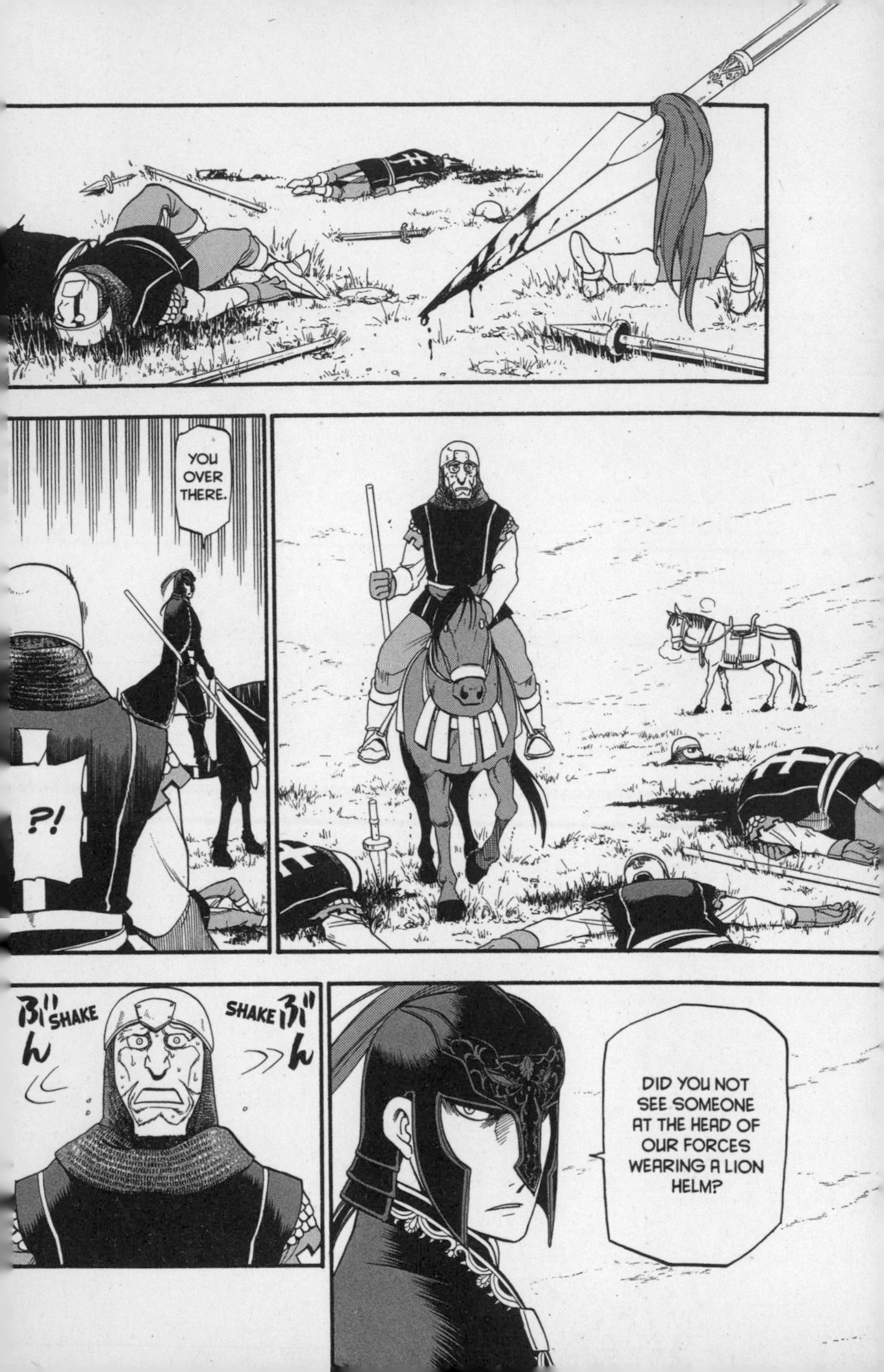
YOU OVER THERE.
?!
DID YOU NOT SEE SOMEONE AT THE HEAD OF OUR FORCES WEARING A LION HELM?
SHAKE
SHAKE

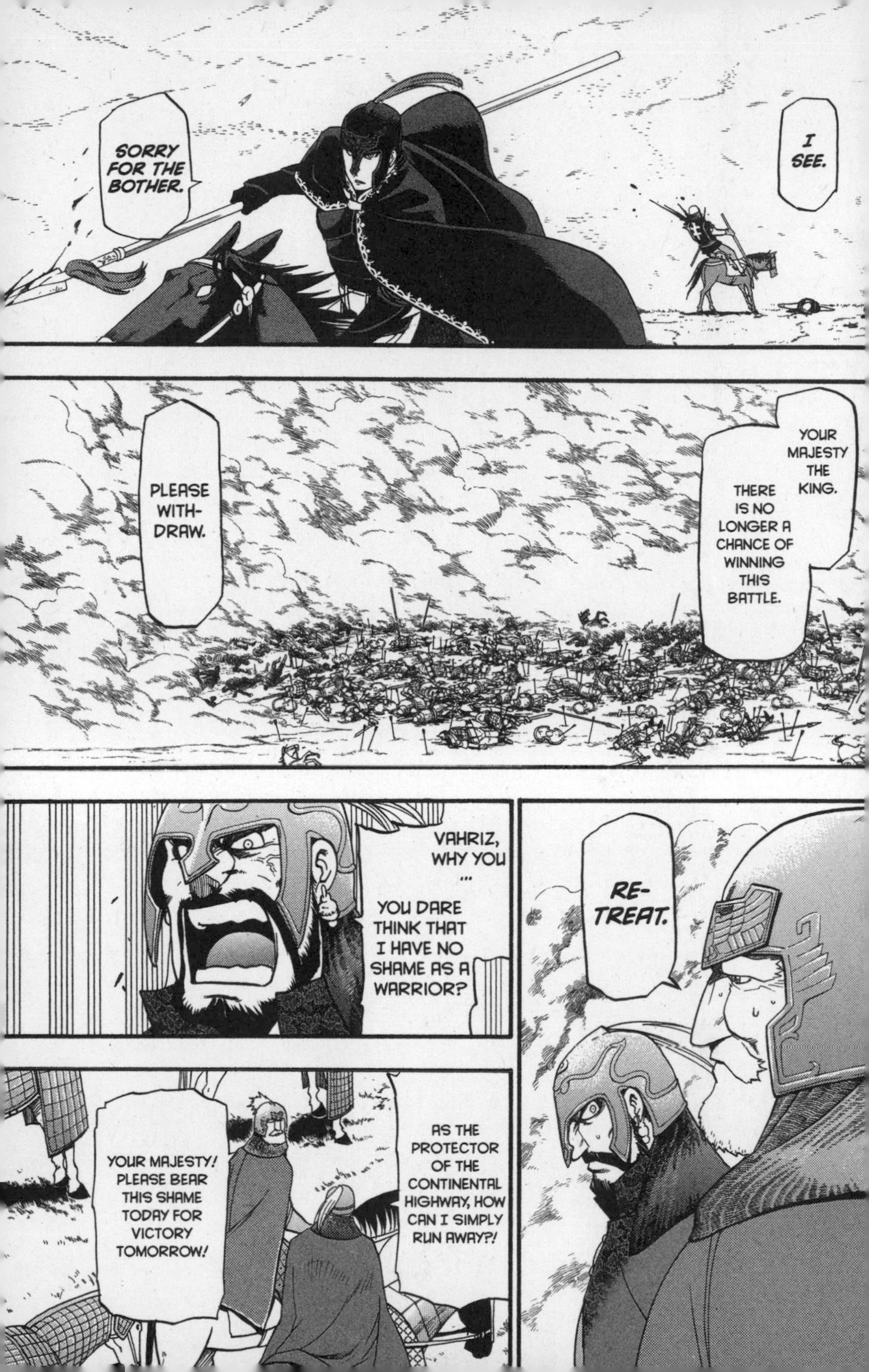
I SEE.
SORRY FOR THE BOTHER.
YOUR MAJESTY THE KING.
THERE IS NO LONGER A CHANCE OF WINNING THIS BATTLE.
PLEASE WITH-DRAW.
RE-TREAT.
VAHRIZ, WHY YOU ...
YOU DARE THINK THAT I HAVE NO SHAME AS A WARRIOR?
AS THE PROTECTOR OF THE CONTINENTAL HIGHWAY, HOW CAN I SIMPLY RUN AWAY?!
YOUR MAJESTY! PLEASE BEAR THIS SHAME TODAY FOR VICTORY TOMORROW!

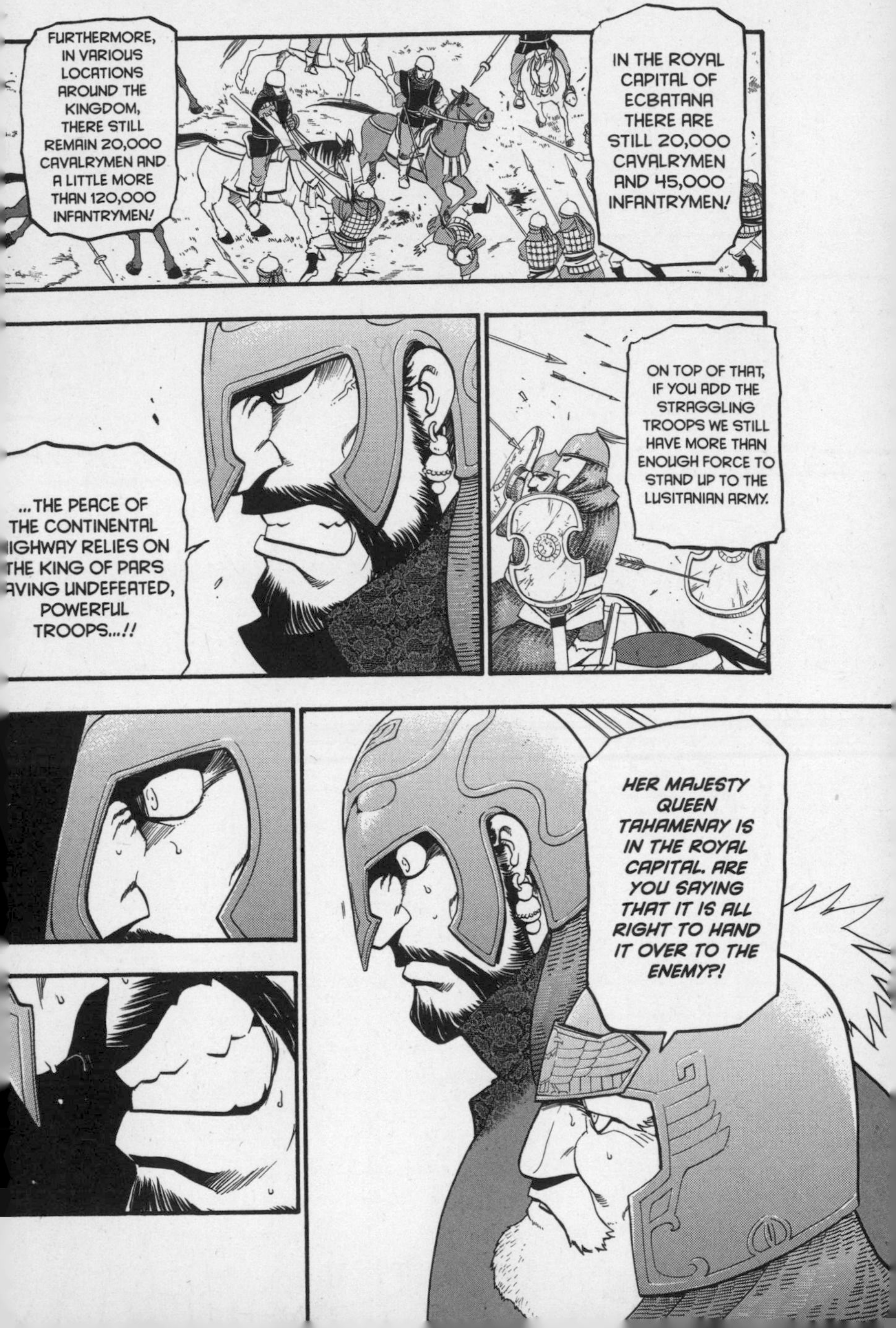
IN THE ROYAL CAPITAL OF ECBATANA THERE ARE STILL 20,000 CAVALRYMEN AND 45,000 INFANTRYMEN!
FURTHERMORE, IN VARIOUS LOCATIONS AROUND THE KINGDOM, THERE STILL REMAIN 20,000 CAVALRYMEN AND A LITTLE MORE THAN 120,000 INFANTRYMEN!
ON TOP OF THAT, IF YOU ADD THE STRAGGLING TROOPS WE STILL HAVE MORE THAN ENOUGH FORCE TO STAND UP TO THE LUSITANIAN ARMY.
...THE PEACE OF THE CONTINENTAL IGHWAY RELIES ON THE KING OF PARS AVING UNDEFEATED, POWERFUL TROOPS...!!
HER MAJESTY QUEEN TAHAMENAY IS IN THE ROYAL CAPITAL. ARE YOU SAYING THAT IT IS ALL RIGHT TO HAND IT OVER TO THE ENEMY?!

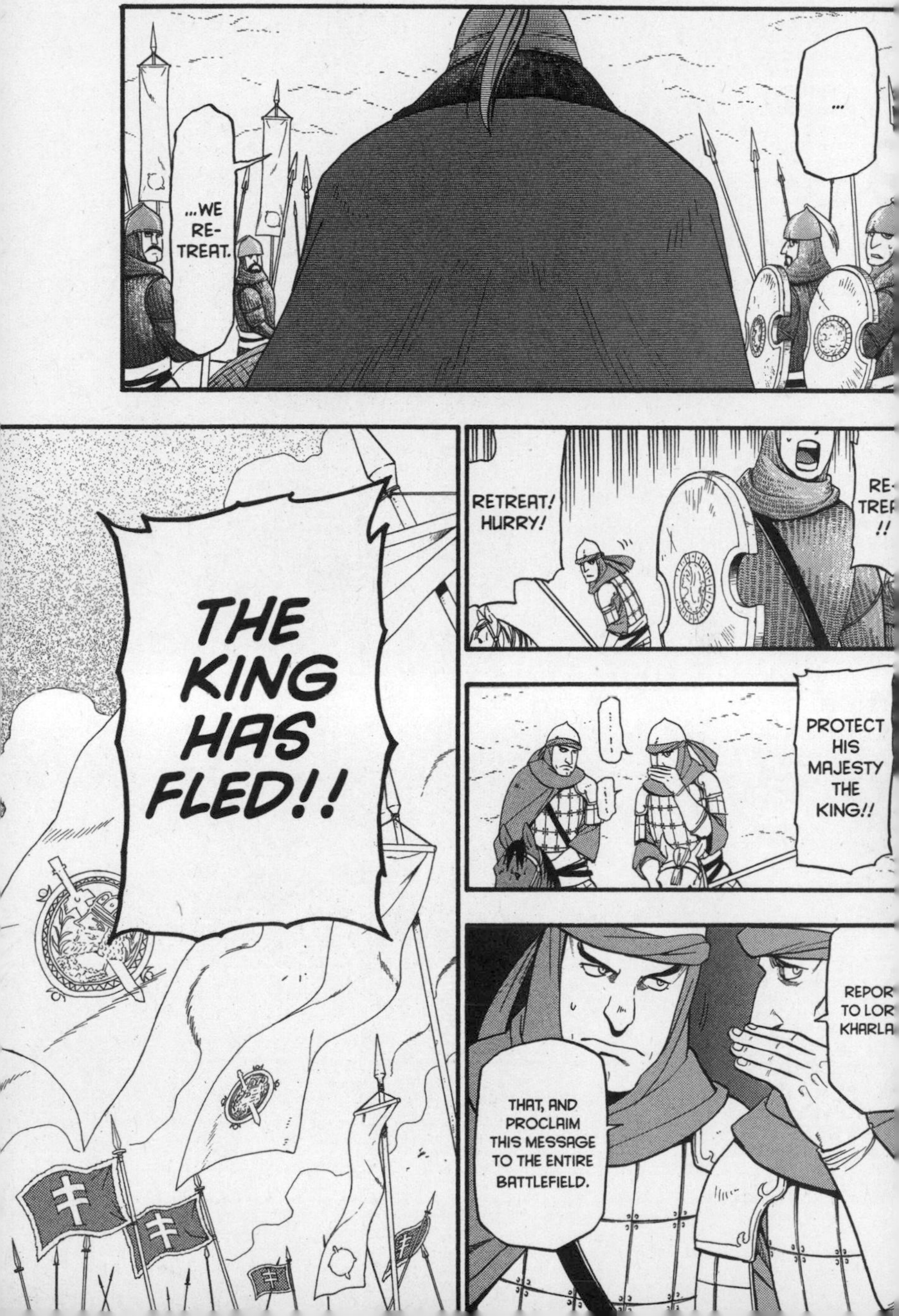
...
...WE RE-TREAT.
RE-TREA !!
RETREAT! HURRY!
PROTECT HIS MAJESTY THE KING!!
REPOR TO LOR KHARLA
THAT, AND PROCLAIM THIS MESSAGE TO THE ENTIRE BATTLEFIELD.
THE KING HAS FLED!!

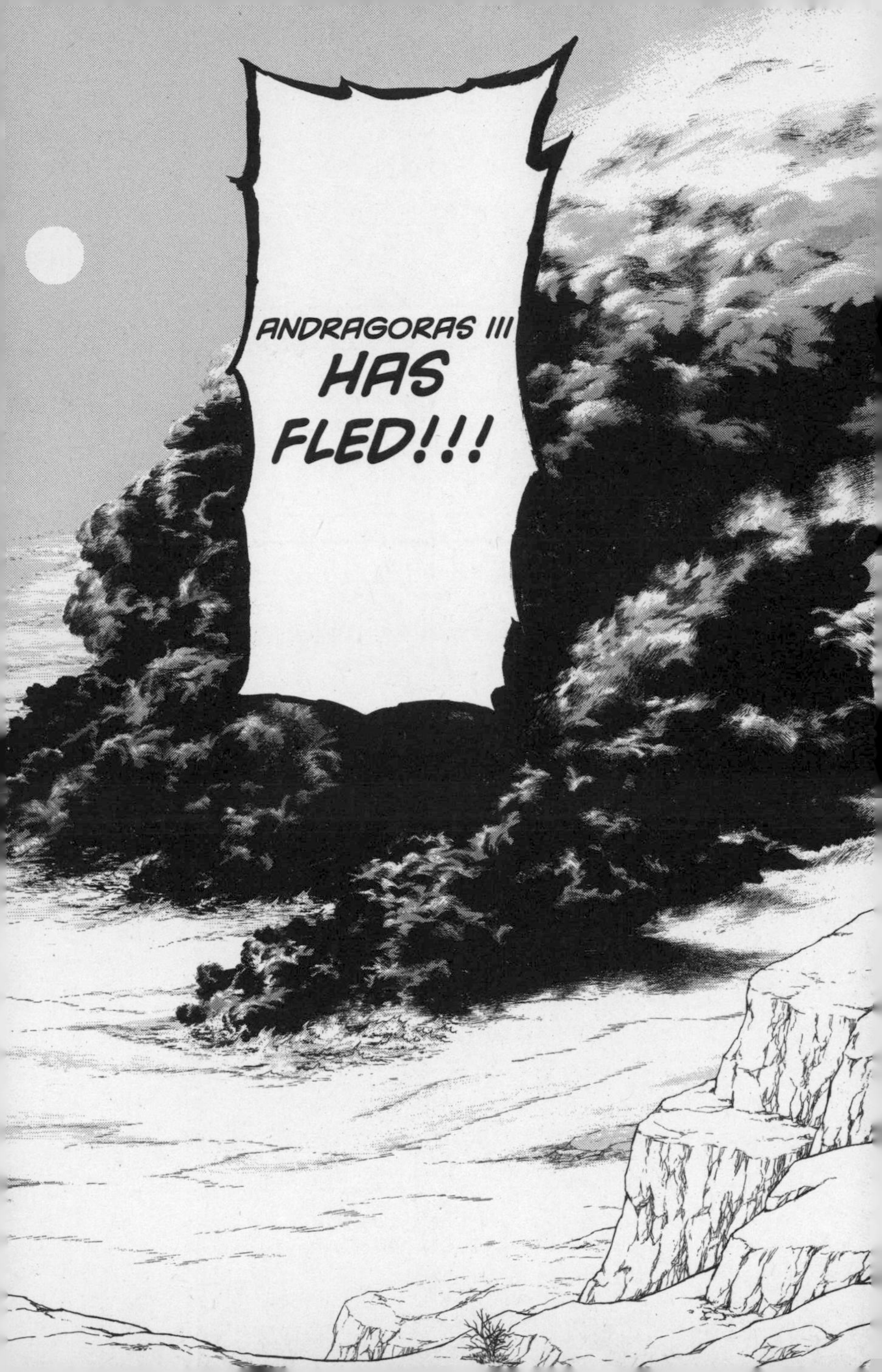
ANDRAGORAS III HAS FLED!!!

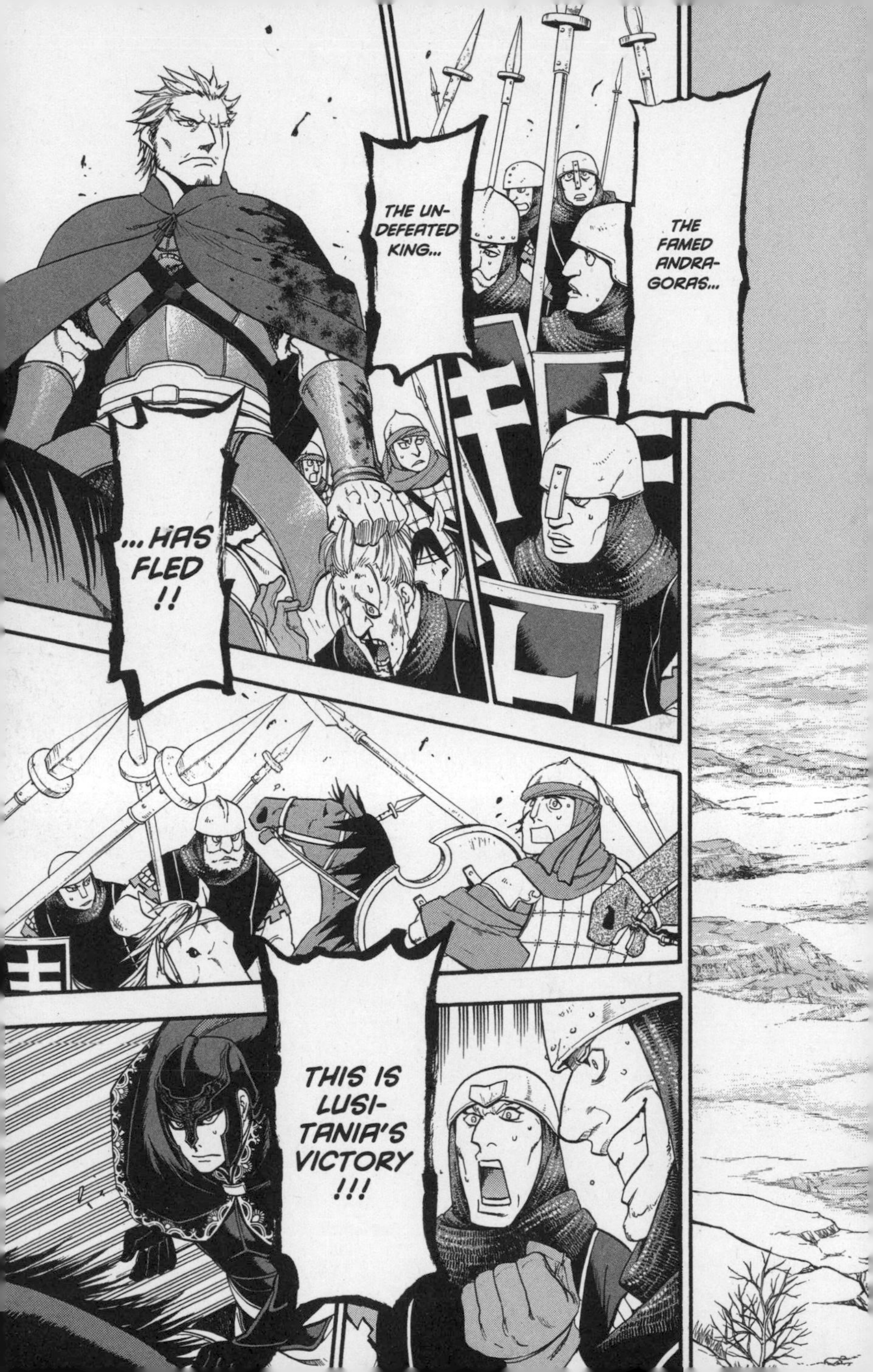
THE FAMED ANDRAGORAS...
THE UN-DEFEATED KING...
...HAS FLED!!
THIS IS LUSITANIA'S VICTORY!!!

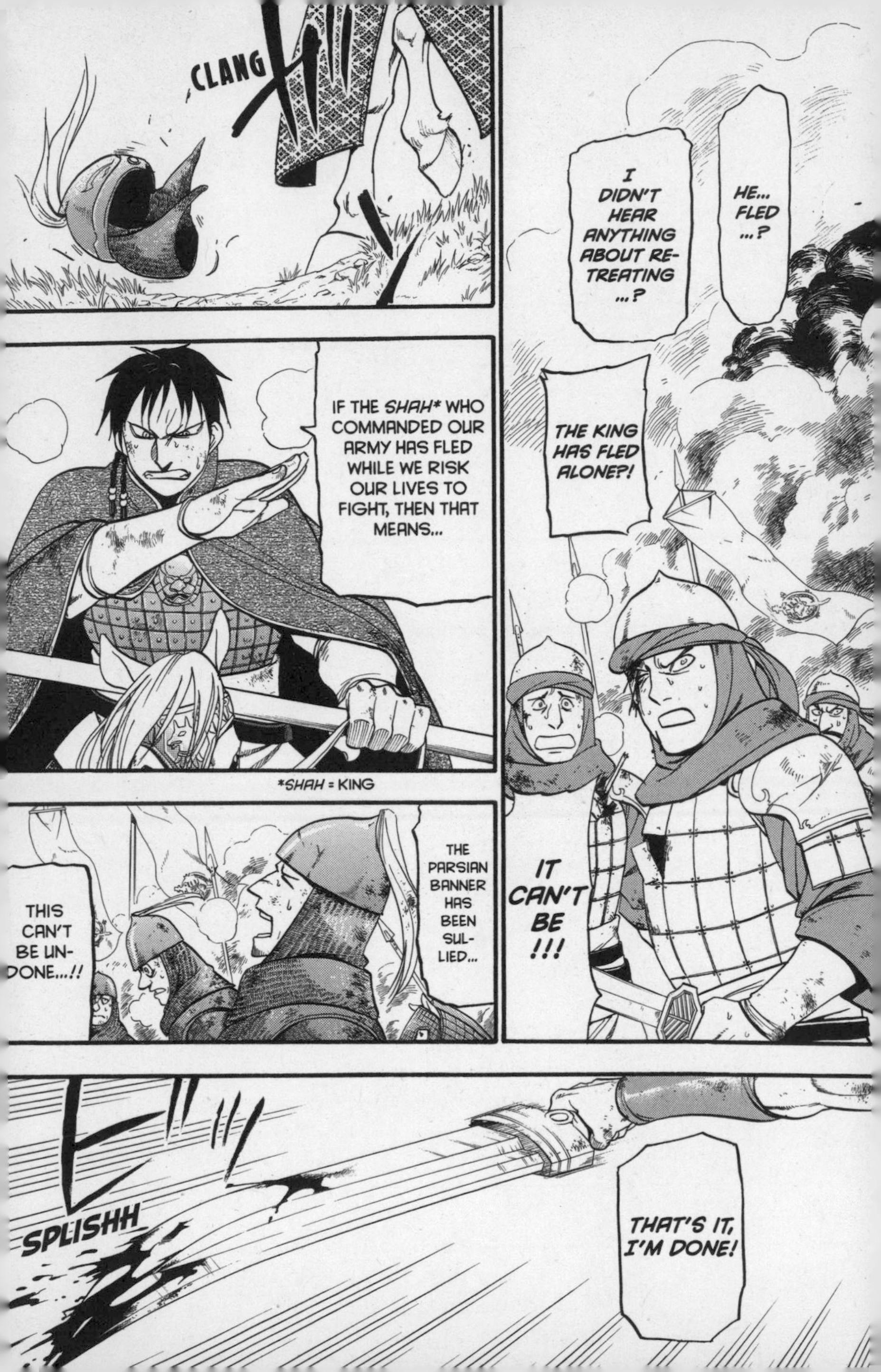
HE... FLED ...?
I DIDN'T HEAR ANYTHING ABOUT RE-TREATING ...?
THE KING HAS FLED ALONE?!
IT CAN'T BE !!!
CLANG
IF THE SHAH* WHO COMMANDED OUR ARMY HAS FLED WHILE WE RISK OUR LIVES TO FIGHT, THEN THAT MEANS...
THE PARSIAN BANNER HAS BEEN SUL-LIED...
THIS CAN'T BE UN-DONE...!!
SPLISHH
THAT'S IT, I'M DONE!
*SHAH = KING

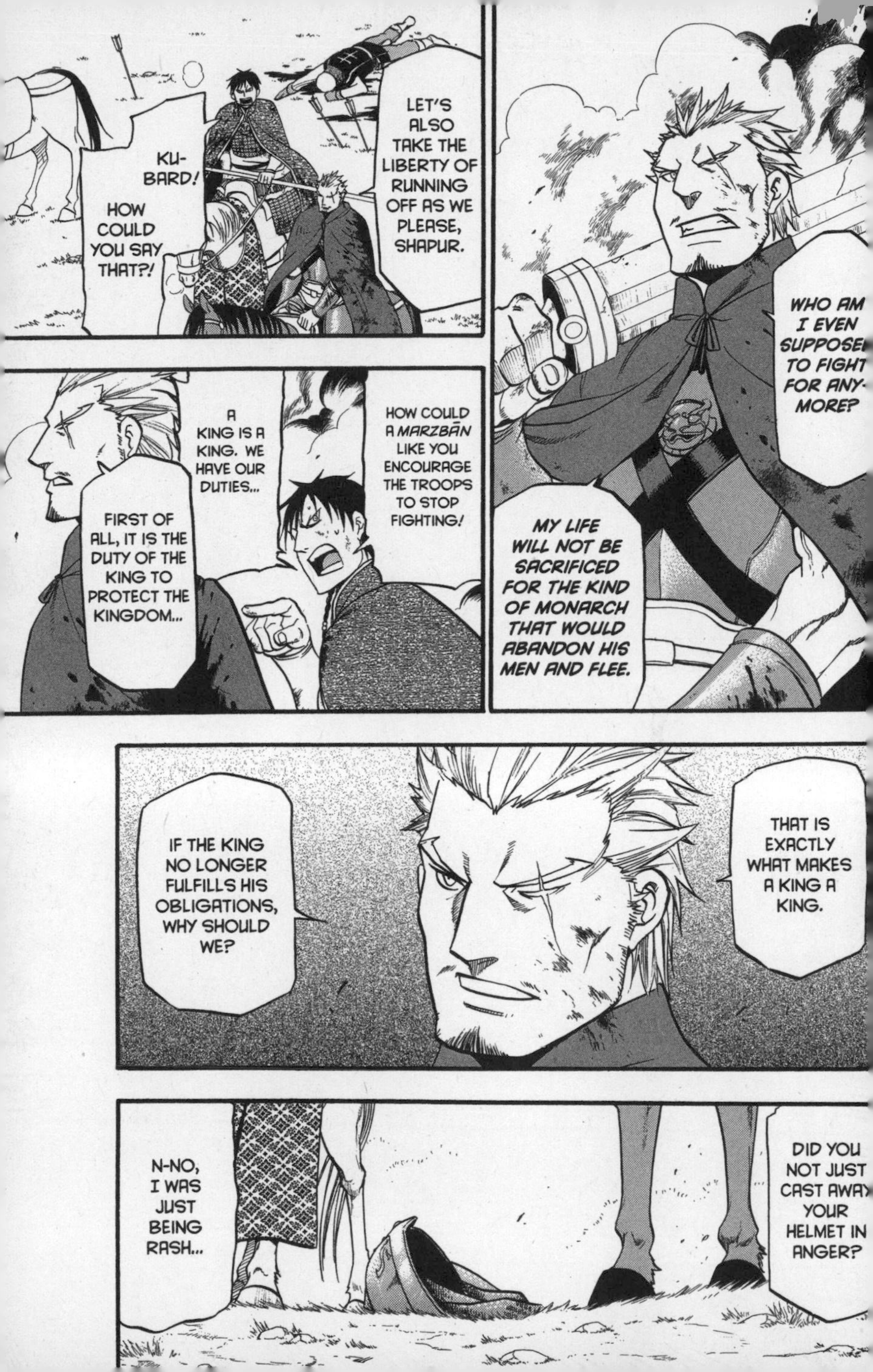
WHO AM I EVEN SUPPOSE TO FIGHT FOR ANY-MORE?
MY LIFE WILL NOT BE SACRIFICED FOR THE KIND OF MONARCH THAT WOULD ABANDON HIS MEN AND FLEE.
LET'S ALSO TAKE THE LIBERTY OF RUNNING OFF AS WE PLEASE, SHAPUR.
KU-BARD!
HOW COULD YOU SAY THAT?!
HOW COULD A MARZBĀN LIKE YOU ENCOURAGE THE TROOPS TO STOP FIGHTING!
A KING IS A KING. WE HAVE OUR DUTIES...
FIRST OF ALL, IT IS THE DUTY OF THE KING TO PROTECT THE KINGDOM...
THAT IS EXACTLY WHAT MAKES A KING A KING.
IF THE KING NO LONGER FULFILLS HIS OBLIGATIONS, WHY SHOULD WE?
DID YOU NOT JUST CAST AWAY YOUR HELMET IN ANGER?
N-NO, I WAS JUST BEING RASH...

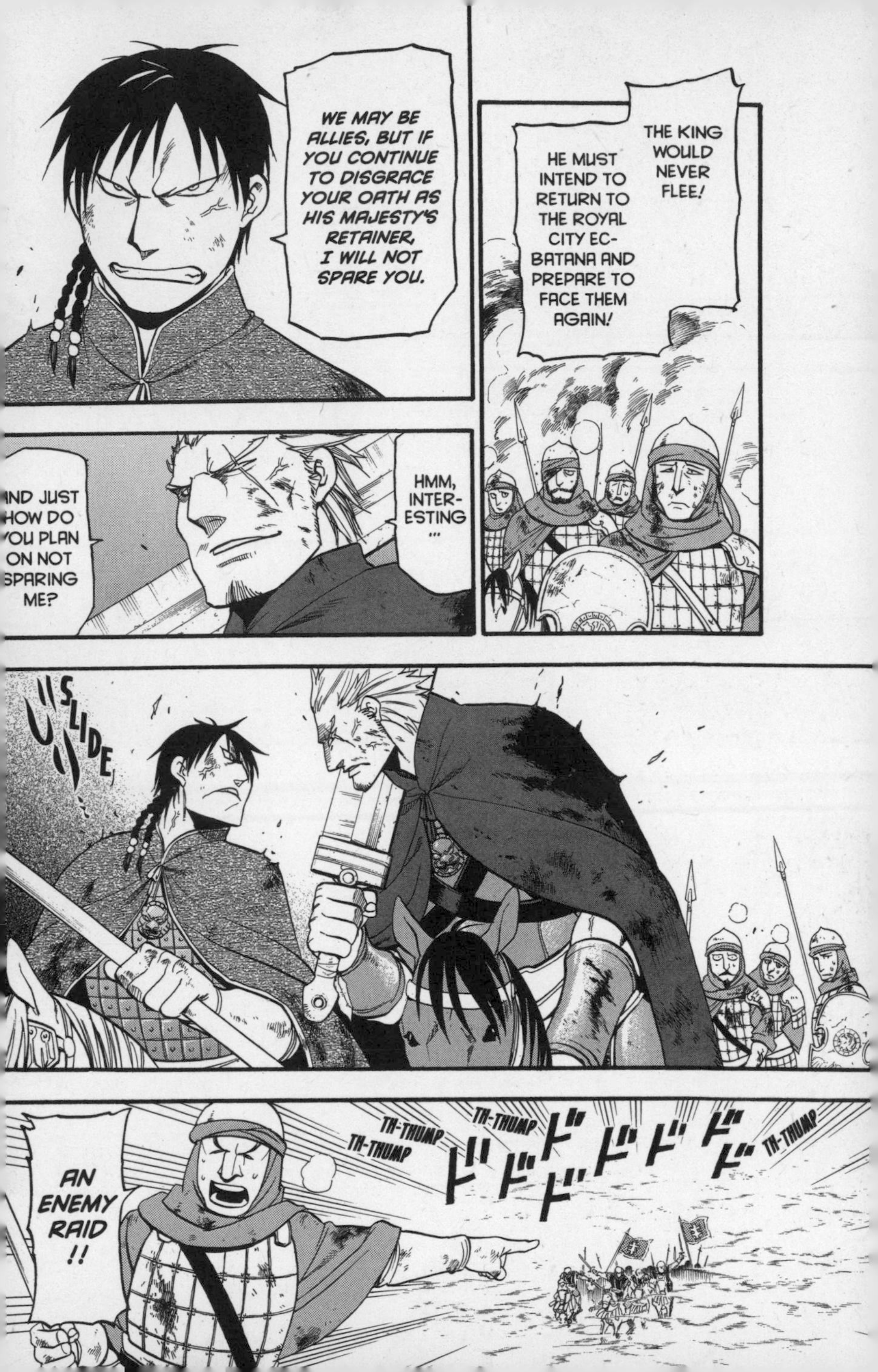
THE KING WOULD NEVER FLEE!
HE MUST INTEND TO RETURN TO THE ROYAL CITY EC-BATANA AND PREPARE TO FACE THEM AGAIN!
WE MAY BE ALLIES, BUT IF YOU CONTINUE TO DISGRACE YOUR OATH AS HIS MAJESTY'S RETAINER, I WILL NOT SPARE YOU.
HMM, INTER-ESTING...
AND JUST HOW DO YOU PLAN ON NOT SPARING ME?
SLIDE
TH-THUMP
ドドドドドドド
TH-THUMP
TH-THUMP
TH-THUMP
AN ENEMY RAID!!

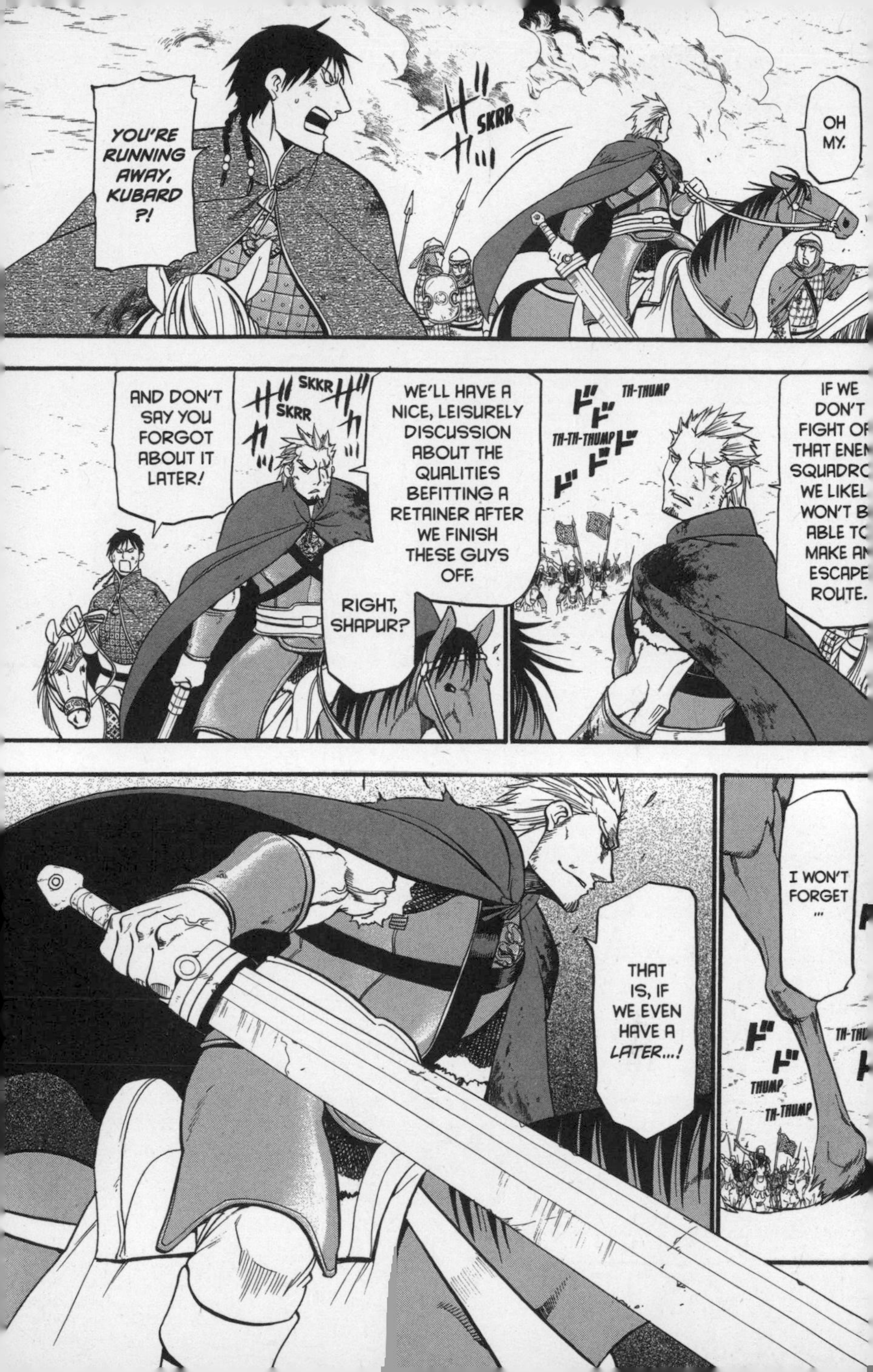
OH MY.
SKRR
YOU'RE RUNNING AWAY, KUBARD ?!
IF WE DON'T FIGHT OF THAT ENEM SQUADRO WE LIKEL WON'T B ABLE TO MAKE AN ESCAPE ROUTE.
TH-THUMP
TH-TH-THUMP
WE'LL HAVE A NICE, LEISURELY DISCUSSION ABOUT THE QUALITIES BEFITTING A RETAINER AFTER WE FINISH THESE GUYS OFF.
RIGHT, SHAPUR?
SKKR
SKRR
AND DON'T SAY YOU FORGOT ABOUT IT LATER!
I WON'T FORGET ...
TH-TH
THUMP
TH-THUMP
THAT IS, IF WE EVEN HAVE A LATER...!

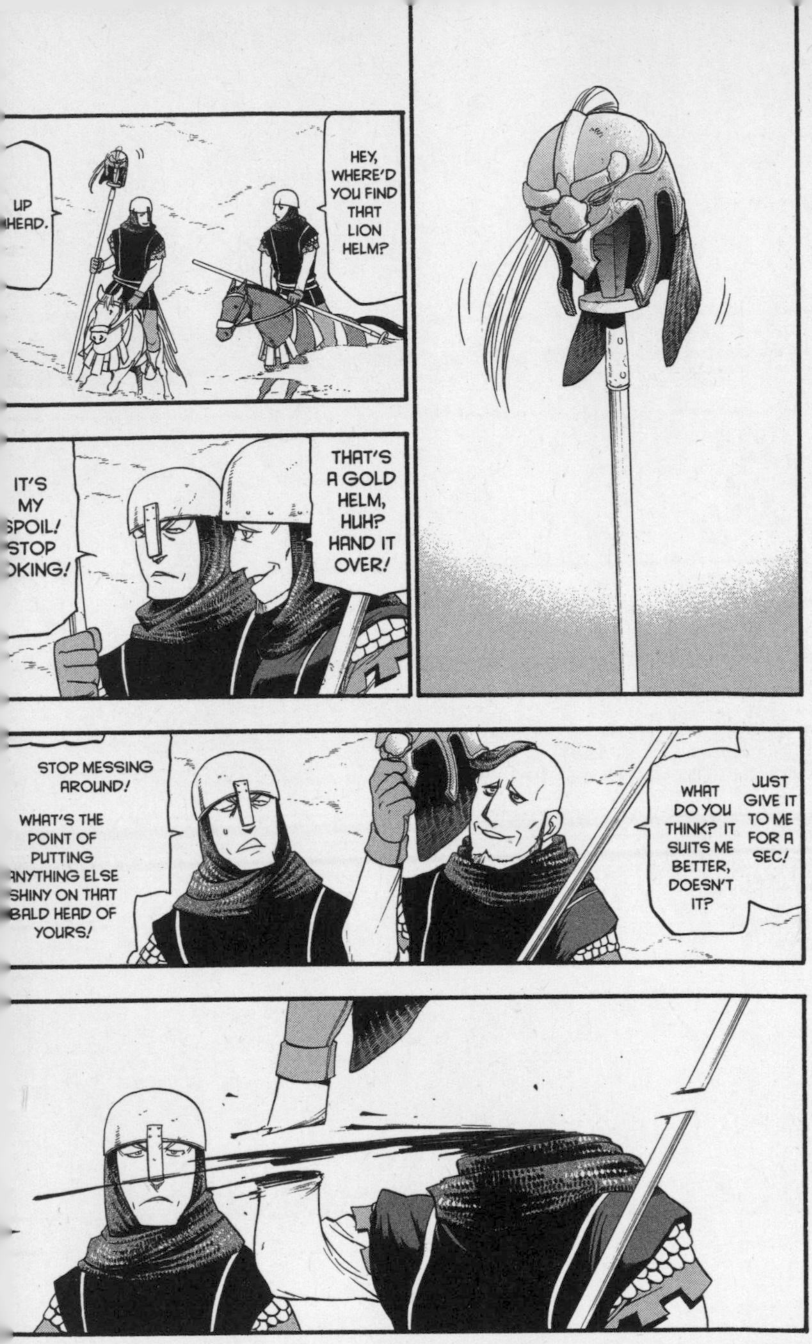
HEY, WHERE'D YOU FIND THAT LION HELM?
UP HEAD.
THAT'S A GOLD HELM, HUH? HAND IT OVER!
IT'S MY SPOIL! STOP OKING!
JUST GIVE IT TO ME FOR A SEC!
WHAT DO YOU THINK? IT SUITS ME BETTER, DOESN'T IT?
STOP MESSING AROUND!
WHAT'S THE POINT OF PUTTING NYTHING ELSE SHINY ON THAT BALD HEAD OF YOURS!

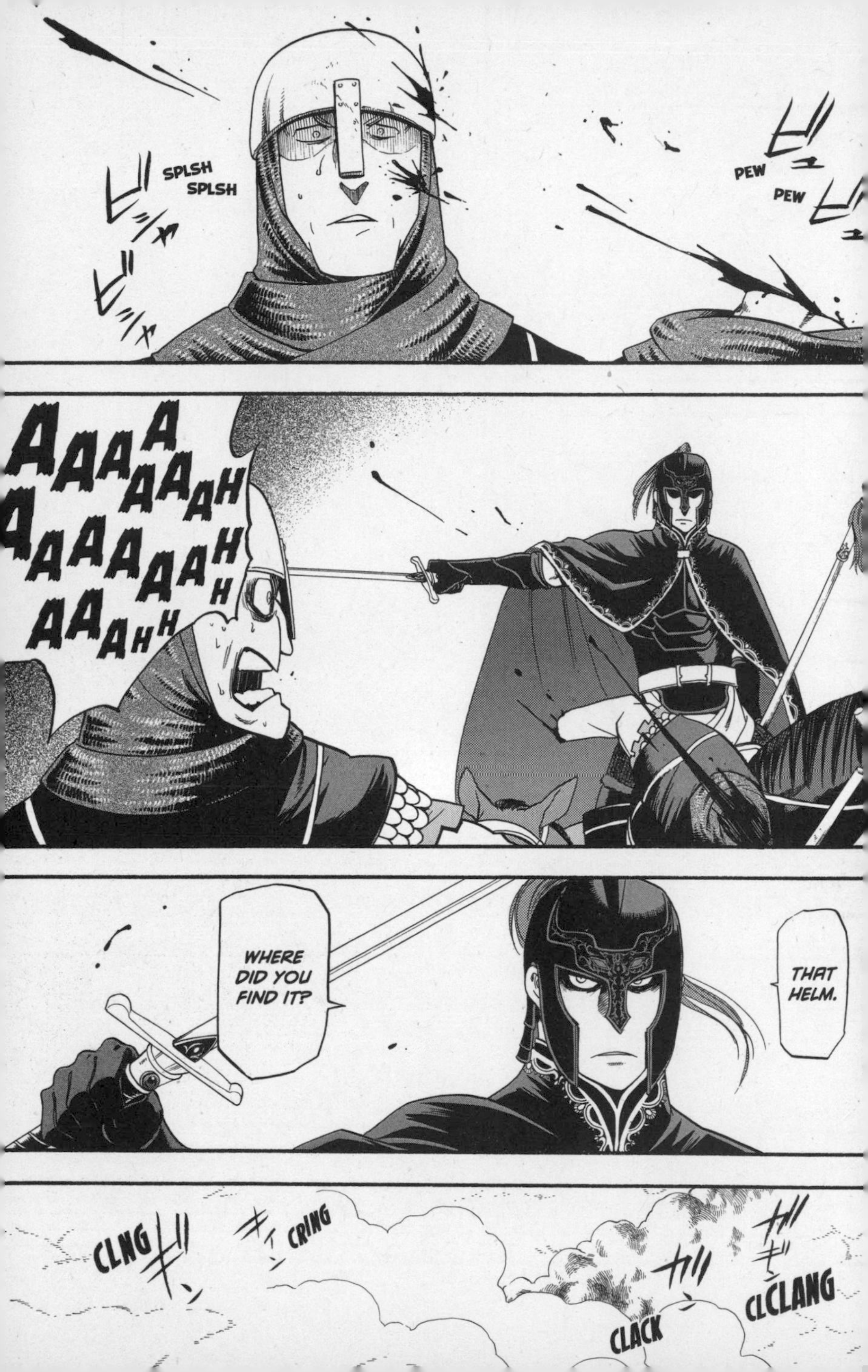
PEW
PEW
SPLSH
SPLSH
AAAAAAAAH AAAAAAAAHH AAAAHH
THAT HELM.
WHERE DID YOU FIND IT?
CLCLANG
CLACK
CRING
CLNG

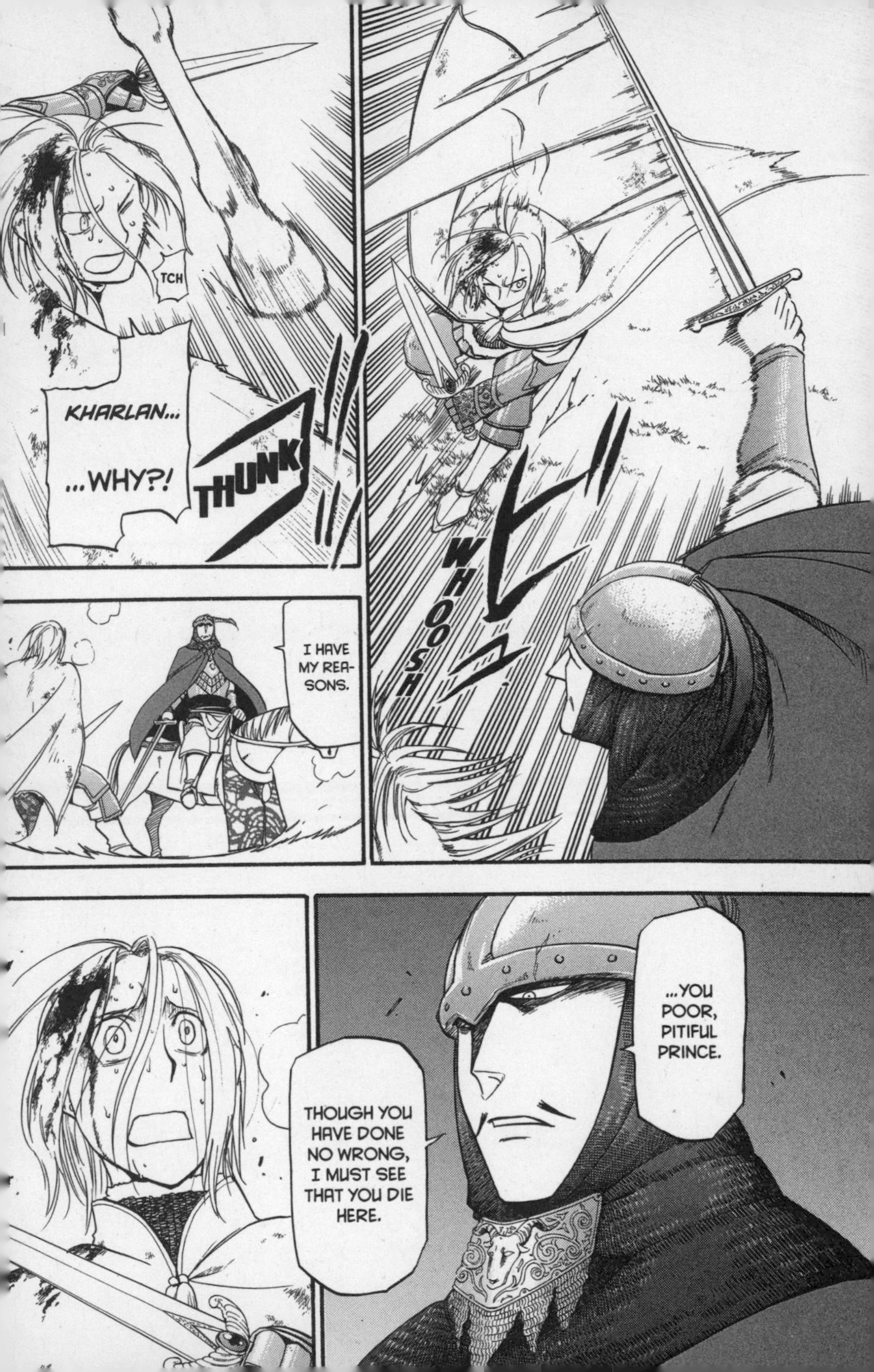
WHOOOSH
TCH
KHARLAN...
...WHY?!
THUNK
I HAVE MY REASONS.
...YOU POOR, PITIFUL PRINCE.
THOUGH YOU HAVE DONE NO WRONG, I MUST SEE THAT YOU DIE HERE.

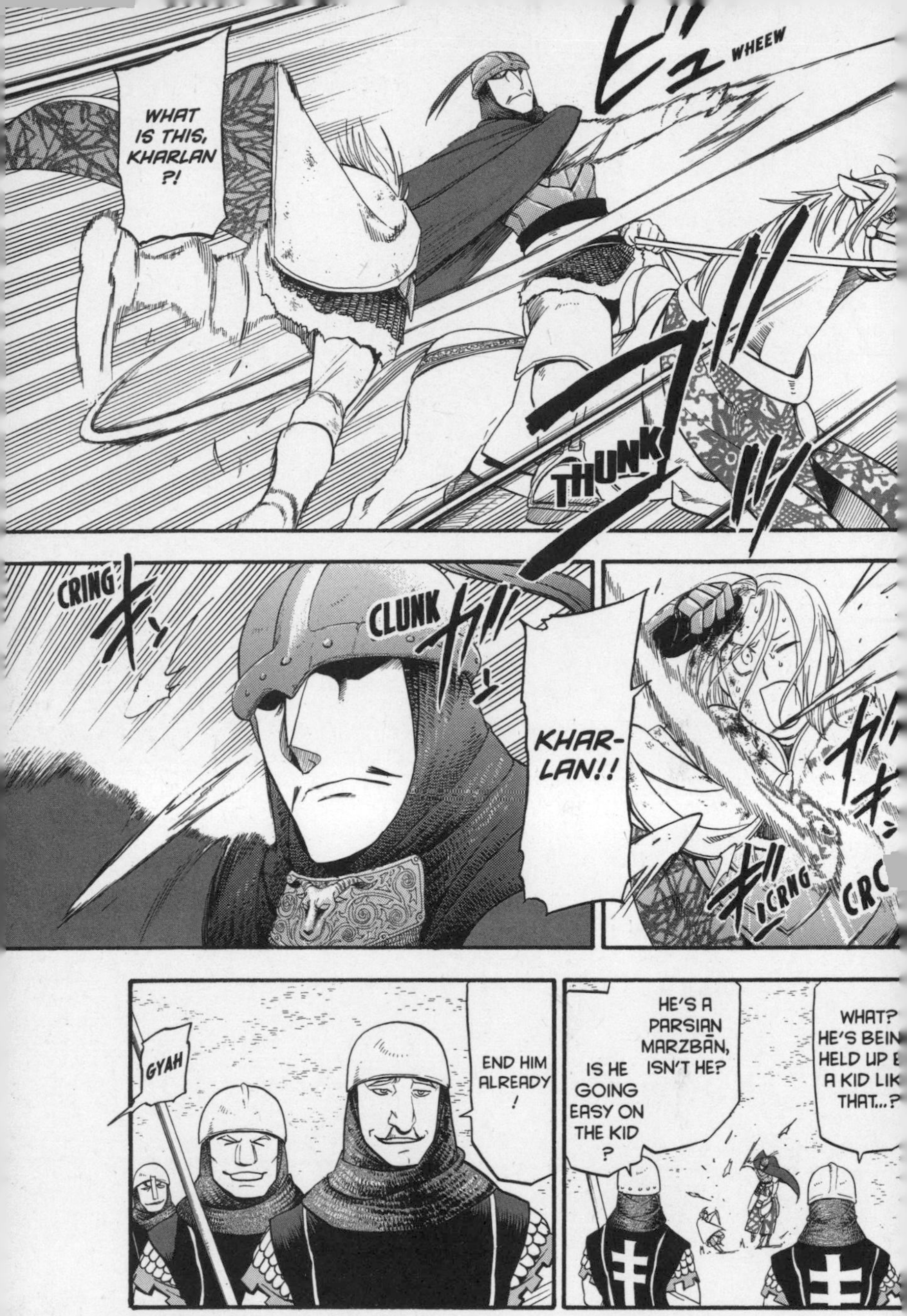
WHEEW
WHAT IS THIS, KHARLAN?!
THUNK
KHAR-LAN!!
CRNG
CRC
CLUNK
CRING
WHAT? HE'S BEIN HELD UP B A KID LIK THAT...?
HE'S A PARSIAN MARZBĀN, ISN'T HE?
IS HE GOING EASY ON THE KID?
END HIM ALREADY!
GYAH

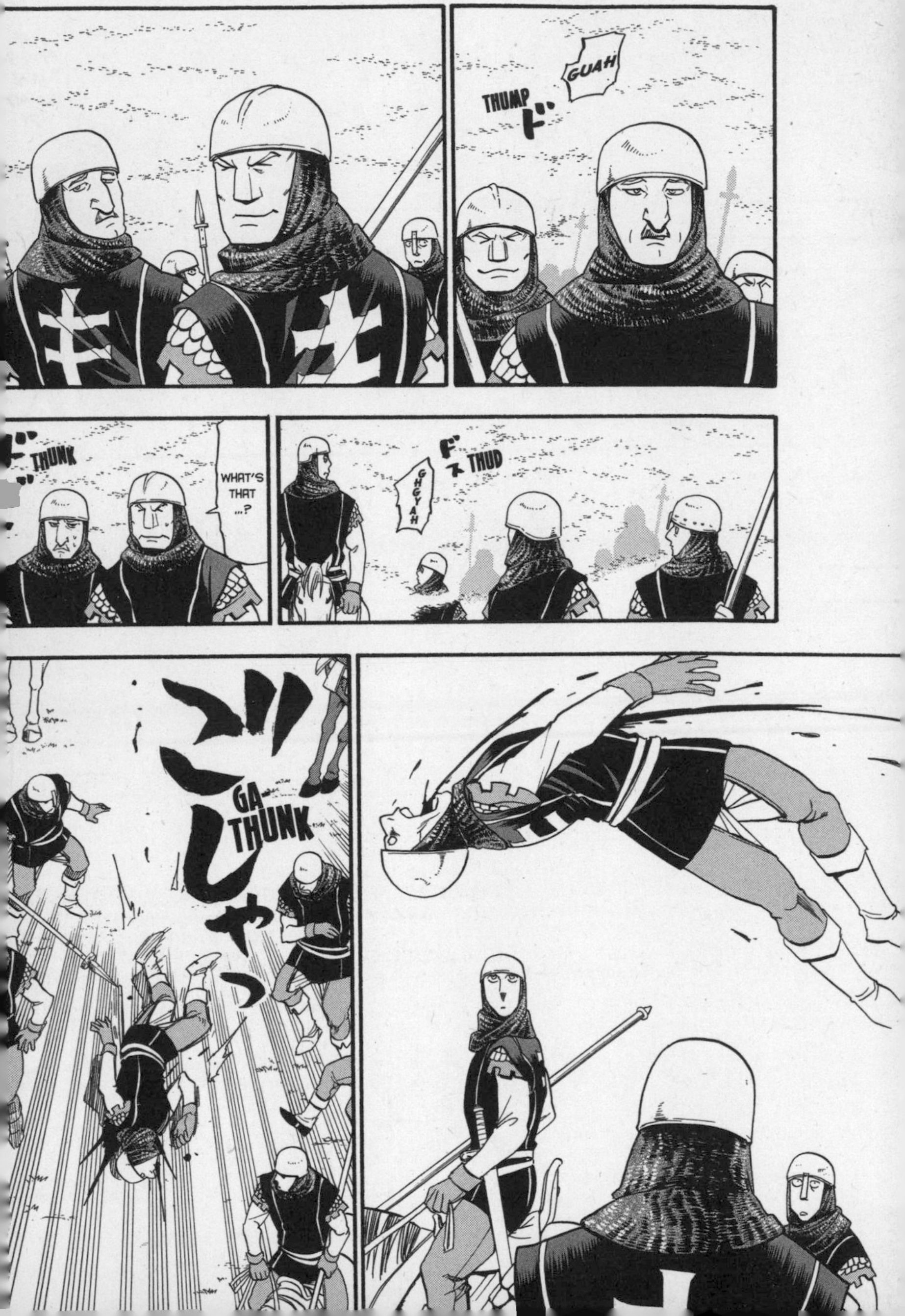
THUMP
GUAH
THUD
GHGYAH
THUNK
WHAT'S THAT ...?
GA THUNK

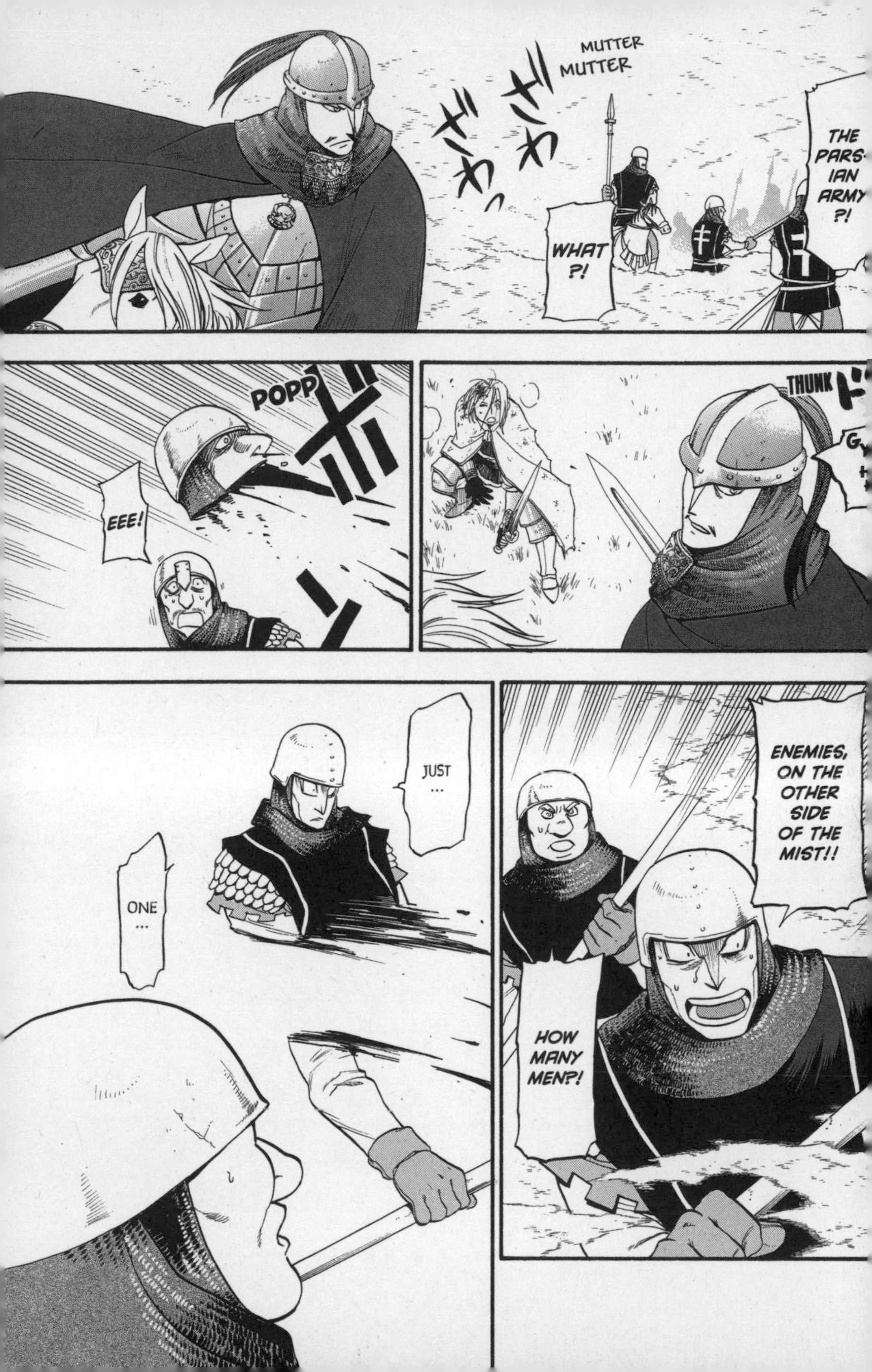
THE PARS-IAN ARMY ?!
MUTTER MUTTER
ざわ ざわっ
WHAT ?!
THUNK ド
POPP
EEE!
ENEMIES, ON THE OTHER SIDE OF THE MIST!!
HOW MANY MEN?!
JUST ...
ONE ...

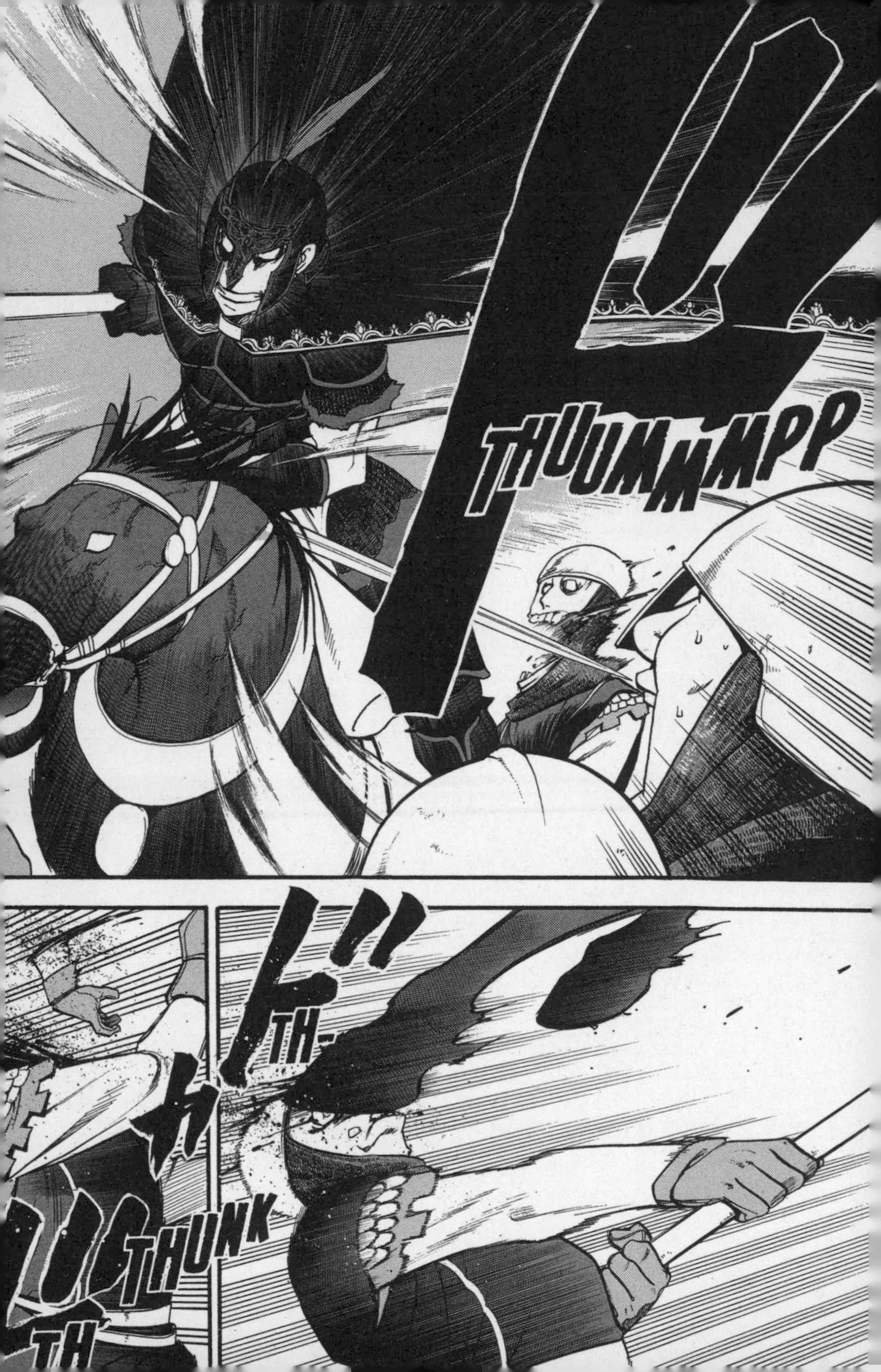
THUUMMMPP
TH-
THUNK
TH

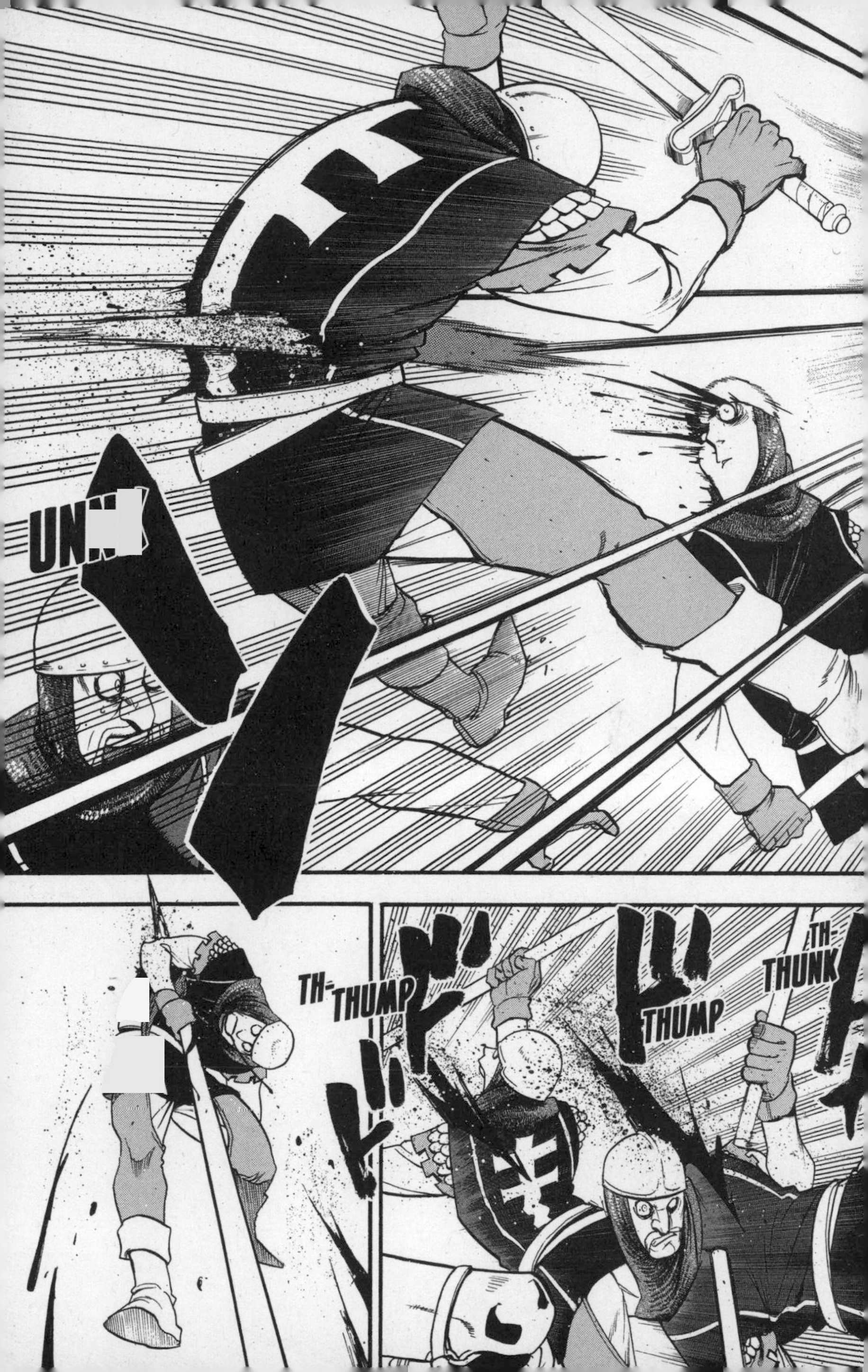
UNN
TH-THUNK
THUMP
TH-THUMP

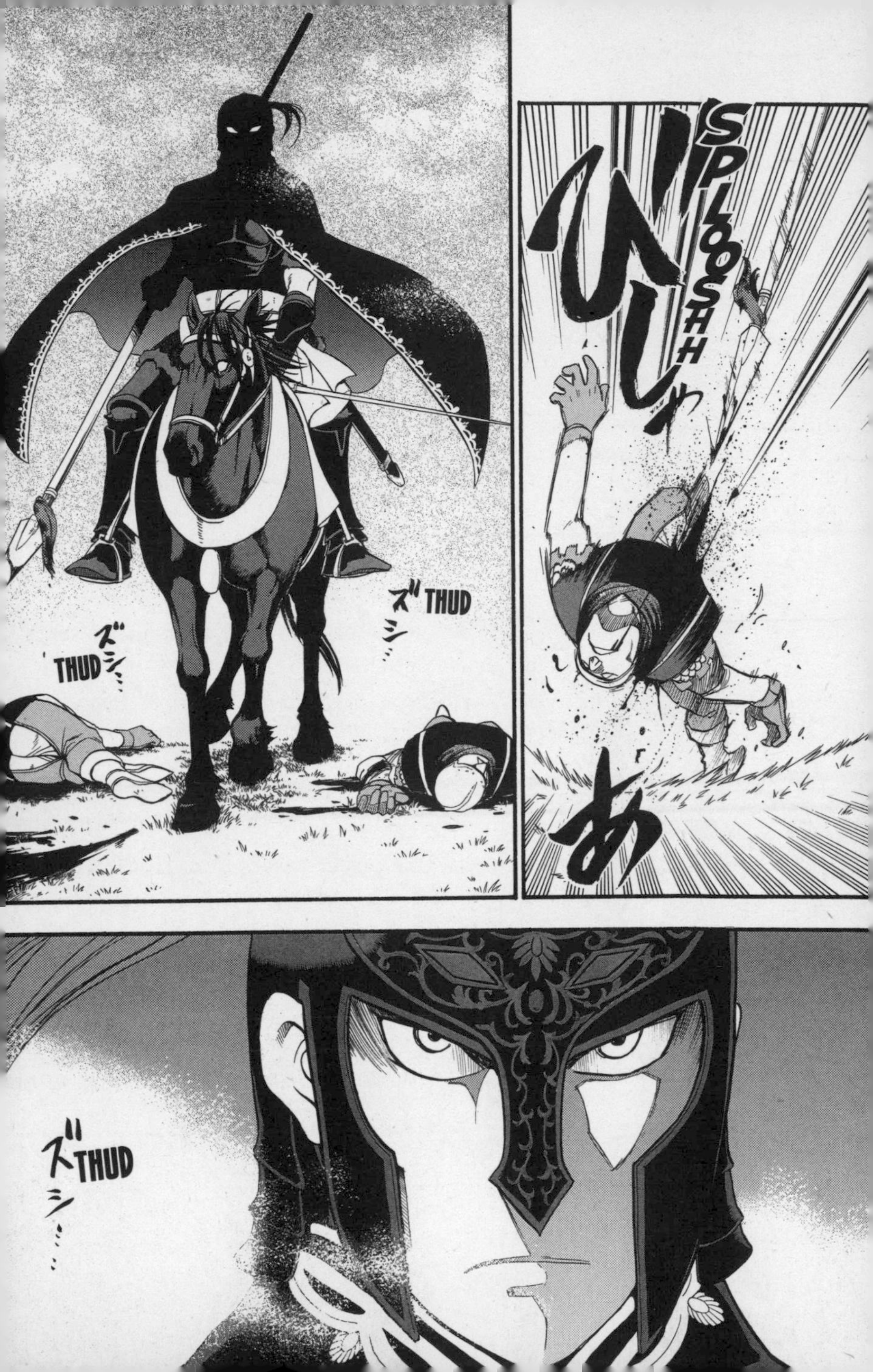
SPLOOSHH
ひしゃ
あ
ズシ…
THUD
ズシ…
THUD
ズシ…
THUD

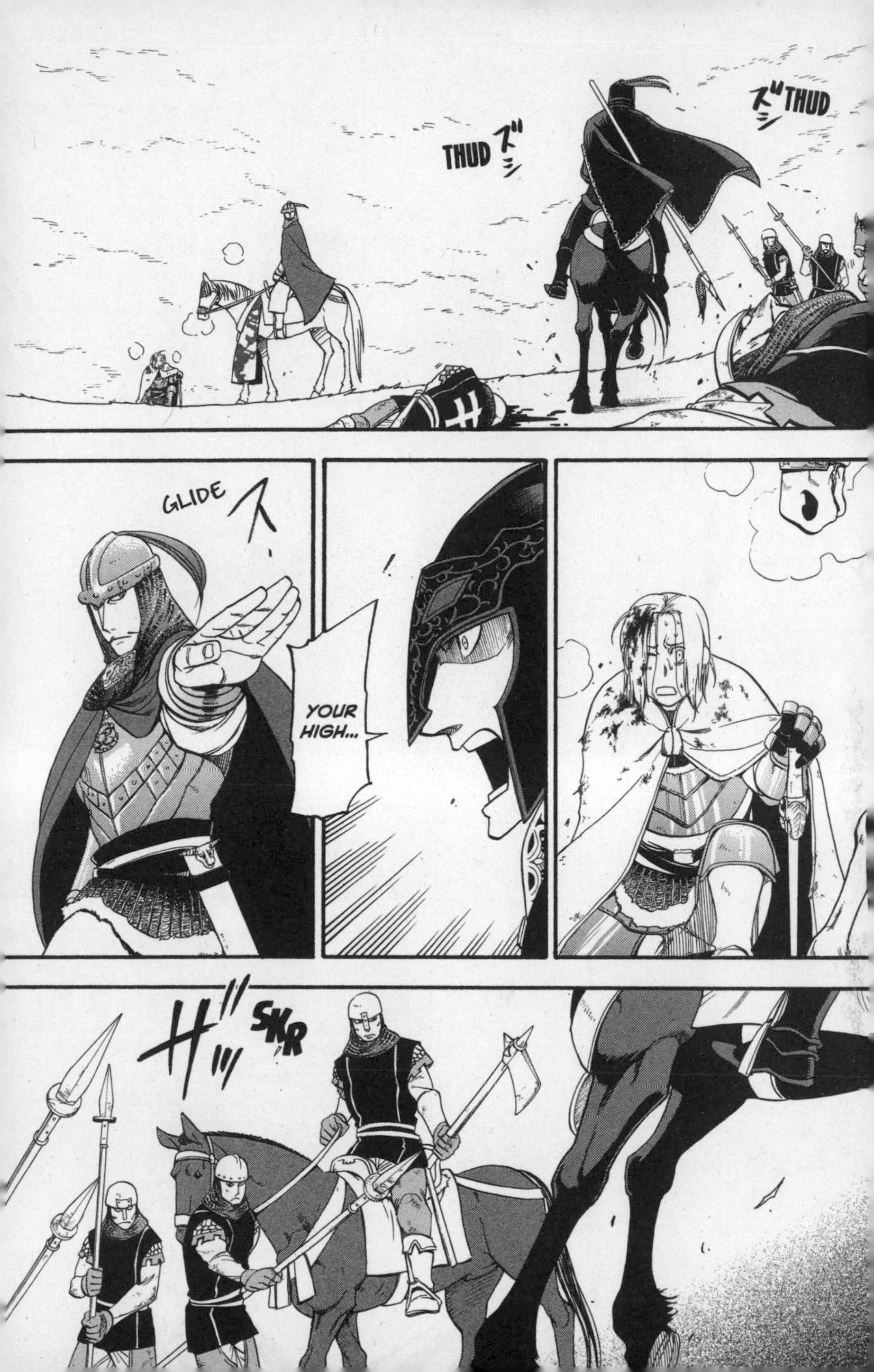
ズシ THUD
THUD ズシ
YOUR HIGH...
GLIDE ス
ザ SKR

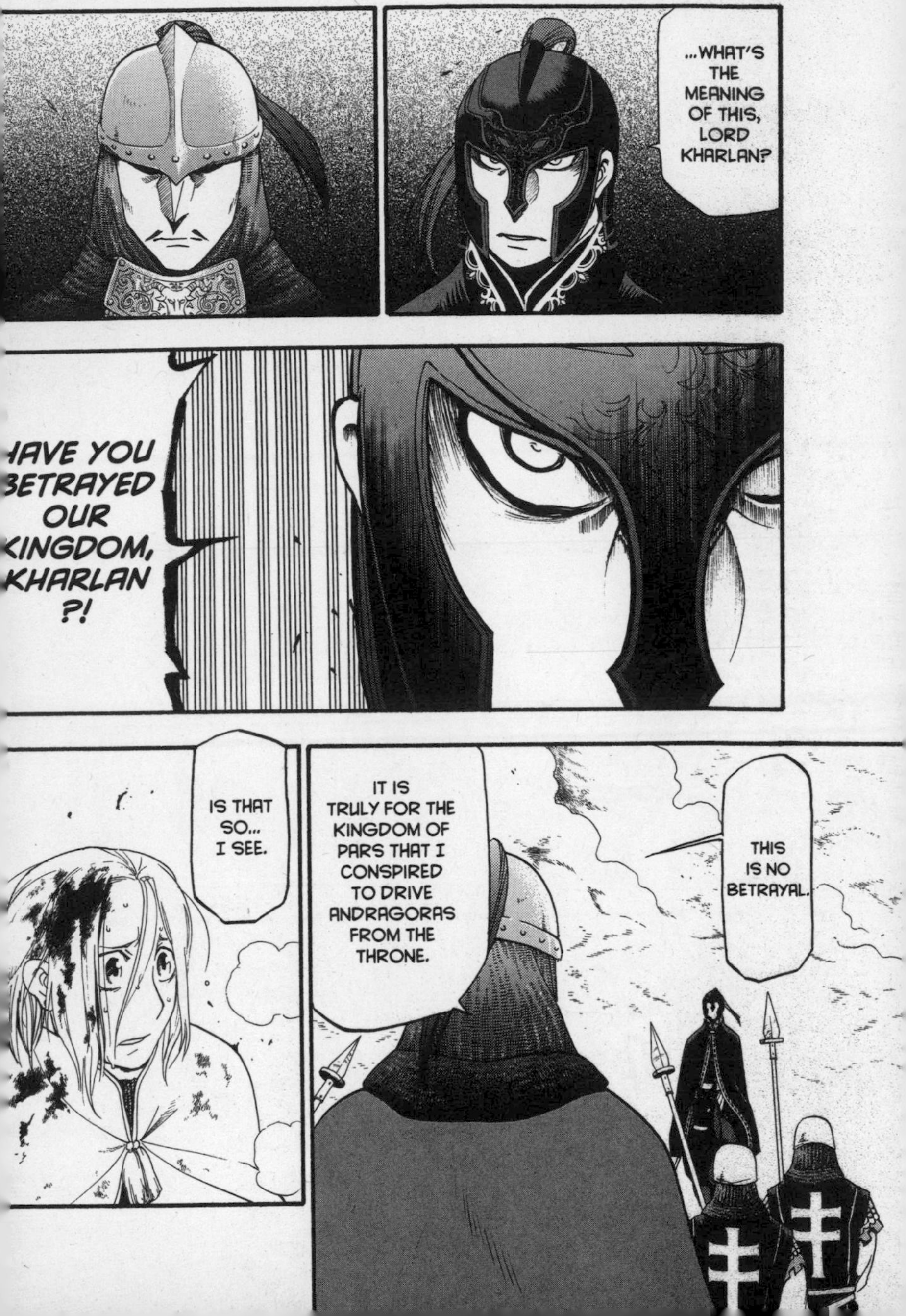
...WHAT'S THE MEANING OF THIS, LORD KHARLAN?
HAVE YOU BETRAYED OUR KINGDOM, KHARLAN?!
THIS IS NO BETRAYAL.
IT IS TRULY FOR THE KINGDOM OF PARS THAT I CONSPIRED TO DRIVE ANDRAGORAS FROM THE THRONE.
IS THAT SO... I SEE.

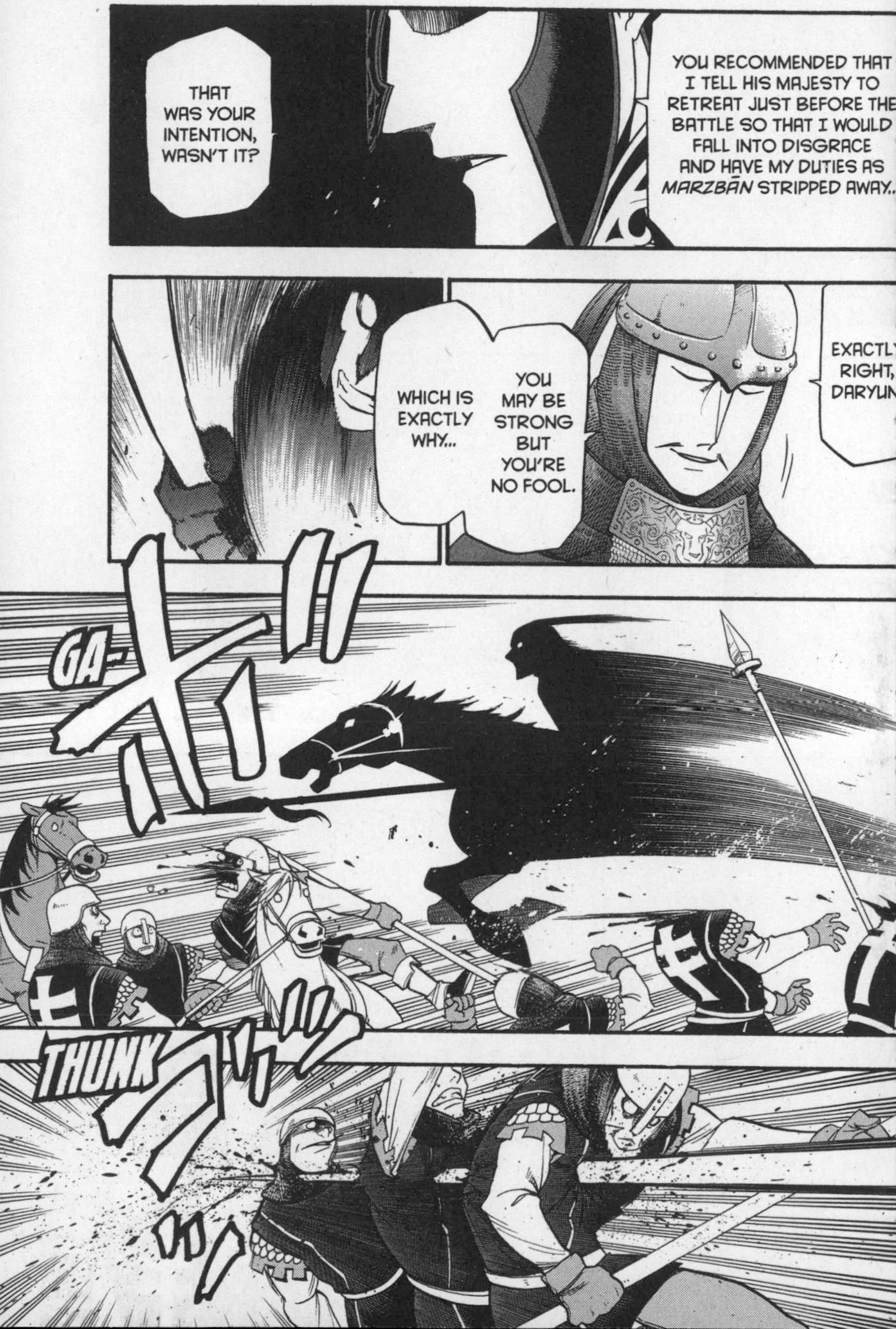
YOU RECOMMENDED THAT I TELL HIS MAJESTY TO RETREAT JUST BEFORE THE BATTLE SO THAT I WOULD FALL INTO DISGRACE AND HAVE MY DUTIES AS *MARZBĀN* STRIPPED AWAY...
THAT WAS YOUR INTENTION, WASN'T IT?
EXACTLY RIGHT, DARYUN
YOU MAY BE STRONG BUT YOU'RE NO FOOL.
WHICH IS EXACTLY WHY...
GA-
THUNK

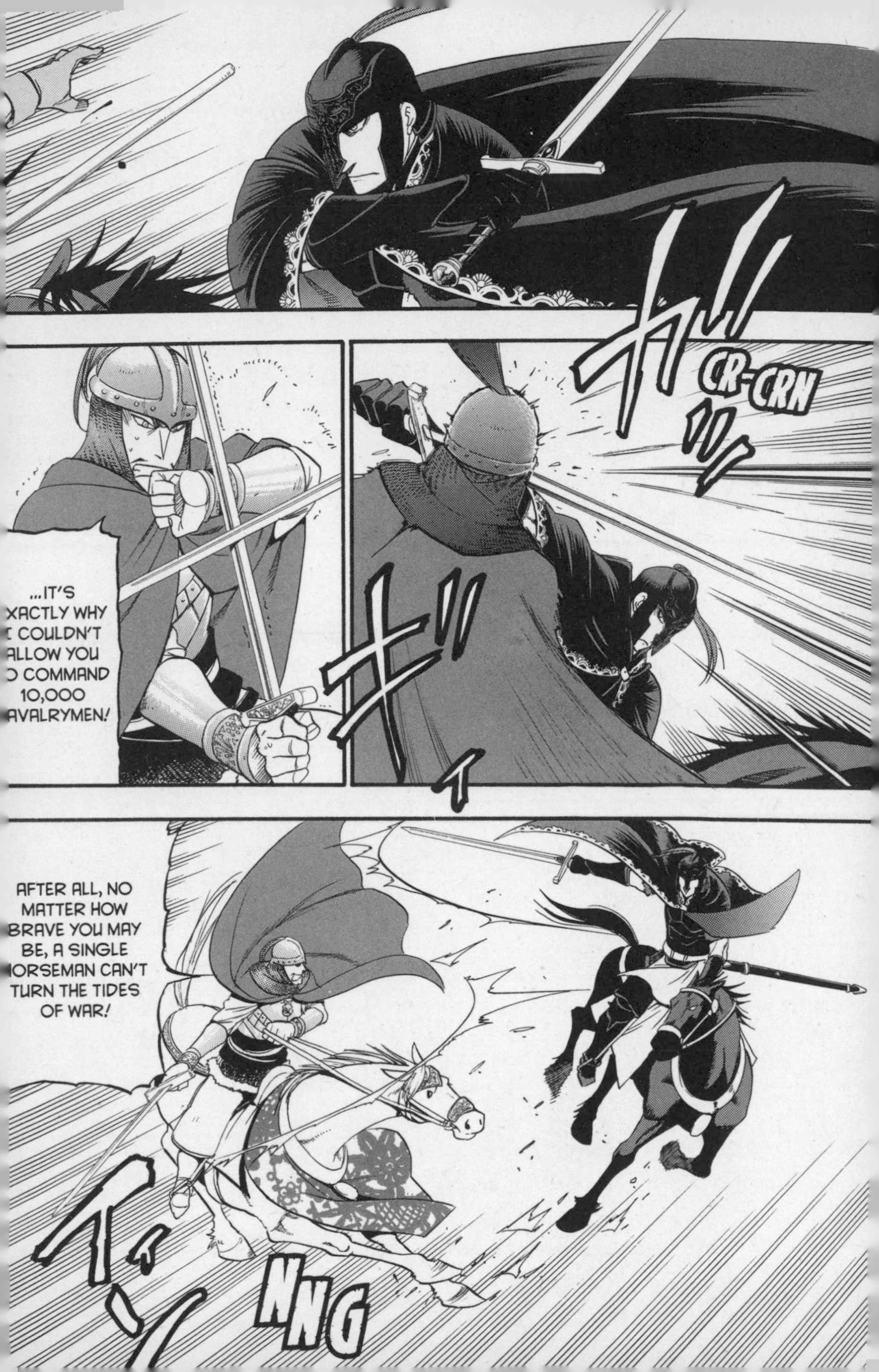
CR-CRN
...IT'S XACTLY WHY COULDN'T ALLOW YOU O COMMAND 10,000 AVALRYMEN!
AFTER ALL, NO MATTER HOW BRAVE YOU MAY BE, A SINGLE ORSEMAN CAN'T TURN THE TIDES OF WAR!
NNG

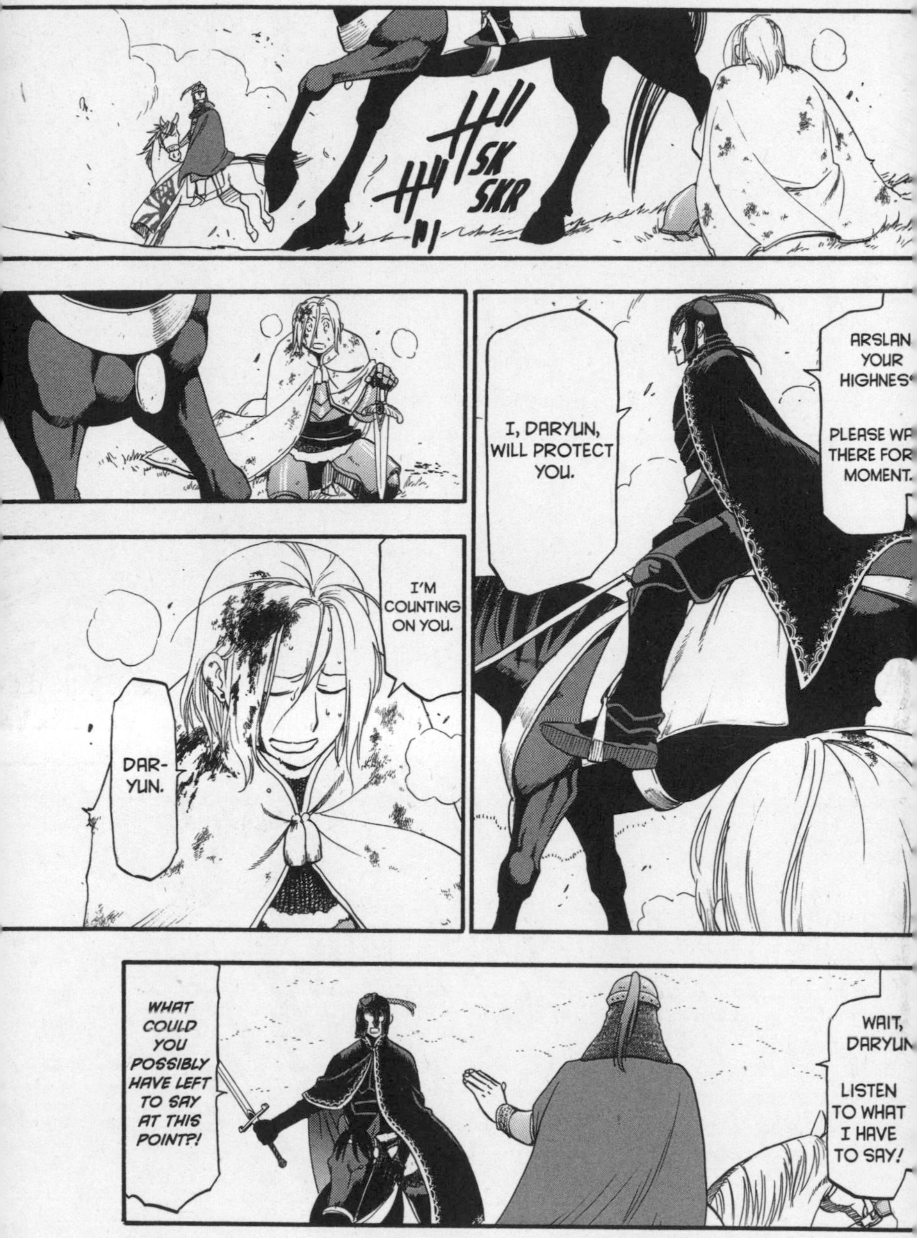
SK SKR
ARSLAN YOUR HIGHNES
PLEASE WA THERE FOR MOMENT.
I, DARYUN, WILL PROTECT YOU.
I'M COUNTING ON YOU.
DAR-YUN.
WAIT, DARYUN
LISTEN TO WHAT I HAVE TO SAY!
WHAT COULD YOU POSSIBLY HAVE LEFT TO SAY AT THIS POINT?!

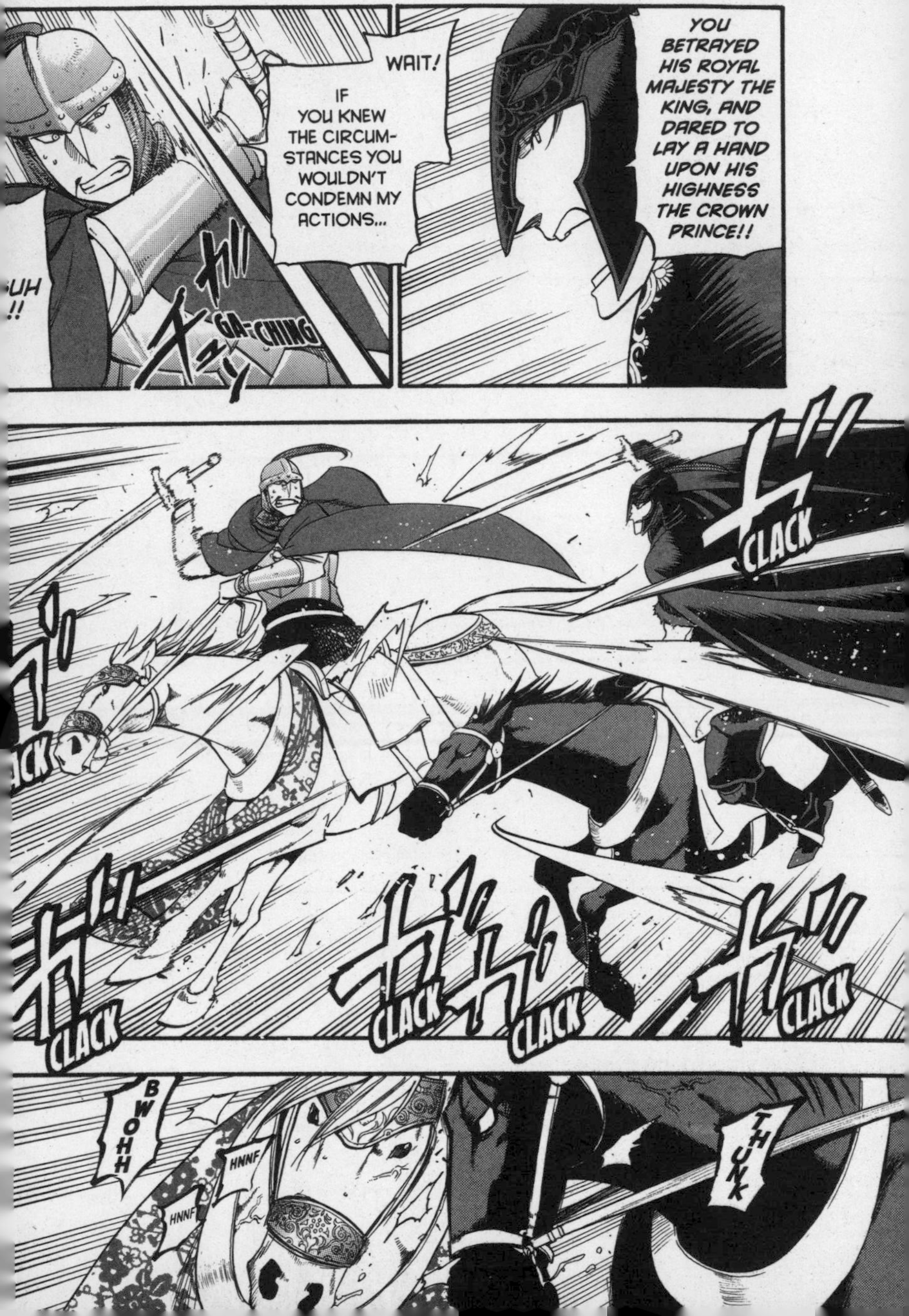
YOU BETRAYED HIS ROYAL MAJESTY THE KING, AND DARED TO LAY A HAND UPON HIS HIGHNESS THE CROWN PRINCE!!
WAIT!
IF YOU KNEW THE CIRCUM-STANCES YOU WOULDN'T CONDEMN MY ACTIONS...
GA-CHING
CLACK
CLACK
CLACK
CLACK
CLACK
CLACK
THUNK
BWOHH
HNNF
HNNF

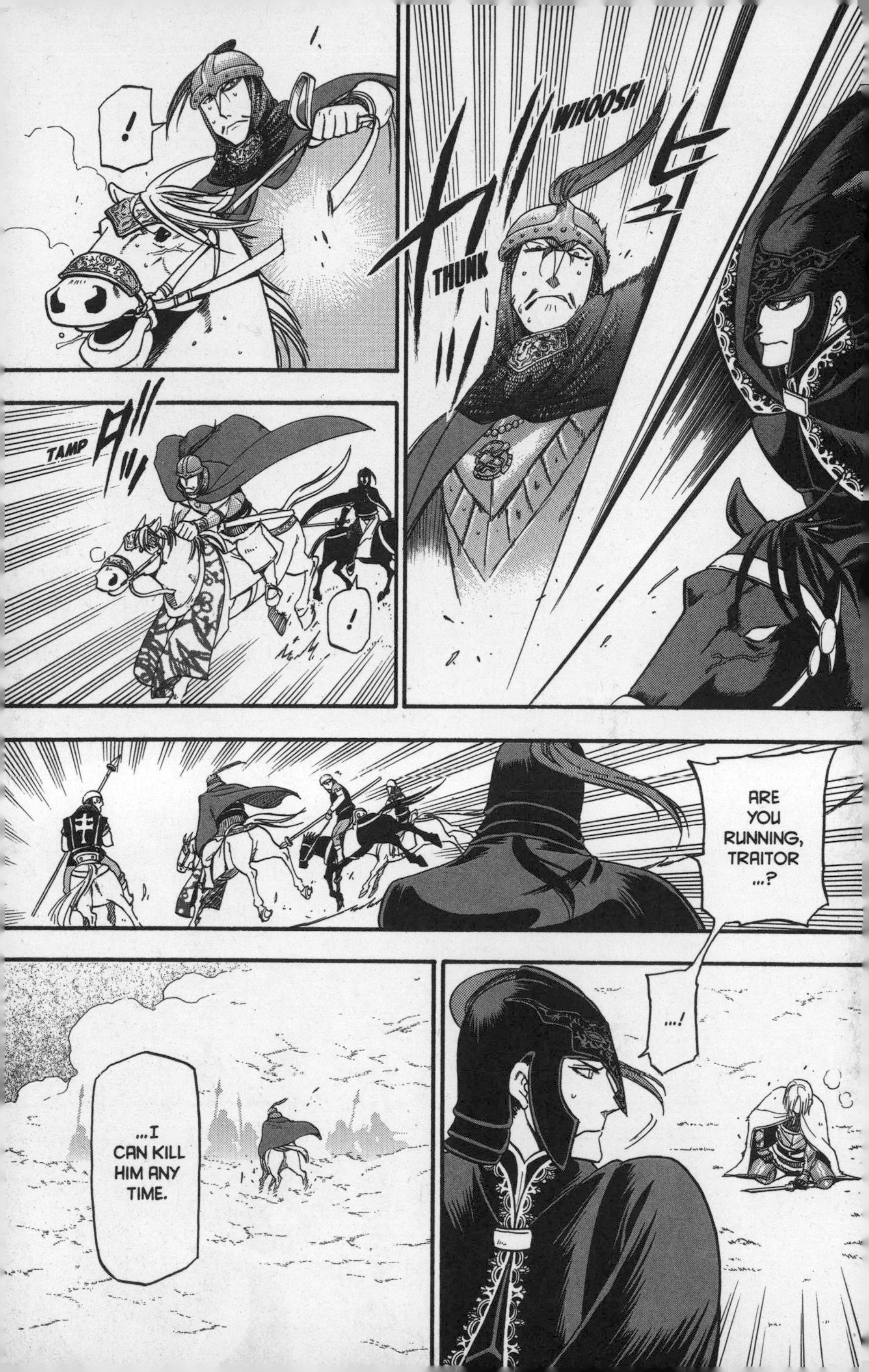
WHOOSH
THUNK
!
TAMP
!
ARE YOU RUNNING, TRAITOR ...?
...!
...I CAN KILL HIM ANY TIME.

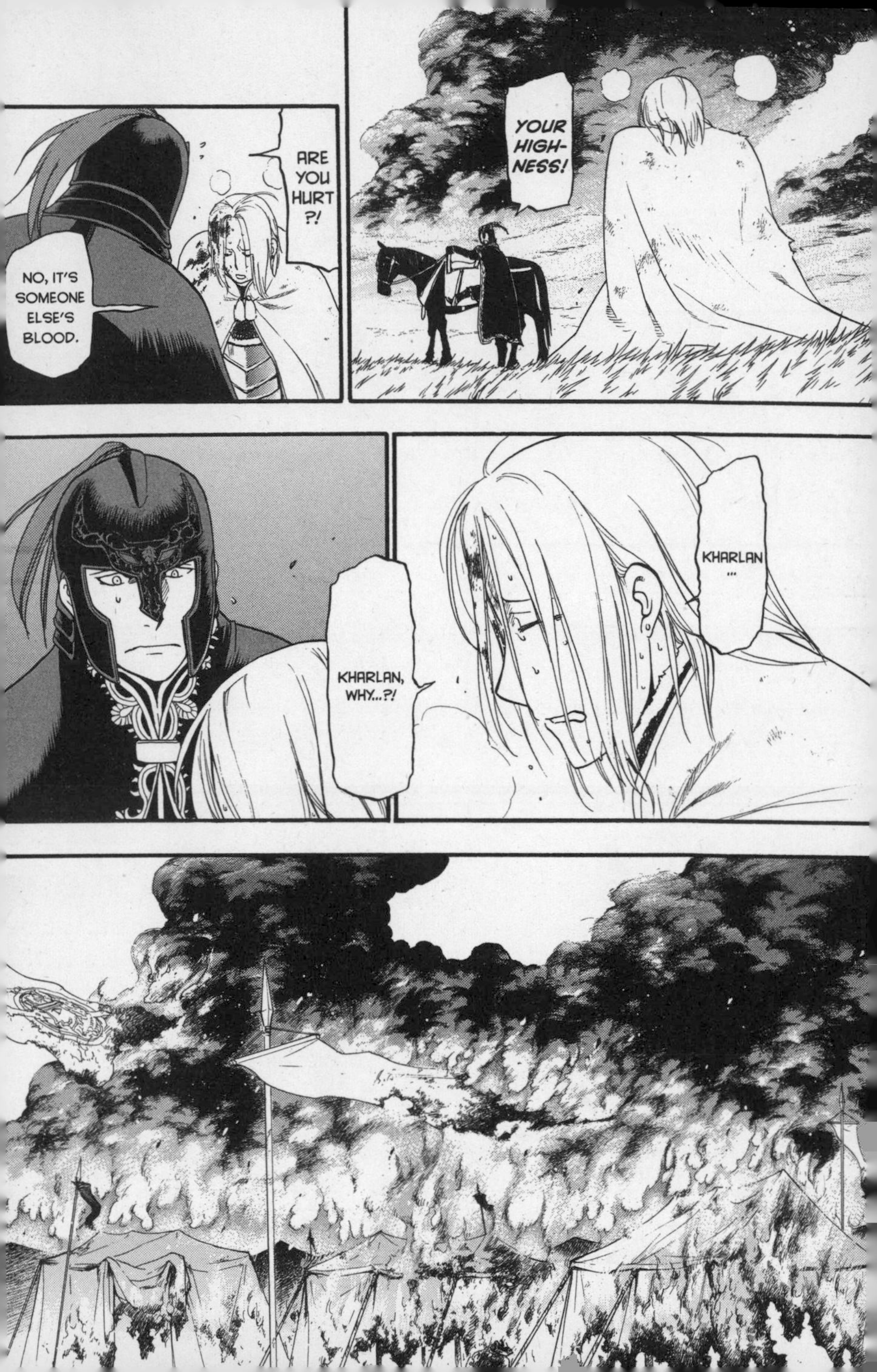
YOUR HIGH-NESS!
ARE YOU HURT?!
NO, IT'S SOMEONE ELSE'S BLOOD.
KHARLAN...
KHARLAN, WHY...?!

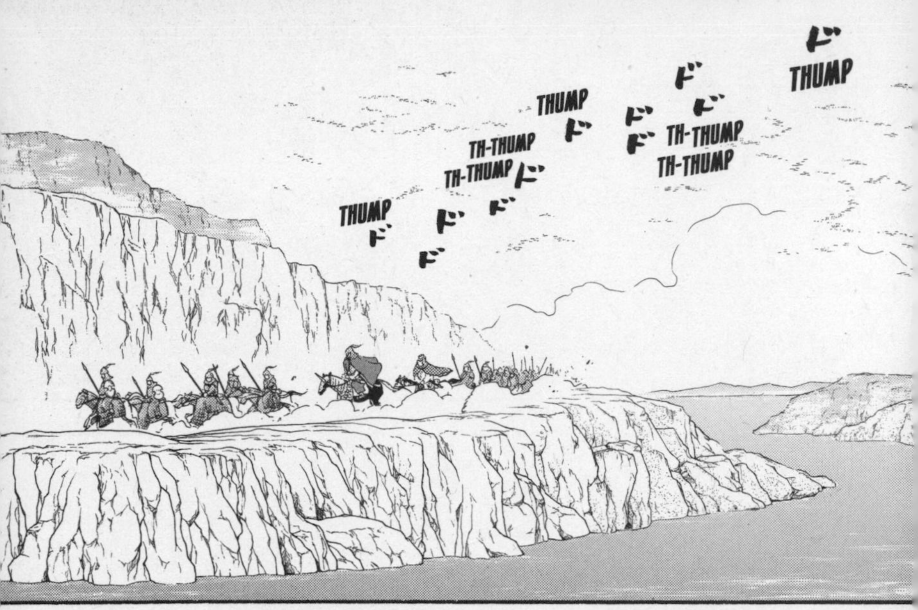
ド
THUMP
ド
ド ド
THUMP
ド
ド ド
TH-THUMP
TH-THUMP
TH-THUMP
TH-THUMP
ド
ド ド
THUMP
ド
ド

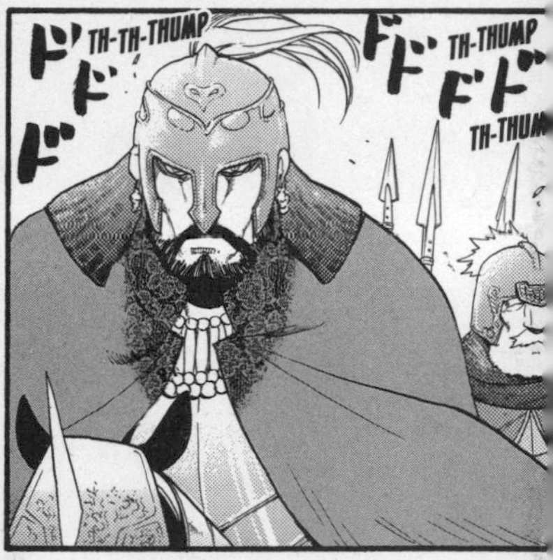
ドド
TH-THUMP
ドド
TH-THUM
ド
TH-TH-THUMP
ド
ド

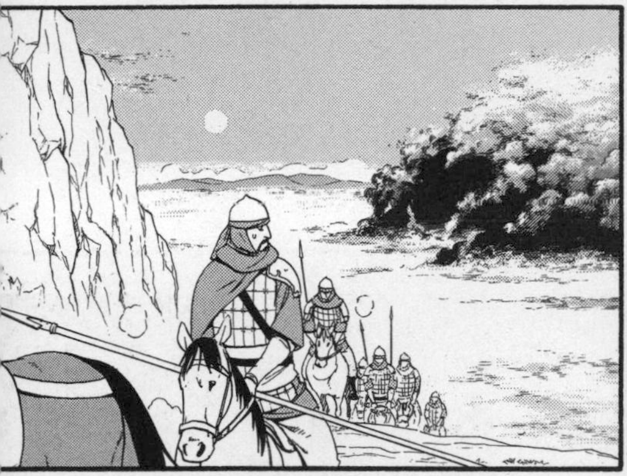

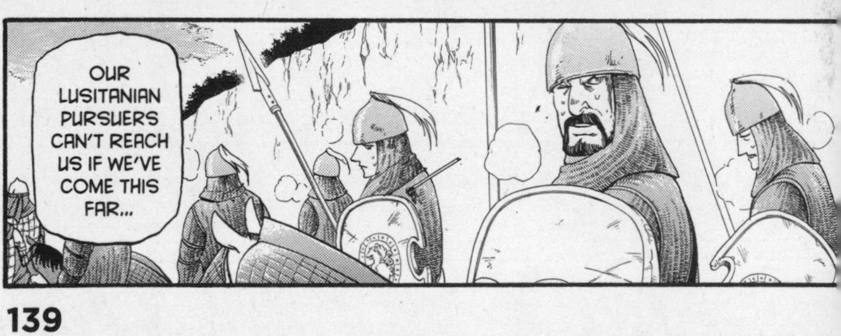
OUR LUSITANIAN PURSUERS CAN'T REACH US IF WE'VE COME THIS FAR...

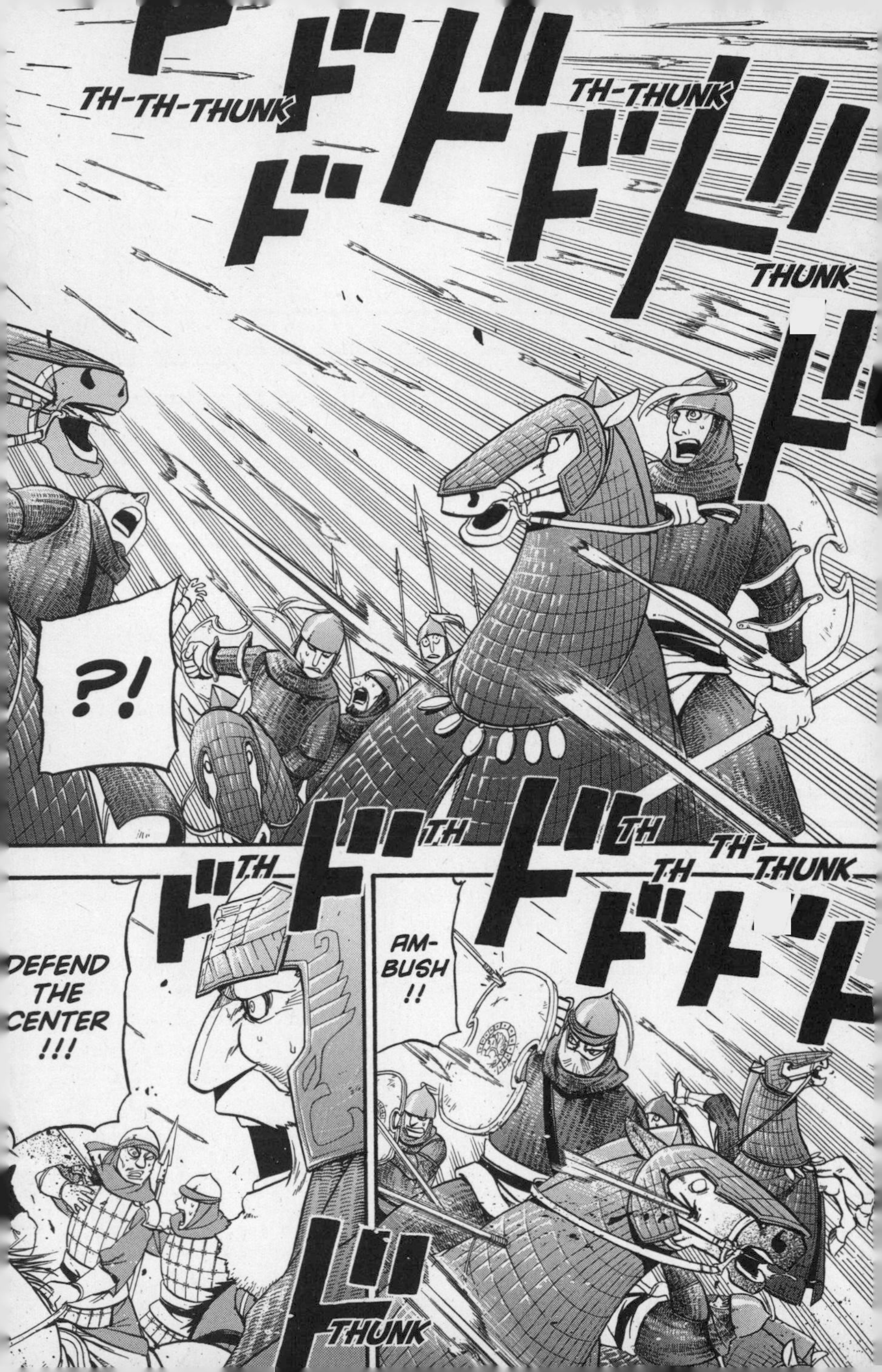
TH-THUNK
THUNK
TH-TH-THUNK
?!
TH
TH
TH-
TH
THUNK
AM-BUSH!!
TH
DEFEND THE CENTER!!!
THUNK

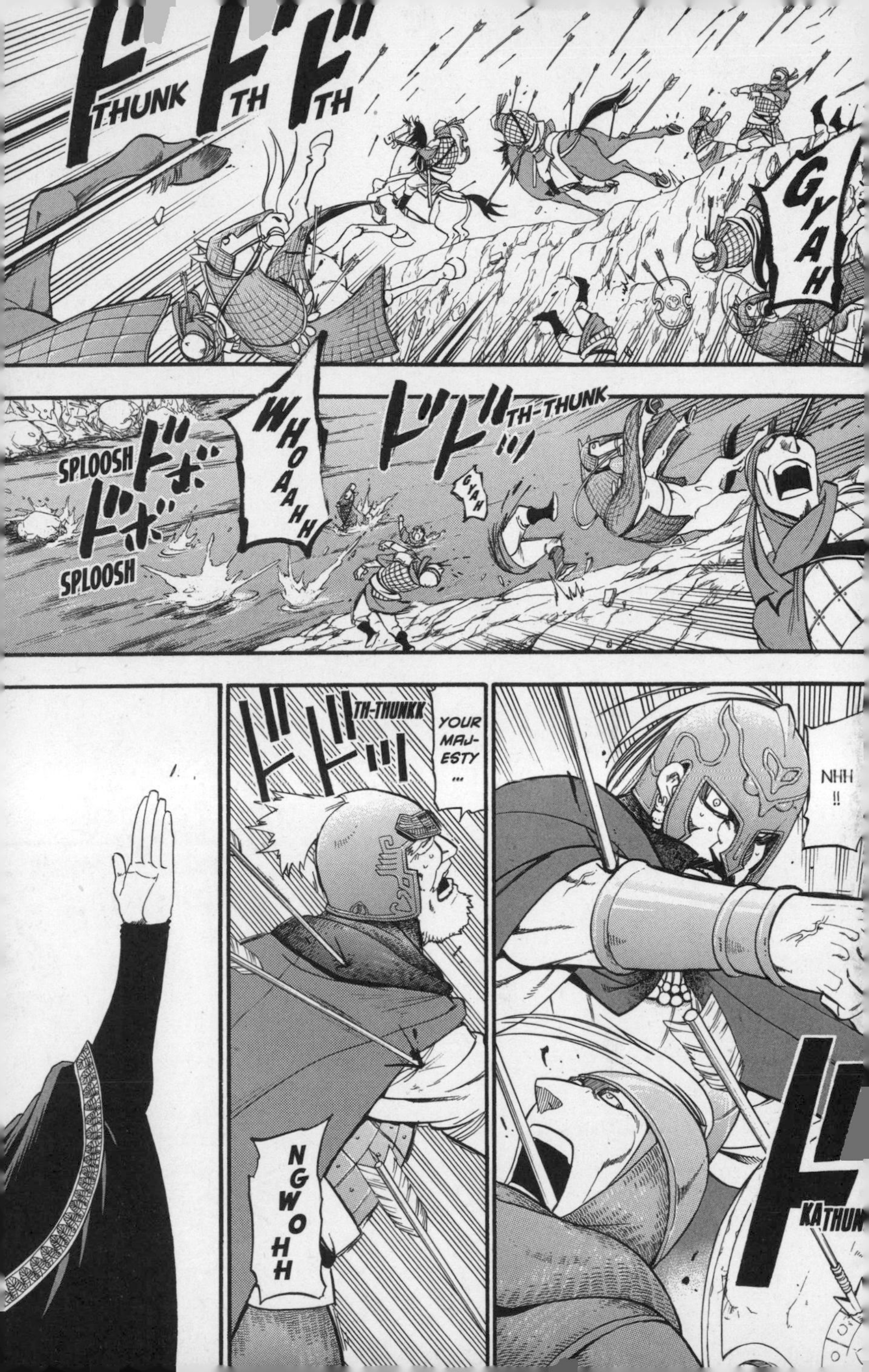
GYAH
ドドド
TH
TH
THUNK
ドドドッ
TH-THUNK
GYAH
WHOAAAHH
ドボドボ
SPLOOSH
SPLOOSH
NHH !!
ド
KATHUNK
YOUR MAJ-ESTY ...
ドドドッ
TH-THUNKK
NGWOHH

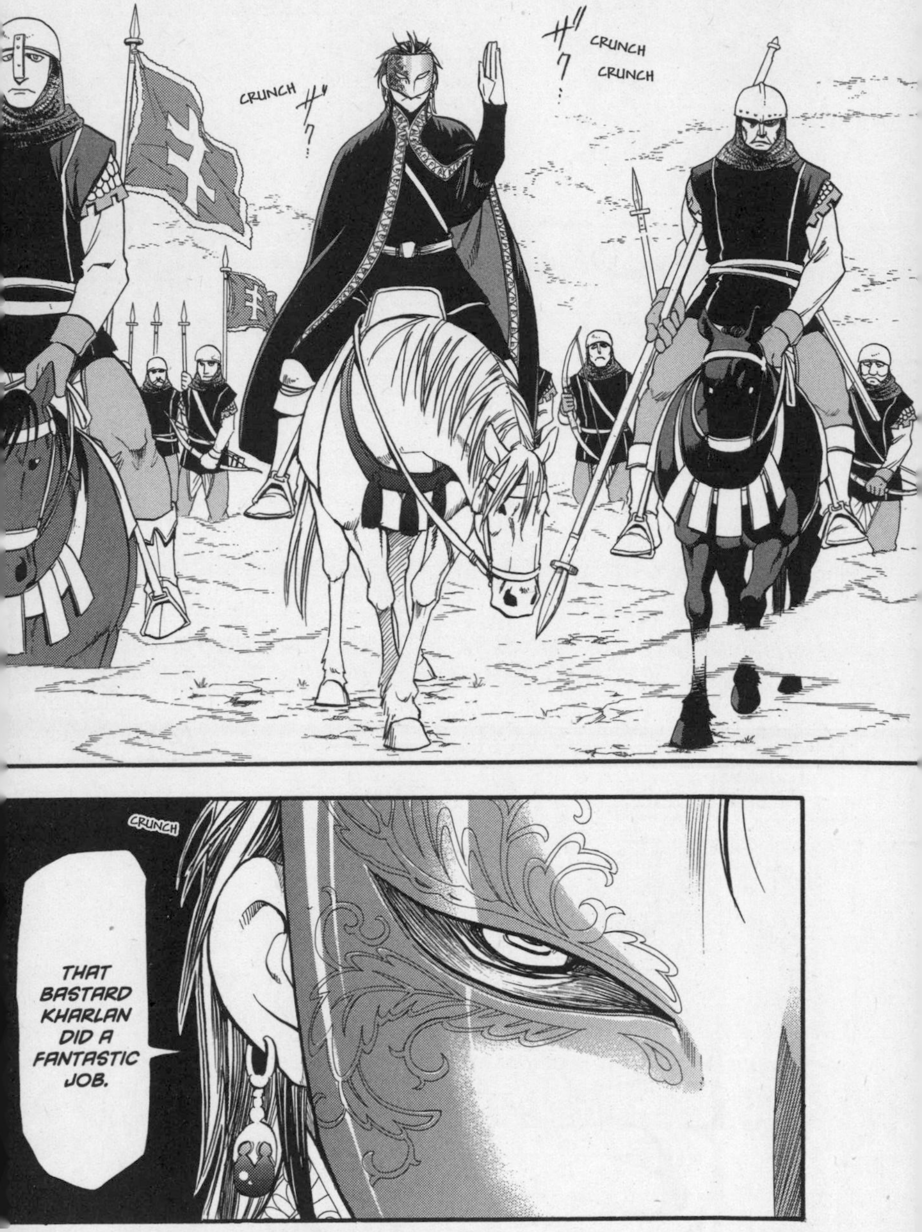
CRUNCH
CRUNCH
CRUNCH
CRUNCH
THAT BASTARD KHARLAN DID A FANTASTIC JOB.

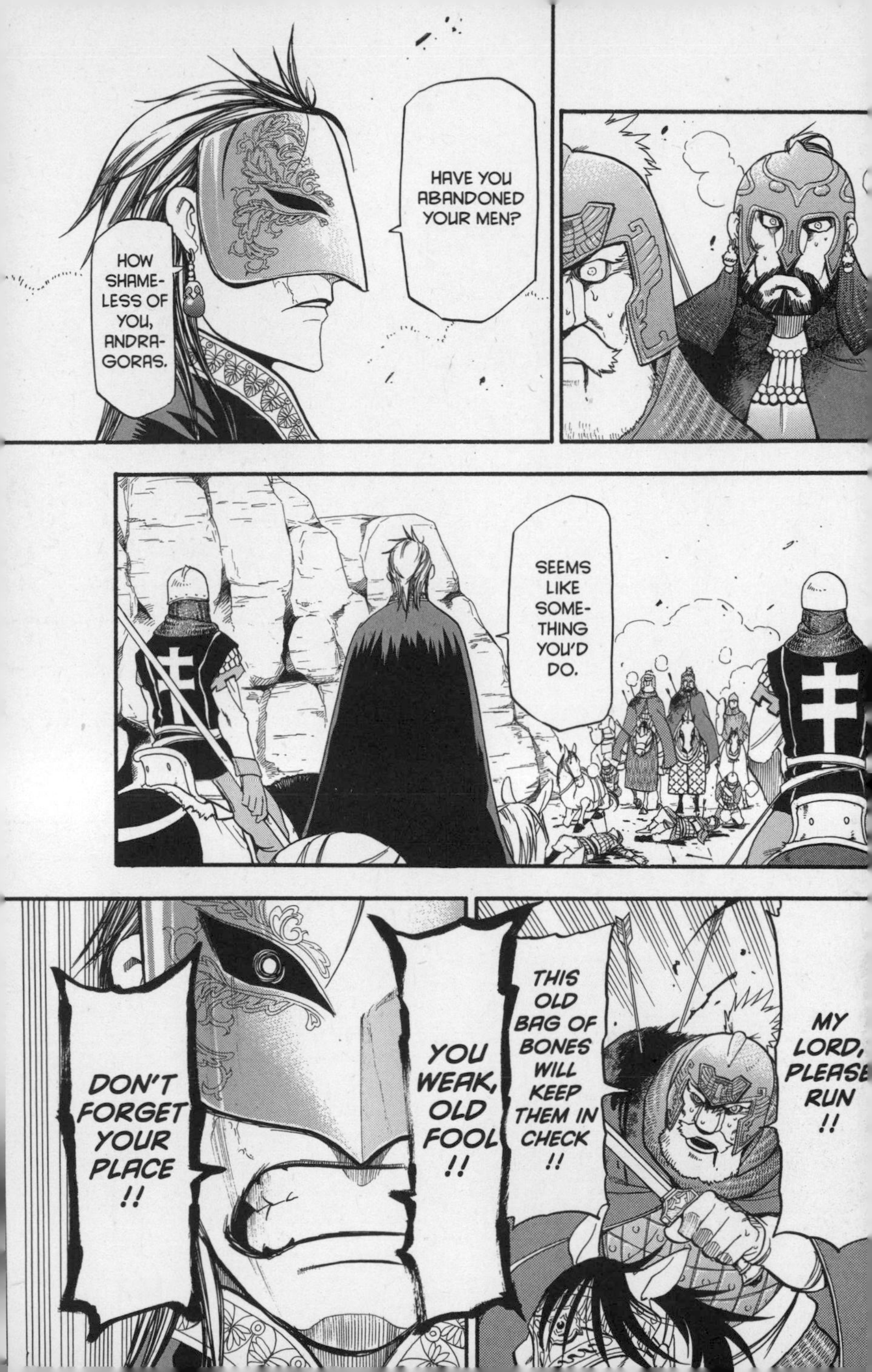
HAVE YOU ABANDONED YOUR MEN?
HOW SHAMELESS OF YOU, ANDRAGORAS.
SEEMS LIKE SOMETHING YOU'D DO.
MY LORD, PLEASE RUN!!
THIS OLD BAG OF BONES WILL KEEP THEM IN CHECK!!
YOU WEAK, OLD FOOL!!
DON'T FORGET YOUR PLACE!!

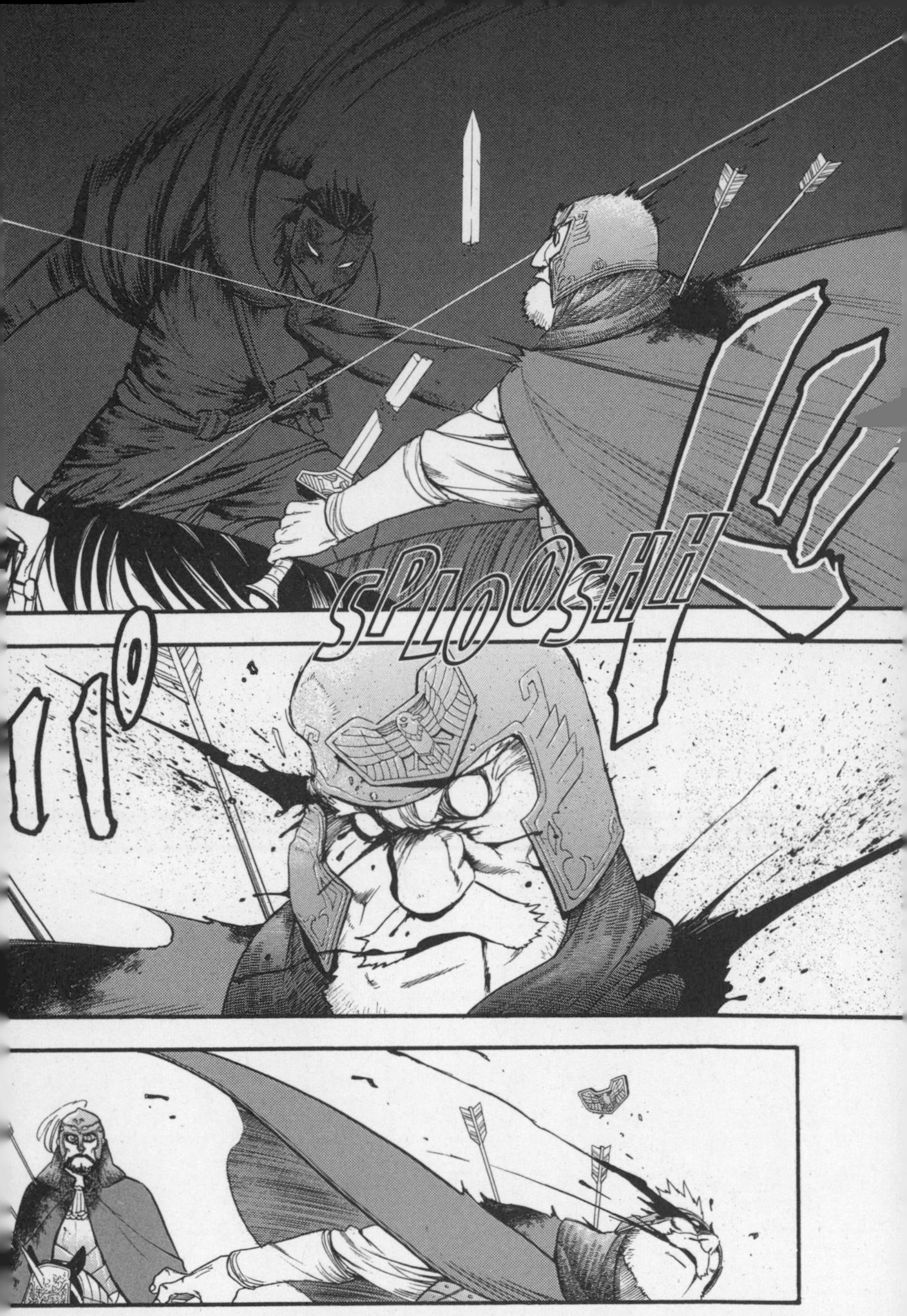
SPLOOSHH

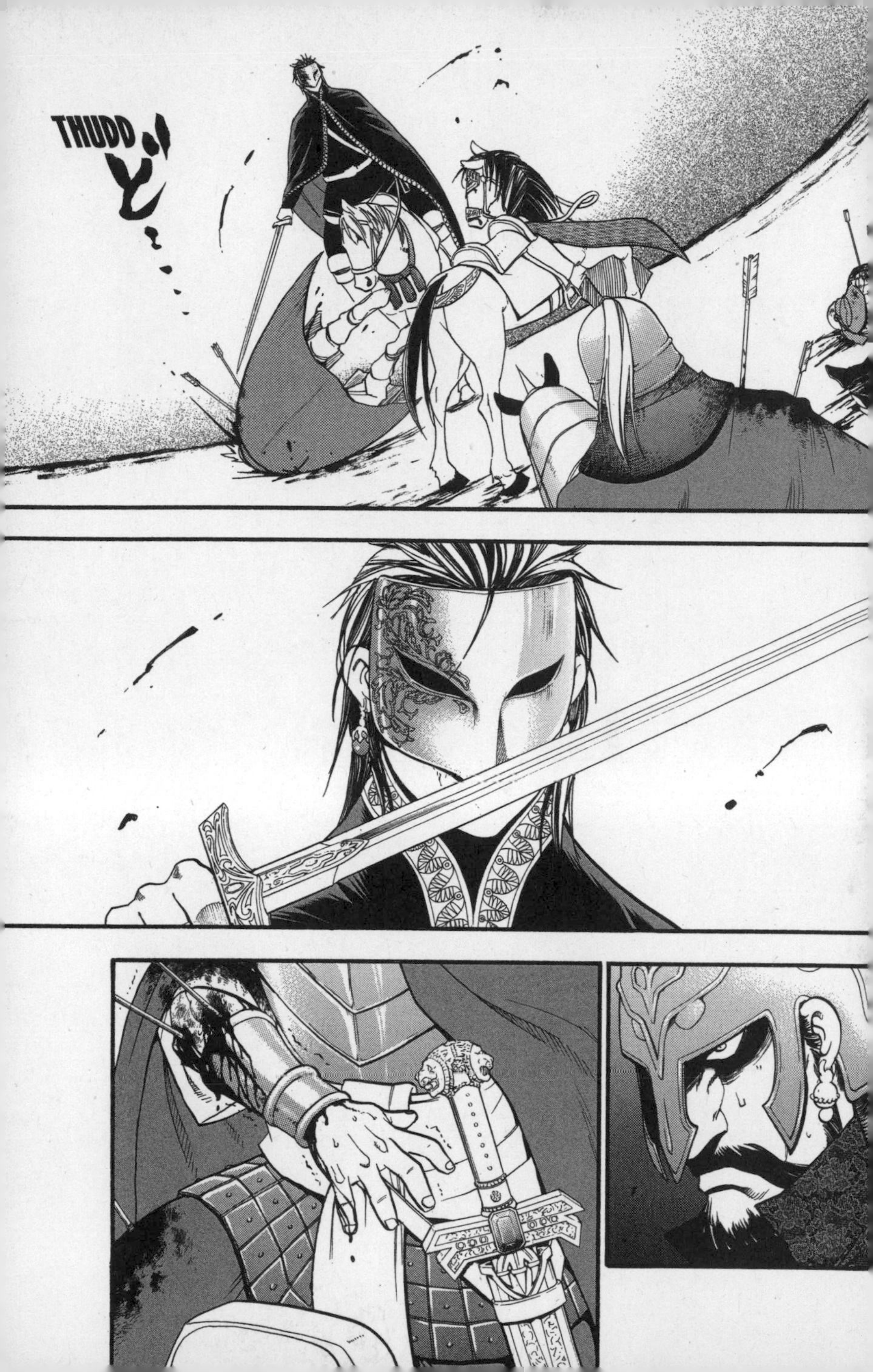
THUDD
ど!

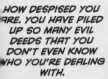
HOW DESPISED YOU ARE. YOU HAVE PILED UP SO MANY EVIL DEEDS THAT YOU DON'T EVEN KNOW WHO YOU'RE DEALING WITH.

YOU...

WHO ARE YOU ...?

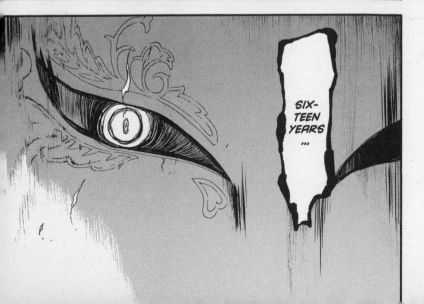
SIX-TEEN YEARS ...

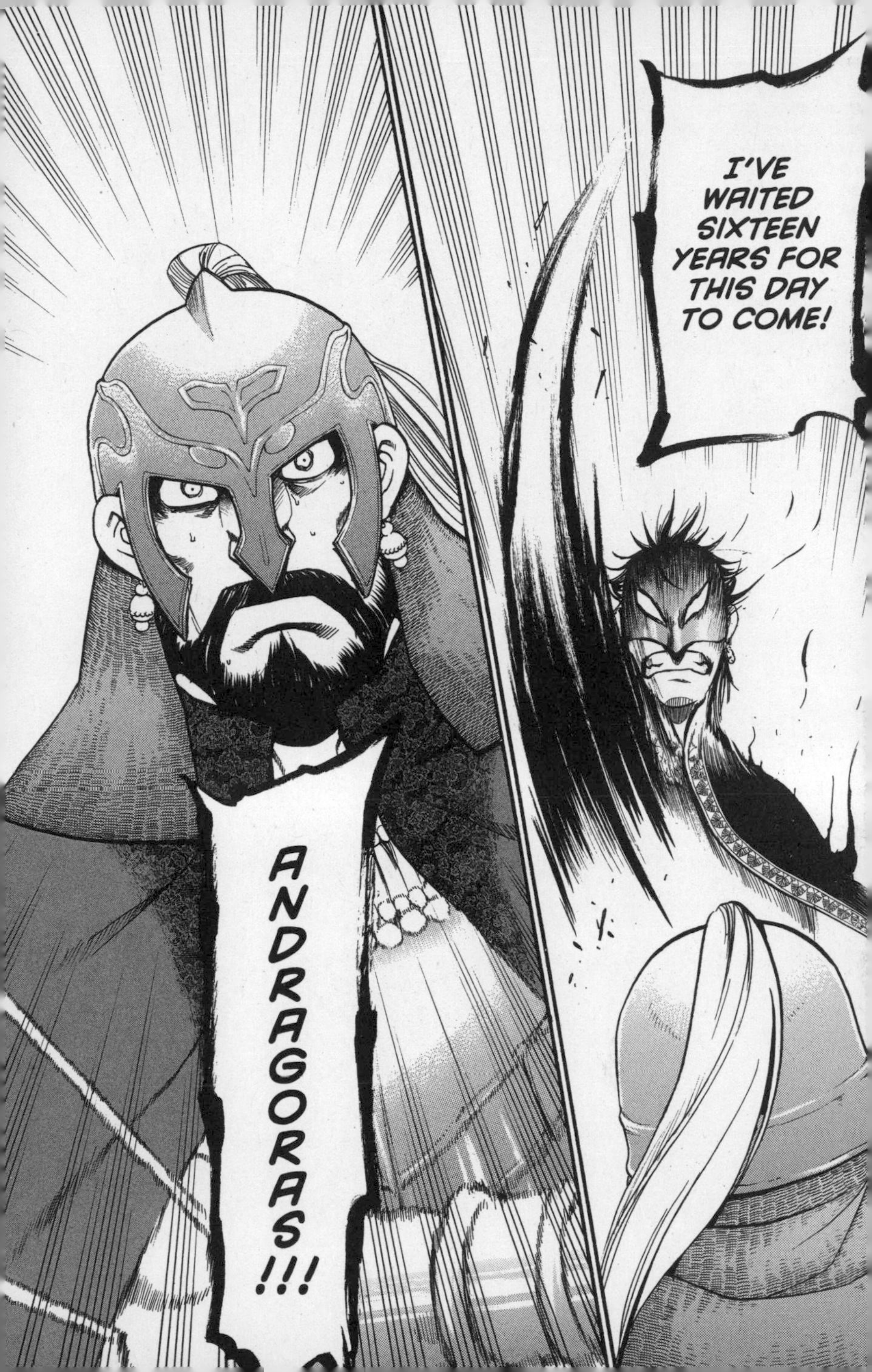
I'VE WAITED SIXTEEN YEARS FOR THIS DAY TO COME!
ANDRAGORAS!!!

THE HEROIC LEGEND OF
ARSLAN

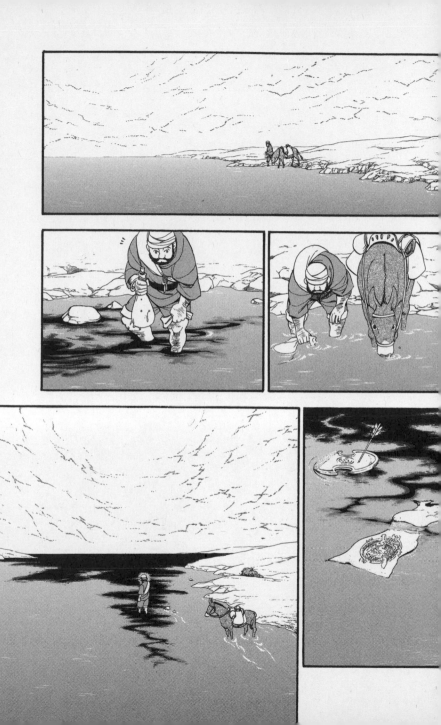

Chapter 4: A Reunion with an Old Friend

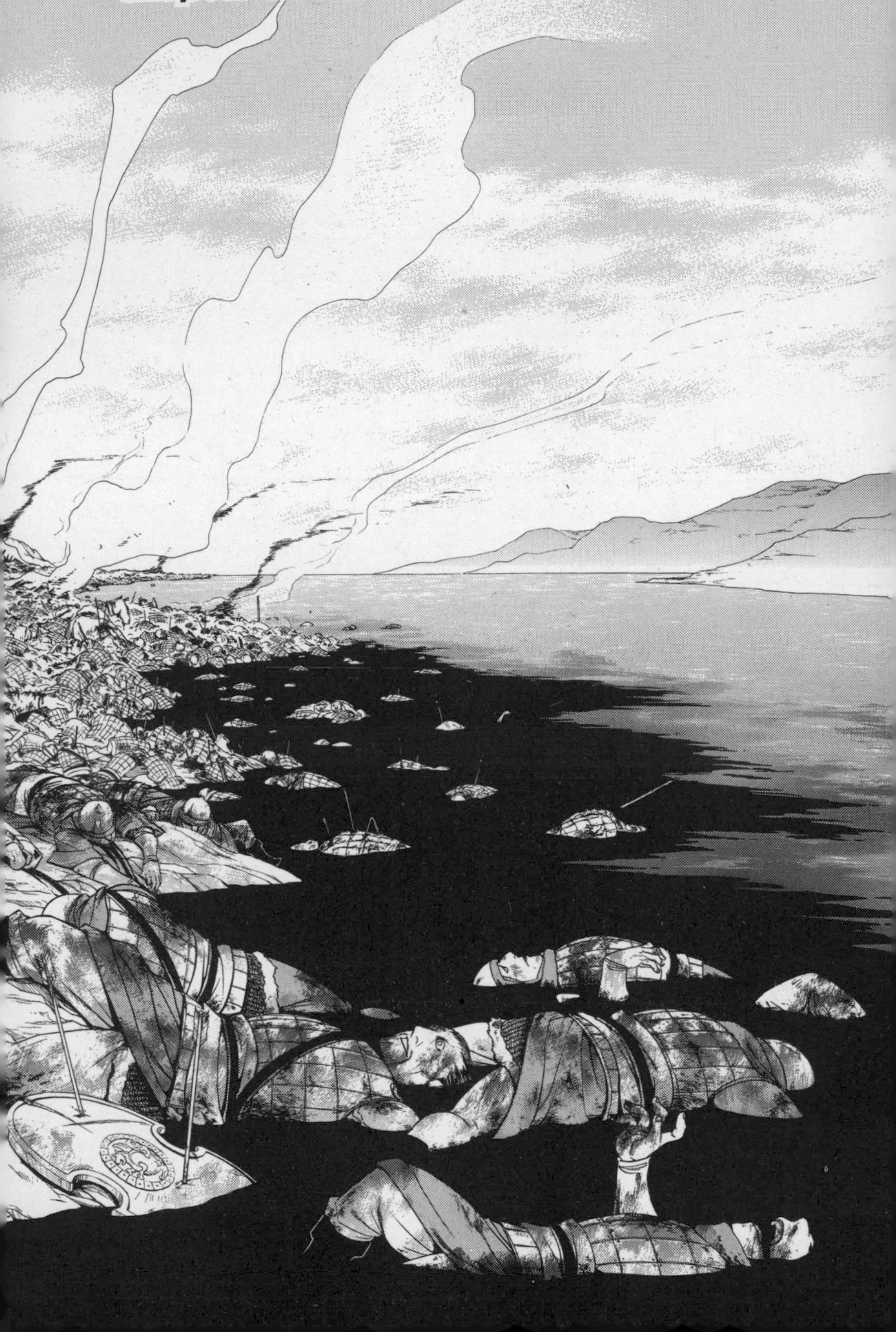

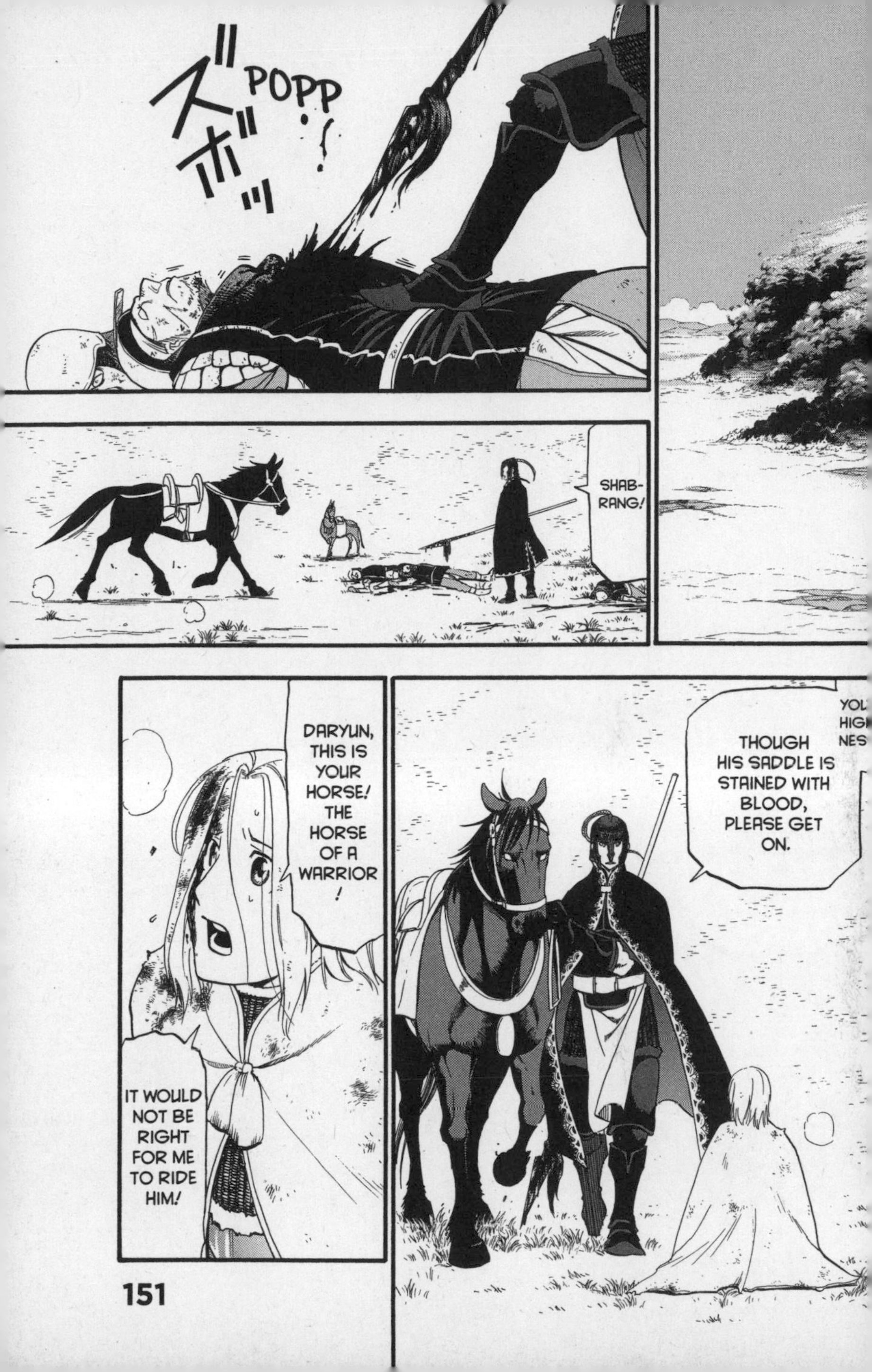
ズボッ
POPP!
SHAB-RANG!
THOUGH HIS SADDLE IS STAINED WITH BLOOD, PLEASE GET ON.
DARYUN, THIS IS YOUR HORSE! THE HORSE OF A WARRIOR!
IT WOULD NOT BE RIGHT FOR ME TO RIDE HIM!

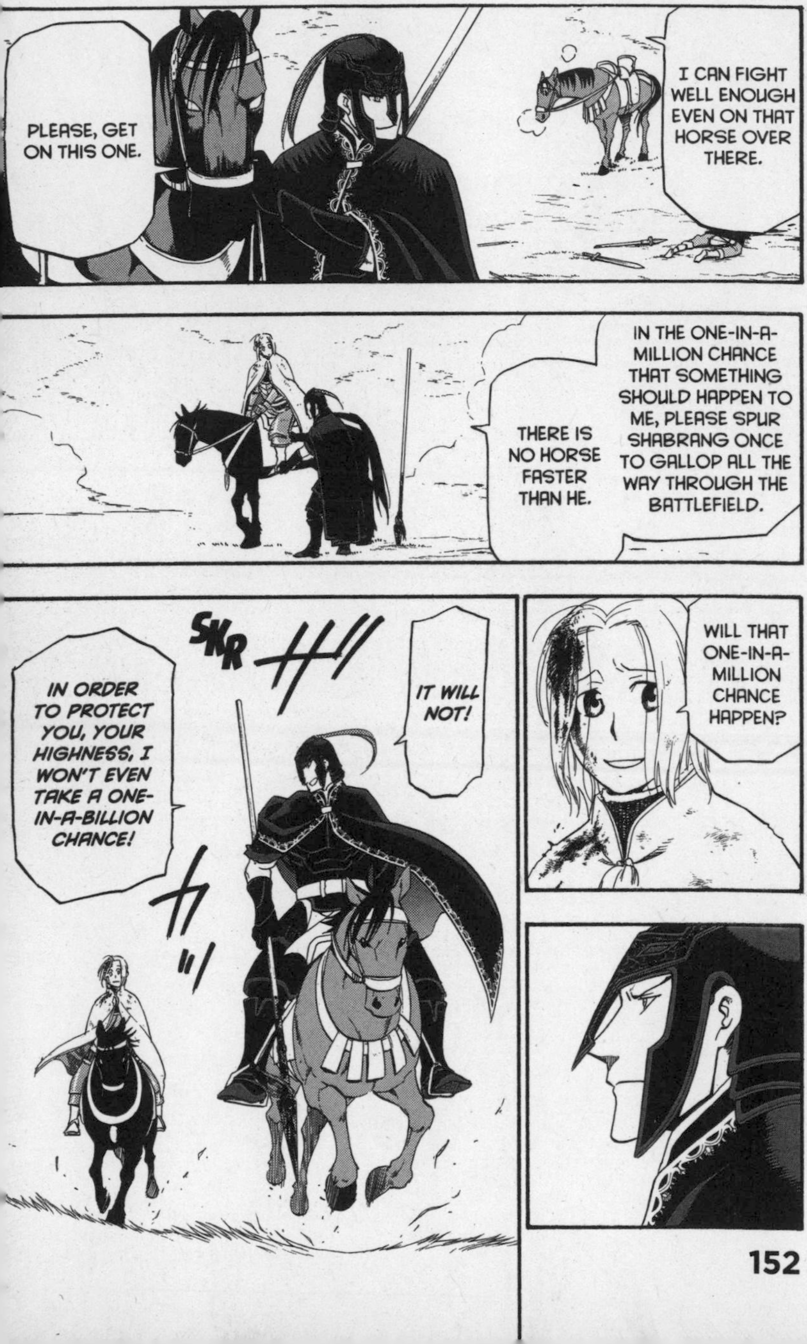
I CAN FIGHT WELL ENOUGH EVEN ON THAT HORSE OVER THERE.
PLEASE, GET ON THIS ONE.
IN THE ONE-IN-A-MILLION CHANCE THAT SOMETHING SHOULD HAPPEN TO ME, PLEASE SPUR SHABRANG ONCE TO GALLOP ALL THE WAY THROUGH THE BATTLEFIELD.
THERE IS NO HORSE FASTER THAN HE.
WILL THAT ONE-IN-A-MILLION CHANCE HAPPEN?
IT WILL NOT!
SKR
IN ORDER TO PROTECT YOU, YOUR HIGHNESS, I WON'T EVEN TAKE A ONE-IN-A-BILLION CHANCE!

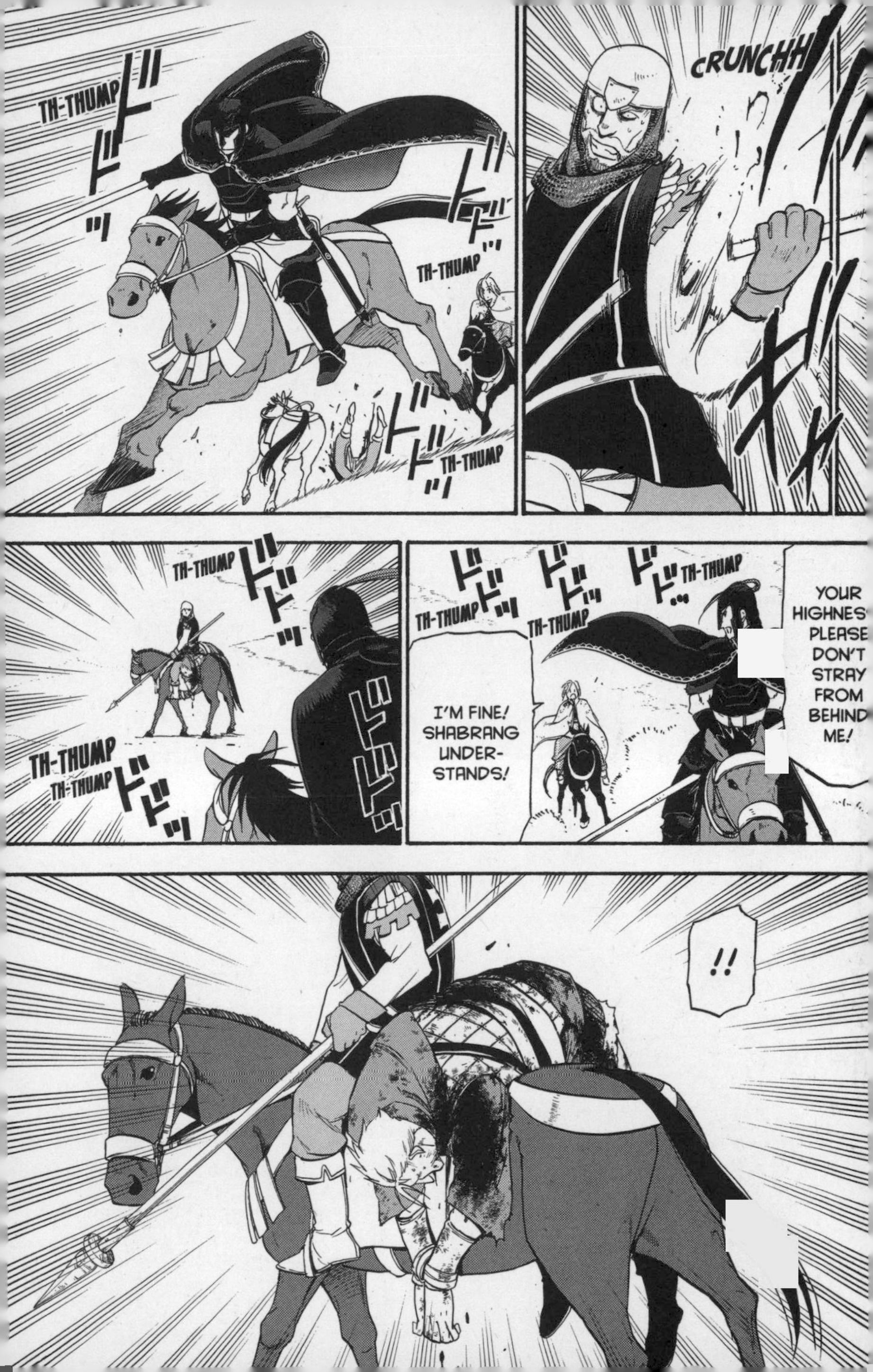
CRUNCHH
TH-THUMP
TH-THUMP
TH-THUMP
YOUR HIGHNES PLEASE DON'T STRAY FROM BEHIND ME!
TH-THUMP
TH-THUMP
TH-THUMP
I'M FINE! SHABRANG UNDER-STANDS!
TH-THUMP
TH-THUMP
TH-THUMP
!!

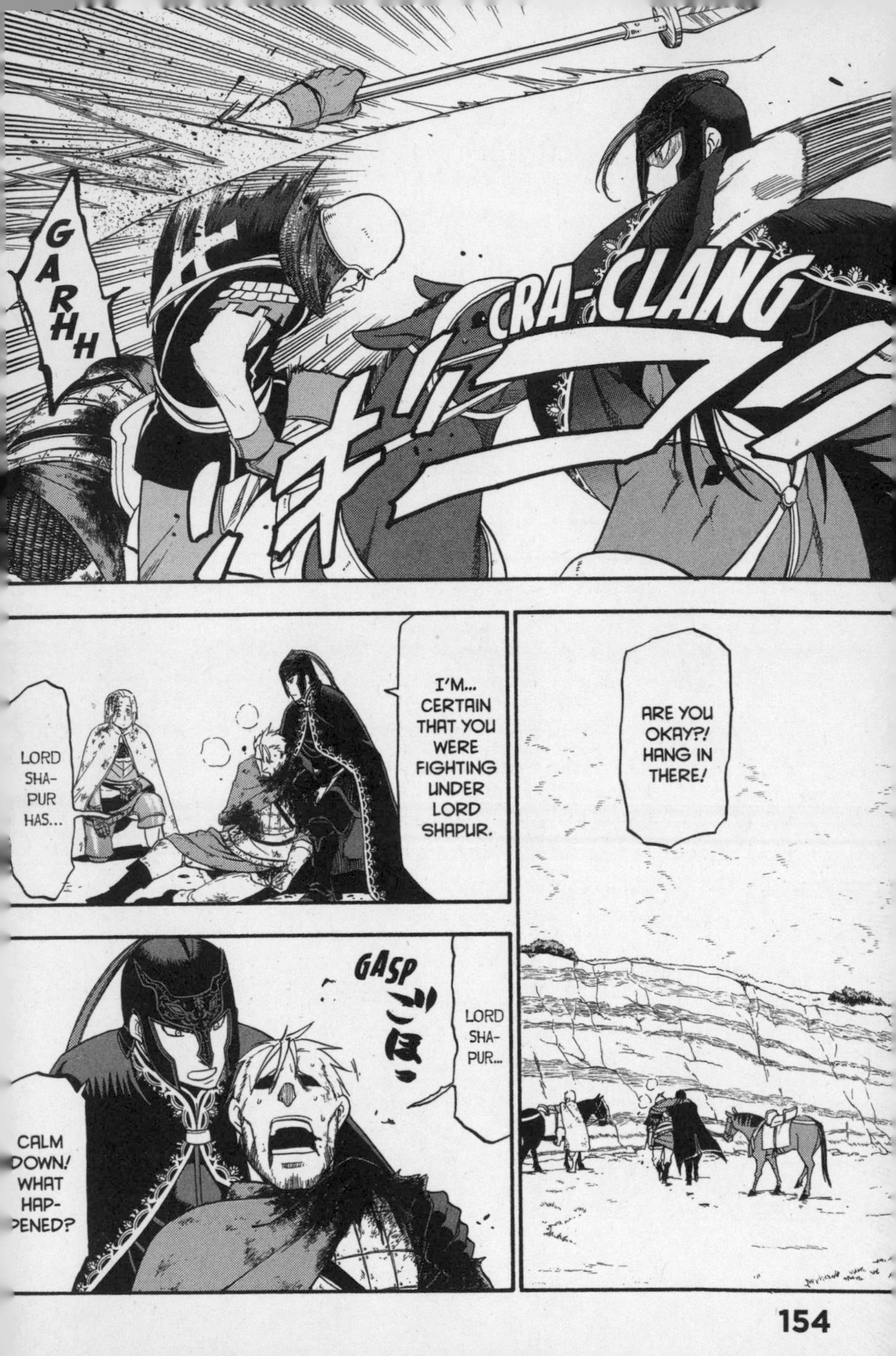
CRA-CLANG
GARHH
ARE YOU OKAY?! HANG IN THERE!
I'M... CERTAIN THAT YOU WERE FIGHTING UNDER LORD SHAPUR.
LORD SHAPUR HAS...
LORD SHAPUR...
GASP
ごほっ
CALM DOWN! WHAT HAPPENED?

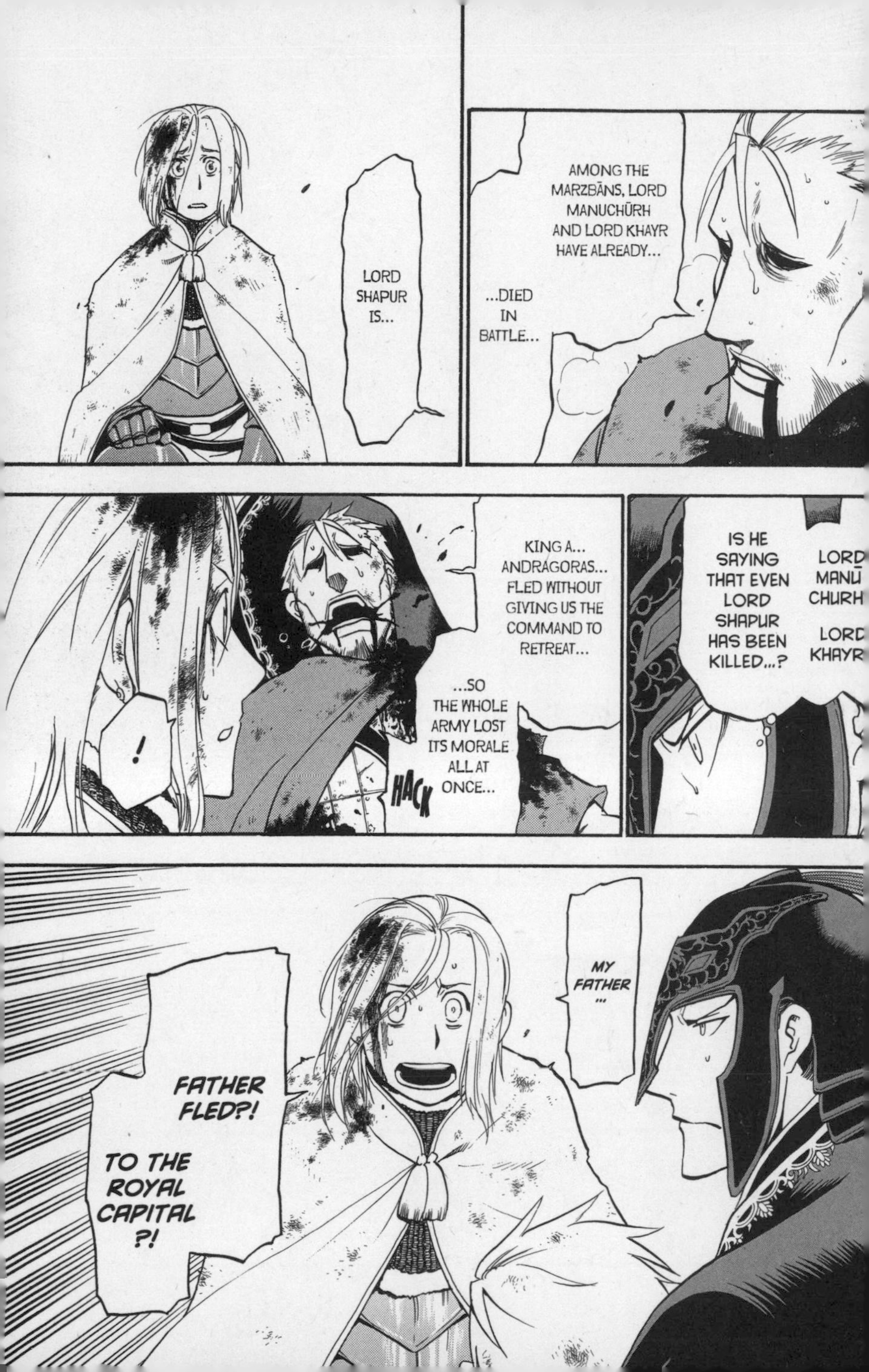
AMONG THE MARZBĀNS, LORD MANUCHŪRH AND LORD KHAYR HAVE ALREADY...
...DIED IN BATTLE...
LORD SHAPUR IS...
LORD MANŪ CHURH
LORD KHAYR
IS HE SAYING THAT EVEN LORD SHAPUR HAS BEEN KILLED...?
KING A... ANDRAGORAS... FLED WITHOUT GIVING US THE COMMAND TO RETREAT...
...SO THE WHOLE ARMY LOST ITS MORALE ALL AT ONCE...
HACK
!
MY FATHER ...
FATHER FLED?!
TO THE ROYAL CAPITAL ?!

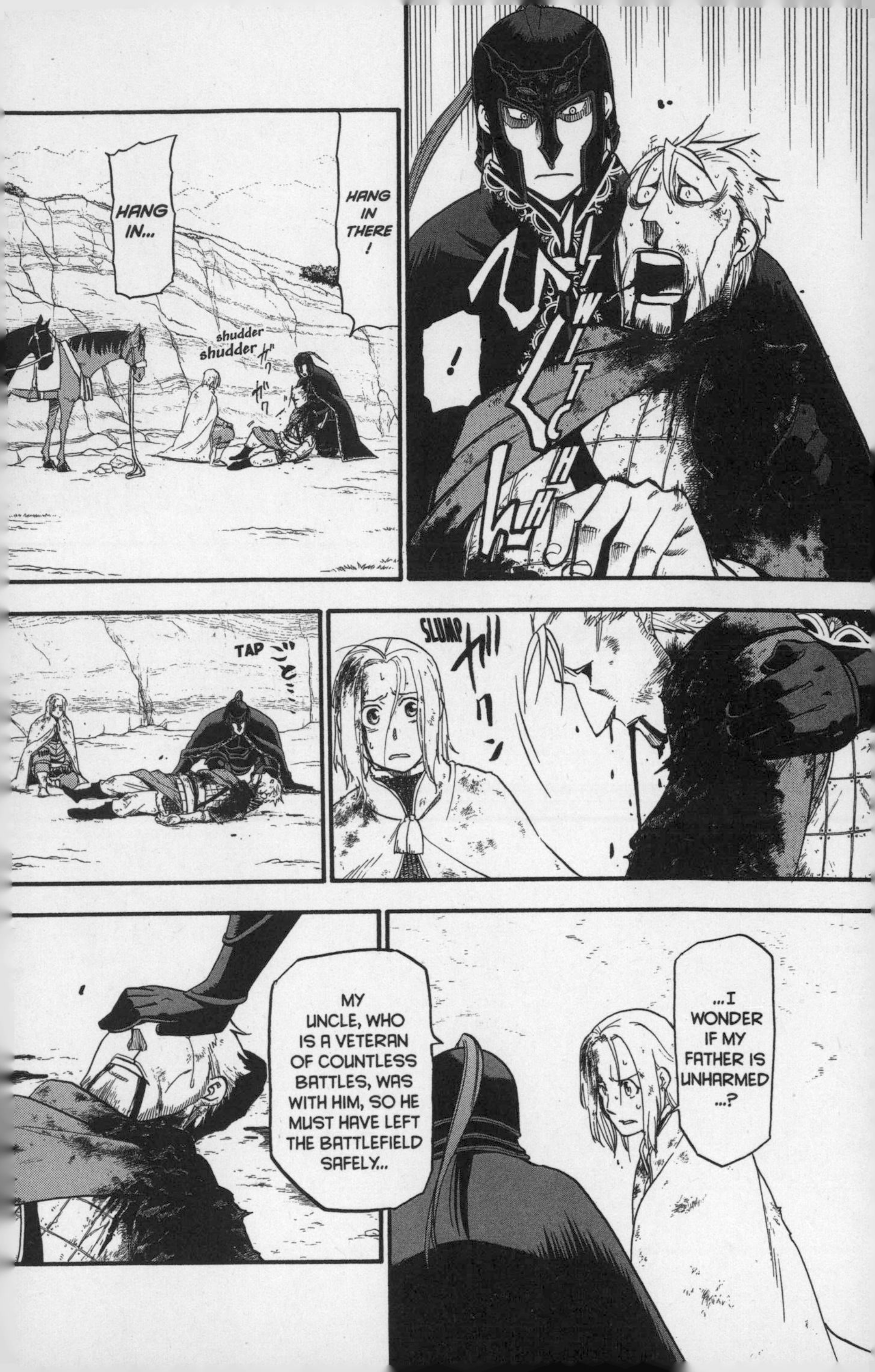
TWITCH
!
HANG IN THERE!
HANG IN...
shudder shudder
SLUMP
TAP
...I WONDER IF MY FATHER IS UNHARMED...?
MY UNCLE, WHO IS A VETERAN OF COUNTLESS BATTLES, WAS WITH HIM, SO HE MUST HAVE LEFT THE BATTLEFIELD SAFELY...

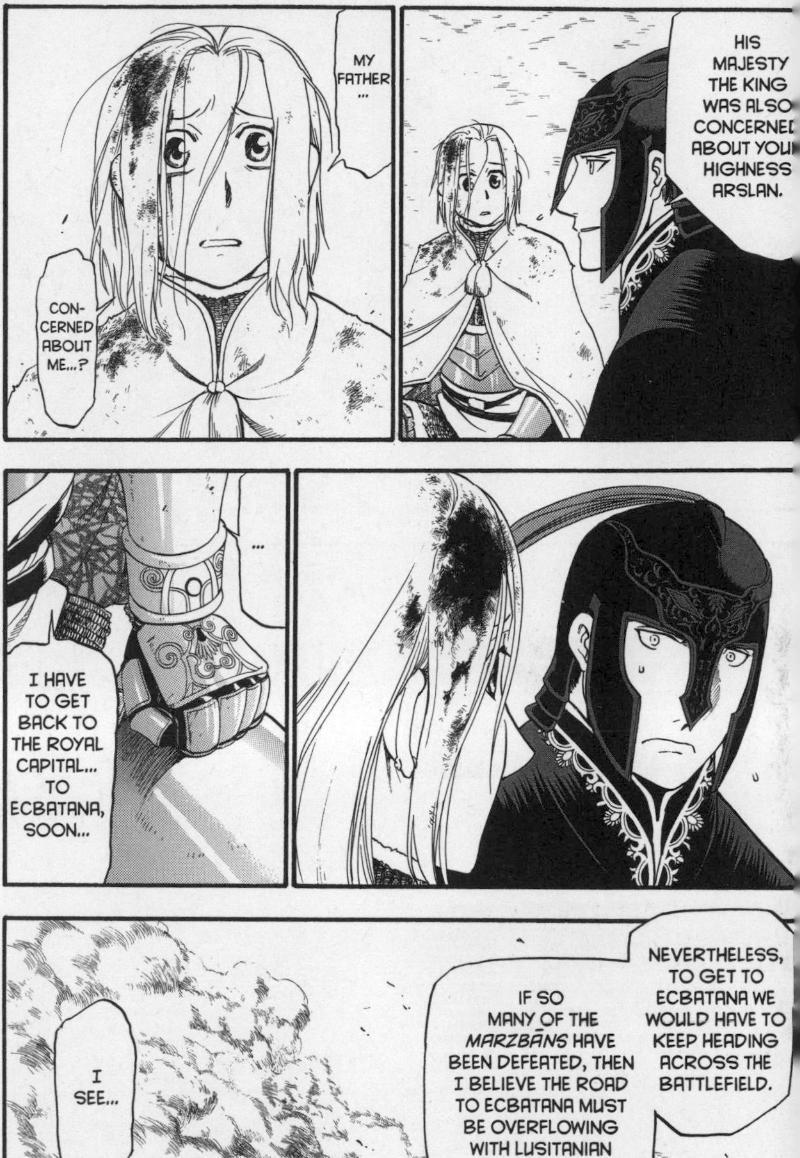
HIS MAJESTY THE KING WAS ALSO CONCERNED ABOUT YOUR HIGHNESS ARSLAN.
MY FATHER ...
CON-CERNED ABOUT ME...?
...
I HAVE TO GET BACK TO THE ROYAL CAPITAL... TO ECBATANA, SOON...
NEVERTHELESS, TO GET TO ECBATANA WE WOULD HAVE TO KEEP HEADING ACROSS THE BATTLEFIELD.
IF SO MANY OF THE *MARZBĀNS* HAVE BEEN DEFEATED, THEN I BELIEVE THE ROAD TO ECBATANA MUST BE OVERFLOWING WITH LUSITANIAN SOLDIERS.
I SEE...

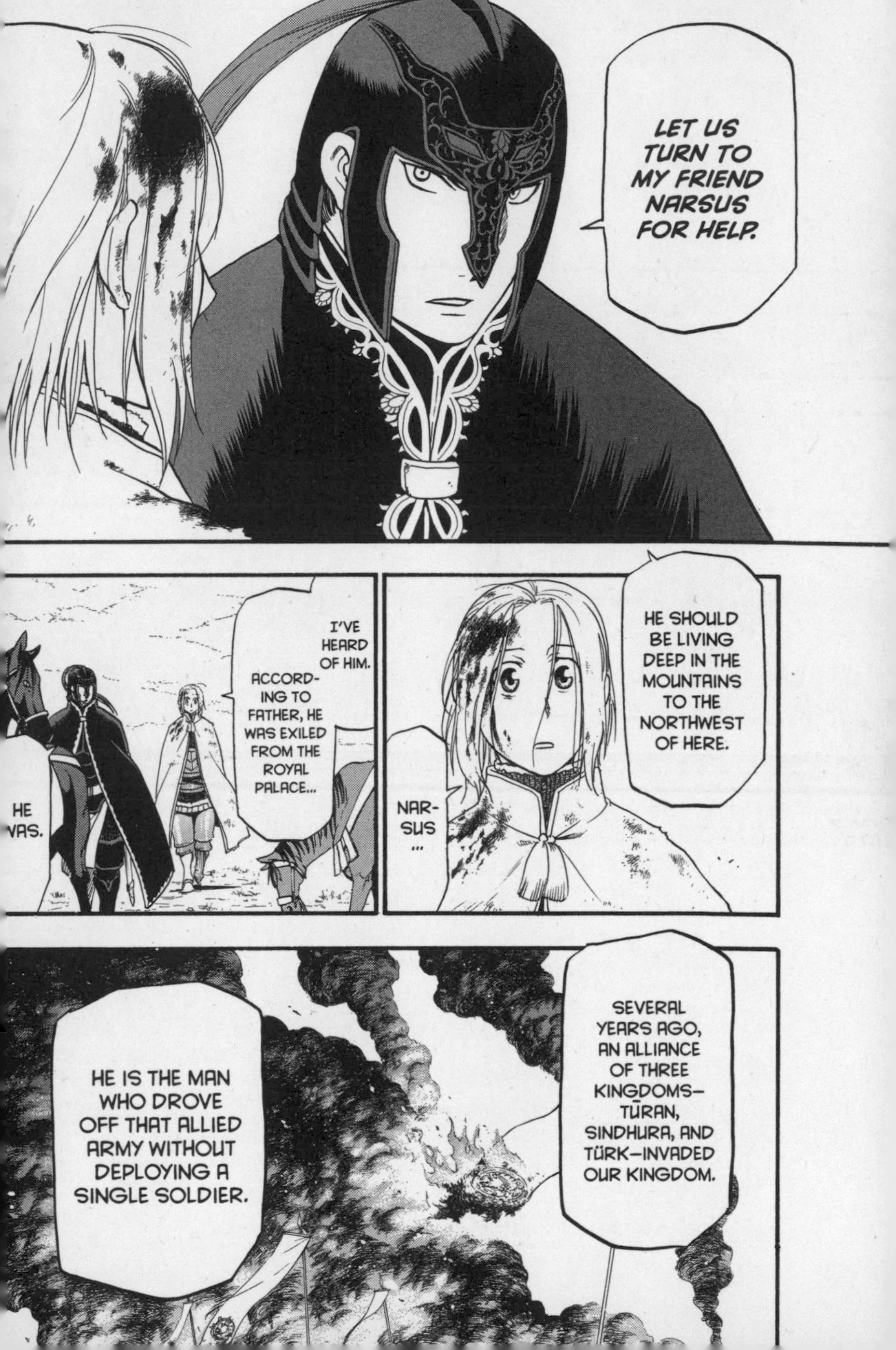
LET US TURN TO MY FRIEND NARSUS FOR HELP.
HE SHOULD BE LIVING DEEP IN THE MOUNTAINS TO THE NORTHWEST OF HERE.
NARSUS...
I'VE HEARD OF HIM. ACCORDING TO FATHER, HE WAS EXILED FROM THE ROYAL PALACE...
HE WAS.
SEVERAL YEARS AGO, AN ALLIANCE OF THREE KINGDOMS—TŪRAN, SINDHURA, AND TÜRK—INVADED OUR KINGDOM.
HE IS THE MAN WHO DROVE OFF THAT ALLIED ARMY WITHOUT DEPLOYING A SINGLE SOLDIER.

WA HA HA
はは は
はは は
HA HA HA HA

I CAN'T HELP BUT LAUGH AT HOW THEY FELL SO NEATLY INTO OUR TRAP!

YEAH!

THIS W
AN OVE
WHELMI
VICTOR
HOW
EXCELLE

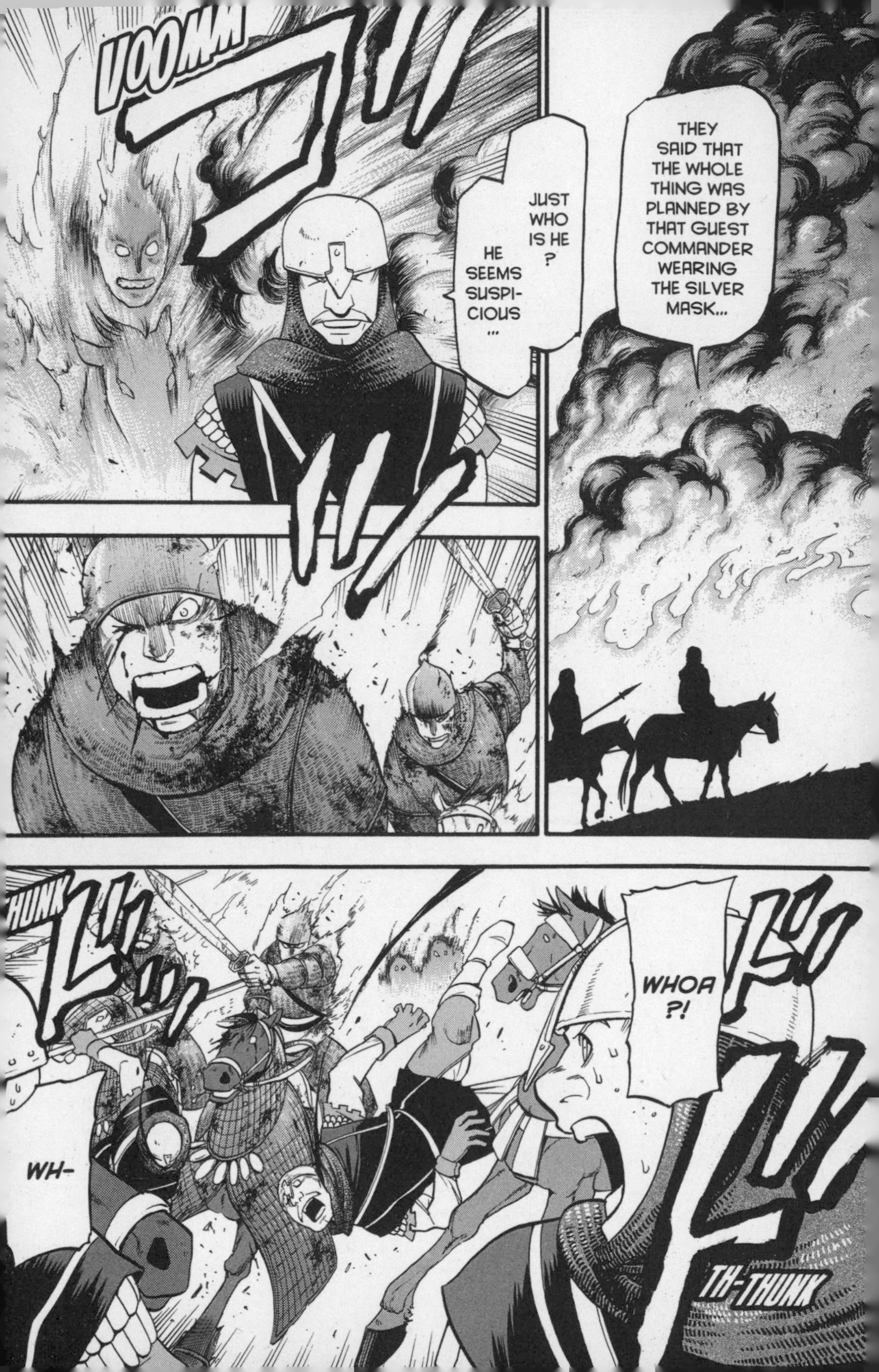
THEY SAID THAT THE WHOLE THING WAS PLANNED BY THAT GUEST COMMANDER WEARING THE SILVER MASK...
JUST WHO IS HE?
HE SEEMS SUSPICIOUS...
VOOMM
WHOA?!
THUNK
WH-
TH-THUNK

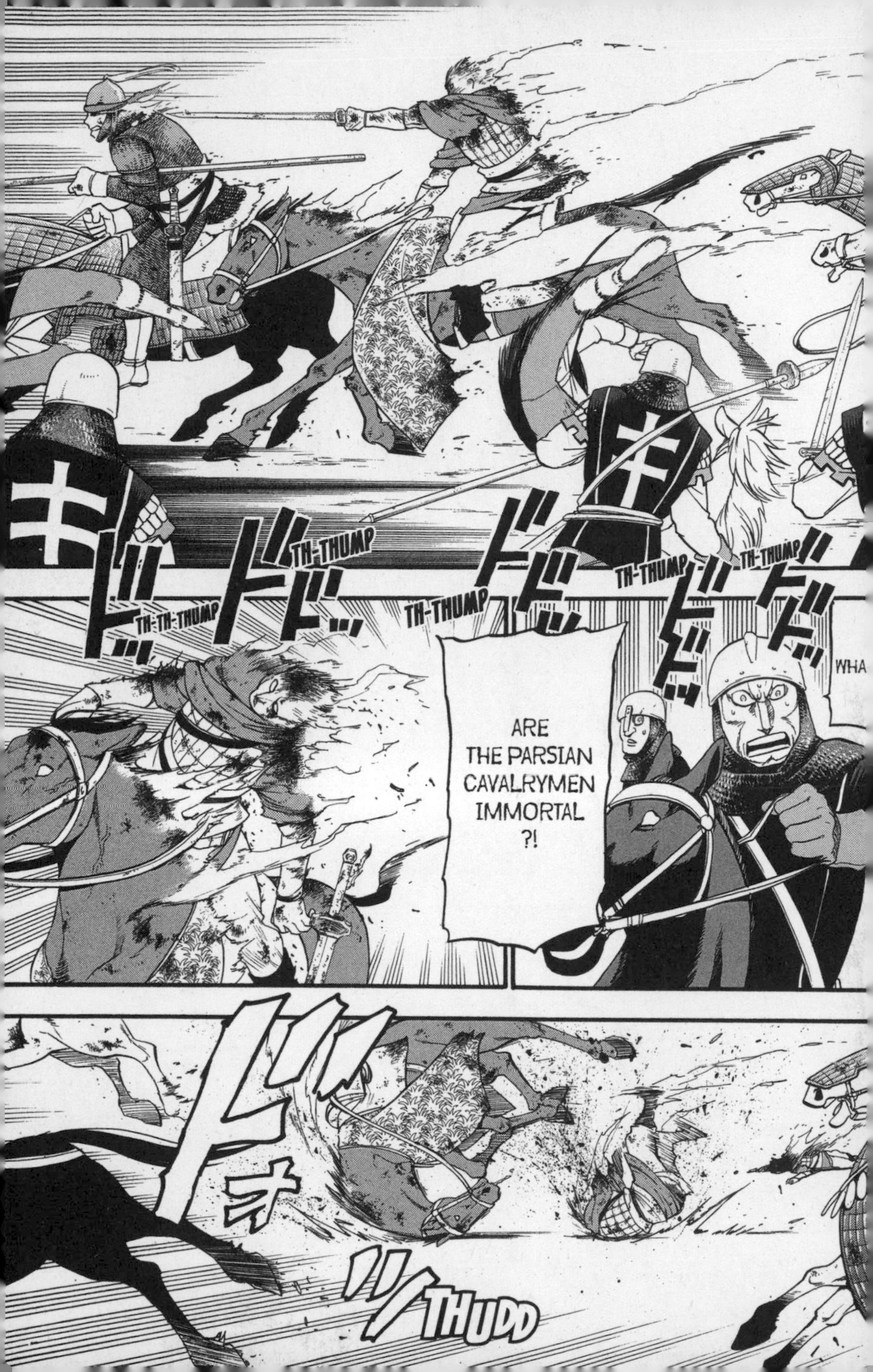
TH-THUMP
TH-THUMP
TH-THUMP
TH-THUMP
TH-TH-THUMP
WHA
ARE THE PARSIAN CAVALRYMEN IMMORTAL ?!
THUDD

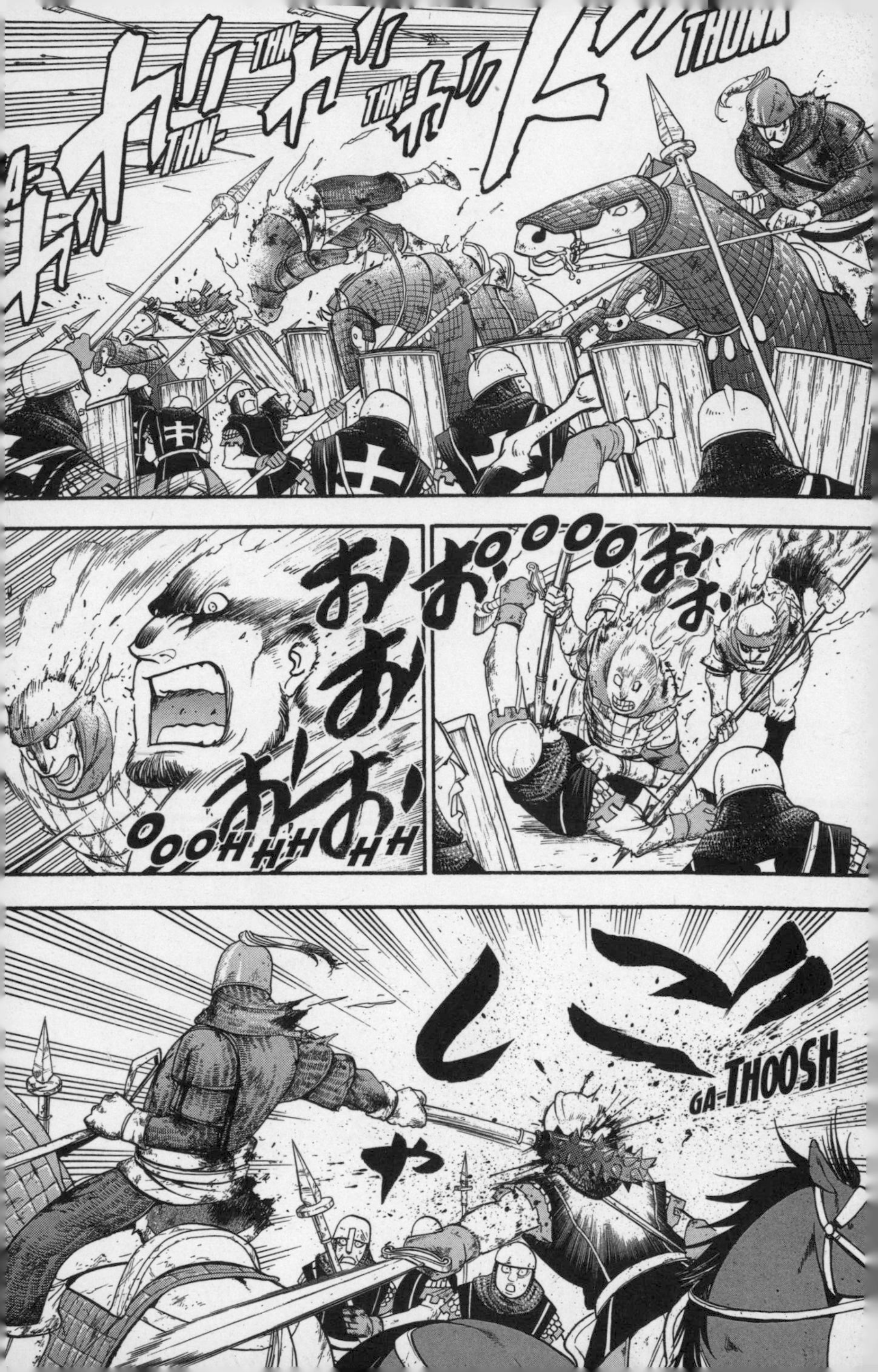
THUNK
THN-
THN-
THN-
OOOHHHHH
GA-THOOSH

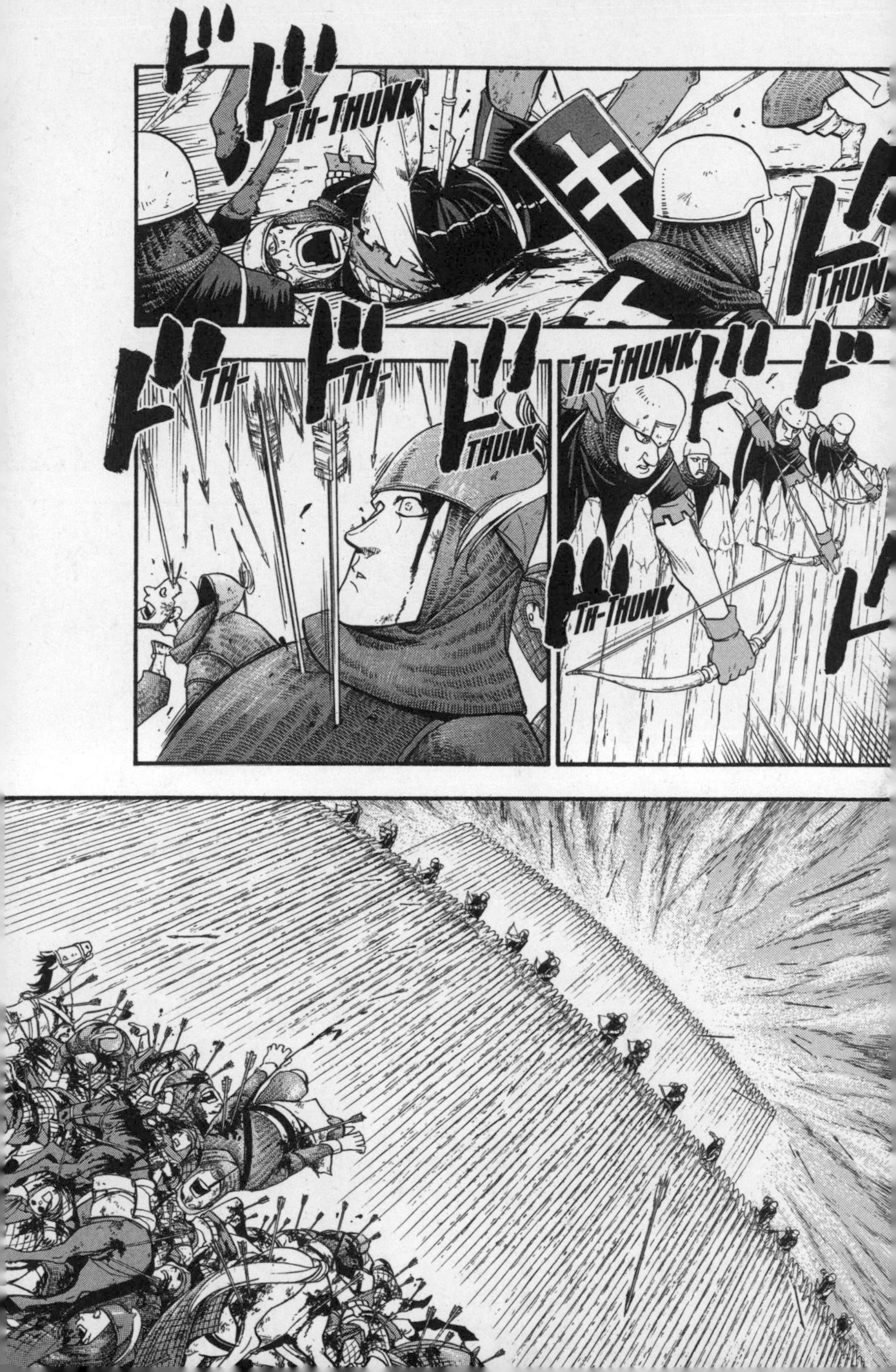
THUNK
TH-THUNK
TH-THUNK
TH-THUNK
TH-
TH-
THUNK

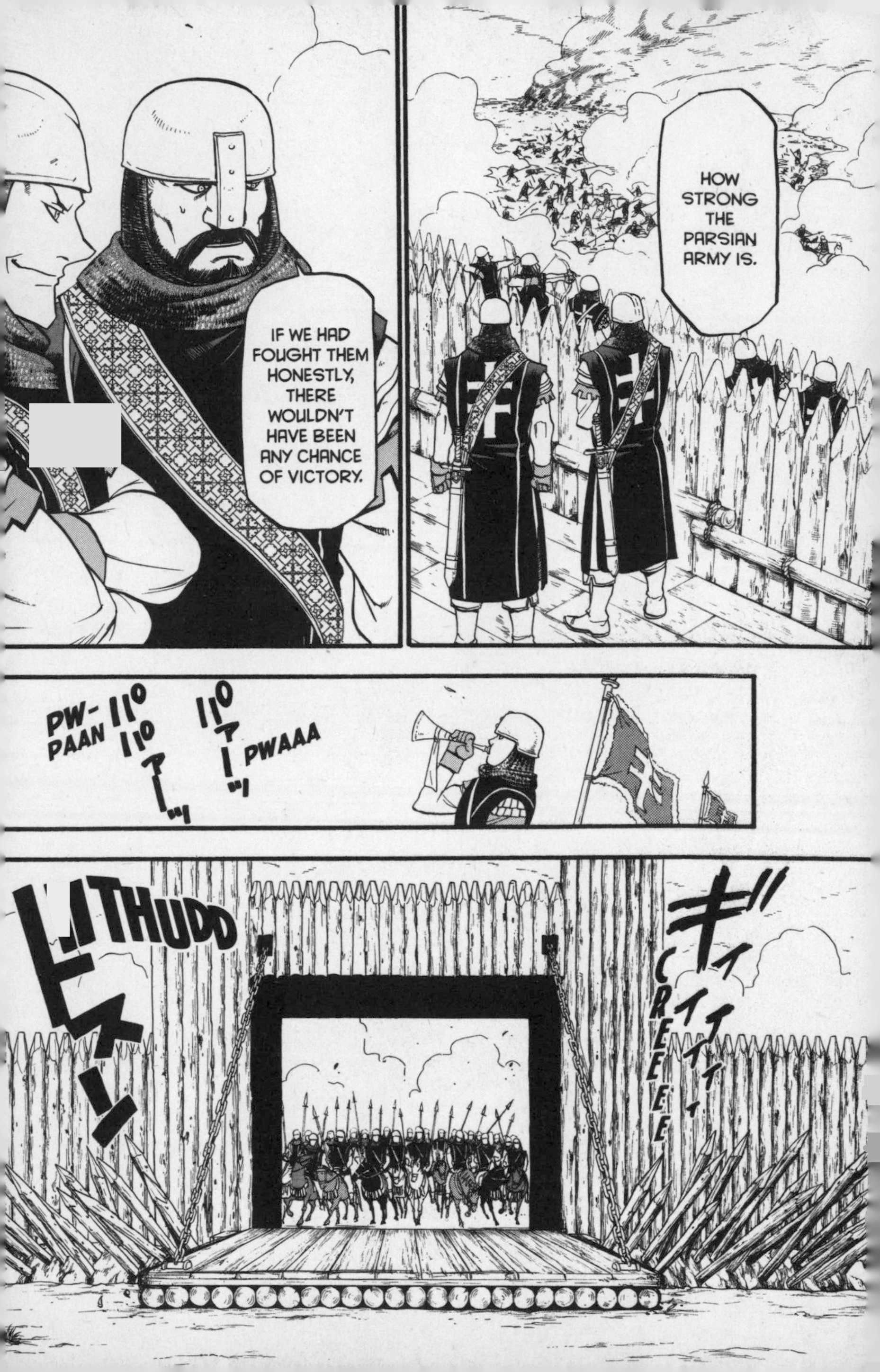
HOW STRONG THE PARSIAN ARMY IS.
IF WE HAD FOUGHT THEM HONESTLY, THERE WOULDN'T HAVE BEEN ANY CHANCE OF VICTORY.
PWAAA
PW-PAAN
CREEEEE
THUDD

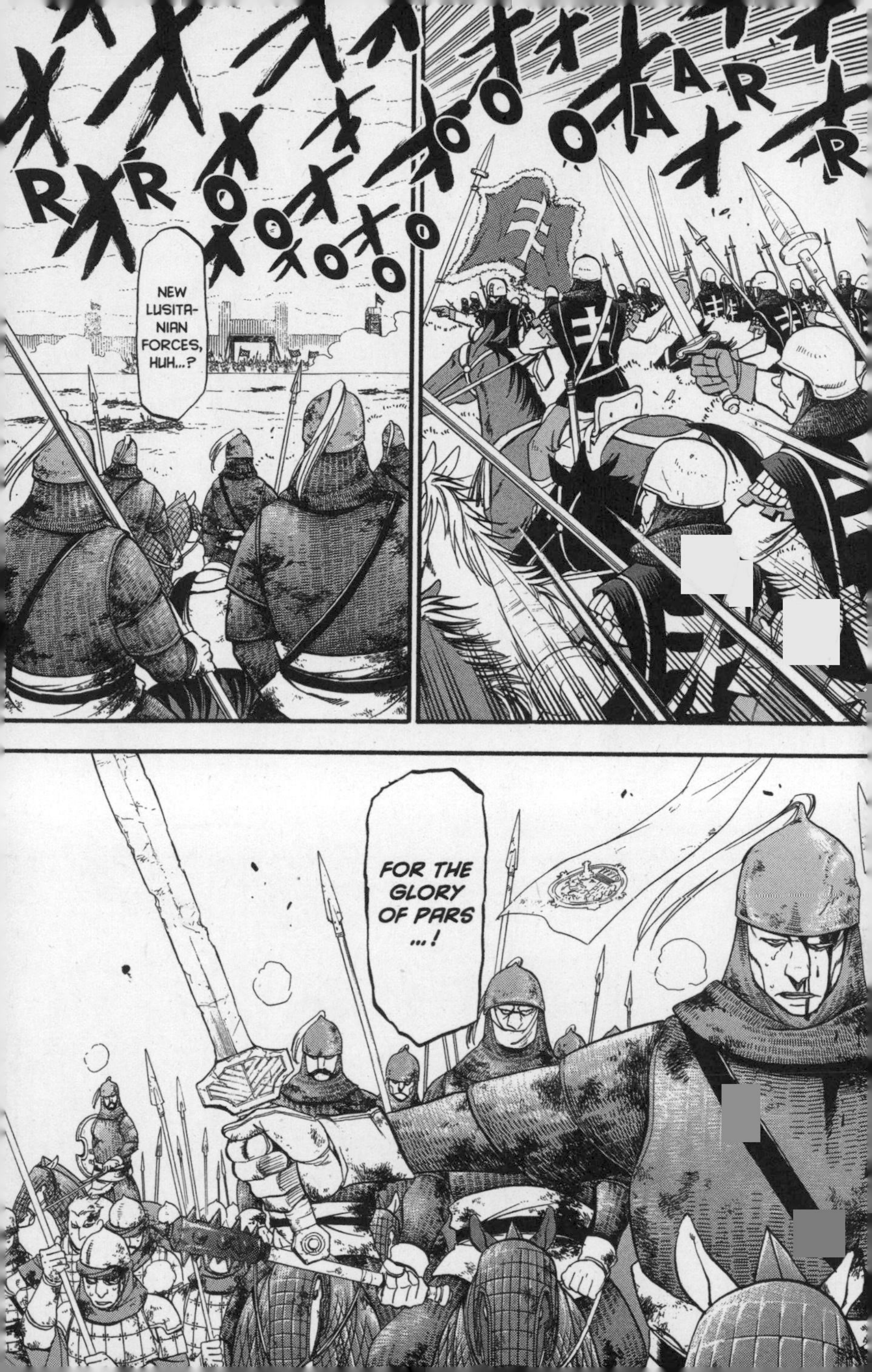
RRROOOOOOOOAARR
NEW LUSITA-NIAN FORCES, HUH...?
FOR THE GLORY OF PARS ...!

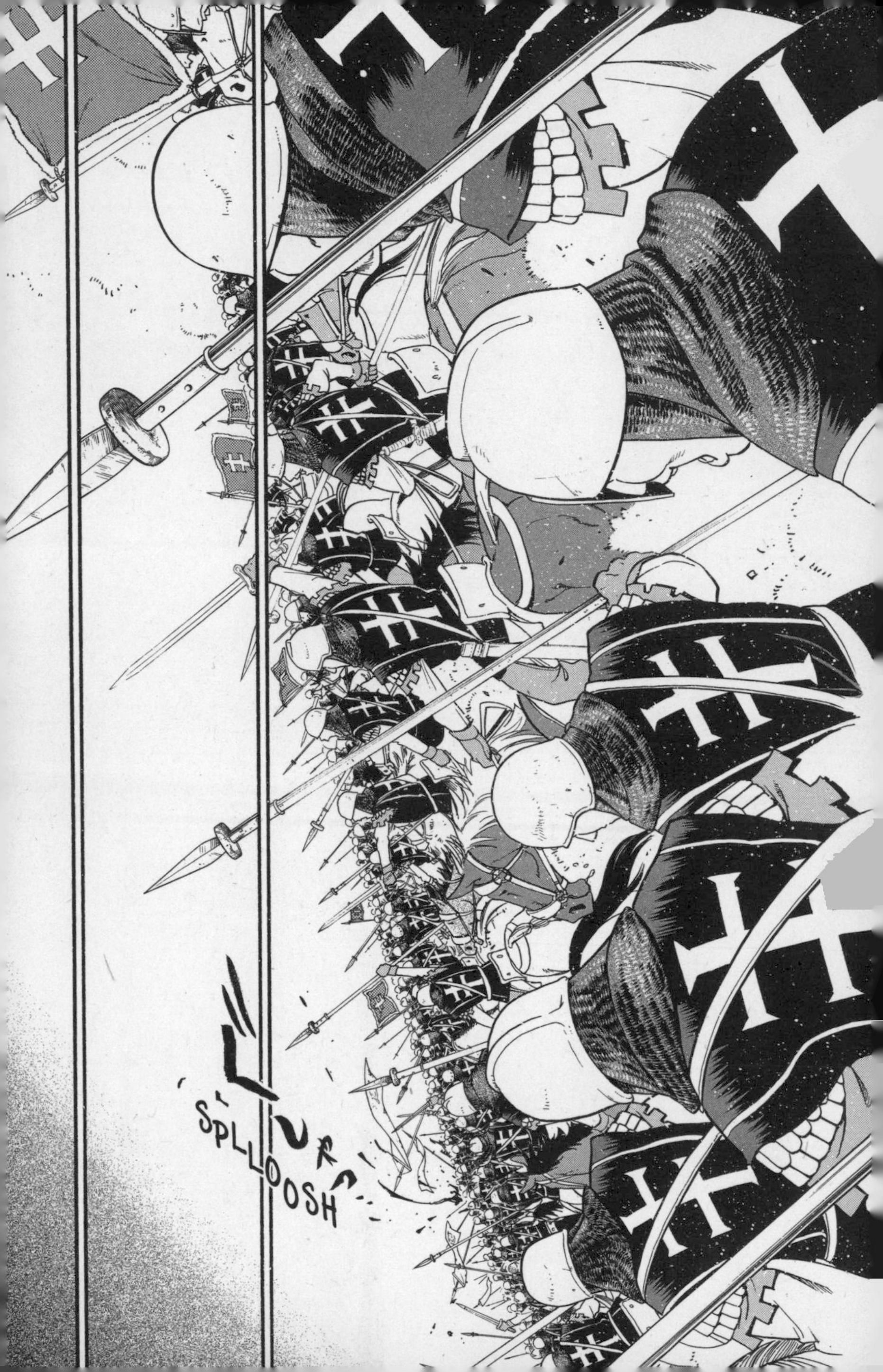
SPLLOOSH

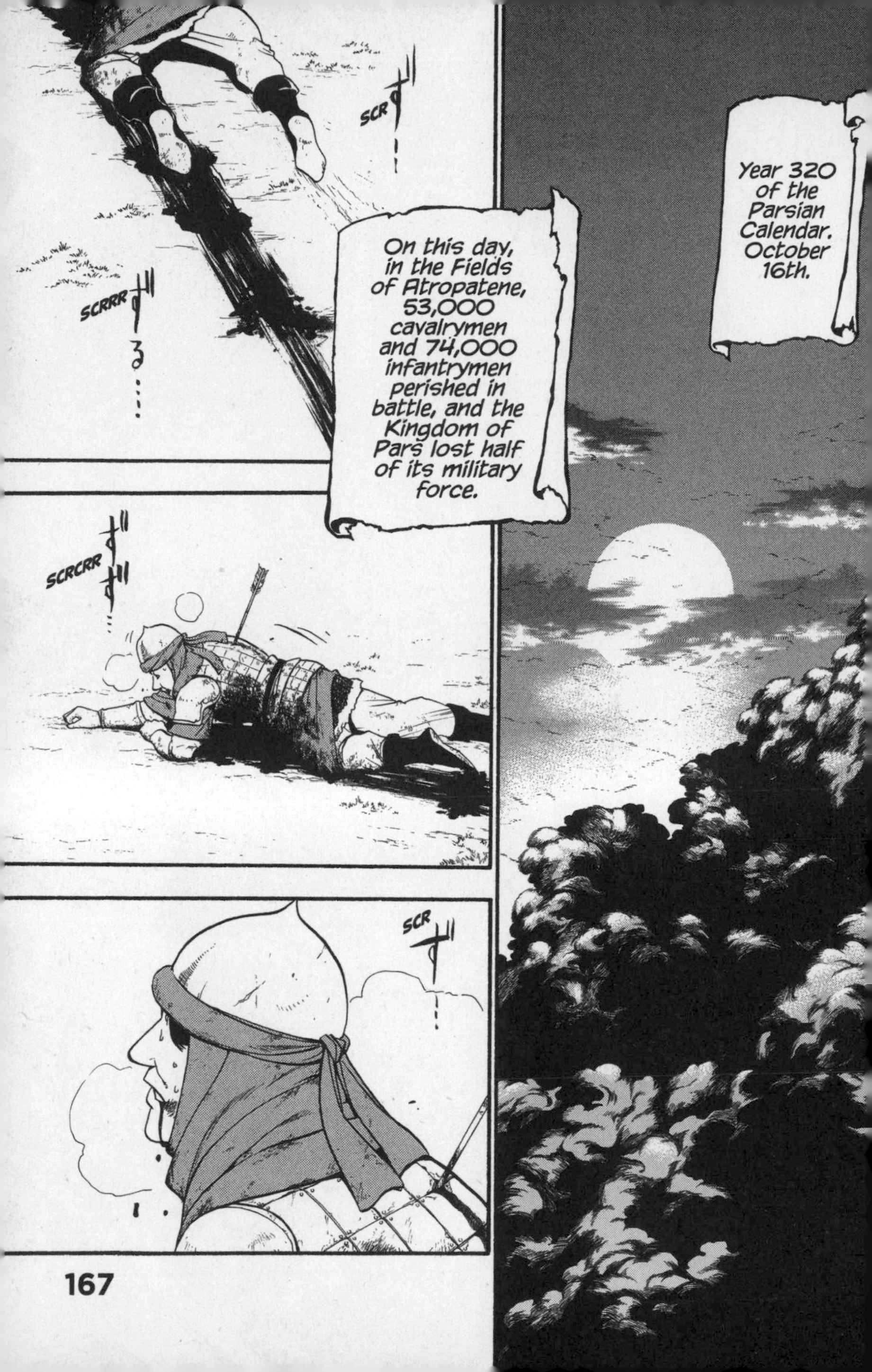
Year 320 of the Parsian Calendar. October 16th.
On this day, in the Fields of Atropatene, 53,000 cavalrymen and 74,000 infantrymen perished in battle, and the Kingdom of Pars lost half of its military force.
SCR
SCRRR
SCRCRR
SCR

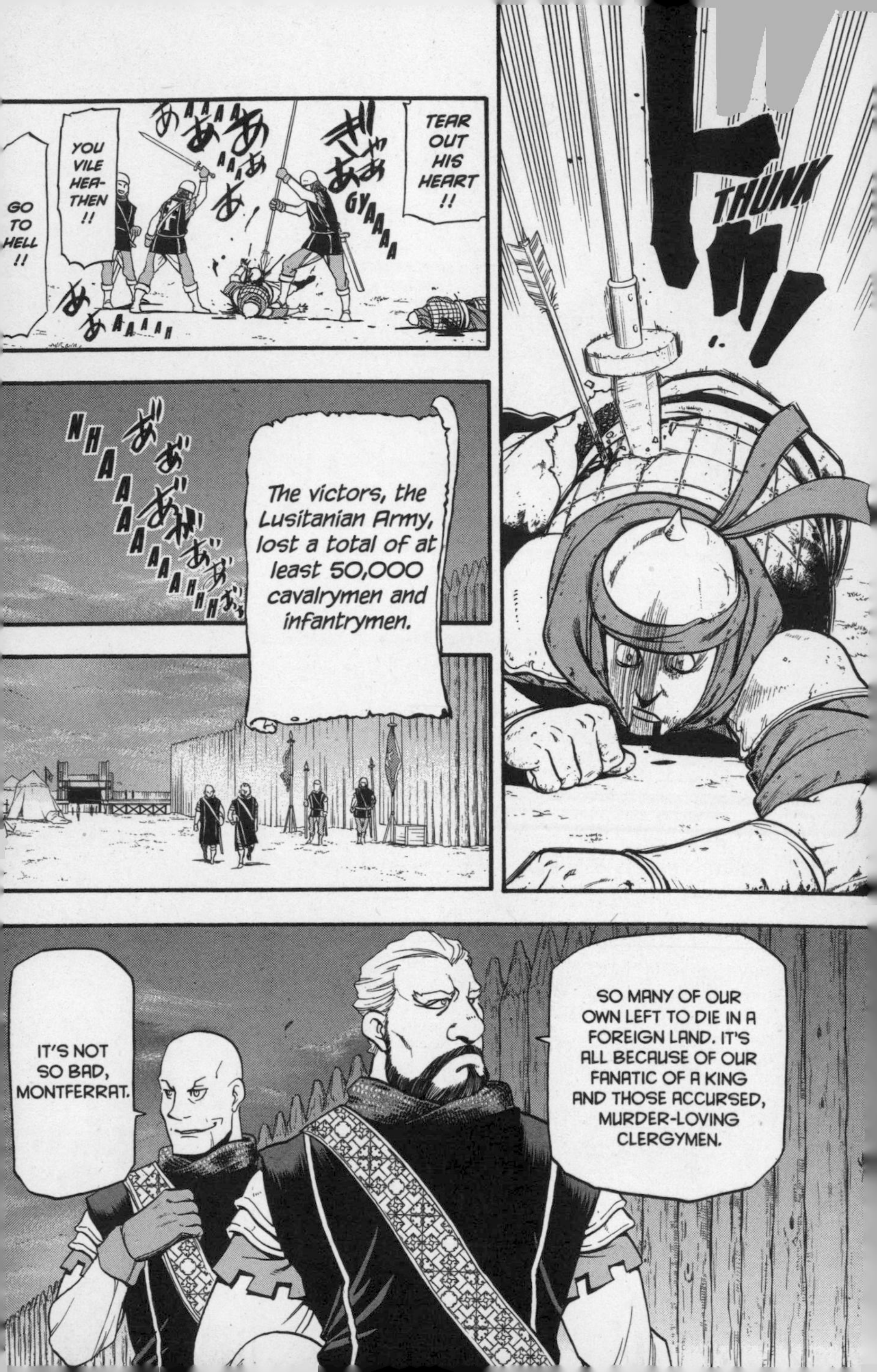
THUNK
TEAR OUT HIS HEART!!
GYAAAAA
YOU VILE HEATHEN!!
GO TO HELL!!
AAAAAH
NHAAAAAAAAAHHH
The victors, the Lusitanian Army, lost a total of at least 50,000 cavalrymen and infantrymen.
SO MANY OF OUR OWN LEFT TO DIE IN A FOREIGN LAND. IT'S ALL BECAUSE OF OUR FANATIC OF A KING AND THOSE ACCURSED, MURDER-LOVING CLERGYMEN.
IT'S NOT SO BAD, MONTFERRAT.

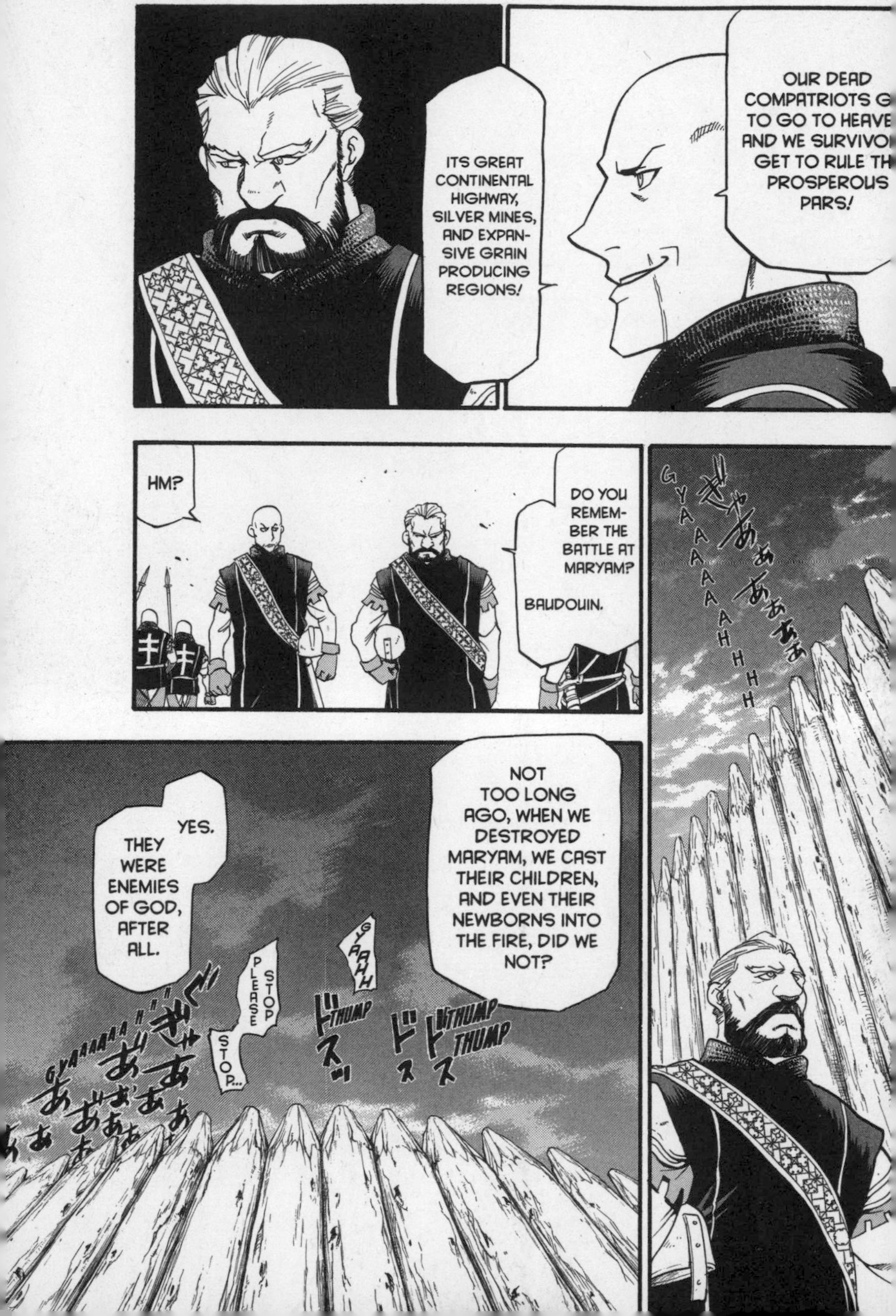
OUR DEAD COMPATRIOTS G TO GO TO HEAVE AND WE SURVIVO GET TO RULE TH PROSPEROUS PARS!
ITS GREAT CONTINENTAL HIGHWAY, SILVER MINES, AND EXPAN-SIVE GRAIN PRODUCING REGIONS!
GYAAAAAAHHHH
DO YOU REMEM-BER THE BATTLE AT MARYAM?
BAUDOUIN.
HM?
NOT TOO LONG AGO, WHEN WE DESTROYED MARYAM, WE CAST THEIR CHILDREN, AND EVEN THEIR NEWBORNS INTO THE FIRE, DID WE NOT?
YES. THEY WERE ENEMIES OF GOD, AFTER ALL.
GYAHH
THUMP
THUMP THUMP
PLEASE STOP
STOP...
GYAAAAAAA

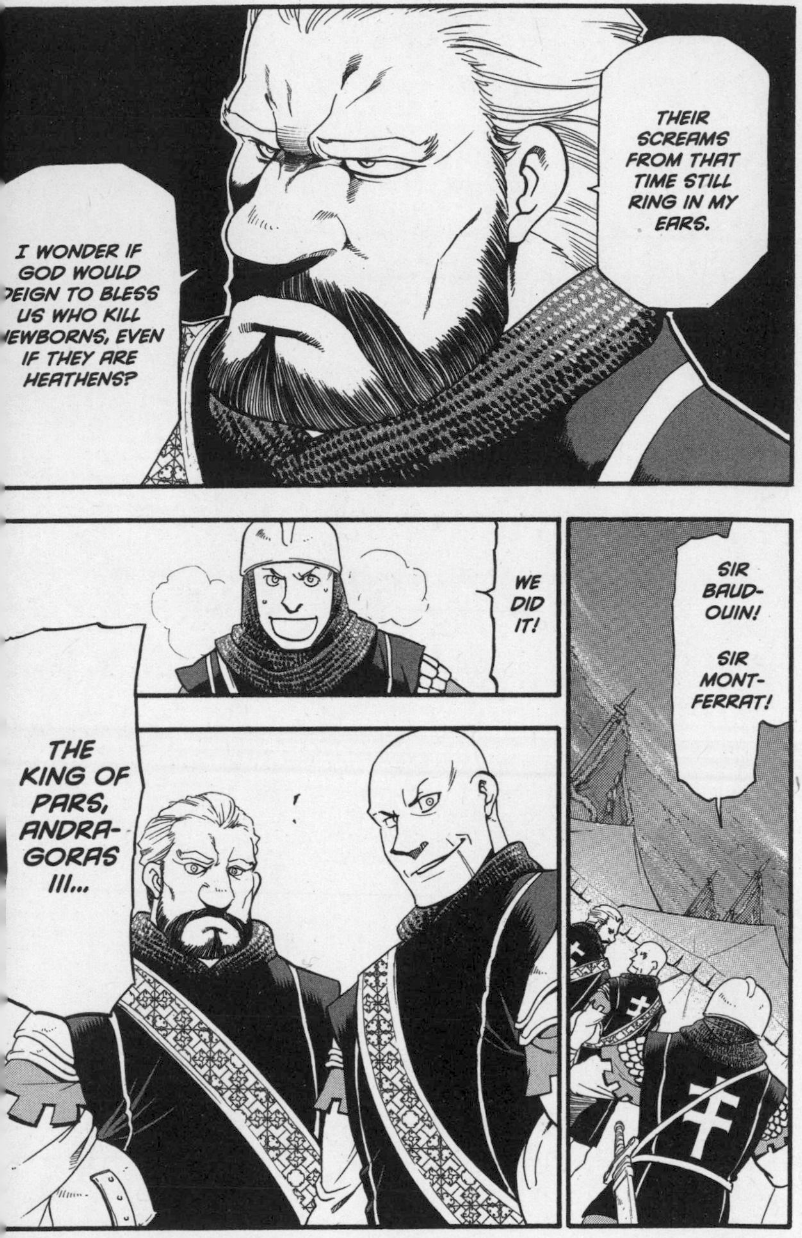
THEIR SCREAMS FROM THAT TIME STILL RING IN MY EARS.
I WONDER IF GOD WOULD
EIGN TO BLESS US WHO KILL
EWBORNS, EVEN IF THEY ARE HEATHENS?
SIR BAUD-OUIN!
SIR MONT-FERRAT!
WE DID IT!
THE KING OF PARS, ANDRA-GORAS III...

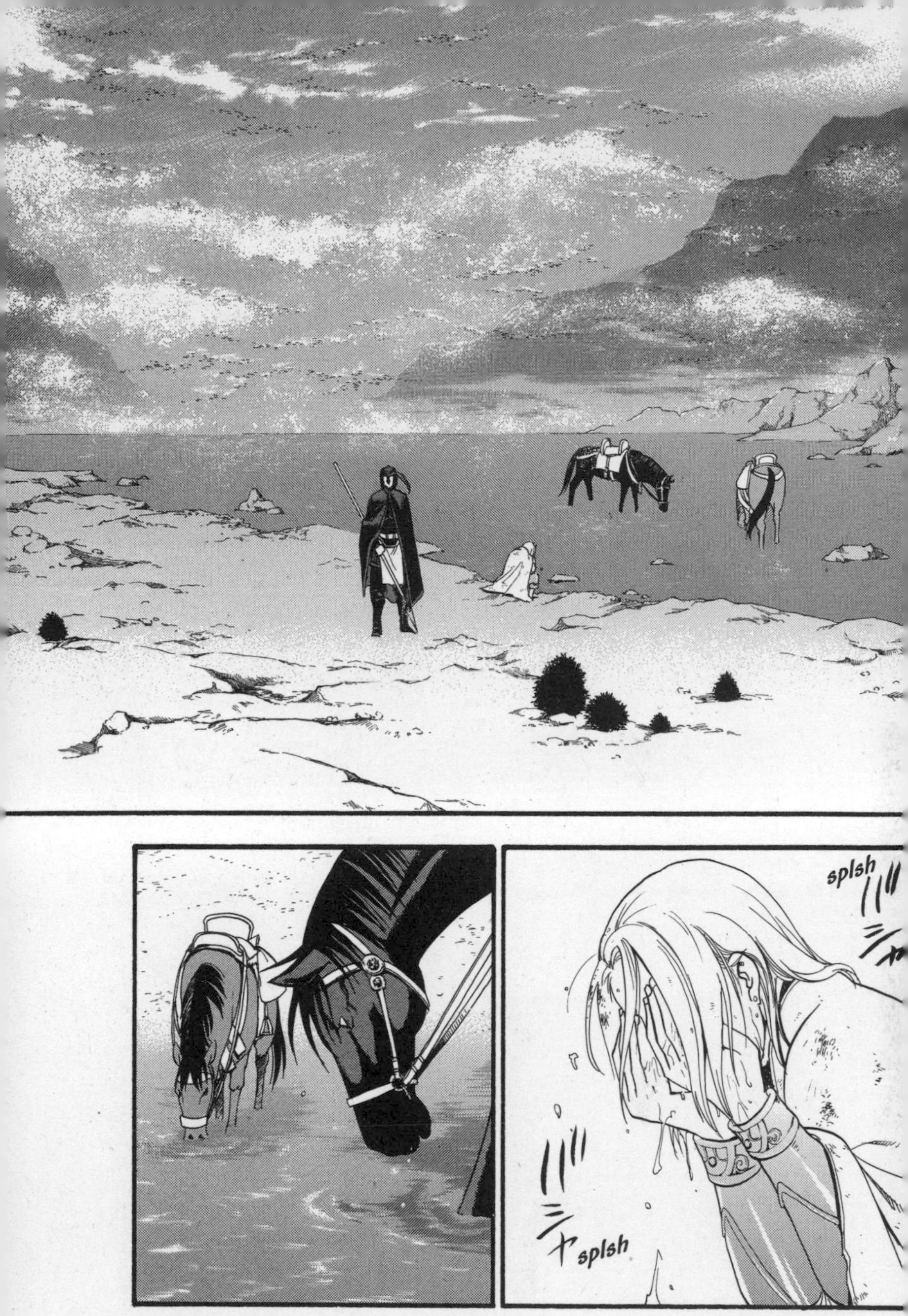
splsh
splsh

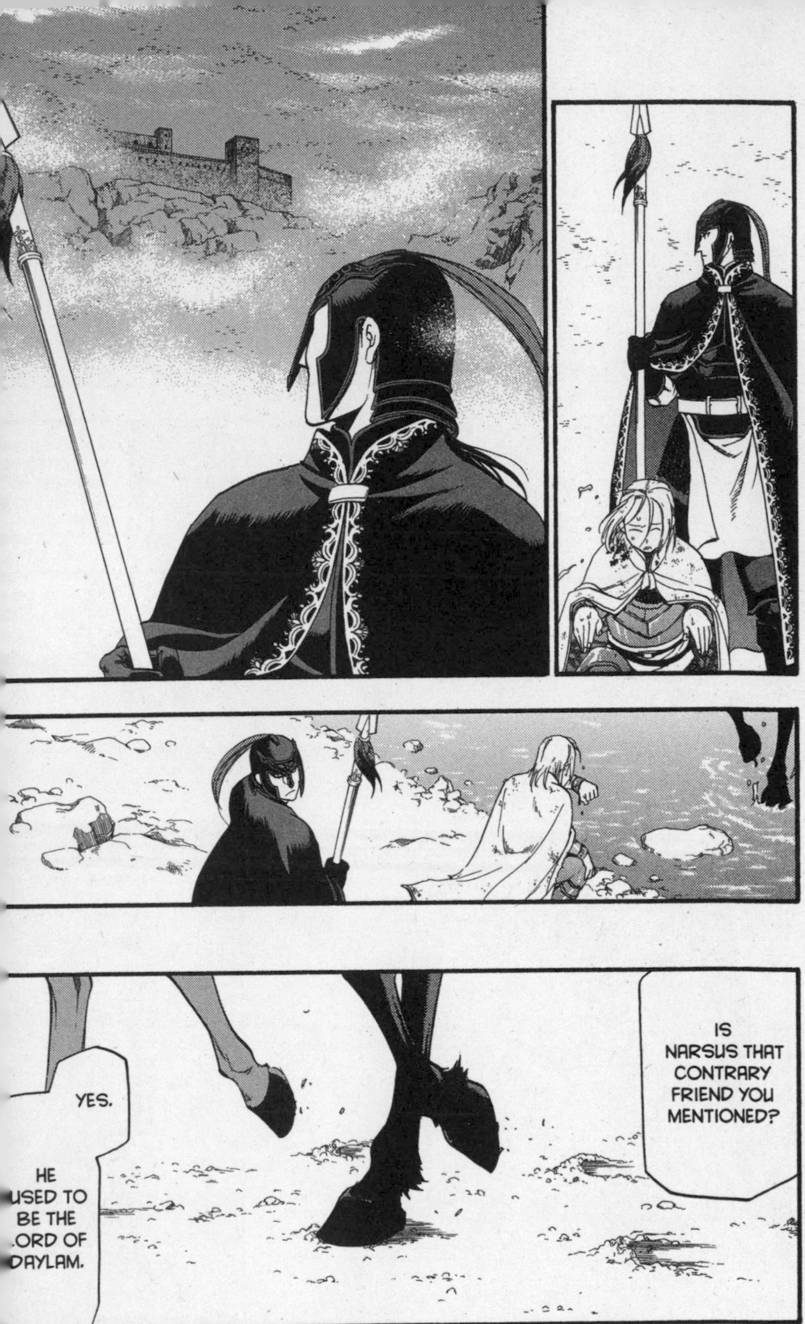
IS NARSUS THAT CONTRARY FRIEND YOU MENTIONED?
YES.
HE USED TO BE THE LORD OF DAYLAM.

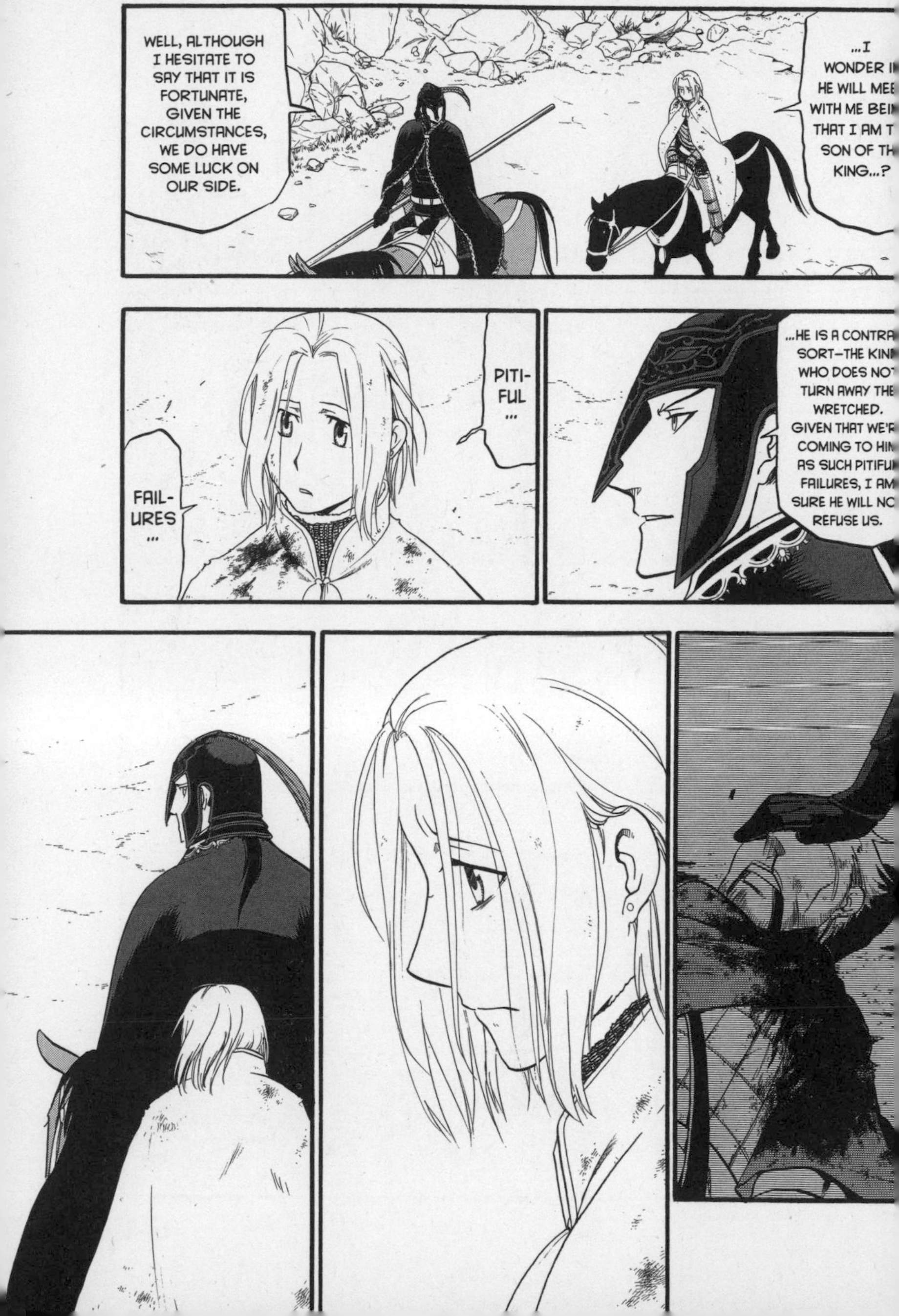
...I WONDER I HE WILL MEE WITH ME BEI THAT I AM T SON OF TH KING...?
WELL, ALTHOUGH I HESITATE TO SAY THAT IT IS FORTUNATE, GIVEN THE CIRCUMSTANCES, WE DO HAVE SOME LUCK ON OUR SIDE.
...HE IS A CONTRA SORT—THE KIN WHO DOES NO TURN AWAY THE WRETCHED. GIVEN THAT WE' COMING TO HI AS SUCH PITIFU FAILURES, I AM SURE HE WILL NO REFUSE US.
PITI- FUL ...
FAIL- URES ...

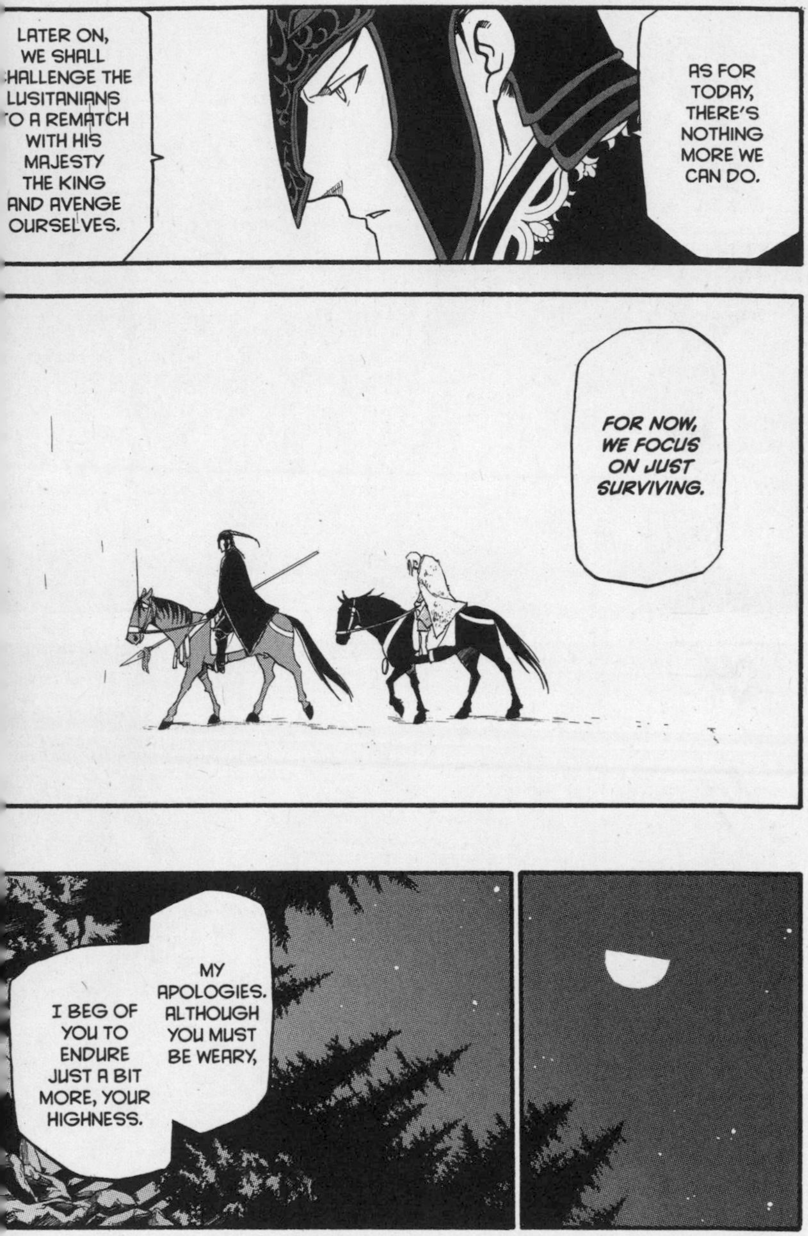
AS FOR TODAY, THERE'S NOTHING MORE WE CAN DO.
LATER ON, WE SHALL CHALLENGE THE LUSITANIANS TO A REMATCH WITH HIS MAJESTY THE KING AND AVENGE OURSELVES.
FOR NOW, WE FOCUS ON JUST SURVIVING.
MY APOLOGIES. ALTHOUGH YOU MUST BE WEARY,
I BEG OF YOU TO ENDURE JUST A BIT MORE, YOUR HIGHNESS.

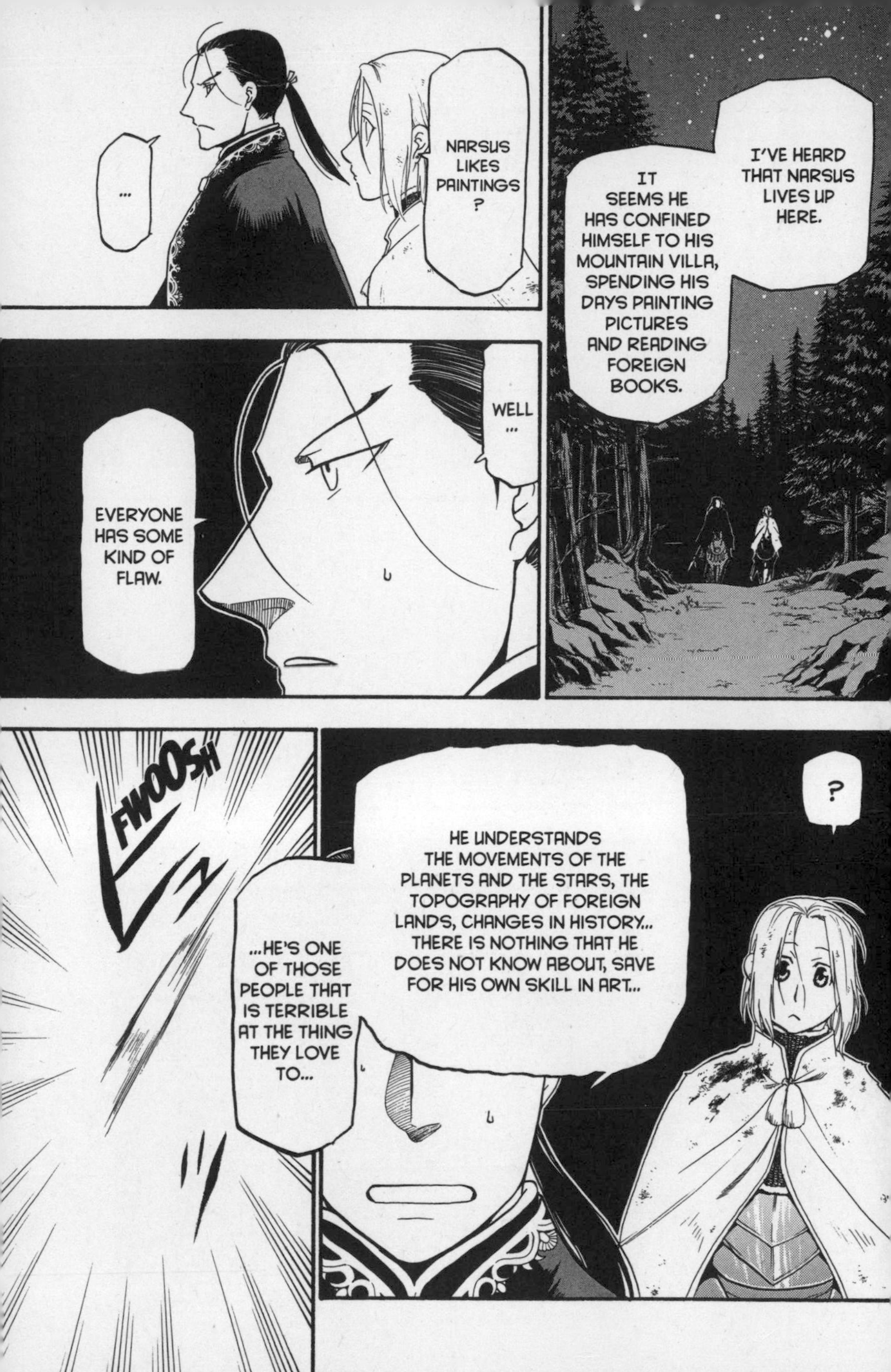
I'VE HEARD THAT NARSUS LIVES UP HERE.
IT SEEMS HE HAS CONFINED HIMSELF TO HIS MOUNTAIN VILLA, SPENDING HIS DAYS PAINTING PICTURES AND READING FOREIGN BOOKS.
NARSUS LIKES PAINTINGS ?
...
WELL ...
EVERYONE HAS SOME KIND OF FLAW.
?
HE UNDERSTANDS THE MOVEMENTS OF THE PLANETS AND THE STARS, THE TOPOGRAPHY OF FOREIGN LANDS, CHANGES IN HISTORY... THERE IS NOTHING THAT HE DOES NOT KNOW ABOUT, SAVE FOR HIS OWN SKILL IN ART...
...HE'S ONE OF THOSE PEOPLE THAT IS TERRIBLE AT THE THING THEY LOVE TO...
FWOOSH

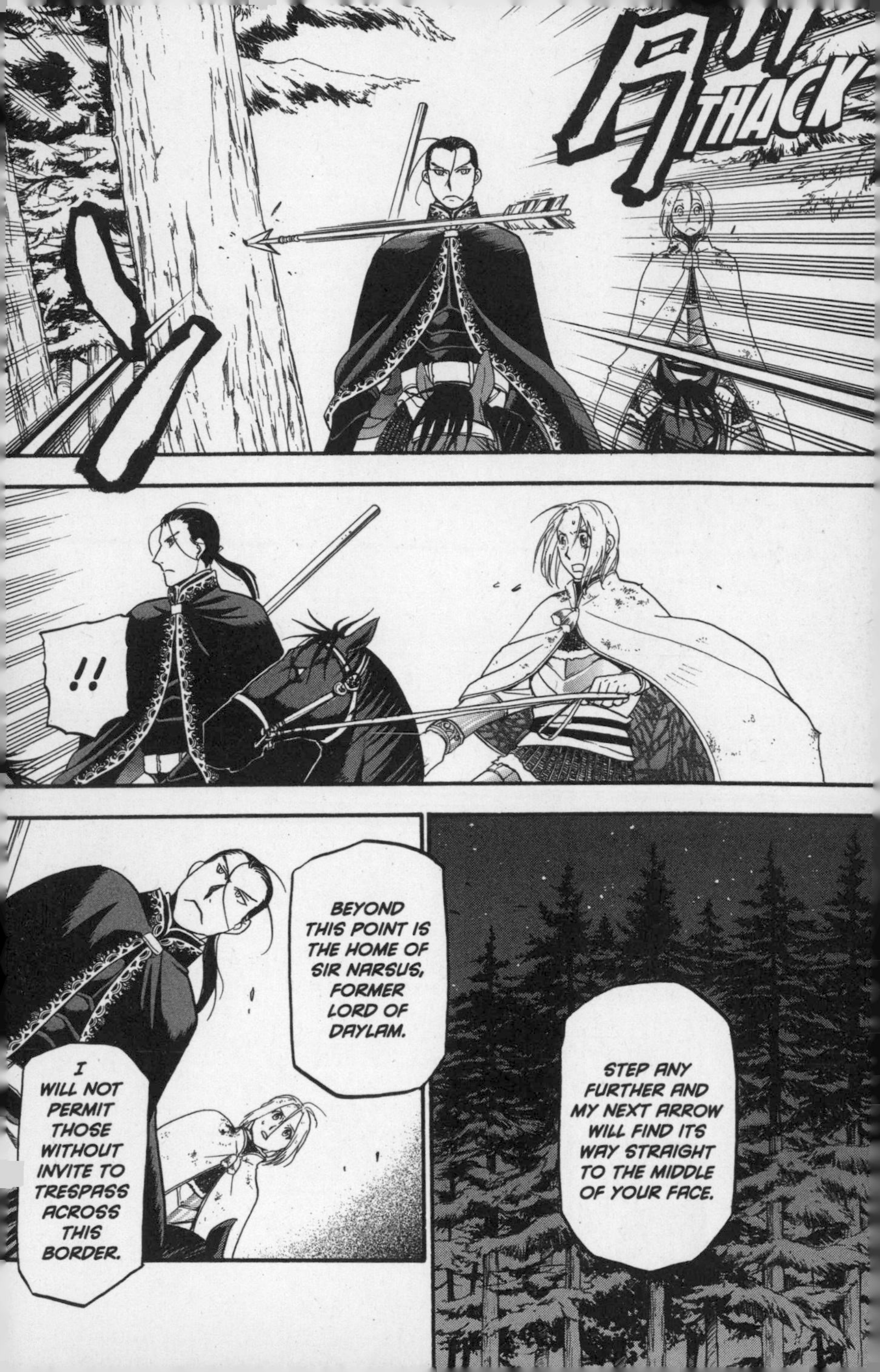
THACK
!!
BEYOND THIS POINT IS THE HOME OF SIR NARSUS, FORMER LORD OF DAYLAM.
STEP ANY FURTHER AND MY NEXT ARROW WILL FIND ITS WAY STRAIGHT TO THE MIDDLE OF YOUR FACE.
I WILL NOT PERMIT THOSE WITHOUT INVITE TO TRESPASS ACROSS THIS BORDER.

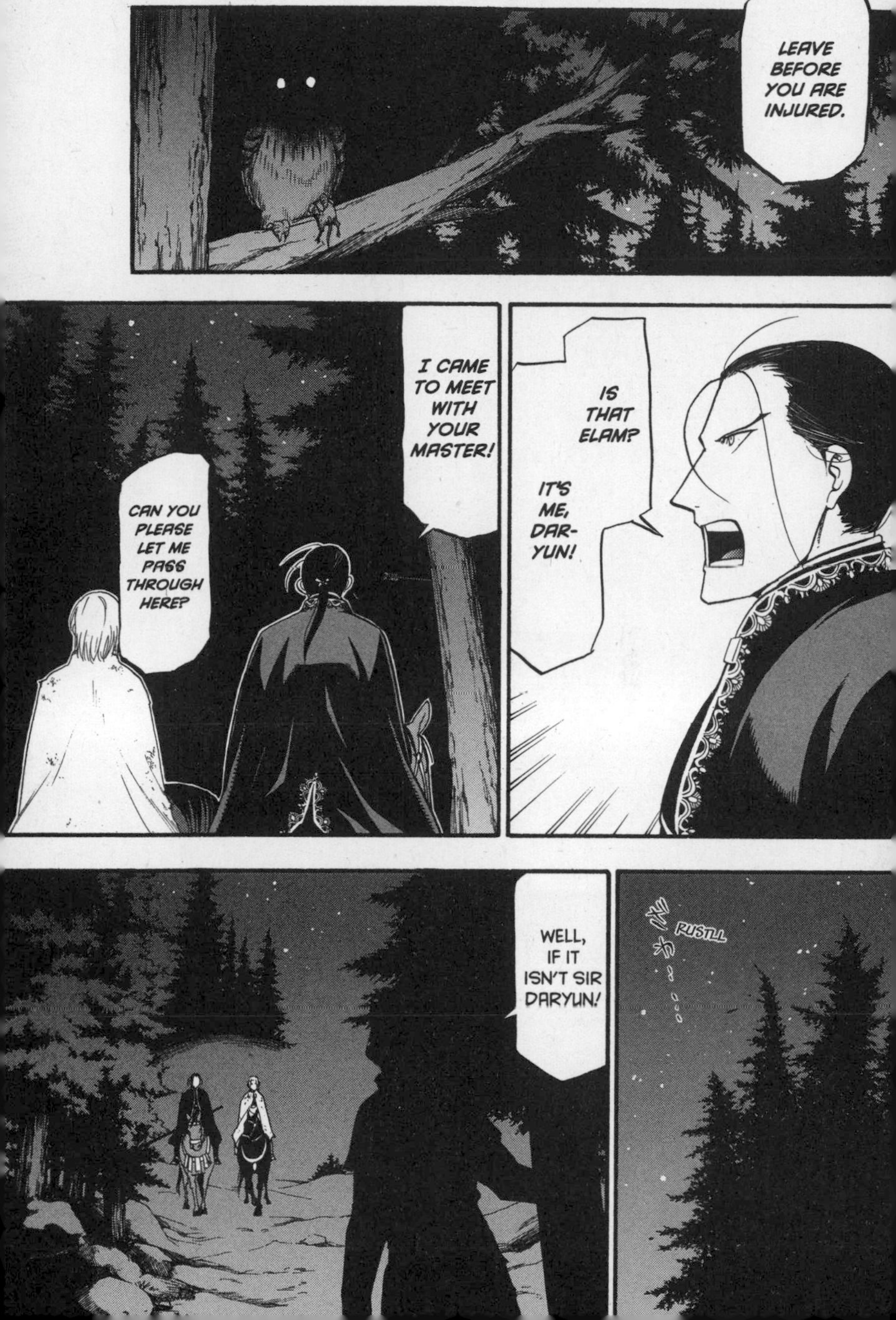
LEAVE BEFORE YOU ARE INJURED.
IS THAT ELAM?
IT'S ME, DAR-YUN!
I CAME TO MEET WITH YOUR MASTER!
CAN YOU PLEASE LET ME PASS THROUGH HERE?
RUSTLL
WELL, IF IT ISN'T SIR DARYUN!

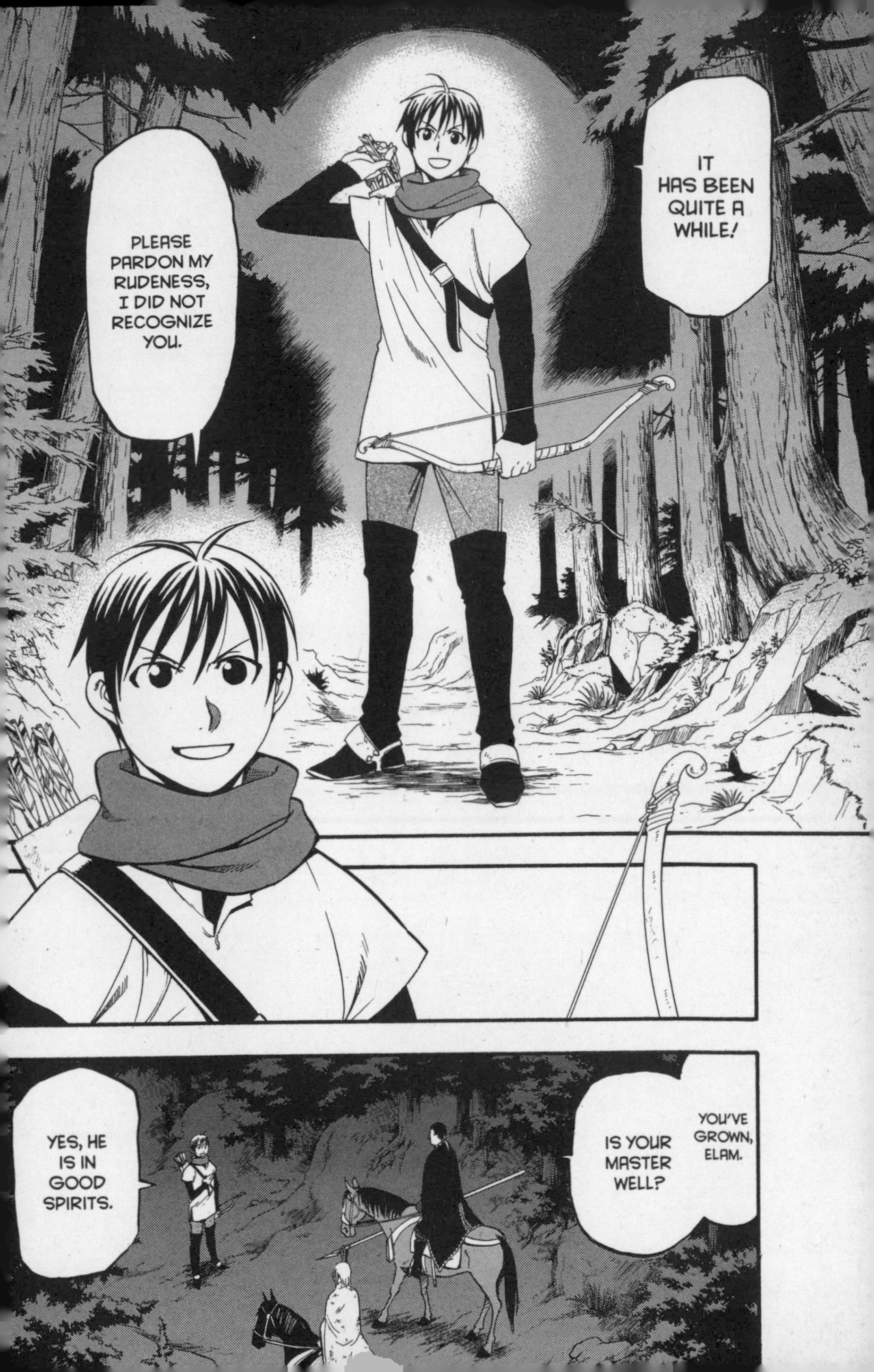
IT HAS BEEN QUITE A WHILE!
PLEASE PARDON MY RUDENESS, I DID NOT RECOGNIZE YOU.
YOU'VE GROWN, ELAM.
IS YOUR MASTER WELL?
YES, HE IS IN GOOD SPIRITS.

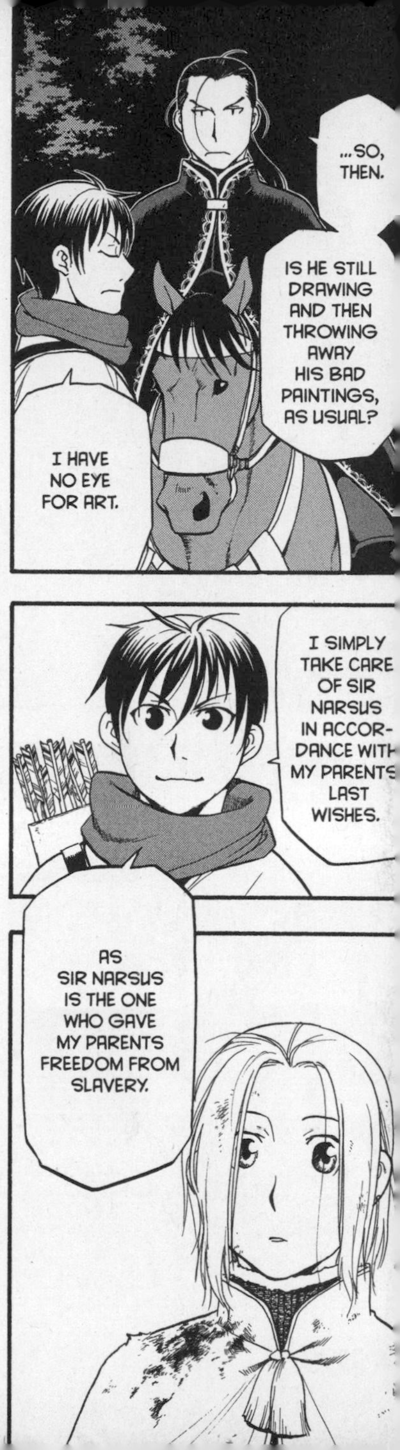
...SO, THEN.
IS HE STILL DRAWING AND THEN THROWING AWAY HIS BAD PAINTINGS, AS USUAL?
I HAVE NO EYE FOR ART.
I SIMPLY TAKE CARE OF SIR NARSUS IN ACCORDANCE WITH MY PARENTS LAST WISHES.
AS SIR NARSUS IS THE ONE WHO GAVE MY PARENTS FREEDOM FROM SLAVERY.
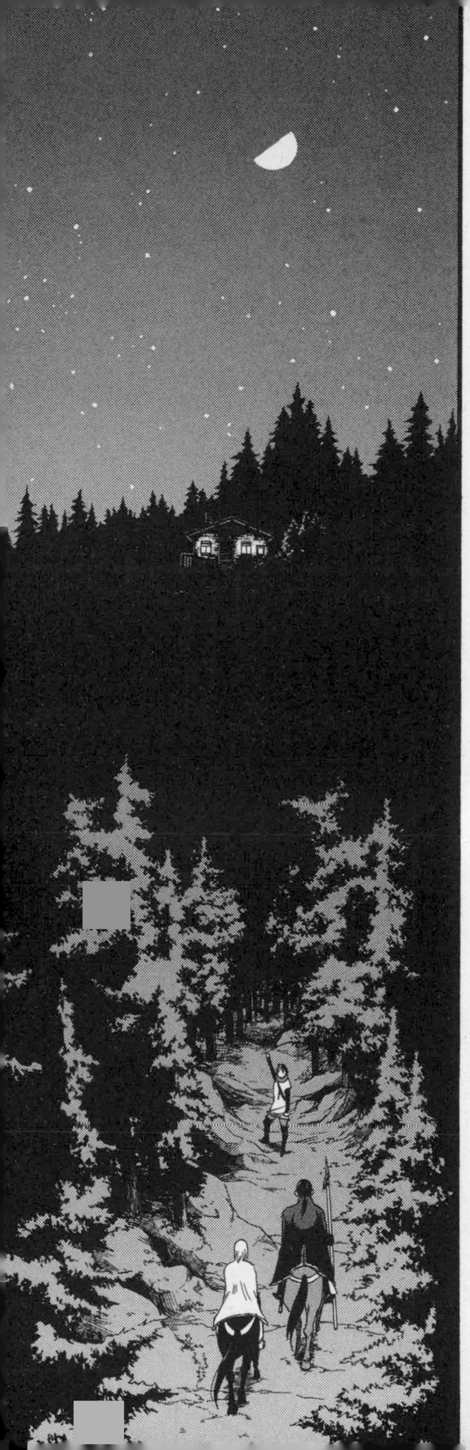

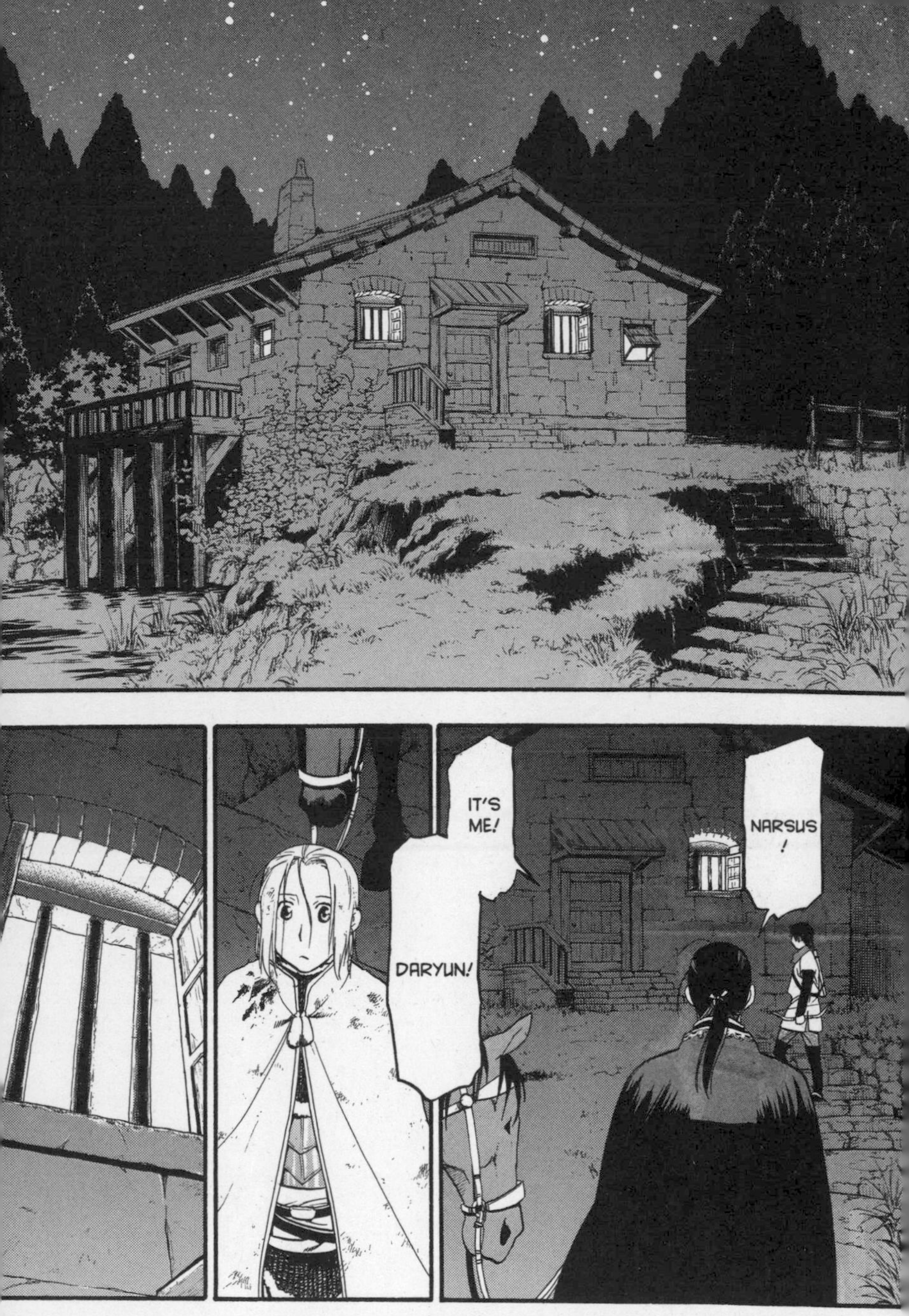
NARSUS!
IT'S ME!
DARYUN!

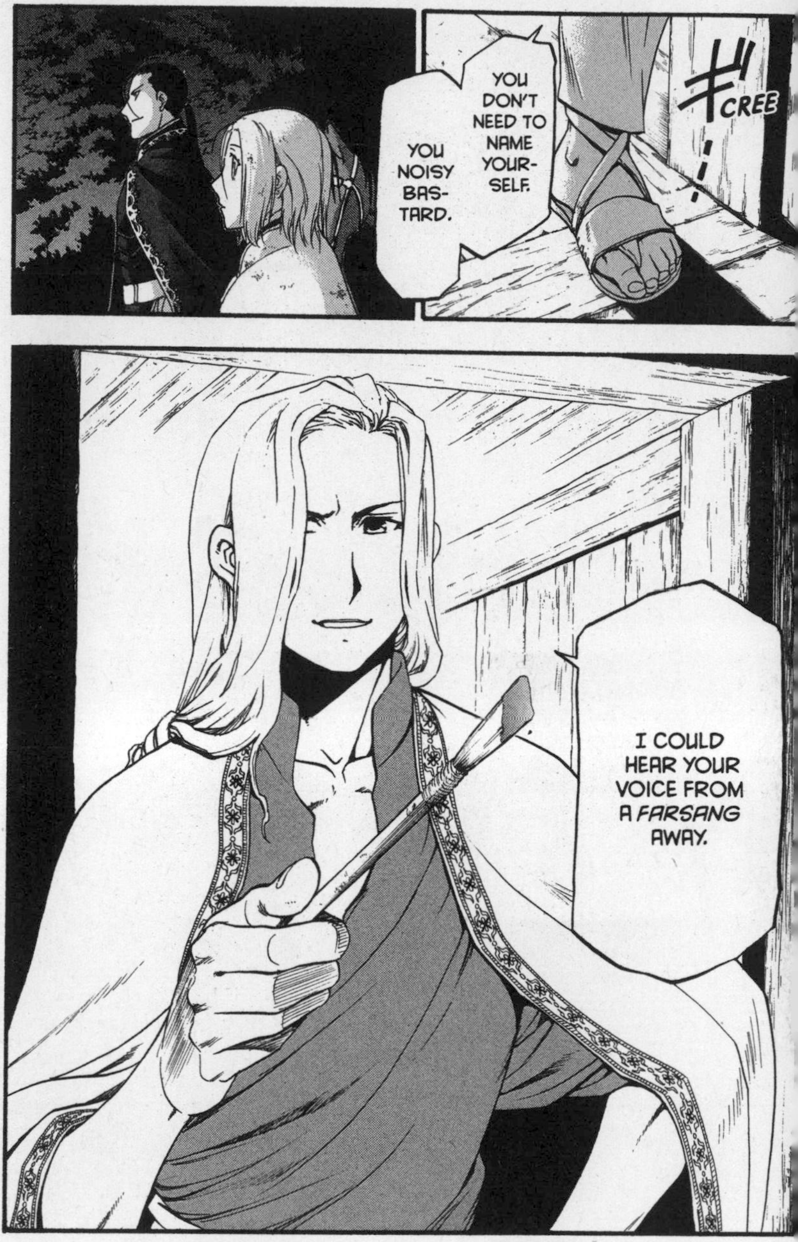
CREE
YOU DON'T NEED TO NAME YOUR-SELF. YOU NOISY BAS-TARD.
I COULD HEAR YOUR VOICE FROM A *FARSANG* AWAY.

THE HEROIC LEGEND OF ARSLAN BONUS FOUR-PANEL COMIC

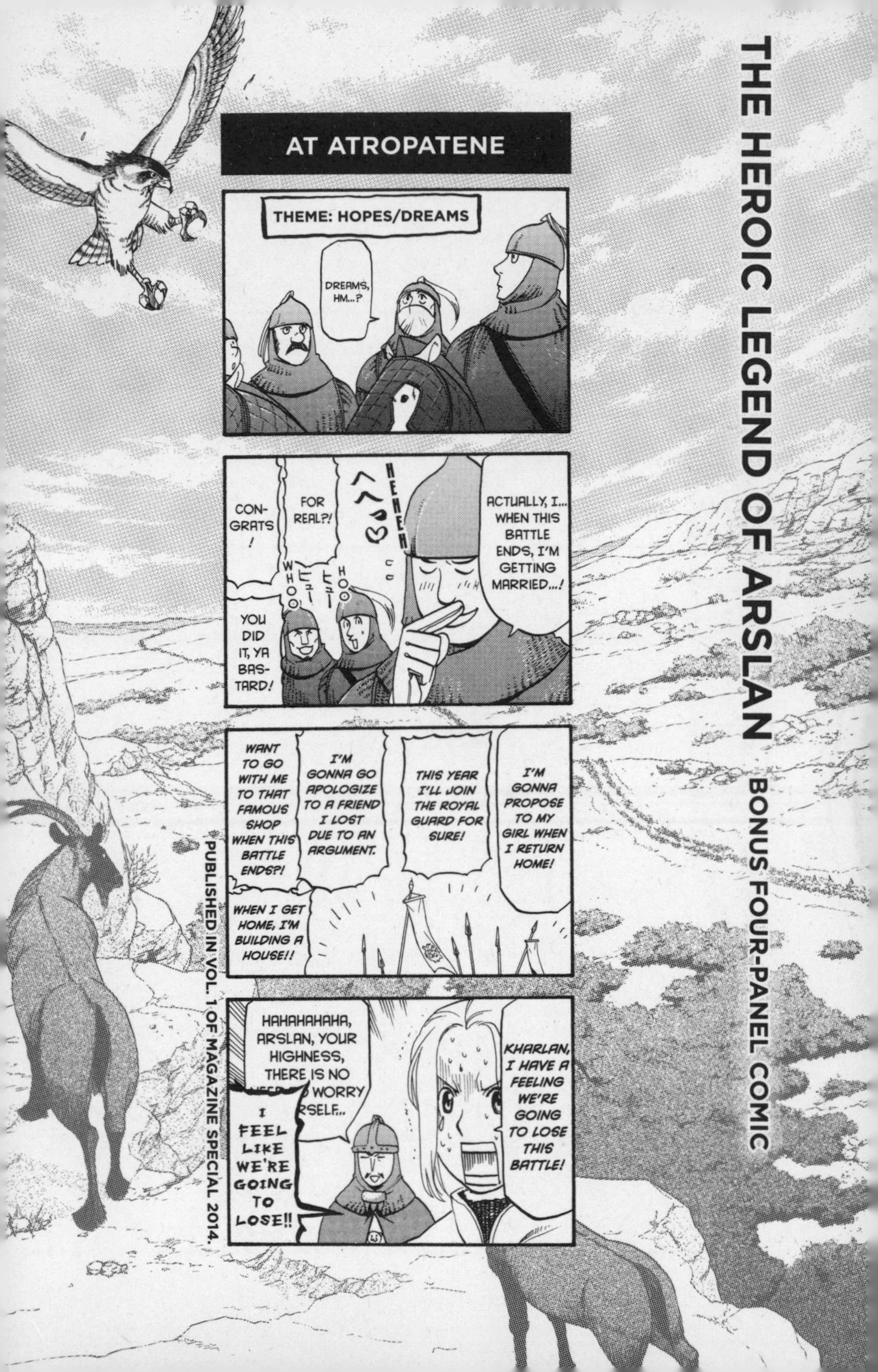
AT ATROPATENE
THEME: HOPES/DREAMS
DREAMS, HM...?
ACTUALLY, I... WHEN THIS BATTLE ENDS, I'M GETTING MARRIED...!
HEHEH
FOR REAL?!
CON-GRATS!
WHOO
WHOO
YOU DID IT, YA BAS-TARD!
I'M GONNA PROPOSE TO MY GIRL WHEN I RETURN HOME!
THIS YEAR I'LL JOIN THE ROYAL GUARD FOR SURE!
I'M GONNA GO APOLOGIZE TO A FRIEND I LOST DUE TO AN ARGUMENT.
WANT TO GO WITH ME TO THAT FAMOUS SHOP WHEN THIS BATTLE ENDS?!
WHEN I GET HOME, I'M BUILDING A HOUSE!!
KHARLAN, I HAVE A FEELING WE'RE GOING TO LOSE THIS BATTLE!
HAHAHAHAHA, ARSLAN, YOUR HIGHNESS, THERE IS NO
WORRY
RSELF...
I FEEL LIKE WE'RE GOING TO LOSE!!

PUBLISHED IN VOL. 1 OF MAGAZINE SPECIAL 2014.

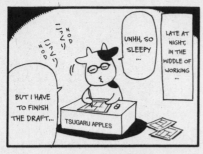

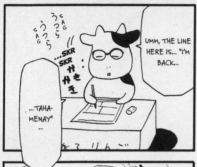

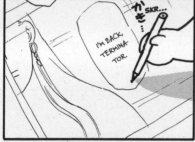

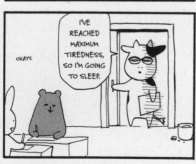

THE HEROIC LEGEND OF POSTSCRIPT

I WAS ABLE TO READ THE ORIGINAL SCRIPT, AND WHILE STILL BEING THRILLED BY THE DESCRIPTION OF "CHARGE!!!" THE STORY UNFOLDED AT A RAPID PACE, AND THOUGH PRESUMPTUOUS OF ME, I ENDED UP BEING GIVEN THIS CHANCE TO DRAW THE MANGA VERSION. RIGHT NOW OUR MAIN HERO, ARSLAN, STILL HAS VERY FEW FRIENDS, BUT THINKING ABOUT THE DAY I CAN DRAW HIM SAYING "CHARGE!!!" MAKES ME EXCITED!

I LOOK FORWARD TO WORKING ON THIS FOR YOU!

ARAKAWA HIROMU

あらかわひろむ

THE HEROIC LEGEND OF ARSLAN 1 -SPECIAL THANKS-

MR. TANAKA YOSHIKI
MR. ADACHI HIROAKI
MR. PARK JONG HIN
MS. TSUCHIYA MOE

EVERYONE WHO HELPED ME WITH MY MANUSCRIPTS. AND YOU!!

LATE AT NIGHT, IN THE MIDDLE OF WORKING...
UNHH, SO SLEEPY...
こっくり NOD
こっくり NOD
BUT I HAVE TO FINISH THE DRAFT...
TSUGARU APPLES
UMM, THE LINE HERE IS... "I'M BACK...
うつら SAG
うつら SAG
...SKR SKR かき かき
...TAHA-MENAY"...
かき SKR...
I'M BACK, TERMINA-TOR.
I'VE REACHED MAXIMUM TIREDNESS, SO I'M GOING TO SLEEP.
OKAYY.

An urgent reprinting stemming from the rush of requests for the special conversation published in “Weekly Shonen Magazine” and “Bessatsu Shonen Magazine”!

ARAKAWA HIROMU X TANAKA YOSHIKI: A BRILLIANTLY BIG CONVERSATION!!

They're both big fans of each other! A special conversation between the miraculous tag eam of “The Heroic Legend of Arslan,” Arakawa Hiromu-sensei and Tanaka Yoshiki-sensei is made into a reality! We bring you Nishimoto Hideo-sensei, who is currently running “Chotto Morimashita” in “Weekly Shonen Magazine” as the famous(ly annoying?) MC, iscussing everything with the pair, from the work itself to the secrets of creation! Wow... aren't the two of you giving a little too much away?!

“THE PRIZE MONEY IS A MILLION YEN. HOW MANY BOXES OF POTATOES IS THAT?!”

THE START OF BOTH CREATOR'S CREATIVE LIVES.

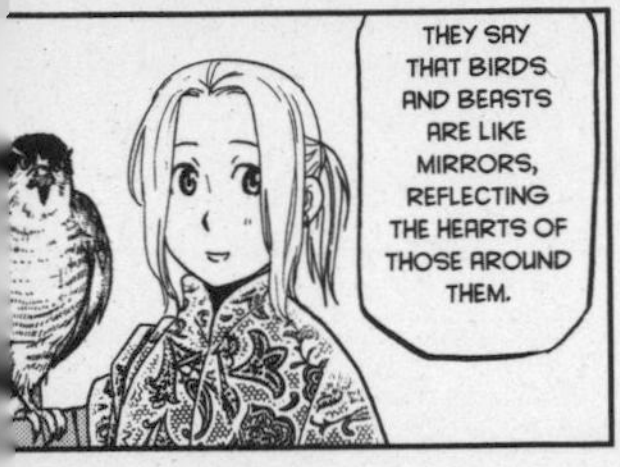
THEY SAY THAT BIRDS AND BEASTS ARE LIKE MIRRORS, REFLECTING THE HEARTS OF THOSE AROUND THEM.

NISHIMOTO: Being surrounded by a pair of industry giants today is enough to make me want to quickly excuse myself due to nervousness. (Laughs). I would definitely like to ask, how did you get started drawing manga, Arakawa-sensei?

ARAKAWA: In the normal way. When I was a kid, if there was white space on the back of fliers, I would just always doodle there.

NISHIMOTO: Tanaka-sensei, did you also, like...write stories on the back of fliers?

ARAKAWA: Th-the backs of fliers are all-purpose. (Big laugh.)

ANAKA: Hahaha. As far as writing goes, I kept a journal during my middle-school days. It seems like my om is still carefully holding on to it, so I feel like I want to find some way to incinerate it. (Laughs.)

ISHIMOTO: Managing editor, you better recover that soon! It's your chance to get a hold of his weakness!

ANAKA: Speaking seriously, apparently, I would scribble down story outlines and other things like that. ccording to my mother I've been like that as long as she can remember, but it's actually something I don't emember too well.

ISHIMOTO: Why, then, did you want to become an author?

ANAKA: During the spring break following my acceptance to graduate school, I wrote a short story for ome reason or another and that started it. I saw an article about a new author's prize in a literary magazine alled “Gen'eijou,” and the idea just suddenly came to me, so I wrote several pages and sent them in. I was sure nat there was no way I'd win, so I completely forgot about it.

ISHIMOTO: But that totally won and led to your debut as a writer.

ANAKA: I was at a funeral when they contacted me about my win. The woman who ran my dorm had uddenly passed away, and they called me right in the middle of the service. So I mean, as I was sitting n the corner of the room with a serious look on my face, the phone rang out. I picked it up and I hear omething like, “Hello, Mr. Tanaka? You've been chosen for the new author's prize...” But it wasn't the kind of tmosphere where I could just say, “I'm happy,” or whatever, so I said “Hmm, is that so?” The person on the hone then said to me, “Aren't you happy?” And even as they asked me that question, you could hear the ound of a priest praying right next to me. (Laughs.)

RAKAWA: That's like some comedy routine. (Laughs.)

ISHIMOTO: Well then, when did you decide to seriously draw manga, Arakawa-ensei?

RAKAWA: I wonder where that seriousness came from. I had all kinds of dreams vhen I was young. I liked animals, so my dreams included being an animal handler

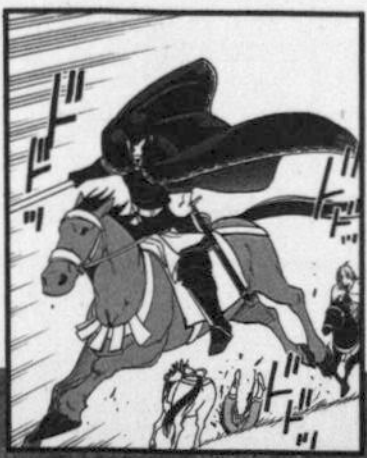

at a zoo, or a veterinarian, or something like that. At the same time, I lik[e] manga, so it was probably around middle school that I started draw[ing] gag comics with animals and such.

NISHIMOTO: Your animal gags, Arakawa-sensei! There's a gold mine he[re] too, everyone. (Laughs.)

ARAKAWA: My family ran a farm. My parents had four girls and one b[oy,] and with my grandparents and aunt we were a huge family. Because [we] weren't too well off financially, I gave up on being a veterinarian when I g[ot] into high school. It was there that I decided that I would become a man[ga] artist in the future, and so we'll say the path got narrowed down to a single one. I entered an agricultural hi[gh] school, and after I graduated, while helping my family, I would draw manga. Stuff like "Romance of the Thr[ee] Kingdoms" dojinshi or stuff related to games; things like that. After that, when my younger brother's path [in] life was decided, I started to submit my work, and moved here to Tokyo using the prize money.

NISHIMOTO: You won a large sum, didn't you?

ARAKAWA: The prize money is a million yen. How many boxes of potatoes is that?! (Laughs.)

NISHIMOTO: No way that you're calculating it using potatoes. (Laughs.)

▮ A SLUMP HAS ARRIVED! WHAT DO YOU DO?!

NISHIMOTO: There's something else I really wanted to ask. Around me... probably including me (laug[hs]) there are quite a few beginner manga artists. They start out writing stories well, but there is an incredib[ly] large number of people who get discouraged in the middle. And I wondering, how do the two of you co[pe] with it when you end up in a slump?

TANAKA: No, I have nothing specific. When I can't write, I just say, "I can't write!" and give up, and I watch the DVDs that have been piling up and such. Just recently I saw a film that was something like "Anacon[da] vs. King Gorilla." (Laughs.) After all, no matter how much you turn the faucet, if the main waterline is clos[ed] nothing will come out. (Laughs.)

NISHIMOTO: How about you, Arakawa-san? I would think you must have days where you don't feel up to [it.]

ARAKAWA: I also am good at giving up, and when I think that I just must be in that mood, I fall asleep. Th[at] or I suddenly start cleaning or something like that. I end up using a toothbrush or something to clean all t[he] way to the corners of the room, and then I go out thinking, "I'll go buy cleaning supplies!" or something, b[ut] in the end I just buy manga and go back home. (Laughs.)

▮ A MIRACULOUS COLLABORATION! "THE HEROIC LEGEND OF ARSLAN."

NISHIMOTO: Well then, it's finally time for me to ask about "The Heroic Legend of Arslan." I feel like the ma[in] character is truly first-rate, but how on earth did you develop him?

TANAKA: A standard in Grimm's Fairy Tales or stories about alternate worlds is for a boy raised in a small h[ut] in the middle of the forest to actually be a descendent of the royal bloodline... there are those kinds of tal[es] in which an exile of noble birth overcomes trial and tribulation to become of value, right? I read several volumes of stuff like that, and thought, "How about trying to write something that's the opposite of this?" In short...

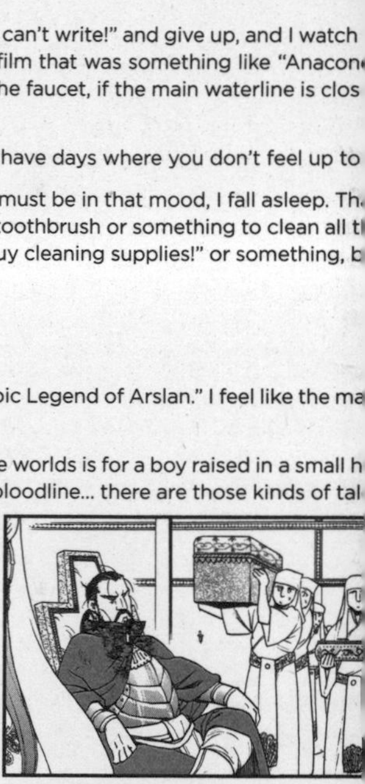

NISHIMOTO: Woah, I'm sorry. I won't ask anything past that point! All of you readers please look forward to it! Arakawa-sensei, I heard that you had difficulty due to a lack of reference materials on Persia, which serves as the backdrop for the story.

(TANAKA) "HOW ABOUT TRYING TO WRITE SOMETHIN[G] THAT'S THE OPPOSITE OF THIS?"

COME ON!!

"SURE ENOUGH, I GOT 'CARRIED AWAY.'" (ARAKAWA)

ARAKAWA: I like research materials, so I'm diligent about searching for them. Things like images, old books... I once had an acquaintance who deals in antiques bring me a statue. I also spend a lot of time at photo collections like the "Persian Exhibitions" they sometimes have at museums. I got all the accessories and such, but I didn't know the colors of the clothing and buildings, so when they told me "Do it in color," it was a bit of a pain. (Laughs.)

■ THE MANGA INDUSTRY IN AN UPROAR! HOW DID THE SUPER HIGH PROFILE TAG-TEAM "START DATING"?

SHIMOTO: Well then, Tanaka Yoshiki-sensei's masterpiece, "The Heroic Legend of Arslan," is being adpated into a comic by Arakawa Hiromu-sensei...this news is unprecedented, but Tanaka-sensei, have you eady read the manga?

ANAKA: I was able to read up to the third chapter. I was really happy when I read the first chapter. I was oved by the scene where Arslan was pulled around by his ear. (Laughs.)

ARAKAWA: My heart is racing is over here, though. (Laughs.)

SHIMOTO: Please tell me about the circumstances around the formation of the tag team that brought the dustry into an uproar.

ARAKAWA: About five years ago, I heard a discussion of this plan from my managing editor. "We heard that u're a huge fan of 'The Heroic Legend of Arslan,' Arakawa-sensei, and really want to request this of you..." what I was told, but I said, "I've never read it..."

SHIMOTO: Huh?! Was it a misunderstanding on the part of your managing editor?

ARAKAWA: It seems like it, but I came to be interested in it myself after often being asked in fan letters, o you like 'Legend of the Galactic Heroes?'" I wondered if that had something in common with the way I eate stories, but I passed the time without really reaching out for the novel, and then this plan suddenly me to me. When I was able to read it, well, sure enough, I got 'carried away,' and soon had devoured all e volumes. (Laughs.)

SHIMOTO: Tanaka-sensei, how did you feel about this plan?

ANAKA: Discussions of turning "The Heroic Legend of Arslan" into a manga had come up from time to ne in the past. And in the middle of everything, I suddenly received the message that "Arakara Hiromu-ensei will do us the favor of drawing it." I couldn't believe it at all, and thought it would end up turning into discussion like, "Arakawa-san's friend's relative will draw it." (Laughs.) I read "Fullmetal Alchemist," and ted her work, "Noble Farmer," also, and I felt it was too amazing that the same person wrote both works. I as able to speak to Arakawa-san, and when I was finally able to believe that I could really ask her to make is into a manga, I ran to the book store and said "Please give me all the volumes of 'Fullmetal Alchemist,'" ecause I wanted to read it once more. (Laughs.) I was able to read the final volume as it was released.

ARAKAWA: Thank you very much. (Laughs.)

ANAKA: After that, "Silver Spoon" began, and I realized "Oh, this person likes horses." On top of that, even hen drawing the same fights, I thought, "She seems to like sword fighting more than shoot-outs." I thought would never be more grateful than to have someone like that draw "The Heroic Legend of Arslan" for me.

ANYWAY, I JUST WANT HER TO DRAW FREELY!

SHIMOTO: At the time of the manga adaptation, did you make ome kind of request of Arakawa-sensei, Tanaka-sensei?

ANAKA: No, as far as I'm concerned, I wanted Arakawa-san to do hat she wanted to do, and wanted her to draw things that only e could draw, that's all. It was a pushy request on my part, but ctually, just by having her draw something in the prologue that as not in the original script, I thought, "I did it!" (Laughs.)

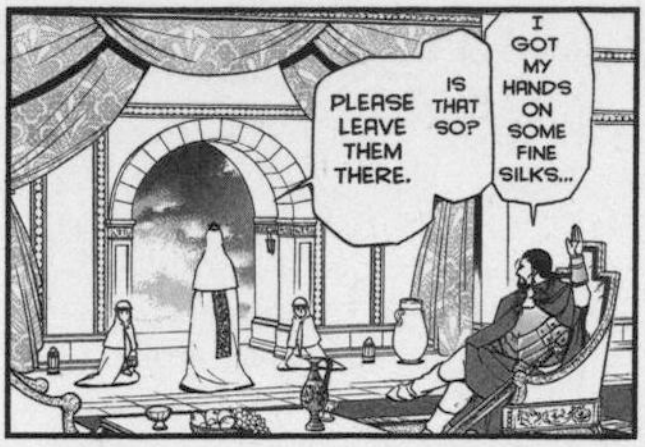
I GOT MY HANDS ON SOME FINE SILKS...
IS THAT SO?
PLEASE LEAVE THEM THERE.

NISHIMOTO: I see. Chapter One is the story of what happens in t days before the original script, isn't it? What made you think abo illustrating that episode, Arakawa-sensei?

ARAKAWA: I started with the structure of the kingdom, of Arsl and his parents, because if I began with the war, then the sto would just go rolling along... I felt I wanted to draw the relationsh between the king and the queen, too. I also wanted to illustra the rich culture of the royal capital Ecbatana, and the kingdo called Pars and so on. I thought, for starters, I would build th foundation.

NISHIMOTO: Drawing a peaceful age makes the misery of war stand out, doesn't it?

ARAKAWA: That's true. It was good that I was also able to create a little bit of a disquieting feeling on t final page thanks to the suggestions of my managing editor.

TANAKA: In the original script, I wasn't able to write much about the peaceful Ecbatana in Andragoras' tim so by having those "streets of splendor" written about so well in the first chapter of the Arakawa versio was given the pleasure of being able to really enjoy seeing it. It really exudes atmosphere. There's a giraf too. (Laughs.)

ARAKAWA: Around the beginning of the second chapter of the original version, the prince is just walki around the city normally, isn't he? I had something like a yearning for that atmosphere and so I drew it wh thinking, "Oh, from chapter two something awful is going to happen here."

■ IN ORDER TO DRAW "THE WORLD OF ARSLAN"...

NISHIMOTO: I really am not up on my studies, and so I thought that Pars was an entirely fictional kingdo But actually, this is set in Persia, and actual events are woven into the story, aren't they? When drawi buildings and clothing and such, did you gather reference materials?

ARAKAWA: That's right. But when we talk about the age of the Persian Empire, this was up until the days the Sasanian Empire (226-651 AD.) After that, they were invaded by Islamic nations and all kinds of thin were destroyed. So even though they were so prosperous, there are surprisingly few research materia left over. There are like, stone monuments and statues, and eating utensils and such, and I can just bare manage to imagine what kinds of clothes they might have worn at that time. Since this is fantasy, there a many points that are supplemented by imagination.

TANAKA: In the end, this is a fictional kingdom based on Persia, so it was best for me to have Arakawa-s draw it in the way that was easiest for her. The strongest thing working for us is the fact that there's no o who has actually seen Pars. (Laughs.)

NISHIMOTO: By the way, when writing "The Heroic Legend of Arslan," did you do on-site research, Tanaka-sensei?

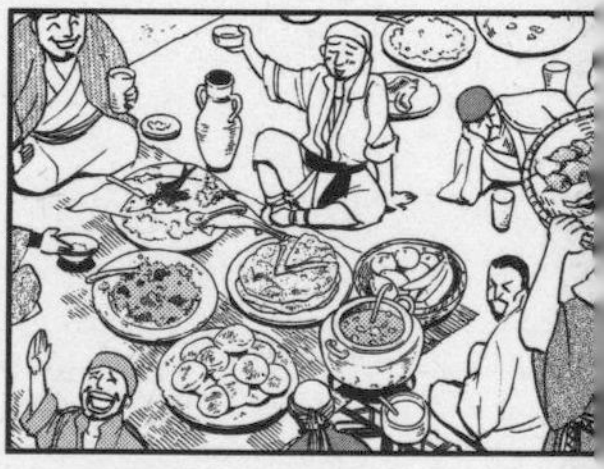

TANAKA: No, I didn't go. I have a strong tendency towards fantasizing, and whenever I come up with any single thing, I feel as though I can see everything around it too.

■ THE INSPIRATION BEHIND THE BIRTH OF THIS WORK.

NISHIMOTO: I would also like to ask how both of you get ideas to create your works. For example, for "The Heroic Legend of Arslan," what caused you to decide to write that?

TANAKA: Having "The Legend of Galactic Heroes," read by an unexpected number of people, I felt like I ha written everything I could about space operas. Then at the same time, I thought, "I'd like to write somethir

(TANAKA)
"THERE'S NO ONE WHO HAS ACTUALLY SEEN PARS. (LAUGHS.)"

"PEOPLE HAVE THE AMAZING POWER TO MOVE STORIES ALONG."

with sword-fighting." Even so, I had no confidence in being able to write Japanese sword fighting, and as far as Western stories go, we already have Kurimoto Kaoru-san's "Guin Saga." When I thought I needed to compete in a different area, suddenly "Persia" was what popped into my head. It might be the effect of books and TV, but I also might have just lost my head. (Laughs.) Even now, it's a mystery to me.

NISHIMOTO: For example, what was the reason that you decided to write "Fullmetal Alchemist," Arakawa-sensei?

ARAKAWA: I planned it after I came to Tokyo. While I was doing all kinds of research about magic and the "Philosopher's Stone," I thought, "This is such an interesting theme, so why has no one done it as their main story? If no one else is doing it, than you do it yourself!" "Silver Spoon," also came from the fact that "No one is doing a manga about an agricultural high school." I'm in a niche industry, a niche business, aren't I? (Laughs.)

■ HOW THE CHARACTERS & STORY WERE CREATED

NISHIMOTO: When turning this into a manga, was there something you were careful about when creating the characters?

ARAKAWA: Tanaka-san's works have "developed characters," or should I say the people have the amazing power to move stories along. Of course there's politics, battles, and so on, but it feels like people are moving the story along. Therefore, it wasn't about "how to inflate the characters," but instead, "how to cut them down," was important. Since there are a lot of interesting episodes, it's difficult to cut them. The people really are active, and so you even develop an attachment to the enemies.

TANAKA: That does develop, it really does.

ARAKAWA: On the enemy's side, there is a kind of evil religion that would even harm babies, and there's this intense archbishop named Bodin, but I look forward to feeling like "I wonder how much of this will I be allowed to draw?" On top of that, when drawing the rough plans for the characters, the first thing I finished was King Innocentis of the enemy kingdom, Lusitania, who only became king because he was the oldest brother, and has forced all the difficult issues on his capable younger brother. (Laughs.)

TANAKA: That guy, he isn't a bad guy, though. (Laughs.) I'm also looking forward to seeing how his younger brother Guiscard is drawn.

ARAKAWA: I'm excited about all the new characters I'll be drawing from now on.

NISHIMOTO: What I first noticed about Innocentis is probably how he seems like he's a little bit of a useless person, I think.

ARAKAWA: Even for a kingdom that slaughters people of other religions, you can feel a bit of sympathy for them having a king like that. Because of that, I started to feel a bit of the charm of Lusitania. (Laughs.)

NISHIMOTO: There really are a lot of characters that show up, but do you model these characters off of the people around, Tanaka-sensei?

ARAKAWA: I wanted to ask that too!

TANAKA: Around me, hmm... Well, there's no one like Bodin around me. (Laughs.)

ARAKAWA: If there was, they'd be too intense. (Laughs.)

NISHIMOTO: The fact that your characters are so human, you must have an observant eye, right? "Tanaka-sensei has a bad personality, probably," or something. (Laughs.)

TANAKA: You have a sharp eye. (Laughs.)

I WONDER IF GOD WOULD DEIGN TO BLESS US WHO KILL NEWBORNS, EVEN IF THEY ARE HEATHENS?

...JUST WHAT IS A PROPER KING, I WONDER?

NISHIMOTO: No, "That's creepy," I think.

ARAKAWA: I'm being observed, aren't I?

NISHIMOTO: Bringing the discussion back to the comic adaptatio[n], what are your thoughts as far as the visual side of things?

ARAKAWA: What's more important than the outward appearance [of] the characters, are the scenes. It's like, the more I read along the scri[pt] the more storyboards pop into my head as I think "Oh, I want to dr[aw] this!" At that point, the characters are still stick figures, but the scen[es] are all ready, even down to the way the frames are split.

NISHIMOTO: Wow, geniuses really are different... Well then, on the other side of things, who did you have t[he] most trouble with being unable to get their character figured out?

ARAKAWA: It was of course, Arslan. Until the end of the manga version was set, I was completely unab[le] to get a visual sense of Arslan. After first discussing the final chapter over several meetings, I then work[ed] backwards and thought it over.

NISHIMOTO: Was "Fullmetal Alchemist" like that too?

ARAKAWA: I started after first getting a broad idea of the final chapter. I created everything with the id[ea] that there was a terminus, and along the way there, were several large stops. I then filled in the trac[k] between them during serialization.

TANAKA: I really understand that. I also liken writing to a journey. In short, you leave Tokyo, and it's decid[ed] that the story will end by arriving in Osaka. But I think, on the way, do you take the Tokaido line, or do y[ou] take the Chuo line, or do you wait until the maglev train passes through? (Laughs.) Rather than deciding [on] a strict path, you decide based on the character's personalities or in response to their circumstances a[nd] you think, do they try stopping by extra stations, or instead, do they try skipping them and passing by? I w[as] a little surprised to hear your story, Arakawa-san. Up to this point, I've heard no end of people telling m[e] "Your way of doing things is unusual." (Laughs.)

ARAKAWA: Right, right. People say the same thing to me. (Laughs.) What do you think, Nishimoto-san?

NISHIMOTO: I've never stopped at even one of those stations, but... were there even stations there? [Or] rather, I might even be walking. (Laughs.)

■ THE INVINCIBLE TAG TEAM'S ULTIMATE COOPERATIVE SYSTEM

NISHIMOTO: As far as the very well-received manga version of "The Heroic Legend of Arslan" goes, we ha[d] Tanaka-sensei say, "Anyway, I just want her to draw freely." At the storyboarding level, did you check in o[n] the contents?

TANAKA: Actually, I am just leaving it all to her.

ARAKAWA: In the beginning, I thought that he would check it over, but I was told, "It won't happen[."] (Laughs.)

NISHIMOTO: Isn't that overly-lenient of you? (Laughs.) Finally, as far as the appeal of this work goes, pleas[e] give us a few words as the author of the original script.

TANAKA: I'm simply looking forward to the continuation, wondering "What will happen after this point[?"] So checking ahead of that would be a waste. It's so interesting that I even want to novelize this mang[a.] (Laughs.)

ALL TOGETHER: (Big laugh.)

The contents of this discussion were published in "Bessatsu Shonen Magazine" December 2013 and "Week[ly] Shonen Magazine" Vol. 49 2013.

(TANAKA) "UP TO THIS POINT, I'VE BEEN TOLD, 'YOUR WAY OF DOING THINGS IS UNUSUAL.'"

- BONUS SKETCHES -

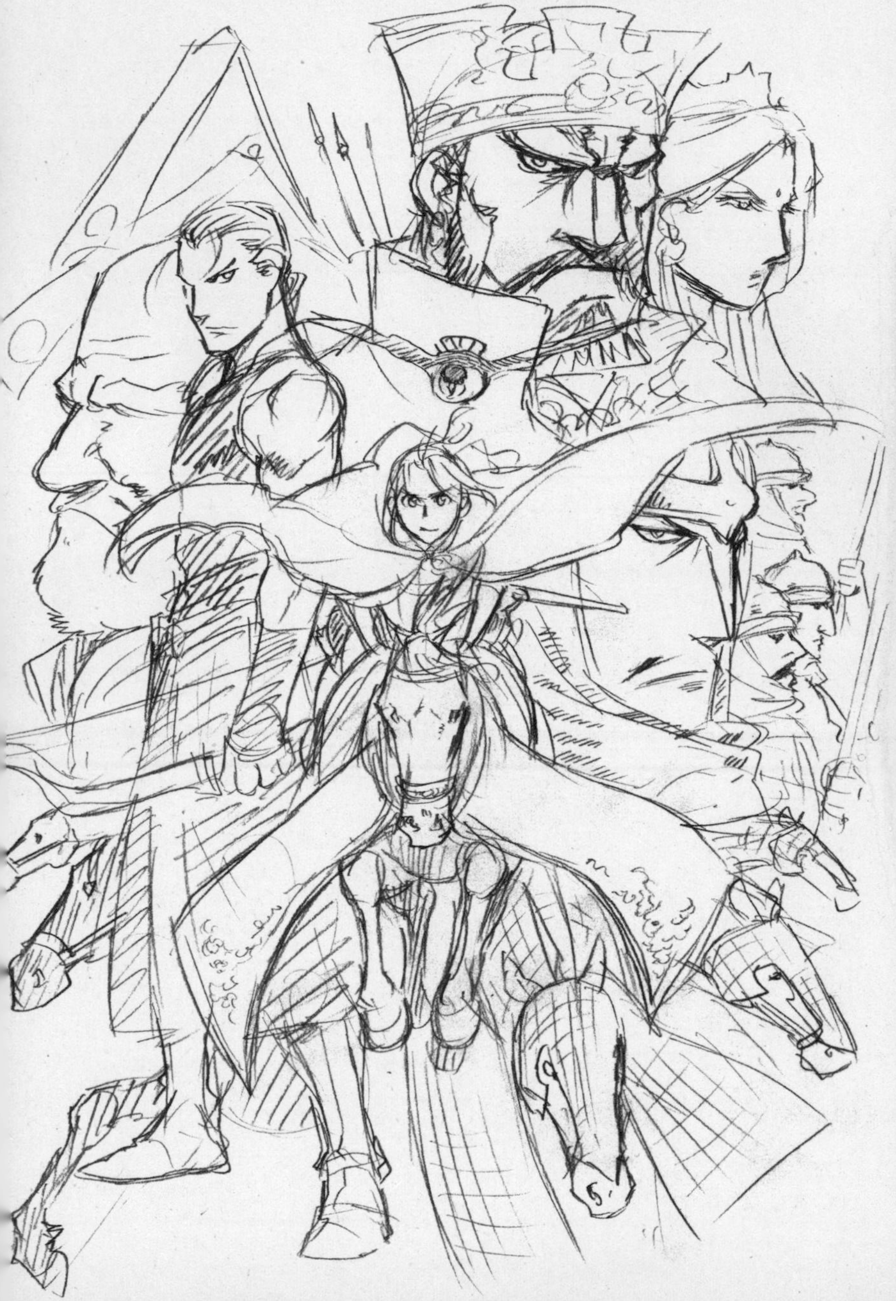

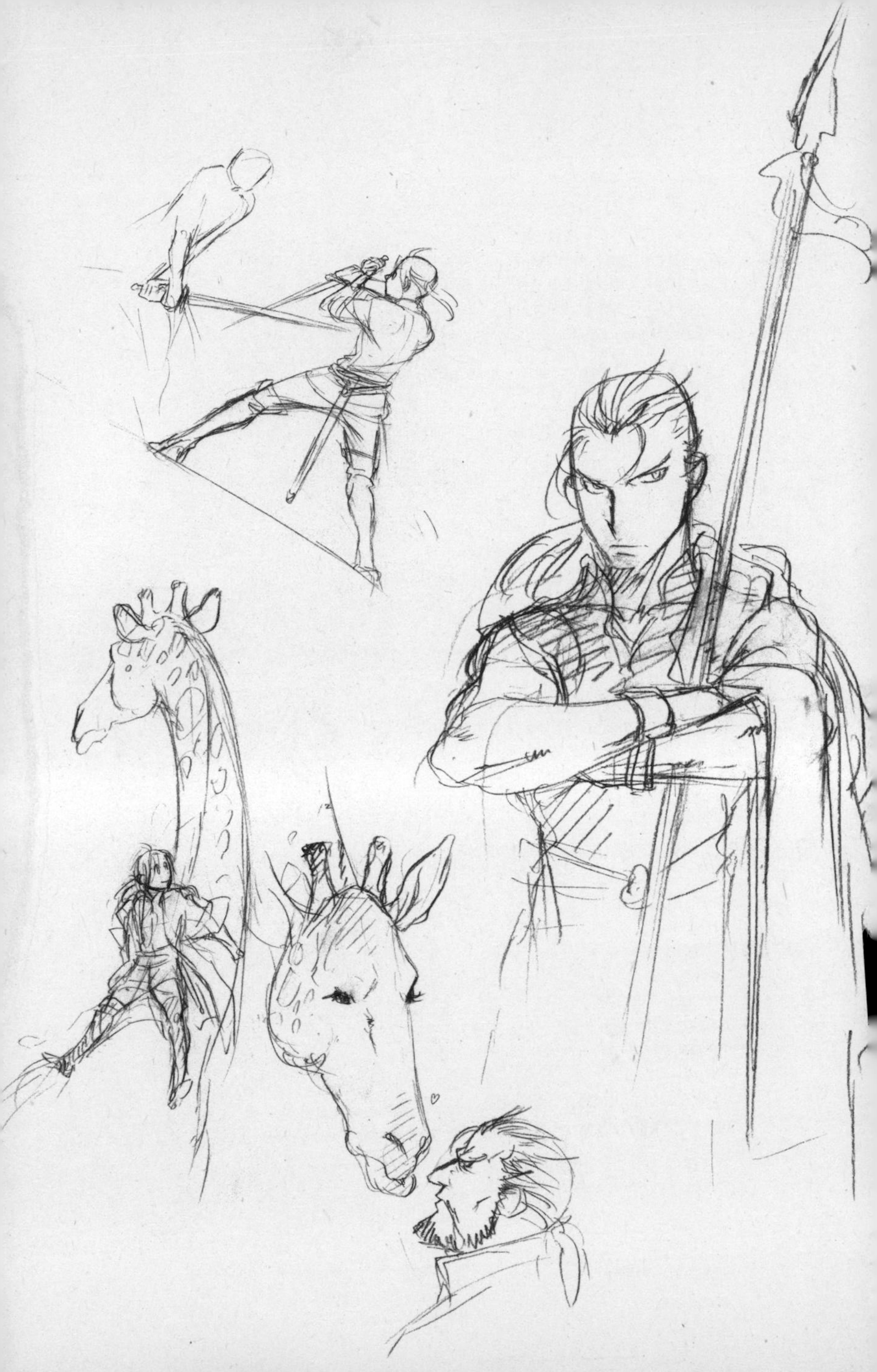

A Kodansha Comics Trade Paperback Original.

The Heroic Legend of Arslan volume 1 copyright © 2014 Hiromu Arakawa & Yoshiki Tanaka
English translation copyright © 2014 Hiromu Arakawa & Yoshiki Tanaka

Published in the United States by Kodansha Comics,
an imprint of Kodansha USA Publishing, LLC, New York.

Publication rights for this English edition arranged through Kodansha Ltd., Tokyo.

First published in Japan in 2014 by Kodansha Ltd., Tokyo, as *Arslan Senki* volume 1.

ISBN 978-1-61262-972-8

Printed in the United States of America.

www.kodanshacomics.com

9 8 7 6 5 4 3 2 1

Translator: Lindsey Akashi
Lettering: Christy Sawyer
Editing: Ajani Oloye